1968

1968

The Rise and Fall of the New American Revolution

Robert C. Cottrell and Blaine T. Browne

ROWMAN & LITTLEFIELD
Lanham • Boulder • New York • London

Published by Rowman & Littlefield
A wholly owned subsidiary of The Rowman & Littlefield Publishing Group, Inc.
4501 Forbes Boulevard, Suite 200, Lanham, Maryland 20706
www.rowman.com

Unit A, Whitacre Mews, 26-34 Stannary Street, London SE11 4AB

British Library Cataloguing in Publication Information Available

Library of Congress Cataloging-in-Publication Data

Names: Cottrell, Robert C., 1950- author. | Browne, Blaine T. (Blaine Terry) author.
Title: The rise and fall of the new American Revolution / Robert C. Cottrell and Blaine T. Browne.
Description: Lanham, MD : Rowman & Littlefield, [2018] | Includes bibliographical references and index.
Identifiers: LCCN 2017059069 (print) | LCCN 2018015324 (ebook) | ISBN 9781538107768 (Electronic) | ISBN 9781538107751 (cloth : alk. paper)
Subjects: LCSH: United States—Politics and government—1961–1963. | Nineteen sixty-eight, A.D. | Protest movements—United States—History—20th century. | New Left—United States—History—20th century. | Radicalism—United States—History—20th century. | Revolutionaries—United States—History—20th century. | Political activists—United States—History—20th century. | Youth movements—United States—History—20th century. | Social movements—United States—History—20th century. | United States—Social conditions—1960–1980.
Classification: LCC E846 (ebook) | LCC E846 .C67 2018 (print) | DDC 973.923—dc23
LC record available at https://lccn.loc.gov/2017059069

Printed in the United States of America

To America's 68ers

Contents

Preface

The year retains its mythic hold on the imagination in the fashion of few others. Like 1789, 1848, 1871, 1917, 1989, and 2011, it is recalled most of all as the year when revolution beckoned or threatened, depending upon one's perspective. For a time, it seemed as if anything were possible in 1968, that utopian visions could be borne out in the political, cultural, racial, and gender spheres.

Leading adherents of the counterculture appeared ready to join forces with political activists envisioning a new American Revolution. At the top of the year, a small band of individuals calling themselves *Yippies*, members of the largely nominal Youth International Party, looked ahead to the Democratic Party National Convention in Chicago. In remarkable but obviously paradoxical fashion, they wanted to promote "disruption or sabotage," albeit in an anarchistic manner. In the process, they hoped to discredit both the Democratic Party and President Lyndon Baines Johnson, who had been instrumental in bringing about a revolution in American law pertaining to race relations and had helped to usher in the largest expansion of the welfare state since the New Deal. At the same time, LBJ and the country's leading political organization had been in power when the worst excesses of the postwar Pax Americana unfolded in Vietnam and race riots beset American cities. The Vietnam War enraged the Yippies, led by Abbie Hoffman and Jerry Rubin, as it did so many young people in the United States and across the globe, as well as a growing number of those who had attained the no longer to be trusted generational dividing point of thirty years of age.

Fervent pacifists had their own idea of revolutionary agitation, operating through the Resistance, the group that had make its first appearance only months earlier and called for draft-eligible men to refuse to adhere to Selective Service guidelines. Declining to accept even designation as conscientious objectors, young men like David Harris and Dennis Sweeney hoped that enough of their age cohorts would as well, thus bringing the draft system to a grinding halt. Several well-known figures, both inside and outside the academy, offered full support for the young men who made up the Resistance or followed its lead. That resulted in the Justice Department's decision to conduct the first of the era's conspiracy trials, with the prosecution of Dr. Benjamin Spock, the nation's best-known pediatrician, and four other anti-war leaders, for violating the Selective Service Act.

The Johnson administration, which targeted Spock and other members of the so-called Boston Five, obviously feared radical challenges regarding conscription, the waging of the Vietnam War, or the carrying out of domestic policies. Overseas, to the dismay of the Johnson administration, revolutionaries were clearly on the march too, as exemplified by the Tet Offensive that erupted in Vietnam in late January, with 84,000 Vietcong (VC) fighters and North Vietnamese Army (NVA) regular troops seeking to topple the South Vietnamese regime of President Nguyen Van Thieu and Vice President Nguyen Cao Ky. The communist Politburo in Hanoi believed the timing was propitious for the long awaited Final Offensive that would expel US soldiers and reunify the Vietnamese homeland. Images from Vietnam shattered the notion of US invincibility, most notably those of Vietcong guerrillas fighting their way inside the American embassy compound in Saigon and a prominent South Vietnamese police official blowing out the brains of a VC suspect.

Reportage from Vietnam dramatically altered the American political landscape, with President Johnson weakened and practitioners of a New Politics threatening his hold on the White House. Having been turned down by other prominent politicians, most notably Senator Robert F. Kennedy, anti-war activist Allard Lowenstein convinced Senator Eugene McCarthy to undertake a virtually unprecedented bid to wrest the Democratic Party nomination from a sitting president. Tet enabled McCarthy to make an unexpectedly strong showing in the New Hampshire primary, where he came close to pulling in more votes than Johnson while capturing twenty of twenty-four delegates to the national convention. Shortly following McCarthy's promising finish, RFK, the former attorney general and the slain president's younger brother, entered the race, to the chagrin of many young people who were considered part of a Children's Crusade for McCarthy. Others were enthused, and Kennedy drew large, impassioned crowds, seemingly possessing the ability to harvest support from various sides of the political spectrum and across racial divides. President Johnson, particularly stung by the entrance into the political race of Senator Kennedy, whom he despised and who disliked him every bit as much in return, delivered a nationwide television address in which he discussed opening peace talks and announced his decision not to seek reelection.

As the American political order was shaken up, Dr. Martin Luther King Jr. continued his own crusade to make over his country. The nation's leading practitioner of the Social Gospel, who passionately adhered to the ideals of the beloved community and racial democracy while other activists disavowed the nonviolence he preached, King undertook a Poor People's Campaign to bring about a measure of economic equality. Long a believer in the need for democratic socialism, he began to voice radical precepts more directly and publicly. Considering the Vietnam War an abomination that prevented a genuine War on Poverty at home, King also became one of the most eloquent spokespeople condemning the horrors being inflicted on a small Southeast Asian land. To the dismay of the Johnson administration, he added his name to the ranks of those openly criticizing US engagement, particularly lauding the young men who made up the Resistance. While displaying more radical stances, King suffered criticism from within the Establishment and the Movement alike, along with constant death threats. In the final several weeks of his life, he gave voice to premonitions about his impending demise, while refusing to temper his radical, even revolutionary messages.

The idea of revolution, and of revolution requiring violence, proved more and more appealing, not simply to young, disaffected Americans but to politically engaged youth around the globe. Revolution, or at least the idea of it, took hold in the United States, Western Europe, Japan, Latin America, Southeast Asia, the Middle East, and the Soviet bloc, especially Czechoslovakia. The recently slain Argentine physician turned revolutionary, Ernesto "Che" Guevara, provided a role model for many, particularly as the Central Intelligence Agency (CIA), much reviled on the left, was blamed for his death. Other inspirations appeared in the prolonged Vietnamese struggle for national liberation, the hope spawned in Prague to meld socialism and democracy, the example seemingly offered by the Chinese Cultural Revolution, and the antics of anarchists ranging from the Yippies in America to the Dutch Provos. Revolution seemed to be looming in the streets or on campuses as far afield as Columbia University in New York City and the Sorbonne in Paris.

Others embraced revolutionary tactics, believing that radical change in government policies, both at home and abroad, was imperative. A small number of radical pacifists, including the Catholic priests and brothers Daniel and Philip Berrigan, and Thomas Melville, a former Maryknoll priest, determined to engage in several steps beyond those undertaken by the Resistance. They targeted draft boards and draft files, relying on direct action tactics that resulted in their being called the Ultra-Resistance. The federal government responded by going after the Berrigans, Melville, and their compatriots, again employing the mass conspiracy trials that had long been used to tear apart or at least badly weaken the American left. While seldom grabbing the attention elicited by both the Resistance and the Ultra-Resistance, unaffiliated young men continued to contest the draft system in their own ways, ensuring that it hardly operated as smoothly as both the White House and the Pentagon desired.

In the United States, a surprising number of radicals viewed Senator Kennedy's presidential bid favorably, but his chance of winning the Democratic Party presidential nomination remained problematic at best. LBJ's departure from the race resulted in Vice President Hubert H. Humphrey's entrance into it and rapid accumulation of pledged delegates from non–primary holding states. Notwithstanding sometimes rapturous crowds, Kennedy failed to win over many McCarthy supporters, who viewed him as an interloper and opportunist lacking the principles that had compelled their candidate to join the Dump Johnson movement.

Meanwhile, Dr. King's Poor People's Campaign sputtered before the nation's apostle of nonviolence fell victim to the politics of assassination that had long seared American politics and would again soon. In Oregon, which was too economically comfortable and too white to favor him, Kennedy proved politically fallible, ending a family winning streak in electoral contests. Recognizing the necessity of prevailing in the California primary, Kennedy campaigned hard there, going head-to-head against McCarthy in a televised debate, while seemingly dabbling in racial stereotypes. All of that led to a narrow but convincing triumph, and a pledge to go on to Chicago where he hoped to become his party's nominee. But the violence that afflicted the nation now visited the Ambassador Hotel in Los Angeles, where RFK delivered an abbreviated victory speech just after midnight on June 5. The fatal shooting of Kennedy by a lurking assassin seemed to bring to an end the New Politics of 1968, shattering the hopes of liberals and radicals alike.

The repeated quashing of the dream and the killing of the dreamers created greater despair, especially among America's young. Many, although certainly not all, of the most politically engaged members of the generation that came of age during the 1960s shifted further leftward in the direction of believing radical, even revolutionary, change was needed. By 1968, even key figures associated with the counterculture, which was often considered apolitical, proved willing to voice political stances, including those of a seemingly radical nature. Politicos associated with an organization like Students for Democratic Society (SDS) supposedly shared little in common with the vast number of young people who seemed enamored with a new American bohemia that had produced events like the previous year's Summer of Love, the turn toward communes and collectives, and the counterculture's potent concoction of sex, drugs, and rock 'n' roll. By 1968, some in the hippie community expressed revolutionary ideas themselves, although sometimes those involved individualistic quests for expanded consciousness rather than raising barricades. Others, however, were surprisingly politically engaged, and willing to make common cause with political radicals, offering the possibility of some type of youth quake transcending the mid-1960s London fashion revolution and the longer hair and Salvation Army attire associated with the counterculture. Implicitly at least, the Beatles and the Rolling Stones waged a battle of a kind regarding such political commitment, with the former offering a cautionary message in "Revolution" and the latter endorsing revolutionary action in "Street Fighting Man."

Events overseas and in America pertaining to the counterculture, social unrest, Establishment politics, war, and revolution, appeared surreal at times during 1968, with virtually apocalyptic happenings taking place. August was a particularly unsettling month in a year such incidents abounded. That month alone witnessed disturbing developments in Prague and Chicago that caused many to draw comparisons between those very different cities. In the wake of the Khrushchev revelations of Stalinist terrors a dozen years earlier, ferment had taken hold in parts of Eastern Europe. Soviet forces had crushed the Hungarian Revolution in the fall of 1956, but opposition to communist rule hardly abated in the region. By the mid-1960s, Czechoslovakia began to experience a loosening of the Communist Party's authoritarian grip, allowing for the unfolding of what came to be known as the Prague Spring. During the spring of 1968, the recently appointed first secretary of the Czechoslovakian Communist Party, Alexander Dubček, who was determined to curb censorship while fostering political participation and economic change, spoke of the need to bring about "communism with a human face." But on August 20, 500,000 Warsaw Pact forces invaded Czechoslovakia to expel "counter-revolutionaries," placing the Prague Spring at great risk of being laid to rest.

As events in Czechoslovakia proved increasingly dire, the Democratic Party held its nominating convention in Chicago from August 26 to 29. With the New Politics having foundered badly following the murder of Robert F. Kennedy, Vice President Humphrey, a strong backer of the administration's Vietnam policy, appeared the near certain nominee of the world's oldest political party. Platform fights ensued between supporters of the Johnson White House and anti-war delegates, but concluded with no happy resolution for Vietnam War critics. Over several days, the Chicago police and anti-war activists battled in the streets as television cameras rolled and voices rang out, "The Whole World Is Watching." A presidential commission later charged that a police riot ensued, with mass arrests and beatings that spilled over to restaurants, hotels, even the convention floor.

Confrontation of another sort continued to take place in American families and homes as the second wave of the feminist movement grabbed attention through a spectacular protest in 1968. The postwar period had ushered in a new cult of domesticity, placing motherhood and the nuclear family in a seemingly sacrosanct position. But sexism suffused the American mainstream, with the expectation that patriarchy necessarily prevailed, whether through male political, business, and cultural leaders or popular cultural representations like the television programs *The Donna Reed Show* and *Father Knows Best*. Some women pushed back against the misogyny that limited occupational expectations even for graduates of the finest women's colleges. By 1968, feminists were holding consciousness-raising sessions. They also established organizations like New York Radical Women and Cell 16, put out the pamphlet *Toward a Female Liberation Movement*, and conducted marches condemning sexism. Most strikingly, they carried out a protest of the Miss America pageant in Atlantic City, charging that it amounted to a "cattle auction."

The women's movement would soon be divided by the issue of how to deal with men, or whether to do so at all. Embedded in that controversy was the manner in which lesbians were perceived both inside and outside the movement. Both women and men had long been involved in the fight to contest the often scandalous way homosexuals were treated in the United States, through groups like the Daughters of Bilitis and the Mattachine Society. During the 1960s, gays engaged in more public campaigns to challenge discriminatory treatment, participating in documentaries, speaking with journalists exploring the status of homosexuals in America, and conducting protests through demonstrations, including "sip-ins" patterned after sit-ins. In 1968, medical diagnoses of homosexuality began to alter, with the American Psychiatric Association (APA) no longer referring to it as "sociopathic." The APA's continued categorization as a "sexual deviation," however, troubled many homosexuals, some of whom pushed for a Homosexual Bill of Rights.

As the women's and gay rights movements grabbed attention in 1968, with talk of the need to revolutionize gender and sexual relations in the United States, so did the environmental campaign. It too had received a spur during the early postwar period, with concerns expressed about major industrial accidents and pollution, new national parks established, and the appearance of new environmental organizations. Rachel Carson's best-selling book, *Silent Spring*, which warned of the dangerous impact of pesticides, provided impetus for the budding environmental movement. By 1968, the meteorologist Elmer Robinson was warning that elevated carbon dioxide counts could result in "serious world-wide environmental changes." Edward Abbey published *Desert Solitaire*, bemoaning man's impact on the desert environment, and Paul Ehrlich released *The Population Bomb*, predicting demographic disasters. In similar fashion, Garrett Hardin's article "Tragedy of the Commons" prophesied a ruinous destiny for a humankind engaged in selfish pursuits. He also wrote, "Long experience has shown that local problems are best dealt with by local action . . . globalism is usually counterproductive."

Notwithstanding such admonitions, the world as of 1968 appeared more interconnected than ever, with events across the globe impacting cultural, political, and social developments. Ideas and tactics seemed to be contagious during 1968, with talk of revolution continuing, the possibility of which exhilarated some while enraging others. Such incongruous responses took place in the United States, Czechoslovakia, France, and Mexico, among various locales. The vision of transforming their society invigorated many of Mexico's high school and college students, dissatisfied with the Institutional Revolutionary Party (PRI), which, despite its name, had governed for decades in a decidedly nonrevolutionary manner. Charging that radicals were leading mass protests and worried about their impact on the Olympic Games to be held in Mexico City in October, the government conducted a brutal crackdown leading to the death of an untold number of demonstrators and bystanders, possibly surpassing 1,000. With student activism quelled, the Olympic Games proceeded, but protest also marked the spectacle.

Best remembered from the 1968 Olympic Games is the quiet, dignified protest involving two American sprinters, Tommie Smith and John Carlos from San Jose State University, medal recipients in the 200-meter dash. With their heads bowed and their feet bare, Olympic champion Smith and bronze medal recipient Carlos held aloft single fists, covered in black gloves. The Smith-Carlos protest was a milder version of what the sociologist Harry Edwards had originally envisioned: a boycott by black athletes spurred by the Olympic Project for Human Rights (OPHR). The OPHR was itself a byproduct of the turn toward black power that had taken hold within the civil rights movement, resulting from growing disenchantment with liberal approaches and seemingly pervasive racial discrimination. By 1968, the Black Panther Party also garnered greater attention, with the release of Eldridge Cleaver's autobiographical *Soul on Ice* and a murder trial involving cofounder Huey Newton. During the fall, students at San Francisco State University, associated with the Third World Liberation Front, initiated the longest-running strike in American public education, demanding greater representation for people of color, the rehiring of a militant black instructor, the admission of any black students who applied, and the setting up of a Department of Black Studies.

Progressive, even radical political, social, and cultural movements attained considerable attention throughout 1968, with talk of revolution heard around the globe. But the revolutionary surge that seemed so imminent when the year opened had ebbed by the early fall, in many instances. The Tet Offensive altered the American political landscape, yet failed to bring about the toppling of the US-backed South Vietnamese regime, and led to the decimation of Vietcong forces. The war itself only intensified, yielding greater death and destruction. The French government of Charles de Gaulle faltered in the face of the May protests, but conservatives solidified control by summer. The Mexican governing party, PRI, remained entrenched, following the Tlatelolco massacre of protesters in Mexico City's Plaza de las Tres Culturas. By contrast, the Prague Spring crashed to a halt with the Warsaw Pact invasion.

In the United States too, the forces calling for revolution, whether political or cultural, had to take a back seat as backlash and assassinations blunted the New Politics and abetted the rise of George Wallace, Ronald Reagan, and Richard M. Nixon. All three benefited from the politics of backlash, with Wallace conducting a vigorous presidential bid through his American Independent Party that saw him deftly if crudely utilize racism and the threat of violence to gain the votes of those angered by the civil rights, anti-war, and women's movements, and dismayed by the counterculture. In California, Governor Ronald Reagan continued governing in a generally moderate fashion while calling on charged rhetoric that endeared him to conservatives and made him the darling of the New Right. Reagan's own attempt to win the Republican Party nomination came too late, allowing Nixon to prevail. The defeated 1960 nominee painted himself as a new Nixon, supposedly more mature and softened in some manner. But his campaign used tactics and rhetoric that attracted many who would otherwise have preferred Reagan or even Wallace. That, coupled with the Democratic Party's propensity for self-destruction, enabled Nixon, who promised a restoration of law and order and insisted he could better handle the Vietnam War, to prevail, however narrowly, in the November election. Helpful too were actions behind the scenes in which Nixon surrogates worked to interfere with peace talks, a violation of the 1799 Logan Act forbidding unauthorized individuals from negotiating with foreign governments. While such shenanigans would not become public knowledge for decades, Nixon's election ensured that the proponents of a new American revolution and the president-elect would clash in the period ahead.

Acknowledgments

Robert C. Cottrell wishes to express appreciation to his wife Susan, their daughter Jordan, and other supportive family members.

Blaine T. Browne extends his thanks to those who schooled him in the arts of historical research and writing, and more immediately to his ever-patient wife Marian, who never falters in her support for his professional endeavors.

The authors want to express their appreciation for Rowman & Littlefield's production team, especially Jon Sisk, Kate Powers, and Elaine McGarraugh.

1

"Yippie!"

Abbie, Jerry, and the Politics of Play

Figure 1.1   Demonstrators protest the Vietnam War in front of the White House. By 1968, such demonstrations had become commonplace. The Yippies took protest to a new level, combining street theater with radical politics. Library of Congress, Prints and Photographs Division, LIC-DIG ppmsca-24300.

Sixteen hippies, spearheaded by Abbie Hoffman and James Fourrat, but including Jerry Rubin and Stew Albert, invaded the sanctity of the New York Stock Exchange on the morning of August 24, 1967. They were connected, intimately or not, with the New York Diggers, an anarchist group known for deliberately provocative actions designed to elicit attention regarding various

1

causes. In a concerted act of guerrilla theater, the band of sixteen tossed dollar bills onto the trading floor. The *New York Daily News* vividly reported, "A shower of green power descended on the heads of the startled capitalists" as protesters appeared to be displaying disdain "for the almighty bucks." Some stockbrokers, clerks, and runners, John Kifner of the *New York Times* reported, responded in good humor, but most "jeered, shouted, pointed fingers and shook their fists." Clerks raced to grab the money, but security guards soon forced the hippies off the floor of the Exchange. One unnamed demonstrator spoke of a desire "to make a loving gesture to these people," while Fourrat more dramatically offered, "It's the death of money." Hoffman later bragged, "In the minds of millions of teenagers the stock market had just crashed," but stocks were already shaky because of the American economy's increasingly fragile nature.

One of the Stock Exchange protest participants, Jerry Rubin, had a well-established reputation as an anti-war activist. Newly arrived in the city, Rubin encountered Keith Lampe, who spoke of Hoffman, explaining, "He's a Digger. He believes it's more important to burn dollar bills than draft cards." Lampe introduced Rubin to Hoffman, who invited him to participate in the Wall Street action, which Fouratt claimed to have plotted. Indeed, Fouratt wanted "to figure out an action that would focus public attention on corporate America's role in Vietnam." However, as Fouratt revealed, "Abbie, like everything else, appropriated it as his." Believing that Wall Street appeared unfazed by the Vietnam War, they determined to carry out a demonstration at the Stock Exchange.

Reporters from both the mainstream and the underground press, having been apprised of the protest—which Hoffman denied—showed up at the New York Stock Exchange office building located in lower Manhattan's Financial District at 20 Broad Street. The protesters, many of whom had never met, appeared at the visitors' gallery, situated above the trading floor, and engaged in various antics, including stuffing money in their mouths. Hoffman, Fouratt, and their companions encountered John Whighton, head of the Exchange's security force, who indicated that no demonstration was possible. Responding to Whighton's obvious perception of who they were, Hoffman retorted, "Who's a hippie? I'm Jewish and besides we don't do demonstrations, see we have no picket signs." When Whighton solicited a name from the group, which called itself ESSO or the East Side Service Organization, Fourrat responded, "George Metesky," an almost mythical name in New Left circles. Metesky was the disgruntled former Consolidated Edison mechanic turned "Mad Bomber," who had terrorized New York City for more than a decade and a half, beginning in November 1940. In setting up a tour of the New York Stock Exchange, Hoffman had also employed the pseudonym George Metesky.

Once at the gallery overlooking the trading floor, the group engaged in its brand of street theater, drawing on the 300 one-dollar bills—or thirty or forty, according to various accounts—Hoffman had collected, while yelling, "Take the money! Here's the real shit!" Confused security guards stated, "You can't do that, you're not allowed to do that. That's illegal, we're going to get the police." Hoffman and company responded, "What do you mean? People throw away money all the time here! This is the way you do it, isn't it?" When a reporter asked who had supplied the money, Fouratt said, "It was from General William Westmoreland's mother who disapproved of her son's military policy in Vietnam." The resulting disruption halted the stock ticker for a few minutes, but elicited considerable attention, as Hoffman had hoped.

After being escorted outside, Hoffman and Rubin lit a $5 bill, which a runner for the Stock Exchange tore away from them. Hoffman, Fourrat, and their compatriots flippantly responded to questions from reporters. When asked who they were, one protester declared, "Cardinal Spellman," referring to the conservative Roman Catholic prelate. "Thousands" was the response to the query of how much money had been thrown around, and "Hundreds," the reply to the one involving how many people were part of the group. But that last answer also included the comment, "We don't exist! We don't exist." When a bystander complained, "This is a disgusting display," Hoffman agreed. "You're right. These people are nothing but a bunch of filthy commies."

The Wall Street protest exemplified how skillfully Hoffman, Rubin, and a small band of political activists-turned-hippies used the media to draw attention for various causes and events, while acquiring greater notoriety themselves. As another Stock Exchange participant, Superjoel, recalled, "It went network. We were elated. That was beyond our wildest dream." Hoffman appreciated how appealing the story, which he considered "a perfectly mythical event," was to the mass media. "It's a natural. Right after the news report . . . comes the human interest story—crazy hippies throwing money." Michael Rossman, a leading activist in Berkeley, considered the demonstration "perfect" due to its simplicity and simultaneous ability to amount to "profound theater." In his autobiography, Hoffman suggested that guerrilla theater was "probably the oldest form of political commentary." The brief incident involving "mind-terrorists" compelled Stock Exchange representatives, for instance, to place bulletproof glass around the gallery. Hoffman also pointed to Antonin Artaud, the French writer and actor who was associated with "the Theater of Cruelty," which emphasized the "total spectacle," seeking to "abolish the stage and auditorium," and foster catharsis. To Hoffman, "protest as theater came natural." For one thing, he and his fellow protesters already dressed "in costume," sporting the often colorful garb associated with the American counterculture. In addition, they operated through street engagement, playing music, asking for spare change, and protesting issues both large and small.

In writing about the Stock Exchange demonstration, Hoffman headlined a chapter "Driving the Money Changers from the Temple" in his book *Revolution for the Hell of It*. At the same time, he thought that something greater had transpired, that "a spark had been ignited. The system cracked a little." As Hoffman saw it, "In the minds of millions of teenagers, the stock market had just crashed."

That very possibility, however hyperbolically considered, delighted both Hoffman and Rubin, who would become the self-proclaimed leaders of a group of media-seeking political activists turned countercultural guerrillas. Hoffman and Rubin, born in 1936 and 1938, respectively, were somewhat older than many Movement activists and hippies, with greater experience in civil rights and anti-war campaigns. Like a disproportionate percentage of Movement activists, both were Jewish, which intensified their identification with oppressed groups, such as Southern blacks or Vietnamese peasants. A recipient of a B.A. in psychology from Brandeis University and an M.A. in the same discipline from the University of California at Berkeley (UC Berkeley), Hoffman participated in the civil rights movement in the Deep South, assisting with Mississippi Freedom Summer (MFS) in 1964. As the United States greatly intensified its role in Vietnam, Hoffman became involved in the anti-war movement. He also proved enamored with the flowering American counterculture, letting his naturally wavy hair cascade around his face, donning colorful garments, and participating in a CIA-sponsored LSD (lysergic acid diethylamide) experiment. Hoffman was drawn to a New York version of the Diggers, an anarchist group that initially appeared in San Francisco's Haight-Ashbury district and extolled the virtues of street theater and provocative actions, including the setting up of Free Stores and the doling out of free food.

Having grown up in a less affluent household than Hoffman, Rubin went to Oberlin College in Ohio and Hebrew University in Jerusalem, before graduating from the University of Cincinnati. He enrolled in the doctoral program in sociology at UC Berkeley but quickly dropped out to engage in full-time political activism. By the spring of 1965, Rubin was helping to orchestrate the Vietnam Day Committee (VDC), which launched a massive teach-in, early draft resistance, and the International Days of Protest. He ran the campaign of *Ramparts* editor Robert Scheer, who sought to oust liberal Democratic congressman Jeffrey Cohelan, a supporter of the Johnson administration's stance on Vietnam. During the summer of 1966, Rubin and several other anti-war activists were ordered before the House Un-American Activities Committee (HUAC) in Washington, DC. HUAC intended to offer legislation "to make it a criminal offense to interfere with troop movements, distribute propaganda affecting troop morale, or provide aid to hostile powers." Rubin had been calling for the VDC to work toward the creation of a "third party" to condemn the administration's Vietnam War policies. On August 16, Rubin appeared at a HUAC session dressed in a Revolutionary War uniform and wearing a tricorn hat. He believed it was necessary to question HUAC's "very legitimacy," and he wanted to appeal to young people throughout the United States. Rubin issued pamphlets declaring that he sought to "symbolize the fact that America was born in revolution," yet was presently "denying the right of others to revolution." The inquiry ended on August 19, with Rubin dragged out of the hearing as he complained about not being called to testify. Rubin was one of a dozen individuals ejected and then "arrested for creating disturbances," according to the *New York Times*. Subsequently, Rubin ran for mayor of Berkeley, amassing 20 percent of the vote and coming in second in the race, although far behind the Republican incumbent. Increasingly influenced by the counterculture, Rubin sought to bridge the gap between political and cultural radicals through the discarding of "games and institutions that oppress and dehumanize" and by nurturing "new values and new human relations."

Hoffman continued to protest the Vietnam War, joining Jim Fouratt in organizing a Flower Brigade of hippies who marched in New York City next to supporters of the conflict conducting a Loyalty Parade. Hoffman later recounted how the hippies were attacked by "Zonk, fists, red paint, kicks, beer cans, spitting—the whole American Welcome Wagon treatment." Writing in *WIN* magazine, published by the War Resisters League, Hoffman indicated, "The Flower Brigade lost its first battle, but watch out America."

As he became more drawn to the counterculture and street theater, Hoffman felt estranged from standard political practices, including those associated with radical, New Left organizations. The American Old Left had emerged after the Bolshevik Revolution, and attained its greatest prominence during the Great Depression and World War II, but dissipated in the wake of Cold War pressures, sectarianism, and a stubborn refusal on the part of Communist Party USA (CPUSA) to question Holy Mother Russia's infallibility. A New Left appeared by 1960, through groups like the Student Nonviolent Coordinating Committee (SNCC) and SDS, no longer beholden to the shibboleths of the left, envisioning instead a beloved community and participatory democracy. However, those ideals themselves lost luster among many young radicals as unrelenting violence and pressure led to the weakening of a belief in nonviolent direct action and the possibility of peaceful change. By 1967, black power proponents possessed greater appeal in certain circles within the civil rights movement, while advocates of Prairie Power, student syndicalism, and revolution attracted increased support inside the New Left as a whole.

By the time SDS gathered for a national conclave in Denton, Michigan, in June 1967, the organization comprised 247 chapters and approximately 30,000 members around the country, having drawn individuals from across the left and libertarian facets of the political spectrum. Hoffman watched in delight as San Francisco Diggers Peter Berg and Emmett Grogan taunted SDS members while Tom Hayden was presenting the keynote address. Berg urged them to avoid organizing particular groups and, instead, to "organize your head." Grogan cried out, "Faggots! Fags! Take off your ties, they are chains around you necks. You haven't got the balls to go mad. You're going to make a revolution?— you'll piss in your pants when the violence erupts." An early SDS leader, Bob Ross, enraged by the Diggers' tirades," hollered, "If the CIA wanted to disrupt this meeting, they couldn't have done it any better than by sending you." By contrast, Hoffman considered the gathering "monumental" and likely one of a kind. "Holy shit," he yelled. "Excitement, Drama, Revolution."

Clearly influenced by the Diggers, Hoffman and Fouratt planned the Wall Street spectacle, then Abbie attended the third Socialist Scholars Conference, held in New York City in early September. There, Hoffman participated in a debate with SDS leader Gregory Calvert, "Hippies Versus Radicals." Discussing the exchange in the *National Guardian*, Gerald Long suggested, "a hip radical and a radical hippie have a lot in common." The philosopher and political theorist Herbert Marcuse, who would later be labeled "the father of the New Left," enjoyed Hoffman's cultural radicalism, but concluded, "Flowers have no power other than the power of the men and women who let them grow and protect them." Seemingly in agreement with Marcuse, Hoffman revealed, "I always held my flower in a clinched fist."

Both Hoffman and Rubin participated in the famed March on the Pentagon that took place beginning on October 21, 1967, and involved approximately 100,000 demonstrators. Rubin served as the march's project director, selected by David Dellinger, the former World War II conscientious objector who edited *Liberation*, the anarchist-pacifist journal, and was coordinator of the National Mobilization Committee to End the War in Vietnam ("the Mobe"). In his account of the march, *The Armies of the Night*, Norman Mailer indicates that Rubin possessed "enormous stature among youth groups and Under-Thirties, second perhaps only to Mario Savio," a leader of UC Berkeley's Free Speech Movement (FSM). The choice of Rubin, in Mailer's estimation, revealed that Mobe leaders were flirting with "that no-man's-land between organized acceptable dissent and incalculable acts of revolution."

Already veering in a more radical direction, Dellinger favored the change in tactics that SDS had opted for: "from protest to resistance." As he saw it, the march would meld "Gandhi and Guerrilla," would somehow blend "conventional mass protest and civil disobedience," and thereby marry the anti-war movement's disparate factions. However, to select Rubin was "to call upon the most militant, unpredictable, creative—therefore dangerous—hippie-oriented leader available on the New Left." Yet Dellinger recognized that Rubin was seen as a creative protest strategist, conversant with the employment of inventive, even sensational tactics. The Mobe intended to hold a rally on the National Mall and possibly set up a People's Congress, but Rubin called for protest centered on the symbol of the US military establishment, the massive Pentagon, situated across the Potomac River in Arlington County, Virginia.

Rubin also was more drawn to Hoffman, who "just revolutionized" him. Abbie, for his part, considered Rubin "the white Rap Brown," referring to the militant SNCC leader who said that "violence is as American as cherry pie." Hoffman talked about guerrilla theater that would involve the purported levitating of the Pentagon. A friend, Paul Krassner, suggests that Bay Area hippies Allen Cohen, editor of the underground *Oracle*, and Michael Bowen, an artist associated with the San Francisco Renaissance, broached that very idea. They had encountered Lewis Mumford's *The City in History*, which indicated that the Pentagon symbolized "evil and oppression." The hippie known as Charlie Brown explained that the five-sided star was connected to "war, murder and apocalypse." Allen Ginsberg, for his part, insisted it was another poet, Gary Snyder, the recent author of a scathing poem, "A Curse on the Men in Washington, Pentagon," who talked about levitating the Pentagon. Rubin and Hoffman, for their part, were already teaming up. "Abbie added the theater, the humor, the sparkle, and I added the purpose," Rubin recalled. "I directed Abbie. . . . I took the Abbie wind up doll. I wound him up and pointed him toward the Pentagon." Together, they ensured that the Mobe's plan for "an orderly, peaceful, middle-class protest" would veer off in another direction altogether. Rubin also turned to Ed Sanders of the New York rock band The Fugs, and "the West Coast contingent."

But Hoffman's influence on Rubin proved paramount. The latter was increasingly drawn to Hoffman's perspective about the New Left. As he subsequently explained in *Revolution for the Hell of It*, published the next year, Hoffman wrote, "I don't like the concept of a movement built on sacrifice, dedication, responsibility, anger, frustration, and guilt. All those down things. I would say, look, you want to have more fun, you want to get laid more, you want to turn on with your friends, you want an outlet for your creativity, then get out of school, quit your job. Come on out and help build and defend the society you want. Stop trying to organize everybody but yourself. Begin to live your vision."

Following Hoffman's Wall Street prank, Rubin appeared alongside other Movement heavyweights as the Mobe revealed its intention at a news conference in Manhattan to carry out a major demonstration that would "shut down the Pentagon." Progressive organizations, including SNCC, Women Strike for Peace (WSP), and the Congress of Racial Equality (CORE), endorsed the Pentagon effort. The executive director of the Episcopal Peace Fellowship, the Reverend Thomas Lee Hayes, indicated, "We will gather in a massive anti-war presence, and some will take on the most serious responsibility of direct dislocation of the war machine." The Mobe's statement pledged, "In the name of humanity we will call the war-makers to task." Dellinger warned, "There will be no government building which will be unattacked." Rubin was quoted as avowing that the demonstration was designed to "build a mass movement to end the war."

Such promises alienated moderate members of the Mobe, but Dellinger felt it necessary to intensify "the militance," to "make it impossible for them to continue business as usual." He also considered it necessary to bolster the spirit of protesters, who were starting "to become dispirited." By contrast, as Dellinger saw it, "something happens when people put their bodies on the line, or when they get arrested." Other Mobe leaders like Doug Dowd and Brad Lyttle agreed with Dellinger's assessment, and reasoned that mass civil disobedience involved "a natural evolution" from large demonstrations. Some important anti-war figures, including David McReynolds and Fred Halstead, were more doubtful and worried still more about plans by Rubin and Hoffman to provoke disruptions. That was precisely what the two increasingly close allies hoped to accomplish by wedding cultural and political protest. They also considered "guerrilla media" essential to pique the interest of the news media, which otherwise would lose interest in yet one more demonstration. Fouratt credits Hoffman with the March on the Pentagon, and his ability to "take the hippie element and weld it with the hard-line political reality." Hoffman believed it was necessary to "disrupt the mind-set of Middle Americans."

Hoffman and his friend, the artist Marty Carey, actually went to check out the Pentagon, encountering a security guard who arrested them for littering. *Time* magazine reported that a General Services administrator "graciously gave his permission for them to raise the building a maximum of ten feet" and dropped the charges. Writing in the *East Village Other*, Hoffman pledged, "We will fuck on the grass and beat ourselves against the doors." Generating more media attention, Hoffman talked about having devised a new drug, LACE, which would be doled out like tear gas but supposedly served as an instantaneous aphrodisiac. At another session, he again insisted the Pentagon would be levitated. Rubin was involved in negotiations with the General Services Administration about the impending demonstration.

By October 20, thousands of demonstrators arrived in Washington, DC, to participate in anti-war protests. The *New York Times* noted that approximately 150 groups were part of the Mobe, which was sponsoring the series of events condemning US engagement in Vietnam. Dellinger revealed that many protesters would not be satisfied with "government-approved protest activities" or "the ritualistic charade of merely stepping across a line and being arrested." He also denied that acceptance of a march permit precluded civil disobedience. The Washington demonstrations were tied to an array of anti-war activity, such as Stop the Draft Week involving the turning in of draft cards, including a "mass burn-in, turn-in" that took place in Boston, and sustained clashes with the police in Oakland and Berkeley. However, attention soon gravitated to Washington, DC, where anti-war activists attempted to turn over 1,000 draft cards to the Justice Department and more than 100,000 protesters eventually appeared. Also readying for the march were thousands of Army troops, as a siege mentality took hold in the White House. Large demonstrations were also slated for London, Amsterdam, Berlin, Copenhagen, Oslo, Stockholm, and Tokyo.

In the afternoon of October 21, with a massive array of individuals situated near the Lincoln Memorial, a hip, sardonic quality was apparent through protest signs such as the one reading "LBJ, Pull Out Now, Like Your Father Should Have Done." Dellinger, who had just been attacked by three American Nazi Party members, proclaimed that peaceful protest was being discarded. Civil disobedience would henceforth be paired with confrontation, Dellinger declared. Dr. Benjamin Spock was among the speakers, stating, "We consider the war Lyndon Johnson is waging as disastrous to this country in every way, and that we, the protesters, are the ones who may help to save our country." Spock went on to claim that "the enemy, we believe in all sincerity, is Lyndon Johnson, who we elected as a peace candidate in 1964 and who betrayed us within three months." Dellinger eventually asserted, "This is the beginning of a new stage in the American peace movement in which the cutting edge becomes active resistance" and he referred to the long needed shift "from protest to resistance."

Thousands headed across the Arlington Bridge to the Pentagon, which was surrounded by thousands of soldiers. An early confrontation occurred, in which some protesters sought entry into the Pentagon but were repelled. Many began an encampment, sang songs, and attempted to win over the military police (MPs), with a daisy placed inside the barrel of a National

Guardsman's rifle. Hundreds of draft cards were lit, amounting to the "largest mass draft card burning in the history of protest against the Vietnam War." Hoffman and several friends from the Lower East Side, including Martin Carey, Keith Lampe, and Ed Sanders, along with "black magic practitioners," handed out "noisemakers, wild costumers, and witches' hats." The small group chanted and sang, and acted as though the Pentagon could actually be raised off the ground. Close to midnight, army paratroopers took over from the MPs, then began attacking protesters "like peasants mowing down wheat." Chaos enveloped the crowd, with individuals scurrying to avoid blows from angry soldiers. Some demonstrators wanted to respond in kind, as Cornell political economist Doug Dowd, a Mobe leader, recognized. He spotted Rubin and some others "goading people on, yelling and screaming, and throwing live, fiery pieces of wood up front . . . at the marshals." Enraged by those antics, Dowd later admitted, "That was one of the occasions on which I would have killed Jerry Rubin if I could have." Nearly 700 individuals were arrested, including such luminaries as Dellinger, Hoffman, Norman Mailer, and Dagmar Wilson, one of the WSP founders. While in jail, Hoffman cried out, "I'm in here with Jews and Commies. Let me out!"

Secretary of Defense Robert McNamara, increasingly disenchanted with the administration's war policy, later acknowledged having been "scared" at the sight of the protesters near the Pentagon, and the CIA's Richard Helms also admitted to discomfort concerning the moblike atmosphere. Mainstream media coverage of the protest all but unanimously condemned the purported "lawlessness" of "extremists," the sociologist Tom Wells notes. President Johnson responded by placing greater pressure on intelligence agencies to uncover foreign subversive ties to the anti-war movement. An early initial report, along with subsequent ones, would refute that very notion.

In late November, Hoffman, Rubin, Paul Krassner, and the folk singer Phil Ochs orchestrated a demonstration in Greenwich Village's Washington Square, "The War Is Over," which culminated in a march to Times Square. The idea derived from Allen Ginsberg's declaration the previous year at the National Student Association's convention, when he affirmed, "I declare the end of the war."

Viewing the March on the Pentagon as a complete success, Hoffman and Rubin began gearing up for the "next national rendezvous": the Democratic Party National Convention slated for Chicago the following August. As Hoffman indicated in his autobiography, the plan was to "stalk" the president as he campaigned for reelection, by constructing "armies of protesters" willing to confront "the policy makers with their own madness." Abbie foresaw "a counterconvention, a pop festival, and an all-encompassing week of protest," as the scholar-activist Jonah Raskin, who befriended Hoffman and Rubin, reveals. Rubin got together with Ed Sanders and Keith Lampe, and they talked about a possible turn toward violence within the anti-war movement. Looking ahead to the Democratic Party's national conclave, Sanders tossed out the idea of a free music festival there. On December 25, Hoffman informed Father Bernard Gilgun from the Catholic Worker Movement, who knew Abbie from his civil rights days, of the desire to draw a quarter of a million individuals to Chicago. "We expect about 100,000 of them to be committed to disruption or sabotage. Both are worthwhile."

That message was sent from Florida, where Abbie, his wife Anita, and their friends Paul Krassner and Ellen Sander, who covered the rock scene for *The Saturday Review of Literature*, had gone for a vacation, drawing on a small book advance Hoffman had received. The two men talked about "violence in the revolution." Hoffman indicated that "violence was necessary," convinced as he was that justice, not peace, was most essential. Rubin remembered calling Hoffman and Krassner, who were tripping on LSD, telling them, "Hey, we gotta go to Chicago." Abbie, Anita, and Krassner decided to head back to New York City, where a meeting took place on New Year's Eve at the Hoffmans' apartment on St. Marks Place in the East Village. Present were the Hoffmans, Martin and Susan Carey, Krassner, Rubin, Jerry's girlfriend Nancy Kurshan, Sanders, Carol Shebar, and Danny Schechter, who like Abbie, had been a civil rights and community organizer.

They all got stoned on Colombian marijuana before discussing future plans. According to the historian David Farber, Rubin was enthralled with replicating Ginsberg's earlier pronouncement about the end of the Vietnam War, viewing it as the finest type of guerrilla theater: "exciting and alive and totally participatory." Intrigued as well, Krassner nevertheless questioned how to hold onto that sensibility as a "convention of death" beckoned. Rubin came up with the idea of a Festival of Life, open, public, and able to compete with the Democratic Party's convention for public attention. As he talked about leadership with the Movement, Hoffman insisted that young people should be inspired "to do their own thing" and everyone encouraged to become an artist. The subject of the mass media arose, with Hoffman claiming it made more sense to avoid staid, tedious protest tactics and to draw on "weirdness, absurdity, and colorfulness" to attract a much wider audience. Then, Krassner evidently blurted out, "Yippie! Yippie!" Rubin thought, "Yip, yippie, hippie, oh, God, it was perfect. Hippie to yippie, yippie to hippie." The name conveyed how hippies were being radicalized. Then, Krassner or Anita Hoffman suggested adoption of the appellation Youth International Party, which would signify the international nature of the struggle by young people as ferment was taking place across the globe. As Krassner recalls, "We would *be* a party and we would *have* a party." The name would also appeal to straights and kids alike, Farber reports. Those gathered at the Hoffman apartment were thrilled, as if they had discovered a means to appeal to disaffected youngsters through a fusion of countercultural and Movement approaches. Krassner believed this was already occurring, leading to "an organic coalition of psychedelic dropouts and political activists." The group also fastened onto the idea of offering a pig as the Yippies' presidential candidate, which would obviously appeal to media outlets, both Establishment and underground.

In early January, Rubin attended the Socialist Workers Party Militant Labor Forum, where he debated the radical organization's presidential candidate Fred Halstead on the subject of "what policy next for the anti-war movement?" The *Berkeley Barb*, one of the leading underground papers, indicated that Rubin's response to Halstead's opening statement was "nonverbal," involving the playing of "I am the Walrus" and "Ballad of a Thin Man," by the Beatles and Bob Dylan, respectively, before he lit both his draft card and a dollar bill. As for Rubin's own statement, it began with his declaration that no anti-war movement existed, but was rather a concoction of the mass media designed "to fuck up our minds." He insisted that the world order was collapsing, pertaining to capitalism, money, bureaucracy, imperialism, the middle class, boredom, exploitation, and militarism. The world looked on admiringly as the United States proved unable to subdue the Vietcong. In America, Rubin chortled, "we are all learning how to become Vietcong." In the manner that Ken Kesey of the Merry Pranksters had earlier derided an anti-war rally in Oakland, Rubin dismissed the movement as "self-defeating," and insisted its negativity needed to be supplanted by "an American Liberation Movement." He extolled "the vanguard of action"; the recent devastating rioting in Detroit; the American teenagers who praised Che; the guerrillas who wanted to replicate his practices. In the fashion of Allen Ginsberg's "Howl" and Jack Kerouac's *The Dharma Bums*, two beat classics, Rubin saluted those who were "freaky, crazy, irrational, sexy, angry, irreligious, childish, and mad." That included draft-card burners, drug sirens, protesters waving Vietcong flags, individuals who carried on Proudhon's belief that property was theft, and people willing to blurt out "fuck" on television.

The Vietnam War could be ended, Rubin believed, thanks to the combining of "youth, music, sex, drugs, and rebellion with treason." As for the Movement, Rubin saw it as "a school," whose teachers included "the Fugs/Dylan/Beatles/Ginsberg/mass media/hippies/students fighting cops in Berkeley/blood on draft records/sit-ins/jail." He considered repression the lifeblood of the Movement, requiring attacks from centrists and reactionaries, and he viewed "the street" as "the stage." Cheered by the generational conflict, Rubin, like a growing number of young people, associated communism not with Joseph Stalin but, instead, "the heroic romantic fidel che vietcong." He and his ilk happily envisioned the future, seeking "a communal world where the imagination reigns supreme, and where human institutions respond to human needs." But before their "great" 1984—distinct from George Orwell's dystopian vision—appeared, disruption and crisis would take hold. Looking ahead to the Democratic Party nominating convention in Chicago, Rubin foresaw the Youth International Party attracting half a million young people, all turned on and radicalized, eventually compelling the withdrawal of US forces from Vietnam to maintain order in Chicago. There, LBJ would be "nominated under the protection of tear gas and bayonets." Eventually, law and order would dissipate across the nation, further threatening the authority of the federal government.

More meetings took place over the next several weeks, resulting in additional Movement activists and media figures becoming involved in the campaign to spread the word about the purported existence of the Youth International Party. Another gathering at the Hoffman apartment in early January included Ed Sanders and Keith Lampe, while Bob Fass, an FM radio personality in New York City, who would be called "a midwife at the birth of the counterculture," was also present. In the middle of the month, a larger meeting occurred at Peggy Hitchcock's posh residence in Manhattan. Hitchcock had become involved with Timothy Leary during his early LSD experiments, while her brothers had allowed Leary and Richard Alpert to reside at the family estate in Millbrook, New York, after their dismissal from Harvard University for conducting drug tests with undergraduate students. Leary and Allen Ginsberg were there, as were Allen Katzman, who edited the underground *East Village Other*, and Marshall Bloom, a cofounder of the Liberation News Service (LNS), the underground press syndicate. Hoffman and Rubin broached the idea of a Yippie Festival of Life during the Democratic Party national convention, and an agreement was made to hold a lengthy benefit, "The Three Ring Yippie," in New York City.

On January 16, LNS included an announcement, devised by Hoffman, Rubin, Krassner, and Sanders, for the birth of the Youth International Party, also referred to as Yip! It called for "an international festival of youth music and theater" to be held in Chicago when "the NATIONAL DEATH PARTY" gathered "to bless" President Johnson. A half-million revelers would supposedly dance in the streets, make love in the city's parks, and celebrate the spawning "of FREE AMERICA." Threats delivered by the president, Chicago mayor Richard Daley, and the director of the Federal Bureau of Investigation (FBI), referred to as "J. Edgar Freako," would not thwart the Yippies, who saw American life being soiled "by the forces of violence, decay, and the napalm-cancer fiend." They offered instead "the politics of ecstasy," holding

themselves out as "the delicate spoors of the new fierceness" soon to transform the country. They intended to establish "their own reality," and would
not tolerate "the false theater of the Death Convention." Signatories included
Ginsberg, Leary, and the musicians Arlo Guthrie, Country Joe McDonald,
Phil Ochs, and the Fugs, Ed Sanders' rock band.

Rubin soon informed the underground editor Allen Cohen, a friend from
the West Coast, that he hoped to rekindle the sense of community that had
been present during the Human Be-In, the gathering of countercultural participants in San Francisco's Golden Gate Park in mid-January 1967.

> Our idea is to create a cultural, living alternative to the Convention. It could be the
> largest gathering of young people ever. . . . We want all the rock bands, all the
> underground papers, all the free spirits, all the theater groups—all the energies that
> have contributed to the new youth culture—all the new tribes—to come to Chicago
> and for six days we will live together in the park, sharing, learning, free food, free
> music, a regeneration of spirit and energy.

The idea was to quell isolation and foster the revolution, Rubin wrote. The
Convention afforded a means for activists to do their "own thing, to go
beyond protest into creative cultural alternative."

The appearance of the Yippies was in keeping with changes that various
aspects of the Movement and the counterculture were both experiencing. The
decade of the 1960s had opened with the appearance of two youth-based
organizations, SNCC and SDS, which seemed to justify the analysis by radical sociologist C. Wright Mills, among others, regarding the emergence of a
New Left in the United States and elsewhere. High-minded ideals drove the
young activists who joined SNCC or SDS, which were associated with the
vision of the beloved community or participatory democracy. They engaged
in sit-ins, freedom rides, voter registration drives, and community organizing,
becoming perceived by some, including the journalist Jack Newfield, as "a
prophetic minority." But by the midpoint of the decade, a change in the tenor
of each organization occurred.

The stress induced by arrests, beatings, killings, and the seeming lack of
support from liberal allies caused some in SNCC and the civil rights movement generally to move away from black-white alliances, to adopt the par-
lance of black power, and to effect more militant stances. New organizations,
such as the Oakland-based Black Panther Party, began to supersede SNCC,
which itself abandoned the adherence to nonviolent direct action associated
with John Lewis, Julian Bond, and Diane Nash, and employed by Bob Moses
in his voter registration campaign in Mississippi. SDS too headed away from
its emphasis on participatory democracy featured in Tom Hayden's Port
Huron Statement, and the Economic and Research Action Program (ERAP)

that led Hayden, Todd Gitlin, Nancy Hollander, Paul Potter, and others, to head into inner cities in the fashion of Russian students, the Narodniks, who "went to the people" to generate support for opposition to the czar and autocratic rule a century earlier. The example set by civil rights activists veering in a radical direction and frustration engendered by the dramatic escalation of the Vietnam War led to transformations of SDS and the New Left. Significant too were early stirrings in American higher educational institutions, particularly at UC Berkeley, where the Free Speech Movement involved an insistence that administrators pay attention to the needs and desires of the student body, a growing number of whom began demanding empowerment.

By 1965, according to the organization's historian, Kirkpatrick Sale, SDS experienced the phenomenon of Prairie Power, with new members from the American heartland and large state campuses exuding an anarchist streak and a greater familiarity with the counterculture not initially associated with early SDSers, many of whom were drawn from elite colleges and universities. Within a short while, the latest SDS leaders Carl Davidson and Gregory Calvert extolled student power through the doctrines of student syndicalism and the "new working class," which supposedly included college students and recent graduates. As the last half of the 1960s began to unfold, SNCC and SDS appeared headed down similar paths, with the former discarding its nonviolent preachments and biracial emphasis and the latter shifting from protest to resistance. The growing militancy was paralleled by the small but influential Resistance, the band of young men who refused to adhere to the mandates of the Selective Service System.

Talk of revolution began wafting through the Movement, during the same time that a countercultural explosion beckoned. With the beats of the immediate postwar period serving as progenitors or even countercultural icons—Allen Ginsberg and Gary Snyder come to mind—a new, far larger wave of American bohemians emerged during the 1960s. Shepherded by figures on the order of Timothy Leary and Ken Kesey, young people in particular were drawn to the not always holy trinity of the American counterculture: sex, drugs, and rock 'n' roll. Freer attitudes toward sexuality, mind-altering drugs ranging from marijuana and hashish to psilocybin, mescaline, and LSD, and musicians homegrown and British-inflected such as Jefferson Airplane, the Grateful Dead, Bob Dylan, the Beatles, and the Rolling Stones, affected the generation coming of age during the 1960s, at a bare minimum. Many took on at least the trappings of the counterculture, while alternative institutions abounded, with the advent of communes, collectives, underground newspapers, and the like. Importantly, the counterculture at its sharpest edges offered a radical counterpoint to established practices and verities, even posing something of a challenge to American capitalism itself. The most radical phase of the counterculture, wrapped around utopian visions and millennial hopes, played out as the Movement was entering its own highly charged period when the possibility of ushering in change, even radical in nature, still inspired many activists.

This was also the time, 1967 leading into 1968, when more politically engaged individuals were influenced as never before by the counterculture, and when even many purportedly apolitical hippies considered the need for some level of political involvement. No group, such as it was, seemed more primed for a melding of political and cultural radicalism than the Yippies, as led by Abbie Hoffman and Jerry Rubin. They had the look, the wild hair, the colorful getups, and the at times frenetic makeup to elicit media attention. They possessed deep roots in the Movement, especially its civil rights, anti-war, and New Left strands. They also seemed to embody a certain facet of the counterculture, with their easy references to taking dope, turning on, and altering people's consciousness. They became media darlings for a time, offering print, radio, and television journalists catchy slogans, colorful escapades, even delusional scenarios capable of reaping substantial audiences. In the process, they seemingly represented a new brand of American radicalism, of both a different hipster and a charlatan variety. Their sincerity could certainly be called into question, and it often was, but Abbie and Jerry's ability to pique interest in causes dear to them proved unerring for an extended period, to the dismay of Establishment forces and various Movement activists alike. Power brokers had to worry that the Yippies might be on to something, with an appeal especially to young people that threatened to become contagious. But serious radicals and genuine believers in the American counterculture also had reason to worry, as Hoffman, Rubin, and their clownish band of outlaws mocked the Movement and key activists less inclined to operate in Yippie-like fashion. Being viewed as jesters enabled the Yippies to corral attention and adherents, but hardly provided a blueprint for a serious assault on American institutions and values, even those sorely in need of a shaking up, if not of sweeping transformations altogether.

2

"Hell No! They Shouldn't Go!"

Dr. Spock's Children

Figure 2.1 Dr. Benjamin Spock leading an anti-war march to the United Nations in New York City. America's best-known pediatrician, Spock was one of a number of luminaries who signed "A Call to Resist Illegitimate Authority," conveying support for draft resisters. Library of Congress, Prints and Photographs Division, LC-USZ62-121468.

On Friday, January 5, 1968—a few days after the founding of Yippie!—a federal grand jury in Boston delivered indictments against Dr. Benjamin

Spock, the famed pediatrician turned anti-war activist, and four other individuals, charging them with having conspired to abet violations of the Selective Service System. Spock's purported co-conspirators, some of whom had never met, were Yale University chaplain William Sloane Coffin Jr., Harvard graduate student Michael K. Ferber, the writer Mitchell Goodman, and Marcus Raskin, cofounder of the Institute for Policy Studies (IPS), a progressive think tank in Washington, DC. The five men were connected to the draft resistance movement that had been involved with widely publicized condemnations of conscription, as exemplified by the recent March on the Pentagon.

The arrest of the sixty-four-year-old Dr. Spock was considered particularly newsworthy. Born in New Haven, Connecticut, he, like his father, was a graduate of both Phillips Academy and Yale University. A member of the rowing crew that won a gold medal at the 1924 Olympic Games in Paris, Spock attended Yale Medical School and graduated from Columbia University's College of Physicians and Surgeons. A specialist in pediatric medicine, Spock taught at Cornell Medical College and wrote *Baby and Child Care* (1946). Its progressive, child-centric approach proved tremendously influential, and the book became a worldwide best seller. Following wartime service in the US Navy, Spock worked at the Mayo Clinic before serving as a professor of child development at first the University of Pittsburgh and then Case Western Reserve. He also became politically active, serving as cochair of the National Committee for a Sane Nuclear Policy (SANE), prior to participating in the anti-war movement. A member of the Committee of Responsibility to Save War-Burned and War-Injured Vietnamese Children, Spock backed calls to provide medical assistance in the United States to Vietnamese orphans victimized by napalm. By the spring of 1967, he expressed a willingness to run as a Peace candidate if the Democrats or Republicans failed to nominate an individual exhibiting a "sincere desire" to bring the Vietnam War to a close. Spock also indicated he would proudly serve as Dr. Martin Luther King Jr.'s running mate. While SANE pledged to "energetically" back an anti-war candidate, Spock had to fend off a call for his expulsion from SANE delivered by civil rights activist Bayard Rustin, annoyed at the good doctor's purported "political naïveté" in working with Maoists and Trotskyists inside the anti-war movement. Testifying at the court martial of Captain Howard B. Levy, charged with failing to provide instruction to Green Beret medics headed for Vietnam, Spock appeared willing to defer to the defendant's belief that the program amounted to "prostitution of medicine." In July 1967, Spock served as an American delegate to the Stockholm Conference on Vietnam. Three months later, he resigned as SANE's national cochair, asserting the need for greater militancy in both the civil rights and anti-war movements.

The other defendants were prominent in their own right. Like Spock, another member of a distinguished family, forty-three-year-old William

Sloane Coffin Jr. was a graduate of Phillips Academy and Yale, where he was initiated into Skull and Bones, the prestigious secret society. After serving in the US military during World War II, Coffin attended Union Theological Seminary, which was presided over by his uncle Henry. He left the seminary during the Korean War, entering the CIA. Resuming his studies after three years of espionage work, he graduated from Yale Divinity School. A strong civil rights advocate, Coffin, who had been named Yale chaplain, became a well-publicized freedom rider. An early opponent of the Vietnam War, Coffin was an important figure in Clergy Concerned about Vietnam (eventually renamed Clergy and Laymen Concerned about Vietnam and known by its acronym CALCAV). He was among a group of eminent clergy and intellectuals who attempted to deliver thousands of draft cards to the Justice Department during Stop the Draft Week in mid-October 1967.

Forty-four-year-old Mitchell Goodman, an acclaimed author, was another World War II veteran, having been an artillery officer, before graduating from Harvard and beginning doctoral work in labor economics. Known for his travel articles, Goodman also taught at colleges across the country and published *The End of It*, an impassioned novel about a US artillery battalion's trek through wartime northern Italy. Rapidly immersed in the anti-war movement, Goodman joined in a public protest against Vice President Hubert Humphrey and helped lead a veterans' march down Manhattan's Fifth Avenue. As he participated in a walkout of approximately fifty writers and publishers at the National Book Award ceremonies, Goodman shouted, "Mr. Vice President, we are burning children in Vietnam, and you and we are all responsible!"

IPS cofounder, thirty-three-year-old Marcus Raskin, received his undergraduate and law degrees from the University of Chicago, before serving as an adviser of sorts for liberal members of the House of Representatives. During the Kennedy administration, he was a top adviser on national security and arms control, then departed to establish the left-of-center think tank. Strongly critical of US operations in Southeast Asia, he, along with the renowned Austrian-French journalist-historian Bernard Fall, coedited the *Vietnam Reader*. Angered by the failure of the American left to contest war crimes in Vietnam, Fall referred to French intellectuals who had decried their nation's atrocities in Algeria. Working with fellow IPS cofounder Arthur Waskow, Raskin helped to draft "A Call to Resist Illegitimate Authority," which would be signed by notable figures across the American left and would appear as an advertisement in *The New York Review of Books* and *The New Republic*. The manifesto conveyed support for young men engaged in draft resistance, placing its signatories in possible violation of the Selective Service Act.

The youngest of the Boston Five defendants, twenty-three-year-old Michael Ferber, a graduate of Swarthmore College, was a doctoral student in English at Harvard. His opposition to the Vietnam War led to Ferber's involvement with the Resistance, the group established by Steve Hamilton, David Harris, Lennie Heller, Dennis Sweeney, and a few others, which urged refusal to go along with the draft system, even if that resulted in prosecution and incarceration. Ferber had become concerned about his own draft status in 1965, the year the United States massively escalated the Vietnam War in the air and on the ground, while increasing its deployment levels from 23,000 to 185,000 soldiers. As he later recalled, "Many of us were still convinced that there was an open way of getting the government to end the war. But we had a hard time thinking of a tactic." As for Ferber, he filed for conscientious objector status, which his draft board denied. He was a leader of an East Coast version of the Resistance, helping to organize a public turning in or burning of draft cards, which took place at Boston Commons during Stop the Draft Week.

Ferber became known for the sermon "A Time to Say No," which he delivered on October 16 at Boston's historic Arlington Street Church. He agreed with the French author Albert Camus who had insisted that the rebel offer both negative and positive pronouncements. Ferber pointed to a "radical" Christian and Jewish tradition that extolled "love and compassion . . . justice and respect . . . facing other people as human beings." He went on to deny that either the Revelation or the Revolution were impending, and then admitted:

> The sun will rise tomorrow as it does every day, and when we get out of bed the world will be in pretty much the same mess it is in today. American bombers will continue to drop incendiary bombs on the Vietnamese people and American soldiers will continue to "pacify" their villages. The ghettos will continue to be rotten places to live. Black and Mexican farm workers will continue to get miserable wages. America's schools will continue to cripple the minds and hearts of its pupils. And the American Selective Service System will continue to send young men out to the slaughter.

Declaring this was only "the Beginning," Ferber insisted on the need "to dig in for the long haul," affirming that transforming America would require lengthy "mean struggles and anguish," as well as result in "great human cost." But it was essential to say yes to the radical religious tradition and the extended battle ahead. Ferber called for coming "together to say No to the United States government." After which he declared, "then let our Yes be the loudest No the government ever heard."

The singling out of the Boston Five, as the codefendants came to be known, was hardly by chance. It involved a conscious decision by the Johnson administration to go after apparent leaders of the anti-war movement.

Such a tactic had been tried before in an effort to cripple organizations viewed as antagonistic to the federal, state, or municipal government or even capitalism itself. During the 1880s, an anti-labor campaign culminated in a trial involving eight anarchists accused of setting off a bomb at Chicago's Haymarket Square that resulted in the killing of eleven individuals, including seven policemen. The Haymarket affair helped to cripple the campaign supporting an eight-hour day for striking workers. During World War I and its immediate aftermath, the federal government went after critics of Woodrow Wilson's war policies, particularly those associated with the Socialist Party of America, the Industrial Workers of the World, and radical publications such as *The Masses* and *Mother Earth*, tied to the Lyrical Left that had thrived in prewar Greenwich Village. Another liberal administration, Franklin Delano Roosevelt's, also employed conspiracy trials to prosecute little-liked figures on opposite sides of the political spectrum. The Justice Department initiated wartime suits against both native fascists and Trotskyists. It operated similarly during the height of the early Cold War, singling out eleven leaders of the CPUSA, accused of conspiring to bring about the violent overthrow of the American government.

Later rulings, including the *Yates* case (1957), by the United States Supreme Court, seemingly restricted usage of the doctrine of conspiracy in politically motivated prosecutions. However, President Johnson's mounting dismay about antipathy to US operations in Vietnam resulted in his insistence that nefarious forces were involved in fostering opposition to his war policies. Following LBJ's orders, CIA director Richard Helms began gathering intelligence information pertaining to American college and university campuses. The White House instructed Helms to "exert every possible effort to collect information concerning US radical agitators who might travel abroad." CIA agents began tracking the anti-war movement still more closely, carefully following the protest involving the Pentagon. Shortly after the March on the Pentagon, the CIA undertook an exploration of the supposed threads connecting anti-war activists and foreign entities. To Johnson's dismay, Helms soon reported that little evidence existed of such entanglements. The president remained unconvinced. He also continued to receive information culled from Project Resistance, another CIA program designed to ferret out anti-war activists on college and university campuses. The US Army maintained its own surveillance of anti-war activity, and continued to infiltrate dissident groups, through Operation Continental US Intelligence.

At the same time, the Johnson administration felt compelled to deal with growing opposition to conscription, as draft calls surged. As of mid-1965, the US Army was inducting approximately 10,000 men a month. With American involvement in Vietnam intensifying, the number jumped above the

34,000-man mark by late 1967. Both the anti-war movement and applications for conscientious objector status escalated as well.

The Resistance particularly troubled government officials, disturbed about deliberate defiance of the Selective Service System. Resistance members intentionally evoked comparisons to the earlier battle against the Nazi takeover of much of Europe. They celebrated a "virile" brand of nonviolence, produced a pamphlet, "We Refuse," and intended to "actively challenge the government's right to draft American men for its criminal war against the people of Vietnam." Refusing to accept deferments, they viewed jail as a "justifiable alternative," hoping to induce others "to resist the crimes done in their names." Those active in the draft resistance movement participated in a mass burning of draft cards in April 1967 in Central Park's Sheep Meadow, an event associated with anti-war rallies sponsored by the Spring Mobilization Committee to End the War in Vietnam (Spring Mobe). On the West Coast, the Resistance founders pledged to bring about a mass turn-in of draft cards in the fall. The group also helped to organize We Won't Go meetings around the country.

By the spring of 1967, the Reverend William Sloane Coffin Jr. was one of the leading religious figures closely identified with the anti-war movement. Just over a year earlier, he had publicly revealed the establishment of CALCAV. Deeming the timing critical, Coffin likened the moral situation of his country with that of the *Titanic* prior to its ill-fated collision with an iceberg. Warning against a massive escalation of the Vietnam War, he called on fellow clergy to back negotiations to bring the fighting to an end.

In addition to Coffin, the National Emergency Committee's board included John C. Bennett, president of Union Theological Seminary; Rabbi Abraham Heschel of the Jewish Theological Seminary; the Reverend Robert McAfee Brown, Professor of Religion at Stanford; and its youngest member, twenty-nine-year-old Richard John Neuhaus, another ordained pastor who served at St. John the Evangelist Church in Bedford-Stuyvesant. The board initially expressed opposition to civil disobedience and refused to call for immediate withdrawal, favoring a moderate, apparently respectable stance on the war, although one that proved controversial with many local congregations. Attempting to provide advice, Coffin urged, "Do not let hawks monopolize patriotism."

At the beginning of 1967, Coffin and Neuhaus determined to devise a proposal regarding civil disobedience and the Selective Service System. Coffin proceeded to debate former US Supreme Court justice Charles E. Whittaker on "Law, Order, and Civil Disobedience." Pointing to Puritan leaders, Founding Fathers, and abolitionists as among those who were once "notorious lawbreakers" but later acclaimed as heroes, Coffin broached the possibility of organizing "massive civil disobedience in opposition to the war." Affirming that "while no one has the right to break the law, every man on occasion has the duty to do so," he exhorted young seminarians and religious leaders to relinquish their own draft exemptions. Coffin also urged more established clergy to publicly call for such a move and thereby also expose themselves to possible prosecution under the Selective Service Act. He envisioned a point when several thousand draft-eligible men would appear in leading American cities "with a moving simple statement to surrender their draft cards" before federal buildings. At the same time, Coffin remained adverse to draft-card burning, viewing it as "unnecessarily hostile."

CALCAV did not officially endorse the Spring Mobe rallies but supported individual members who chose to participate. Reverend Brown offered a position paper, "The Religious Community and the War in Vietnam," which stated, "A time comes when silence is betrayal. That time has come for us in Vietnam."

During the spring of 1967, an array of "declarations, manifestoes, calls for support, confessions of 'complicity,' and appendices to We Won't Go statements" materialized, Michael Ferber and Staughton Lynd indicate. The most appealing and influential proved to be "A Call to Resist Illegitimate Authority," released in the summer, crafted by IPS' Marcus Raskin and Arthur Waskow. Among those signing the manifesto were Robert MacAfee Brown, Noam Chomsky, Coffin, Allen Ginsberg, Mitchell Goodman, Dwight Macdonald, and Benjamin Spock.

Goodman took on the task of organizing intellectuals to provide support for draft resisters. While lecturing at Stanford in the spring, he encountered members of the Resistance, including David Harris, and reached out to other faculty members to solicit support for "a pledge of mass civil disobedience designed to stop the war." He considered that "the germ of the idea of adult support to the draft resisters." In mid-September, Goodman became aware of non–draft eligible backers of the Resistance like Chomsky, the noted MIT linguist, and Macdonald. Visiting Chomsky, Goodman first came upon "A Call to Resist Illegitimate Authority," discovering both his name and that of his wife, the poet Denise Levertov, included among the signers, although neither at the time knew anything about it. Following Chomsky's suggestion, Goodman went to talk with Coffin, who suggested they gather "the draft cards that are turned in from all over the country" and submit them to the Justice Department.

On October 2, Coffin spoke at a press conference at the Hilton Hotel in Manhattan, held to deliver "A Call to Resist Illegitimate Authority," complete with over 300 signatures of noted intellectual and artistic figures. As his biographer Warren Goldstein indicates, Coffin connected that document to civil disobedience by the Resistance planned for eight cities two weeks later. Chomsky proclaimed, "What justifies an act of civil disobedience is an intolerable evil. After the lesson of Dachau and Auschwitz, no person of conscience can believe that authority must always be obeyed. A line must be drawn somewhere. Beyond that line lies civil disobedience." He warned, "It may be quite passive. . . . It may involve symbolic confrontation with the war-making apparatus. . . . It may go well beyond such symbolic facts." Continuing, Chomsky declared, "Those who refuse to serve in Vietnam are at the forefront of the struggle to salvage what remains of American honor. Their refusal is an act of courage and high principle." Goodman announced that a group calling itself Conscientious Resistance would submit an array of draft cards to the Department of Justice on October 20. Following the lead of committed clergy, Goodman stated, those "elders" would demonstrate a "commitment, in conscience, to aid, abet, and counsel" resisters.

On October 16, the New England Resistance carried out its rally on the Boston Commons, having asked Coffin to speak and take hold of draft cards young men turned over to him. Coffin had recently admitted to attempting to convince Yale undergraduates to "at least confront the possibility" of relinquishing their draft cards. Before a crowd of 5,000, Coffins spoke of churches and synagogues affording draft resisters sanctuary. He asked, "Are we to raise conscientious men and then not stand by them in their hour of conscience? And if there is a price to pay, should we hold back?"

Four days later, Coffin appeared at the Justice Department, with hundreds of other anti-war protesters, for an interview with Assistant Deputy Attorney General John McDonough, Attorney General Ramsey Clark having declined to meet. McDonough refused to accept the draft cards that were tendered, particularly enraging Arthur Waskow. The group of "elder" anti-war spokespersons and four resisters, all determined to subject themselves to arrest, included Mitchell Goodman, Marcus Raskin, and Spock. Claiming that the Justice Department officials had been "derelict in their duties," Coffin explained, "We came here for a moral, legal confrontation. If our government cannot accept such confrontation, it cannot have much conviction of its own morality. Then it must accept responsibility for less responsible, less nonviolent demonstrations."

The massive rallies at the Lincoln Memorial and the Pentagon that began the following day suggested a more concerted turn toward "active resistance," as David Dellinger phrased it. Dellinger spoke of the deliberate provoking of "confrontations" through civil disobedience, and the encampment at the Pentagon demonstrated the determination of many to make the waging of the war more difficult for the Johnson administration. Clashes took place on and near the steps of the Pentagon, while military police and US marshals swept in, beating demonstrators and arresting nearly 700 individuals, among them Dellinger, Abbie Hoffman, and Norman Mailer.

Refusing to back down, Reverend Coffin helped convince CALCAV to release a statement on October 25 offering "active support to all who in conscience and through nonviolent means decide to resist" conscription. Throwing down the gauntlet, the statement declared, "We hereby publicly counsel all who in conscience cannot today serve in the armed forces to refuse such service by nonviolent means. We pledge ourselves to aid and abet them in any way we can. . . . [W]e too must be arrested, for in the sight of the law we are now as guilty as they."

The federal government, in responding to the anti-draft movement, had certain weapons at its disposal, some dating back centuries like the doctrine of conspiracy and others of quite recent vintage. By August 1965, President Johnson had favored amending the Selective Service Act to criminalize the deliberate destruction or mutilation of a draft card. It allowed prosecutors to charge draft card burners with a criminal act, with violators subject to incarceration for as long as five years and fines as substantial as $10,000. The first individual tried under the new amendment, twenty-two-year-old David Miller, was a pacifist belonging to the Catholic Worker Movement, which strove to usher in a "new society within the shell of the old, a society in which it will be easier to do good." In April 1967, Miller began his prison sentence, a fate eventually shared by over 3,000 young men who were among 8,000 tried for draft resistance or evasion.

Subsequent events in 1967, particularly Stop the Draft Week and the March on the Pentagon, convinced the White House of the need to respond more forcefully to the anti-war movement, which was picking up greater support and displaying heightened militancy as the end of the year approached. Almost immediately following Stop the Draft Week, General Lewis Hershey, director of the Selective Service System, delivered a memorandum and sent a notice, dated October 26, to the nation's 4,081 local draft boards. That system, the memo emphasized, was designed to ensure "the survival of the United States" by mandating "universal" fulfillment of military obligation by age-appropriate men. Deferments were available only to "serve the national interest," and should be withheld if an individual interfered with military recruitment or induced others to refuse military duty. Moreover, such an individual should be prosecuted, along with those who failed to report for military service or refused induction into the armed forces. The seventy-four-year-old Hersey went on to add that participation in illegal demonstrations by "misguided registrants," even those who had previously been labeled unfit for military service or unqualified except in times of declared war or national emergency, might result in reclassification of registrants. That would apply to registrants "up to 35 years of age."

Hershey had acquired an unseemly reputation within the anti-war camp, for heading the dreaded Selective Service System but also for the infamous "channeling memo" that had been printed several months earlier in *New Left Notes*. Actually issued back in 1965, that document by General Hershey declared the Selective Service classification system led to "the channeling of manpower into many endeavors and occupations; activities that are in the national interest." A congressional document the following year attempted to deflect criticism from the Selective Service director, emphasizing that the system he oversaw was essential for America's security. Deferments, according to Congress, were only issued "in the national interest."

In early November, the *New York Times'* B. Drummond Ayres Jr. indicated that General Hershey promised to induct or assist in the prosecution of those who violated draft laws. Pledging to adhere "to the letter of the laws," Hershey denied any desire for "revenge" but sought instead to "discourage some of the excesses we have had in the past." Very quickly, however, the *Times'* Neil Sheehan noted that attorneys in both the Justice and Defense departments determined that inducting anti-war protesters would likely involve an unconstitutional abrogation of free speech. The American Association of University Professors assailed Hershey for striving to quash dissent, and for dismissing due process of law. An appellate court ruling had mandated rescission of an earlier Hershey determination to reclassify students from the University of Michigan who had participated in a sit-in at an Ann Arbor draft board.

Rabbi Israel Margolies, who had helped to establish the New Jersey chapter of SANE and had marched with Martin Luther King Jr., denounced Hershey's "directive" as a "disgrace to our democracy." The Johnson administration's failure to oppose Hershey's recommendation, Margolies believed, suggested that the president, "despite his frequent deference to every American's right to dissent, approves of a plan that is clearly intended to deter and punish dissent." The rabbi feared that President Johnson, lacking popular support, had determined to employ "the war as a means of bludgeoning our young people into silence." Margolies considered this "a brutal form of blackmail" antithetical to democratic principles and "unworthy of the president." Supreme Court Justice Abe Fortas, a close friend of and adviser to the president, stated that Hershey was "a law unto himself and responds only to his own conversation." In a speech at Colgate University, Fortas offered that Hershey's pronouncement probably lacked "the approval of the executive branch of government." Yale president Kingman Brewster Jr. denounced Hershey's position as an "absolutely outrageous usurpation of power." In his estimation, the draft director's action served as "a real damper on free discussion and dissent," and "destroys the whole notion of military service being a privilege and an obligation and not a punishment." Hershey responded by asserting, "Under the First Amendment," which his critics "treasure so much, I have just as much right as they do to state my opinion." Massachusetts Senator Edward M. "Ted" Kennedy also criticized Hershey, while insisting that graduate students from all disciplines "be exposed equally to the draft." Hershey's recommendation, the youngest of the Kennedy brothers complained, all but likened service in the US Armed Forces "to serving a jail sentence."

In an editorial on December 10, the *New York Times* discussed the Selective Service director and his recent attempts to target anti-war demonstrators. It revealed that the judicial overturning of his attempt to punish the sit-inners in Ann Arbor didn't trouble him. "His objective was not to observe the legal niceties but to frighten the demonstrators into leaving his draft boards and the military recruitment alone." The *Times* thus understood perfectly why Hershey sought to threaten the possibility of reclassification as a bludgeon to cripple the anti-war movement, something that must have endeared him to the Johnson White House. However, the resulting political flak was disturbing and led the *Times* to conjecture that the administration might be seeking to force Hershey's retirement.

Attorney General Ramsey Clark battled with Hershey over the director's determination to punish registrants engaged in the anti-draft movement. "I felt that you could not accelerate on the grounds of an exercise of free speech or protest, or unrelated conduct, even criminal conduct," Clark informed Tom Wells. In addition to being pressured by Hershey to expedite prosecution of draft resisters, Clark received instructions from the White House to quickly deliver information about ongoing FBI investigations of Selective Service Act violations, and concerning what he was doing to indict "lawbreakers." Rightly viewed as an opponent of the war, Clark believed his resignation was called for if he were unable to prosecute important figures associated with draft resistance.

Attorney General Clark joined with General Hershey in issuing a statement regarding the Selective Service System, hoping to display solidarity with the director and deliver a warning to those associated with the Resistance. Clark and Hershey now revealed that the Department of Justice's Criminal Division had set up a special prosecution unit, to be headed by former US attorney John Van de Kamp, designed to target those who knowingly violated the Selective Service Act. The unit would single out those who deliberately counseled, aided, or abetted others in refusing to register with the Selective Service System or serve in the US military. Furthermore, US attorneys were instructed to facilitate the investigation and prosecution of such cases, and to urge local police forces "to vigorously prosecute violations of local laws" that might have transpired during demonstrations opposing the Selective Service System. The joint statement stressed that the law had long made a "delinquent" registrant in breach of duties pertaining to his draft status subject to reclassification. Attorney General Clark noted that present prosecutions of Selective Service violations were "at an all-time high," while the percentage of individuals failing to report for induction was far lower than during the Korean conflict. At the same time, Clark and Hershey stated that "lawful protest activities," related to the draft or not, did "not subject registrants to acceleration or any other special administrative action." The lawful employment of First Amendment rights would result in "no penalty or other adverse action." The Constitution protected such rights, which were "vital to the preservation of free institutions," something American soldiers in Vietnam were "fighting to protect," the joint statement affirmed.

In a telephone interview with Neil Sheehan, General Hershey quickly acknowledged that he and the Attorney General differed regarding if young men who hindered the draft and military recruitment were subject to expedited conscription. Hershey also revealed he would not rescind his recommendation of October 26 concerning possible reclassification of registrants. He pointedly stated, "When a fellow goes into a draft board and pours ink on his own file, then there's no disagreement—he's affecting his own status." The disagreement arose regarding "when he goes in and pours ink on his brother's file," Hershey declared.

The *New York Times* criticized the general for placing "himself above the law." A small number of liberal congressmen insisted the president compel Hershey to withdraw his recent recommendation and then induce him to resign. They charged that the director had chosen "to wage a personal crusade against opposition to the war in Vietnam." By contrast, South Carolina's L. Mendel Rivers, the House Armed Services Committee chair, asked when it had become "a disservice to serve in the armed forces of your country" and he defended Hershey's response to "these buzzards."

The Department of Justice's Criminal Division, acting at Attorney General Clark's behest, began pursuing prosecution of Dr. Spock and his codefendants. Van de Kamp admitted to Jessica Mitford, who produced an early, revealing analysis of the trial of the Boston Five, that the decision resulted because of the department's battle with Hershey. "The prosecution . . . was thought to be a good way out—it was done to provide a graceful way out for General Hershey." The defendants were selected, Van de Kamp revealed, due to "their names and personalities." In addition, the FBI had tracked them for months, at a minimum. Television coverage of the defendants was also helpful. But equally significant was the government's clear desire to deliver a warning to activists, even ones as famous as Spock and Coffin, about the potential costs of supporting draft resistance. In addition, the administration was willing to use Justice Department resources to cripple—financially and psychologically—an increasingly important, visible segment of the anti-war movement. Mitford recognized that the prosecution of prominent figures was designed to provide "a pointed warning to the respectable dissenters" seen on television screens agitating against US involvement in Vietnam.

The Attorney General's role in the case was complicated, as a number of analysts and the defendants themselves acknowledged. Clark, who was opposed to the war and would undergo a decided shift leftward after leaving government service, wanted "a draft resistance 'control case' or 'test case'" that "would justify deterring other aggressive actions" by the Justice Department toward "innocent" but not well-known draft resisters. He sought to avoid going after pacifists or conscientious objectors, who had no real support system and were generally viewed as traitors or cowards. Spock and his codefendants, who possessed an abundance of resources, "had thought things through for a long period of time, and had firm—even passionate—understanding and commitment of what they were doing and why." The Justice Department, Clark noted, "could have ground up tens of thousands of youngsters and nobody would ever notice it."

The high profile nature of several of the Boston Five defendants— particularly Benjamin Spock—obviously troubled the Johnson administration. Dr. Spock had been intimately involved with Stop the Draft operations, before offering a very visible presence during the siege at the Pentagon that failed to result in his arrest, to his chagrin. Soldiers appeared to deliberately avoid the famed pediatrician, as he complained to David Dellinger, who was being carried out by police. Dellinger offered, "Apparently he was too popular a figure to be included in the list of disreputable people who would appear in the next day's news accounts." Shortly after the march, Spock was back in the news, expressing his discontent about a planned investigation of New Left activities, including the National Conference for New Politics (NCNP), which he cochaired. Spock bristled that if the "undemocratic investigation" occurred, "it could mark the death knell for traditional dissent in this country." In late October, SANE, which he had also led, called for a "Dump Johnson" movement within the ranks of the Democratic Party. On November 11, Spock joined with other health professionals in visiting Captain Howard B. Levy, who had been court-martialed for "willfully disobeying lawful command of his superior officer" to provide dermatological instruction for Special Forces aidman trainees. The purpose of the visit was to display "solidarity with Captain Levy."

Two days later, Dr. Spock was among a small group at John F. Kennedy

Airport awaiting the return from Cambodia of Tom Hayden, the New Left leader and anti-war activist who had helped bring about release of three US soldiers by Vietcong guerrillas. Spock next held a news conference with the radical social critic Dwight Macdonald, David McReynolds, head of the War Resisters League, and other activists, to publicize an impending blockade of the armed forces induction center at 39 Whitehall Street in Manhattan. Apparently seeking "a major federal prosecution," according to the *New York Times'* Sidney E. Zion, Macdonald indicated that those speaking at the press conference "had 'clearly' violated" federal law in attempting to convince young men to engage in draft resistance and military avoidance. "But the government is not likely to prosecute us," Spock predicted. "Its bankruptcy in the moral sense is proved by its refusal to move against those of us who have placed ourselves between the young people and the draft." Both Macdonald and Spock denied that the anti-draft movement wanted "a martyr," while Macdonald also refuted the notion that the Justice Department failed to prosecute owing to its unwillingness to quash dissent. Macdonald declared, "No. What we're doing is not just free speech, it's not just dissent, it's a deliberate violation of the law." At the same time, the participants indicated they would draw on First Amendment protections if prosecuted.

On December 5, Dr. Spock, Allen Ginsberg, and the Irish diplomat Conor Cruise O'Brien were among 264 people arrested at the Whitehall Street demonstration, which was part of five days of protest involving the induction center. McReynolds had reluctantly broached the idea of Spock's participating in an act of civil disobedience, as the famed pediatrician had yet to be arrested and was still viewed as something of a moderate. As his biographer Thomas Maier explains, Spock went out of the way to ensure that he engaged in civil disobedience on that occasion by literally crawling past a police barricade. Spock and David Dellinger were singled out from other older anti-war participants offering counsel to draft resisters. News accounts also indicated that the NCNP, which Spock cochaired with James Rollins, a black community organizer from St. Louis, had issued a seven-column advertisement that appeared in the *New York Times* calling for the Democratic Party to refuse to renominate President Johnson. Signed by Spock and Rollins, the ad warned, "If necessary, we are also prepared to mobilize the largest demonstration this country has ever seen. It would descend upon the National Democratic Convention" to unveil "the strength of the opposition." Unlike Paul Booth, the former SDS officer who had worked with the NCNP, Spock didn't foresee a gigantic New Left gathering culminating in violence. "I can't think of a reason why we would be inflammatory in this sense. Our demonstration would involve no violence or civil disobedience."

The Justice Department was hardly the only government body following

Dr. Spock's political antics. On December 10, Spock revealed having been visited by two FBI agents seeking "delicate harassment." The agents had called to ask if they could interview him, and Spock said, "I'd be *delighted*, that is, I should be very glad to tell them what I was doing and why." He informed the agents of having supported LBJ as a peace candidate four years earlier, but feeling betrayed as the president massively expanded American military operations in Vietnam. "They asked me if I was aware I was risking jail," Spock reported. "I told them I certainly was. I know I am risking five years in jail," referring to the federal statutes that criminalized advocacy of draft avoidance. Viewing the FBI session as "an attempt at intimidation," Spock said, "It was to be expected that the administration would strike back, but they're mistaken if they think this will intimidate anyone." Speaking to friends about the session, Spock predicted, "Oh, they'll never go after an old pediatrician like me." Shortly after meeting with the FBI agents, who indicated they had come to see him "at the request of the Attorney General," Spock talked to a pair of young men about "this unjust and immoral war," and blasted the president and his Vietnam policy.

Government operatives, inside and outside of the White House, must not have been pleased when Dr. Spock delivered his New Year's resolution to the *New York Times*: "Terrified that Lyndon Johnson will escalate us into war with China this year, and respectful of his indefatigability in overcoming opposition, I will redouble my efforts to end his Presidency and the insane war he prosecutes."

News of the subsequent indictment of Dr. Spock and four other important figures in the anti-war movement reverberated around the country. The *New York Post* prominently displayed the news, "SPOCK INDICTED." While many were dismayed that such a distinguished group of individuals had been selected for prosecution for political stances, others were hardly displeased. After acknowledging he had no idea regarding their guilt or innocence and indicating he took "no pleasure in seeing anybody get indicted," General Hershey praised the Department of Justice for the indictments. "It's a job that ought to be done."

Speaking from his small Upper East Side apartment, Dr. Spock pointed to the Nuremberg principle involving the moral necessity of refusing to go along when "your government is up to crimes against humanity." Affirming, "I certainly don't feel myself guilty," Spock acknowledged, "The government is not going to quit easily and neither are we." The indictments had been issued, he charged, as "Lyndon Johnson and the administration are feeling more desperate all the time because the war is still going against them." While admitting to providing succor to young war resisters, Spock also stated, "I'm not a pacifist. I was every much for the war against Hitler and I also supported the intervention in Korea, but in this war we went in there to steal Vietnam." US engagement in Southeast Asia, Spock insisted, was "'illegal,' 'detrimental,' and 'disastrous.'" Consequently, he saw his own involvement in the anti-war movement as "legal in the highest sense," and lauded anti-draft activists for engaging in "a very patriotic endeavor requiring enormous amounts of courage," while amounting to "the most effective way of opposing the war." Dr. Spock expressed hope "that 100,000, 200,000 or even 500,000 young Americans either refuse to be drafted or to obey orders if in military service." That would create "a very awkward position for the government." Another possibility involved the American people rejecting President Johnson.

Dr. Spock's codefendants and other important members of the American left also responded to news of the indictments. Having received word of his indictment from the UPI, Michael Ferber was "delighted that there was an indictment of such famous people." He thought, "Oh, boy, *Dr. Spock*. The government's actually going after Dr. Spock" and Reverend Coffin. He feared the government "might really crack down," yet he also believed the prosecutions would assist the student movement. The government, he hoped, had "screwed it up." Referring to the sermon he delivered on October 16 at Arlington Street Church, Ferber soon informed the press, "I gather they have moved against the big shots, although I do not consider myself one of those but rather a middle-man." He subsequently called the indictments "the best thing that ever happened to us" and could be turned "to good use." Ferber soon told a group he was speaking to, "Maybe we have a friend in high places," alluding to the selective prosecution of a small number of distinguished anti-war activists. Having recently received an induction order, Ferber was refusing to report.

Promising to fight all the way to the US Supreme Court, Mitchell Goodman said, "I consider it very important to test the legality of the draft law and the constitutionality of Mr. Johnson's war. I suppose that the only way they can be tested is if people of some repute are arrested and tried." He continued, "The United States government is involved in illegalities and that's what we're fighting. People like me believe the government has committed atrocities in Vietnam. We are attempting to save the moral integrity of this country." Goodman wondered why the Justice Department failed to prosecute more of the 2,000 signatories of the statement "A Call to Resist Illegitimate Authority." He asked, "Why has the government been selective? Have they [sic] begun a picking off process?"

The Reverend William Sloane Coffin Jr. spoke on January 12 in Manhattan, alongside Dr. Martin Luther King Jr. at a CALCAV-sponsored news conference. The codefendants, Coffin declared, "welcome the chance to confront the government in the courts of the United States in the traditional American way." He added, "Of course we are prepared to go to jail. When throughout the ages men have suffered death rather than subordinate their allegiance to conscience to the authority of the state, to go to jail is obviously a small thing." Denying that any conspiracy was afoot, Reverend Coffin asserted, "There was no stealth, no guile in anything we did." Instead, "everything we did we did as publicly as possible." The prosecution, he hoped, would not dissuade others from protesting the war. He remained convinced "that an aroused America will see that what we are doing in Vietnam is a deeply wicked thing." Both Coffin and King promised to keep counseling young men to adhere to "their consciences" about conscription. The prosecution of Dr. Spock heightened King's opposition to the draft.

Longtime Socialist Party leader Norman Thomas indicated that the impending trial might serve as "a landmark" in the battle against conscription. "I admire the brave thing" the defendants had done, eighty-three-year-old Thomas declared. Dwight Macdonald, Paul Goodman, David McReynolds, and other anti-war figures held a news conference in mid-Manhattan to offer support for the defendants. A number of anti-war activists, including Noam Chomsky, Martin Luther King Jr., Dwight MacDonald, and Boston University history professor Howard Zinn, expressed solidarity with the Boston Five: "We stand beside the men who have been indicted for support of draft resistance. If they are sentenced, we, too, must be sentenced. If they are imprisoned, we will take their places and will continue to use what means we can to bring this war to an end."

Ramparts magazine warned that should Spock and his codefendants be jailed and thousands fail to "follow them, we can forget about serious opposition to the war and civil liberties." The radical publication, which had increasingly shifted leftward over the past couple of years, added, "If these five men are conspirators, then we must become a nation of conspirators" to stave off domestic repression and oppression overseas.

Discussing the recent indictments, *New York Times* columnist James Reston stated that they carried "the fundamental philosophical issue of the Vietnam War into the courts." In the process, the Johnson administration had triggered an ancient query: "When personal conviction and public law clash in a democracy, how far can the individual go in opposing the government?" This possessed "practical political" implications as well, likely to spur the anti-war movement as the presidential campaign began, Reston noted. As he read the indictment, the journalist believed the defendants did indeed "unlawfully, knowingly, and willfully" implore draft registrants to avoid military service and "asked publicly to be prosecuted for doing so." However, the philosophical conundrum involved the charge of conspiring "to commit offenses against the United States." The defendants insisted that the war constituted the leading offense against their nation. They were responding to a "'higher' moral law, and" stood ready to pay the price. The government contended that it was not contesting the defendants' right to speak out in opposition to the Vietnam conflict or the draft but rather their "inciting and organizing young men to defy the law." As Reston pointed out, the government now agreed with the defendants' argument that they should be arrested alongside those who burned draft cards. Thus, the question arose if the Selective Service provisions were themselves unconstitutional or if "a higher moral law" existed. The defendants, Reston believed, had pushed for this confrontation, hoping "to paralyze the draft and the war by organizing defiance of the law."

The *New York Times* offered a general editorial, "Challenge to the Draft," arguing that the federal government had moved to prosecute Dr. Spock and his fellow defendants to avoid anarchy. At the same time, the paper's editorial staff recognized that "the moral questions raised by the far-reaching acts of deeply troubled citizens are matters of concern for every American."

When the codefendants gathered at the legal office of Spock's attorney Leonard Boudin, brother-in-law of the muckraking journalist I. F. Stone, it was the initial time the supposed coconspirators had all gathered together. They grappled with the government charge of criminal conspiracy, a slippery legal concept long used against mobsters and financial scammers, but more occasionally against those viewed as outside the political pale in the United States. Believing a trial would energize the anti-war movement, Ferber revealed that his previously displeased parents, who resided in Buffalo, now thought "there must be something wrong in America when the best baby doctor in the land is on trial." Coffin recognized the importance of Spock's having been indicted. "He was this respected baby doctor who becomes one of the nation's most principled dissenters, the icon of principled dissent." The youngest and the oldest defendants wanted to turn the case into "a political trial" regarding the Vietnam War. Coffin discussed contesting the constitutionality of both the war and the draft.

An attorney himself, Raskin seemed the most unhappy with the discussion, warning that their indictments would be followed by many others targeting anti-war activists. He feared that individuals such as Goodman, King, Mailer, Noam Chomsky, and the poet Robert Lowell would also be arrested. "It's a decimation of the intelligentsia," Raskin warned and then urged presenting a legal challenge to the conspiracy doctrine. Others, particularly Ferber and Spock, didn't agree with that approach, wanting to contest the war altogether in the manner Coffin suggested. Ferber stated, "But, but, we did this to get *into* this. You guys knew what you were doing. You knew it was illegal. The whole point was to take a stand with us."

Dr. Spock and Reverend Coffin appeared on NBC's *Meet the Press* on January 28, where they confronted a hostile panelist, Lawrence E. Spivak, who also produced the show. At one point, Spivak grilled Spock about whether each citizen in a democracy should be afforded the right to choose whether to engage in civil disobedience. Spock responded, "This is the obligation in a democracy—for everyone to make the judgment. And just because the majority of people go along with the administration doesn't mean that that is right." When Spivak asked if that included an obligation to both violate a law and seek its protection, Spock countered, "Not an obligation to break the law, but to do everything that he thinks is right to try and change the course." Explaining that he had delivered speeches, written letters, and participated in demonstrations, Spock added, "Now I am testing the law in another way." After a testy exchange, Spock charged that his nation was being guided down a disastrous course "by a belligerent administration that had deliberately misinterpreted the history in Vietnam." He saw himself as attempting "to save" his country. Responding to the accusation he was goading others to violate the law, Spock denied that. "I am not urging them to break all laws. I am only saying the young men who are refusing to be drafted to fight an illegal war, which is harmful to the United States, need moral and financial support, and I stand by that."

Notwithstanding his public pronouncement, Spock was not immune to doubts about his course of action. As he admitted to one author, "I've lived sixty-four years without going to jail and somehow I can't imagine it now. Intellectually I can, but not really." He also worried that his indictment would tarnish his standing as a respectable war critic.

On January 29, the Boston Five defendants were arraigned before a federal district court in Boston, charging with having conspired to assist young men in evading conscription. Following a hearing that lasted about ten minutes, Judge Francis J. W. Ford released the defendants, subject to the payment of separate thousand-dollar bonds. Each proclaimed "Not guilty" in response to the indictments. Ferber and Spock went on to a rally at Manhattan Center, attended by more than 4,000 people. To the enthusiastic crowd, Spock asserted that the Vietnam War was "illegal from every point of view" and had resulted in the United States relinquishing "its leadership in the free world."

Spock remained in the news as one of 448 writers and editors who signed a full-page newspaper advertisement pledging not to pay the percentage of their taxes, including a proposed 10 percent surcharge, which helped to fund the war. Other literary witnesses included James Baldwin, Betty Friedan, Norman Mailer, and Susan Sontag. Another eminent figure who signed the manifesto, Eric Bentley, a literature professor at Columbia, noted that the *New York Times*, the *Washington Post*, and the *Boston Globe* were among the newspapers that refused to publish the ad, believing it "was advocating an illegal act."

Word of the prosecution of Dr. Spock, William Sloane Coffin Jr., Michael Ferber, Mitchell Goodman, and Marcus Raskin afforded a spur to the Resistance, which picked up new members and carried out additional actions. Also providing support was the adoption of General Hershey's plan to reclassify resisters for induction. The historian Michael S. Foley indicates that induction centers served as "the ultimate test of a resister's commitment to the cause." Resistance groups attempted to offer support as resisters prepared to refuse induction. They also wanted to make it clear that the federal government was unable to "silence the American people by resorting to intimidation and bogus conspiracy charges." Foley contends too that draft resistance intensified owing to a belief that the indictments of Dr. Spock and his codefendants likely meant repression was worsening. "There was a great hurry to get something accomplished," the philosopher Hilary Putnam notes.

The young men who made up the Resistance demonstrated tremendous élan and determination, along with a radical, even revolutionary sensibility. Their refusal to participate in the Selective Service System placed them in direct opposition to the then-current administration in Washington, but also centuries-long practices regarding the responsibility of community members or citizens to participate in colonial militias, the Continental Army, either the Grand Army of the Republic or the Confederate States of America, or the United States Armed Forces. A tradition of contesting America's wars and even military service altogether also existed, but conscientious objectors, resisters, evaders, and deserters were seldom held in high regard. Over the course of American history, many who fell into those camps had been reviled, abused, incarcerated, or even executed.

The young men coming of age during the 1960s were often the children of proud World War II and Korean War veterans, perplexed by the reluctance of their progeny to engage in military service for their country. Members of the Resistance especially astonished them, not simply for opposing the war but in condemning the Selective Service System entirely, while subjecting themselves to criminal prosecution. The potential penalties for violating the Selective Service Act were quite harsh in terms of both fines and incarcerations. Older supporters of the Resistance, who included four members of the Boston Five, also placed themselves at risk of criminal prosecution, and did so deliberately. The federal government chose to go after certain friends of the Resistance, while not prosecuting many it might have. They included academics like Noam Chomsky, Gabriel Kolko, Christopher Lasch, Staughton Lynd, and

Howard Zinn; writers on the order of Robert Bly, Lawrence Ferlinghetti, Allen Ginsberg, Robert Lowell, Dwight Macdonald, Norman Mailer, Mary McCarthy, Nat Hentoff, Grace Paley, Philip Roth, and Susan Sontag; civil rights leaders Julian Bond and Martin Luther King Jr.; ministers James Bevel, Robert McAfee Brown, and Thomas Merton; the artist Alexander Calder; and the Nobel Prize–winning scientist Linus Pauling.

Ramsey Clark's tenure as attorney general ensured that prosecution for draft avoidance remained selective. Another head of the Justice Department or a different administration might well have opted to behave differently, going more forcefully against members of the American intellectual community who protested both the war and the Selective Service System. A fully reactionary federal government could have crippled the American intelligentsia, much as had taken place during World War I and its immediate aftermath.

3

"We Had to Destroy the Town in Order to Save It"

The Impact of the Tet Offensive

Figure 3.1   In what was described as "the photo that lost the war," Saigon Police Chief Nguyen Ngoc Loan executes a Vietcong suspect on a city street during the Tet Offensive. Photographer Eddie Adams's prize-winning photo, which was featured on the front page of newspapers around the world, seemed to capture the wanton brutality of a war spinning out of control. Library of Congress, Prints and Photographs Division, LC-DIG-ppmsca 19373.

New Year's Eve always brought loud celebrations in Saigon, capital city of the Republic of South Vietnam, as the inhabitants marked the arrival of the Lunar New Year with fireworks. On January 30, 1968, however, a group of around twenty men prepared to usher in the Year of the Monkey in a way that would send shock waves around the world and mark a turning point in the American War in Vietnam. Meeting in a run-down auto repair shop about five blocks from the fortress-like US embassy, members of the South Vietnam People's Liberation Army C-10 Battalion readied weapons and explosives that had recently been smuggled into Saigon. Their mission was to attack the six-story American Embassy Chancery building, situated in a walled compound. These revolutionaries were the vanguard of concerted assaults by Vietcong and the Hanoi-directed People's Army of Vietnam (PAVN) throughout South Vietnam. The Tet Offensive was designed to cripple the Army of South Vietnam (ARVN) and win over the South Vietnamese people, thereby destroying the morale of the American interlopers.

Shortly before 2:45 a.m., the Vietcong guerrillas loaded their weapons into a taxicab and a truck and undertook the short drive to the embassy. As the lead vehicle turned onto Reunification Boulevard, dominated by the embassy's eight-foot wall, the occupants opened fire on the two American MPs stationed outside the night gate. The MPs returned fire as the VC, who wore armbands and neckerchiefs for identification, piled out and began unloading anti-tank rockets and explosive charges. Seconds later, one of the charges blew a three-foot hole in the compound wall. As the communist soldiers poured through, MPs inside the compound opened fire and issued a radio call for reinforcements at the lightly defended facility. Within the first couple of minutes, American and Vietcong dead alike were sprawled in the courtyard and on the street outside. The siege of the US Embassy, which would stun the American public, was under way.

The seven-hour battle at the embassy rapidly unfolded as the assailants seemed on the verge of overcoming the small US Marine Security Guard detachment that provided security inside the walls. External security had been turned over to the South Vietnamese police in mid-December, which now proved of little help. A request for local police reinforcements from US Ambassador Ellsworth Bunker's office was refused by the commanding officer, who argued that because of the darkness, it would be impossible to tell friend from foe. With additional American MPs still minutes away, the attackers launched an assault on the front of the chancery building, riddling the doors and windows with bullets and blasting holes. As additional MPs arrived, they engaged in a shootout with VC out on the embassy lawn. Inside the building, the few Marine guards, CIA officers, and State Department personnel had only light weapons to hold off the invaders. Ironically, while the VC were roaming at will through the compound, MP reinforcements found their entry blocked by the locked gate, which the now-dead American sentries could not open. A firefight intensified on the lawn, with neither side having a clear picture of the situation.

Saigon Associated Press (AP) bureau chief Robert Tuckman issued the first teletype bulletin about the attacks at 3:15 a.m., able to provide only fragmented, sometimes contradictory details. A visiting State Department representative dismissed the first report regarding the Saigon embassy as a joke before subsequent reports confirmed the story. On the embassy grounds, the fighting continued as General William Westmoreland, commander of US forces in Vietnam, ordered the 716th Military Police Battalion, the largest in the city, into action. That force, together with the armored vehicles and helicopters requested by the beleaguered embassy security force, took time to arrive, however. The first helicopter to attempt a landing on the embassy roof was driven off by VC gunfire. At 6:15 a.m., a second chopper succeeded in unloading ammunition and evacuating wounded from the embassy roof, but the building's defenders remained poorly armed.

As the communist assault on the Saigon embassy unfolded, the first televised reports were broadcast from NBC's New York facility, as anchorman Chet Huntley led off the evening's *Huntley-Brinkley Report* with an account of the events occurring in South Vietnam. Brinkley informed his audience that "the Vietcong seized part of the US Embassy in Saigon early Wednesday" and that "twenty suicide commandos are reported to be holding the first floor of the Embassy." Huntley continued to note that "other key installations" were under attack as part of what appeared to be "the enemy's biggest and most highly coordinated offensive of the war." The one-and-a-half-minute report did little to clarify the situation in Saigon for officials and citizens alike, but it was evident that something major was in the offing.

American efforts to regain control of the situation at the embassy improved shortly after dawn when MPs managed to break down the locked front gate with a Jeep. The soldiers charged into the compound, followed by a crowd of reporters and cameramen, who saw that most of the VC already lay sprawled dead or wounded on the grounds. The situation improved further when an Army helicopter deposited onto the embassy roof five US paratroopers, who quickly began clearing the building. Despite numerous media reports that the VC had penetrated the chancellery, the troops found none of the enemy. The situation was somewhat different for Army Colonel George Jacobson, who resided in a villa on the embassy grounds. Armed only with a grenade, Jacobson discovered signs that a guerrilla had indeed made it onto the first floor of his house. MPs outside began a gun battle with the lone VC fighter and lobbed teargas into the residence. Pleading for a weapon from US troops outside, Jacobson caught a pistol that was tossed through his second-story window. Minutes later, he killed the VC on the stairwell. Shortly afterward, at 9:45 a.m., the embassy was declared secure. Fifteen minutes later, United Press International (UPI) announced that "a Vietcong suicide squad" had occupied the first five floors of the embassy. The "fog of war" proved crucial in shaping American responses to the Tet Offensive in subsequent weeks, as the American media struggled to construct an accurate account of what was happening in Vietnam and what it meant.

The assault on the US Embassy in Saigon, though one of the most dramatic episodes of the Tet Offensive, was in reality a small part of an operation mapped out by the Lao Dong (North Vietnam's Communist Party) months earlier. The plan was to launch attacks on more than one hundred South Vietnamese cities and towns, as well as most provincial and district capitals. More specific targets included the US Embassy, South Vietnam's presidential palace, and the Joint General Staff headquarters, along with the headquarters of all four of the South's military regions. The objectives were several: to stun, humiliate, and perhaps shatter the ARVN troops; to discredit and weaken the South Vietnamese government (GSVN); and to bring the South Vietnamese people into the revolutionary fold. These developments, it was believed, would force the hand of the US government, which would be compelled to either make an unpopular decision to ramp up its military commitment or abandon its war effort. North Vietnam's communist leadership believed this "General Offensive and General Uprising" would mark the beginning of the final phase of Vietnam's long war.

July 1967 was the crucial month for planning the operation. That month the Lao Dong Party's Central Committee agreed to move ahead with the offensive. A resolution adopted by the Political Bureau Congress proclaimed that the General Offensive would "decide the fate of the country" and "end the war." That same month, a North Vietnamese delegation departed for Beijing to secure weapons from China and other communist nations. The following month, North Vietnam signed an aid agreement with China and a military pact with North Korea. In the South, military leaders connected to the communist-dominated People's Revolutionary Party gathering in July at the headquarters of the Central Office for the South, also communist-led, on the Cambodia–South Vietnam border. They began planning the offensive, which required reorganizing military cadres, communications, and transportation, as well as rearming southern fighters for the coming struggle. Employing psychological warfare, Hanoi also attempted to convince both Saigon and Washington, DC, that it was willing to discuss the possibility of a coalition government in the South.

In the North, party leaders undertook steps to silence potential opposition. At one level, this necessitated suppression of any possible dissent, leading to the arrest of several hundred party officials who had unwisely questioned the direction of the war. This was ironic, given that both General Vo Nguyen Giap, longtime commander of Vietnamese communist military forces, and Ho Chi Minh questioned the advisability of a general offensive. Regardless, draconian decrees, including the death penalty, were enacted against a wide variety of "counterrevolutionary crimes." A more public initiative involved a public appearance by the aging and infirm Ho, who addressed a Hanoi crowd in December 1967 on the twenty-first anniversary of the start of the First Indochina War against the French. Ho declared that the sacrifices of the Vietnamese in both the North and the South would overcome American aggression, and he predicted "even greater feats of battle." The official newspaper of the Lao Dong proclaimed Ho's speech "an order to advance in our victorious drive . . . a signal for a new wave of attacks." Hanoi Radio also broadcast a poem by President Ho on January 1, 1968, promising, "Total victory shall be ours."

Only the day before, North Vietnam's Foreign Minister Nguyen Duy Trinh had dangled the carrot of peace negotiations during a reception for a delegation from the Mongolian People's Republic. Remarkably, given Hanoi's previous refusal to comment on what might follow a US bombing halt, Trinh announced that after the unconditional cessation of bombing, North Vietnam would hold talks with the US in Washington. American officials were puzzled by the apparent proposal for peace talks even as intelligence sources detected Hanoi's preparations for aggressive action. Nonetheless, as President Johnson had long expressed receptiveness to positive signals from Hanoi, US bombers were ordered to cease attacks on the Hanoi-Haiphong area as a show of good faith. This limited bombing halt was still in effect when the Tet Offensive began.

In the months before Tet, American policy makers were giving serious thought to the direction of the war, which Johnson had Americanized by the summer of 1965 through massive infusion of US troops and supplies. In January 1967, the president felt encouraged by reports from US ambassador Henry Cabot Lodge and the CIA that communist strength in the South was diminishing. Later that month, Joint Chiefs of Staff chair General Earle Wheeler confirmed that "the adverse military tide has been reversed" and predicted that the war could be won "if we apply pressure upon the enemy relentlessly in the north and the south." Nevertheless, the president had been cautious in his public assessments, warning during his State of the Union Address on January 17, "We face more cost, more loss, and more agony."

The United States could yet prevail, however, if Americans remained firm in their resolve.

It was becoming evident that America's public resolve was not unshakable. Harrison Salisbury's series of reports in the *New York Times* about the devastating impact on civilian targets in North Vietnam caused by US bombing stoked simmering anti-war sentiment, especially demands to end aerial assaults. University administrators and faculty at major institutions across the country gathered signatures and petitions protesting the war. Martin Luther King Jr. lent his eloquent voice to the anti-war movement. Equally worrisome to the administration was increased congressional doubt about the war. Senators George McGovern, William Fulbright, Wayne Morse, Frank Church, Albert Gore, Ernest Gruening, and Gaylord Nelson numbered among the growing fold voicing doubts or criticism. New York Senator Robert F. Kennedy drew Johnson's personal ire after a European trip during which the senator was said to have been the recipient of a "peace feeler" from Hanoi not predicated on halting US bombing. Summoned to the president's office, Kennedy was chastised by a furious Johnson, who believed that the senator had leaked the story to undercut him. His personal disdain for Kennedy clearly evident, Johnson promised, "I'll destroy you and every one of your dove friends in six months." "Look, I don't have to take that from you," Kennedy retorted before abruptly walking out of the meeting.

By the spring of 1967, President Johnson, who had to a significant degree personalized the issue of Vietnam, seeing in the failure of US policy his administration's likely political demise, faced a dilemma. Secretary of Defense Robert McNamara agreed to increase deployment levels there to just over 450,000, undercutting General William Westmoreland's request for even more troops. Some 13,000 Americans had died in Vietnam by the summer of 1967 and the war's annual cost exceeded twenty billion dollars. In August, shortly after the president proposed a 10 percent surtax to cover the war's escalating costs, both the Gallup and Harris polls showed declining support for Johnson's Vietnam policies. More alarming, Gallup revealed that 46 percent of those interviewed saw the war as "a mistake." Congressional defections, even among Democrats, were growing. Congressman Thomas "Tip" O'Neill typified the growing skepticism, noting, "We are dropping $20,000 bombs every time someone thinks he sees four Vietcong in a bush. And it isn't working." Dependably supportive newspapers such as the Richmond *Times-Dispatch*, the Cleveland *Plain Dealer*, the *Los Angeles Times*, and the Minneapolis *Star and Tribune* voiced doubts about the war's direction and necessity. *Time* and *Life* magazines likewise began stepping away from their previously reliable support of the war.

Massive escalation had simply not worked as envisioned. In addition to the

400,000 troops in Vietnam, the United States had rained 1,630,000 tons of bombs across Vietnam, more than the American tonnage dropped on Europe in World War II, amounting to a hundred pounds of explosives for every Vietnamese, North and South. The Johnson administration also confronted questions by congressional hawks. Perplexed by growing criticism of a war he himself privately questioned, Johnson brought together a circle of experienced foreign policy advisers on November 2, 1967. The "Wise Men," as the group of seasoned Cold Warriors was known, affirmed that the president was on the right track, despite McNamara's growing doubts about the war's winnability. Reassured, Johnson proceeded to organize a campaign to bolster public morale through assurances that the United States was winning the war.

"We are winning—get the message out." Such was the decree from the Johnson White House, which that fall set up the Psychological Strategy Committee chaired by Walt Rostow. In early November, as North Vietnam's high command finalized preparations for the Tet Offensive, President Johnson set off on a speaking tour of eight military bases to whip up support for the war effort. In Saigon, American newsmen were subjected to lengthy official briefings, often derided as the "five o'clock follies," where they were assured that communist fighting strength had progressively declined. Vice President Hubert Humphrey enthusiastically proclaimed on NBC's *Today Show*, "We are beginning to win this struggle. . . . We are making steady progress."

However, Johnson intended to rely on the new US Ambassador to South Vietnam Ellsworth Bunker, and General William C. Westmoreland, both summoned stateside to proclaim the good news. As commander of US forces in Vietnam, Westmoreland garnered more coverage, beginning with initial comments at Andrews Air Force Base on November 15, when he remarked, "I have never been more encouraged in the four years that I have been in Vietnam. We are making real progress." At a briefing for the House Armed Services Committee the next day, the general went further, claiming that "if present trends continued" a "phase-out" of American troops could begin within two years. Speaking at the National Press Club on November 21, Westmoreland declared that the war was now entering the final stage, in which the burden of fighting would gradually be turned over to South Vietnamese forces. The "Success Offensive" may well have achieved its goal of reassuring many Americans that their lengthy efforts in Vietnam were not in vain. But ironically, the "Success Offensive" ensured that the Tet Offensive would have a devastating impact on American morale.

Contrary to his glowing assurances to domestic audiences, Westmoreland warned the Johnson administration in late December that the very precariousness of the communist position in the South might compel the enemy to initiate "an intensified countrywide effort, perhaps a maximum effort," shortly. Johnson feared some sort of communist initiative, possibly "kamikaze tactics" and "a wave of suicide attacks," as he informed Australian officials. Journalists such as Joseph Alsop likewise predicted that something was afoot when Vietcong and North Vietnamese troops launched assaults along the Demilitarized Zone (DMZ), in the Que Son Valley and at scattered sites, mainly in South Vietnam's northern regions. On January 20 and 21, the US base at Khe Sanh came under heavy artillery bombardment, confirming to Westmoreland and other military officials that the communists intended to press an offensive near the DMZ. General Frederick Weyand convinced Westmoreland to bolster South Vietnam's northern sector with troops withdrawn from the Cambodian border.

The Hanoi regime had declared in October that it would honor a truce between January 27 and February 3, and the GSVN had granted holiday leave to half of ARVN's forces. Westmoreland presciently canceled the US observance of the truce and urged South Vietnam's President Nguyen Van Thieu to do so in Saigon, but Thieu only agreed to reduce the truce to a thirty-six-hour period.

Questions regarding an impending attack were answered in the early hours of January 30, 1968, as the American media struggled to piece together the first alarming reports of a communist offensive across South Vietnam. A complicating factor was the thirteen-hour time differential between Saigon and New York City, a major media center, especially for television. The three top networks—NBC, ABC, and CBS—all scheduled their evening news broadcasts for 6 p.m. on the East Coast and depended heavily on the leading wire services—the AP, the UPI, and Reuters—as well as on their own on-site correspondents. Before the age of videotape or digital recording, film shot in Vietnam was often available for broadcast only several hours after the occurrence of events. The earliest AP bulletins reported that the presidential palace, the US embassy, and other government buildings were under attack in the capital, and that several provincial capitals as well as the American base at Da Nang had also been targeted. Subsequent bulletins focused on the fighting at the US embassy, where "Vietcong suicide guerrillas" were said to be "holed up inside the embassy building." Shortly after the first AP reports, UPI issued bulletins confirming their veracity and declaring that "the Vietcong's greatest offensive of the war swept into the heart of Saigon early Wednesday."

Late-edition city newspapers soon spread the news, often with alarming headlines such as one in the *New York Times* that read "FOES INVADE U.S. SAIGON EMBASSY / RAIDERS WIPED OUT AFTER 6 HOURS / VIETCONG WIDEN ATTACK ON CITIES." CBS's Walter Cronkite, who aired his news show before word of the offensive arrived, reported instead on a major attack on the American airbase at Da Nang, where VC sappers destroyed or damaged some $25 million worth of US aircraft. NBC and CBS quickly put together special televised reports about the offensive, titled respectively "Viet-Cong Terror: A Guerrilla Offensive" and "Saigon Under Fire." A later examination of the reporting of the Tet Offensive concluded that the earliest accounts largely focused on the fighting at the US embassy, chiefly because it was American, easily covered, and, perhaps most of all, dramatic. Soon enough, however, American television viewers were witness to the expanded fighting that swept through much of the city and its environs as well as to a uniquely horrifying demonstration of the war's brutality.

In addition to films of the fighting at the US Embassy, American television viewers also witnessed the effort by ARVN troops to recapture the government radio station in downtown Saigon, which had been taken over by a VC squad tasked with broadcasting the official beginning of the "General Uprising." The invaders held the station for six hours, unable to complete their mission because the transmitter had been shut down and they were eventually overwhelmed and killed by government troops. Viewers then saw the ARVN troops loot the bodies of the dead VC and what remained of the badly damaged station.

These scenes might have inspired mixed reactions, but an episode that occurred on February 1 left an indelible imprint on the minds of those who witnessed it. NBC-TV crew members, accompanied by photographer Eddie Adams, was navigating the debris-strewn street near Saigon's An Quang Pagoda, when they observed a group of South Vietnamese soldiers turn a raggedly dressed VC suspect over to the chief of South Vietnam's National Police, General Nguyen Ngoc Loan. Quickly and unexpectedly, Loan withdrew a pistol, placed it to the suspect's head, and pulled the trigger. With only a brief grimace, the man, later identified as VC officer Nguyen Van Lem, fell to the street, a fountain of blood spurting from the head wound. Adams captured the precise moment of death in a still photograph that won a 1969 Pulitzer Prize, while cameraman Vo Suu filmed the execution. The photo appeared on the front page of newspapers worldwide the following day. Less than two days later, NBC executives agreed to air the film, edited to exclude the final bloody moments, on the *Huntley-Brinkley Report*. To many of the estimated twenty million Americans who watched that night, the film seemed to perfectly capture the arbitrary brutality of an increasingly incomprehensible war. Adams's still photo was later characterized by a historian as "the picture that lost the war."

Savage fighting raged for days in Saigon and across much of the South, with one of the grimmer battles playing out at Ben Tre, where the journalist Peter Arnett quoted a US Army officer as saying, "It became necessary to destroy the town in order to save it." Though the quote's authenticity would later be questioned, the incident seemed to capture the futility of the American effort in Vietnam. Elsewhere in the South, with one major exception, US and ARVN troops ultimately crushed the communist assault, inflicting severe casualties on the enemy but leaving many villages and towns in ruins.

In the ancient imperial capital of Hue close to Vietnam's geographic center, a very different scenario played out as communist troops gained control of the city for an extended period. When the battle ended twenty-five days later, the murderous consequences of communist rule there were shockingly evident. In the early morning hours of January 31, the city, defended only by a small force of ARVN and US troops, was easily overrun by an initial force of VC fighters and 7,500 North Vietnamese troops, whose foremost objective was to seize the Citadel, a nineteenth-century fortress complex. Though US forces were quickly diverted to the city, its recapture took more than three weeks, and was slowed by the dilemma concerning whether to employ widespread air or artillery attacks due to Hue's historical significance. During that time, the Lao Dong Party's draconian plan for securing the city and eliminating "cruel tyrants and reactionary elements"—ill-defined categories that allowed for widespread arrests, imprisonments, and executions—was put into effect. Essentially, anyone suspected of loyalty to the Saigon regime, as well Catholics and most foreigners, was at risk. As the battle for control of the city escalated, with both sides pouring in more troops, thousands of Hue's citizens disappeared, supposedly taken away for "re-education."

Only after the communists were driven from the city in late February did the magnitude of the horror become obvious. Mass graves were eventually uncovered. Officials ultimately estimated that some 2,800 South Vietnamese civilians had been murdered. The intense fighting accounted for about 5,800 civilian deaths, and much of the once-beautiful city lay in ruins. The battle for Hue was the longest, and perhaps bloodiest of the Tet Offensive, costing over 600 US and ARVN lives. Estimates of North Vietnamese deaths ranged from around 1,000 to 5,000.

However, as horrific as the battle for Hue was, American attention was increasingly drawn to the siege at Khe Sanh, where a disturbing historical parallel was taking shape. Journalist and historian Peter Braestrup wrote, "No event during the Tet period was to generate more sustained journalistic output . . . than the PAVN's 77-day siege of the US Marine Combat Base at Khe Sanh." Reportage of the battle gripped the American public's attention for several key reasons. Though the fighting on January 21 preceded the Tet Offensive, Khe Sanh remained relatively quiet as the New Year arrived. But in subsequent weeks, as fighting around Saigon diminished and especially after the recapture of Hue on February 24, the fate of the 6,000 US and

ARVN troops occupying the base in the mountainous northern countryside again became a central concern for the American public and in US government circles. Elements of an unfolding drama were in place: an allied contingent outnumbered and surrounded by some 20,000 NVA fighters, under siege in an isolated area and, perhaps most important, similarities involving the French debacle at Dien Bien Phu in 1954, as the media frequently mentioned. During the spring of 1954, some 12,000 French troops had been besieged by more than 50,000 Viet Minh fighters, who eventually overran the isolated firebase, killing or capturing all of its defenders. The defeat led directly to French withdrawal from the First Indochina War. Now, a similar grim fate possibly awaited American Marines.

The seeming historical parallel with Dien Bien Phu was tenuous at best. The crude runway at the base remained open and resupply was possible. Public perception of a hopeless situation was fed by film of the few aircraft that were damaged or destroyed by enemy fire and through interviews with Marines hunkered down in bunkers or sheltered from steady artillery barrages. In addition, the troops at Khe Sanh possessed air support unavailable to the French, as American aircraft dropped more than 39,000 tons of ordnance on enemy positions around the base. Finally, though there were periodic attacks on the base perimeter, there was no large-scale assault on the Marine positions as had occurred at Dien Bien Phu. Nevertheless, film-crew images of the gloomy, fog-shrouded mountains, seemingly endless jungle, and churned-up red soil at the base presented a picture of a potentially hopeless situation. As Braestrup notes, the "highly unfavorable conditions for accurate and impartial firsthand coverage" at Khe Sanh created circumstances in which "speculative excess, fed by ignorance, bloomed as a substitute." The battle at Khe Sanh ended in early April when an allied relief expedition reached the base as NVA troops withdrew. The fighting cost an estimated 5,500 North Vietnamese and 977 American lives. In July, the US departed from Khe Sanh, no longer deemed of strategic importance.

Long before the siege at Khe Sanh was lifted, American opinion about the war, both public and private, had begun to shift significantly. The general reaction of shock to the Tet Offensive was compounded by a broad perception that the Johnson administration had misled the public about progress in Vietnam. The *Washington Post*'s Art Buchwald captured the latter sentiment in a satirical February 6 column that had General George Custer telling a reporter, "We have the Sioux on the run. . . . Of course we still have some cleaning up to do, but the Redskins are hurting badly and it will be only a matter of time before they give in." Despite the administration's claims, including one directly by the president on February 2 that the communists had failed to

achieve objectives related to Tet, influential voices challenged such asser-
tions. Reacting to the president's pronouncement that the offensive was a
"complete failure," Senator Eugene McCarthy retorted, "If taking over a sec-
tion of the American embassy, a good part of Hue, Dalat and major cities of
the Fourth Corps area constitutes a complete failure, I suppose by this logic
that if the Vietcong had captured the entire country, the administration would
be claiming their total collapse." Republican Governor George Romney of
Michigan concurred, noting, "If what we have seen this past week is a Vietcong failure, then I hope they never have a victory." Senator Robert F. Kennedy, clearly testing the political waters for a presidential campaign, told a
Chicago audience on February 8, "It is as if James Madison were able to
claim a great victory in 1812 because the British only burned Washington
instead of annexing it to the British Empire." Kennedy, whose brother John
had played a major role in shaping the American effort in Vietnam, now
repudiated it, admitting that "for twenty years we have been wrong." The
American war amounted to a "lengthy and consistent chronicle of error,"
the senator proclaimed. "It is time to discard so proven a fallacy and face the
reality that a military victory is not in sight, and that it probably never will
come." In coming weeks, Kennedy became an increasingly impassioned critic
of the war.

Though various congressional war hawks argued for escalation and a few
continued to support administration policy, the chorus of criticism grew in
volume, especially among Democrats. Senator Majority Leader Mike Mansfield of Montana stated that the Tet Offensive demonstrated that no area of
Vietnam was secure. Senator Gore observed that the US was destroying the
nation it "profess[ed] to be saving." Republican Senators Charles Percy and
Jacob Javits challenged the truthfulness of earlier administration character-
izations of the war's progress. Debate sparked by the Tet Offensive was further inflamed by Senator McCarthy's televised warning that there might be
"a demand for the use of tactical nuclear weapons." Despite White House
denials, the controversy attained a life of its own, especially during the prolonged battle of Khe Sanh. When General Wheeler declined on February 14
to categorically rule out the use of nuclear weapons to defend Khe Sanh, the
issue simmered for two more days until President Johnson announced that no
such request had ever been made. During that same week of February 11 to
17, 543 Americans died in Vietnam, making it the deadliest of the war.

In the print media and on television, American anxieties and doubts about
the Vietnam War were broadly aired only days after the beginning of the Tet
Offensive. On February 1, Joseph Kraft wrote in the *Washington Post*, "The
war in Vietnam is unwinnable, and the longer it goes on the more the Americans . . . will be subjected to losses and humiliations." Later that month, the

Wall Street Journal editorialized, "We think the American people should be getting ready to accept, if they haven't already, the prospect that the whole Vietnam effort may be doomed." Widely read weeklies such as *Time* and *Newsweek* proved less willing to declare the war lost, but focused on the enemy's "psychological gains" and ability to launch additional attacks.

Perhaps the most influential commentary on Tet came from the broadcast networks. Initially, NBC's Chet Huntley and David Brinkley, together with ABC's Howard K. Smith, were reserved in their criticisms, Smith even advocating a major escalation of the US effort. The trajectory of network commentary changed, however, following the broadcast of Walter Cronkite's hard-hitting televised special on February 27, *Report from Vietnam*. Taken aback by Tet, the veteran anchorman arrived in Saigon on February 11 for a firsthand look. Shocked at the extent of destruction and death, the widely respected journalist made clear his change of mind during the thirty-minute CBS special. Some nine million Americans watched film of the rubble that now despoiled sections of Saigon, along with interviews of Americans and Vietnamese, who offered a variety of perspectives. The greatest impact came from Cronkite's summation, in which he conceded that he was unsure of who had emerged from the carnage victorious, but concluded, "It seems now more certain than ever that the bloody experience of Vietnam is to end in a stalemate." The only alternative to disaster was negotiation, he advised. Otherwise, "with each escalation, the world comes closer to the brink of cosmic disaster." Tet might well be the enemy's "last big gasp," Cronkite speculated. "But it is increasingly clear to this reporter that the only rational way out then will be to negotiate, not as victors but as an honorable people who lived up to their pledge to defend democracy, and did the best they could." On March 10, NBC's Frank McGee seconded Cronkite's analysis, stating in his network's special that "the war is being lost by the administration's definition" and that American policymakers needed to decide whether "it's futile to destroy Vietnam in order to save it." By that point, both *Newsweek* and *Time* had adopted a much more pessimistic perspective on the course of the war.

As the debate on Vietnam played out in the media, the Johnson administration faced the daunting task of crafting a response to the communist offensive. The president had only authorized deployment of an additional 11,000 troops but in the same week as the Cronkite special, General Wheeler flew to Vietnam to confer with General Westmoreland about strategy. They agreed to request fifteen fighter aircraft squadrons, additional naval support, and more ground troops among the 206,000 additional personnel Westmoreland was requesting. When that information leaked to the *New York Times*, which headlined the troop request on March 10, a firestorm of public and congressional dismay erupted. Moreover, the request occurred at a point when the Defense Department was under new leadership, Secretary Robert McNamara, having resigned or been pushed out by President Johnson in late January, in favor of Clark Clifford, who now headed a task force charged with evaluating the proposed escalation.

As internal debate continued, a rapid succession of events reshaped President Johnson's thoughts about the war. On March 4, Clifford met privately with the president to recommend against the troop increase, convinced in the wake of a discussion with military chiefs that there existed "no plan for victory in the historic American sense." Meanwhile, on March 12, Eugene McCarthy captured a surprising 42.4 percent of New Hampshire's Democratic primary vote as opposed to Johnson's 49.5 percent, highlighting the president's political vulnerability. On March 16, Robert Kennedy announced his candidacy for the presidency.

That same day, anxious, poorly led, and understaffed US Army troops ravaged the village of Son My, located in central Vietnam and considered friendly to the Vietcong, tearing through huts, conducting mass rapes, and killing more than 500 civilians, amid frustrated searches for elusive VC fighters. Vietnamese men of fighting age were not present. American soldiers particularly wreaked havoc on the hamlet of My Lai, slaughtering the old and the young, male and female alike, including babies. Few soldiers declined to participate as war crimes were conducted. A helicopter crew, led by Warrant Officer Hugh Thompson, managed to prevent one small group of Vietnamese from being killed, threatening to fire on American soldiers clearly determined to kill them. Nevertheless, the initial report called the American assault on My Lai "well planned, well executed, and successful."

On March 22, Johnson formally rejected Westmoreland's troop request and scheduled a meeting with the Wise Men for March 26. Reversing their November position, a majority of the eleven advisers now urged de-escalation. Although momentarily furious, Johnson pondered a new direction for both Vietnam policy and his presidency. On the evening of March 31, President Johnson went before the television cameras again, prepared to deliver one of the greatest political surprises of the year. Cognizant that the latest polls showed only 26 percent of those interviewed supporting his Vietnam policies, Johnson opted for a new approach. The first hint of a shift in direction came in the speech's opening paragraph. "Tonight I want to speak to you of peace in Vietnam and Southeast Asia," the president somberly intoned. "No other question so preoccupies our people." LBJ cited the long American efforts to bring peace to the region, then noted North Vietnam's deceitfulness and the failure of its Tet Offensive. He warned of the futility of any future communist assaults and the horrors of endless war before revealing his hopes for bringing the carnage to an end. "We are prepared to move immediately toward peace through negotiations," the obviously weary president declared. The United States would take the first step "to de-escalate the conflict . . . unilaterally and at once." All bombing north of the DMZ, with minor exceptions, would be immediately halted. Johnson went on to confirm the American commitment to liberty across the globe and to call for national unity, his country now divided by the war.

TV listeners hardly knew what was coming as the president expressed an unwillingness to permit his office "to become involved in the partisan divisions that are developing in this political year." "With America's sons in the fields far away," Johnson continued, "with our hopes and the world's hopes for peace in the balance every day, I do not believe that I should devote an hour or a day of my time to any personal political causes." Johnson concluded by announcing he would not seek the Democratic Party's presidential nomination for another term. The Johnson presidency was the latest casualty of a very costly war.

Though the North Vietnamese regime responded positively to Johnson's offer of negotiations, the fighting in Vietnam actually intensified throughout the year. Hanoi launched two "mini-Tets" in May and August in hopes of strengthening its bargaining position. The costs of the Tet Offensive for both North and South Vietnam were significant. Much of the damage in the North was political, as party leaders were compelled to confront both the failure of their major goals and extensive battlefield deaths. Though the VC guerrillas expanded their control of the southern countryside after Tet, resulting in a dramatic setback to the US pacification program, their numbers were greatly reduced. The Military Advisory Command Vietnam estimated that over 180,000 North Vietnamese and VC fighters died in 1968, compelling Hanoi to replenish VC ranks with Northerners. The damage, psychological and otherwise, was worse in the South, where the fighting took place. Confidence in the GSVN was shaken and President Thieu's subsequent declaration of martial law, together with an unpopular new draft law, eroded his popularity. Worse, the GSVN estimated that 14,300 civilians had been killed and 24,000 wounded. 630,000 new refugees sought shelter. Nearly 5,000 ARVN troops were estimated to have died during the offensive.

The cost of the Tet Offensive for the United States went beyond the immediate casualties, which numbered over 4,000 killed and more than 19,000 wounded, in addition to over 600 missing in action. Though analysts have agreed that the Tet Offensive concluded as a US military victory, the negative psychological impact of the event was undeniable. The most immediate casualty was the Johnson administration, which had spent the last weeks of 1967 assuring Americans that the war was being won. Johnson's Democratic Party subsequently tore itself apart over the issue during 1968, a presidential election year. The American public, though in general agreement that the war could not continue as it had since 1965, remained bitterly divided as to how it might be ended, torn between those who still advocated an elusive military victory and others who sought disengagement. Hope that the war might end soon diminished as the year continued. 1968 would be the deadliest year of the war for Americans, with 16,000 dying in a conflict that increasingly fewer of their fellow citizens supported or understood.

4

"The Impossible Dream"

The New Politics

Senator Robert F. Kennedy's attacks on the administration's war policy, which followed his belated entrance into the 1968 presidential race, received rapturous responses at times, including in unexpected places. Shortly after announcing his candidacy, Kennedy appeared at Kansas State University, in Manhattan, Kansas, and at the University of Kansas, in Lawrence, on March 18. Calling the administration's Vietnam policy "bankrupt," Kennedy met up with 14,500 "wildly cheering" college students at Kansas State and 20,000 "frenzied" onlookers at the University of Kansas. Young supporters "mobbed" the senator at airports and on the two campuses. After his talk in Manhattan, Kansas, fans attempted "to touch him or get his autograph." John Herbers of the *New York Times* reported, "Some tore at his sleeves, ruffled his hair and shouted 'Bobby!' as the senator made his way out of the fieldhouse."

During a rally on March 23 in Sacramento, California, Kennedy again faced "a mass of shoving, screaming and frantic people—both youths and adults," according to Herbers. The next day, "a riotous crowd" in Los Angeles greeted Senator Kennedy, many screaming, "Bobby, Bobby!" On March 25, African Americans appeared in large numbers to see RFK as he passed through Watts, the Los Angeles neighborhood that a massive race riot had ravaged three summers before. "Hundreds of black hands reached to touch him." The *Los Angeles Times* indicated that Kennedy's reception in the city proved "uproarious, shrieking and frenzied." In Stockton, California, teenagers yanked "off the senator's cufflinks and ran their fingers through his hair." Herbers subsequently discussed what many believed, that those drawn

Figure 4.1   New York Senator Robert F. Kennedy and Donald F. Benjamin of the
Central Brooklyn Coordinating Council converse at a playground. Drawn to increasingly
progressive and at times radical perspectives, RFK was associated with the New Politics
that briefly flourished in 1968. Library of Congress, Prints and Photographs Division,
LC-USZ62-133299.

to RFK desired "the fulfillment of a mandate cut short at Dallas" on November 22, 1963, the site and date of the assassination of his brother, President John F. Kennedy.

Robert F. Kennedy's campaign would be associated with the idea of a "New Politics" that emerged during the 1968 presidential contest. As the journalist and Columbia University professor Penn Kimball observes, the New Politics of the 1960s was tied to new-styled charisma of the sort emanating from Bobby Kennedy. In Kennedy's case, it was connected to the "moral indignation" he experienced regarding poverty in America and the Vietnam War. It was displayed through "his identification with students, the poor and oppressed" who resided in Third World lands.

But the New Politics was also characterized by a shift in tactics. A Justice Department attorney who acted as a speechwriter for RFK, Adam Walinsky, told reporters, "Our strategy is to change the rules on nominating a president. We're going to do it a new way. In the streets." Walinsky was referring to the need for citizen engagement, or something along the lines of the participatory democracy SDS had called for earlier in the decade. It was true, as the journalist Evan Thomas writes, that Kennedy believed Chicago mayor Richard Daley, one of the last of the old-fashioned political bosses, "means the ball game." And yet RFK reached out to those who had long been or felt themselves to be disenfranchised, including African Americans, Latinos, Native Americans, young people, even members of the white working class.

Along the way, Kennedy engendered, for good and ill, a degree of passion largely unprecedented in the annals of American politics, at least for a generation and probably longer. Westbrook Pegler, a conservative, well-respected journalist who nevertheless ended up in the camp of the John Birch Society, appeared cheered by the chance that "some white patriot of the Southern tier will spatter [Kennedy's] spoonful of brains in public premises before the snow flies." Jackie Kennedy expressed trepidation to family friend Arthur Schlesinger Jr. "Do you know what I think will happen to Bobby? The same thing that happened to Jack. . . . There is so much hatred in this country, and more people hate Bobby than hated Jack." Having conveyed that sensibility to her brother-in-law, Jackie said, "But he isn't fatalistic, like me." After Kennedy's rousing speech at the University of Kansas, *Look* magazine photographer Stanley Tretick shouted, "This is Kansas, fucking Kansas! He's going all the way. He's going all the fucking way!" Jimmy Breslin questioned other reporters, "Do you think this guy has the stuff to go all the way?" The *New York Times*' John J. Lindsay responded, "Yes, of course, he has the stuff to go all the way, but he's not going to go all the way. The reason is that somebody is going to shoot him."

As indicated by the March on the Pentagon and a surge in draft resistance, opposition to the Vietnam War continued to mount by early 1968 and led to the adoption of more militant tactics by some within the Movement. Activists like Jerry Rubin and Abbie Hoffman favored increasingly outlandish approaches, gearing up for the Democratic National Convention in Chicago. The appearance of the Resistance demonstrated the readiness of both young activists and older supporters, several quite renowned, to place themselves at risk of prosecution for contesting the Selective Service apparatus. Others opted to continue to work within the "system," believing they could help to reshape the American nation through the election of progressives, including one to the presidency itself. That resulted in a challenge to the Democratic Party's renomination of Lyndon B. Johnson, and led to the emergence of what came to be known as the *New Politics*. The catalyst for the New Politics, which would be exemplified in the presidential candidacies of Senators Eugene J. McCarthy and Robert F. Kennedy, was the "Dump Johnson" movement that began months before the start of the 1968 presidential campaign. That effort, the historian William H. Chafe contended, involved a small number of reformers, driven by conscience, to gather "enough political power to achieve, in essence, a peaceful coup d'état."

No individual was more identified with that phenomenon than thirty-eight-year-old Allard Lowenstein, whom Chafe referred to as "the source, the inspiration, and the genius that made it all happen." Lowenstein had received his J.D. from Yale Law School and taught or performed administrative duties at a series of universities, including Stanford, North Carolina State University, and City College of New York. He served as a senatorial aide for both Frank P. Graham and Hubert Humphrey, helped to kick off the Freedom Vote Project in Mississippi and MFS, and worked for the liberal political organization Americans for Democratic Action (ADA). Increasingly troubled by US policy in Vietnam, Lowenstein began mobilizing "mainstream" opposition, which included student leaders, college editors, and Peace Corps veterans. In late January 1967, Lowenstein and a group of student body presidents—among them, Stanford's David Harris—met with Secretary of State Rusk, who informed them, "We are fighting monolithic communism and we will escalate until they capitulate." Responding to a query of what would transpire if that didn't occur, Rusk stated, "Someone is going to get hurt." Believing Rusk indicated that a nuclear option would be considered, Colgate's Rick Weidman surmised that the top cabinet officer was "nuts."

Follow-up visits with Vice President Hubert Humphrey and National Security Adviser Walt Rostow discouraged Lowenstein even more, with the latter session illuminating the administration's "worst little blindnesses." Lowenstein determined that "the administration was hopeless," unwilling to negotiate. Consequently, Lowenstein and his colleague at ADA, Curtis Gans, began to look into the possibility of denying President Johnson renomination. Gans, who had joined in the sit-in campaign in the American South and been an early member of SDS, worked for UPI and the ADA, and provided logistical support for "nonviolent, nonconfrontational, and persuasive" mass rallies. In early 1967, Lowenstein and Gans joined with Gerald N. Hill, who led the liberal California Democratic Council, to set up the Conference of Concerned Democrats (CCD) in Gans's home in Washington, DC. While Gans became the CCD's lone employee, Lowenstein, then teaching at City College, traveled across the country to speak with liberal and anti-war activists and discuss the need to remove Johnson from the 1968 Democratic Party ticket. By late spring, Lowenstein informed friends, "It is now clear what must be done. Dump Johnson. We can do it. No one wants him out there and all that we have to do is have someone say it. Like, 'The emperor has no clothes.' There's a movement within the party that is dying for leadership." An early hope that a third party bid could coalesce behind Martin Luther King Jr. soon dissipated. Gans had informed Andrew Young, the civil rights activist, "Dr. King is probably the only person who could bridge the gap between the left and right wings of the movement."

The *Village Voice* columnist Jack Newfield, an SDS charter member who had written *A Prophetic Minority*, an illuminating account about the early 1960s New Left, compared Johnson to former heavyweight boxing champion Sonny Liston, twice bested by Muhammad Ali in title bouts. "He is a bully with a quitter's heart . . . he will not run if he thinks he cannot win." Newfield referred to a child at Auschwitz screaming at a German guard, with death impending, "You won't be forgiven anything." The journalist added, "This is my saying the same thing to Lyndon Johnson. He is not my President. This is not my war."

It was clear by the first half of 1967 that the war was tearing at the fabric of American liberalism, just as it was rending the Vietnamese landscape. Writing in the *New York Review of Books*, Noam Chomsky delivered a scathing indictment, "The Responsibility of Intellectuals," in which he insisted they had "to speak the truth and . . . expose lies." Chomsky went on to eviscerate intellectuals like Arthur Schlesinger Jr., Walt Rostow, Henry Kissinger, Irving Kristol, and McGeorge Bundy for having provided cover for "the deceit and distortion surrounding the American invasion of Vietnam." The legendary journalist Walter Lippmann refuted the Johnson administration's insistence that communists had to be stopped in Vietnam to prevent Munich-like appeasement of the sort Allies engaged in when they allowed Hitler to carve up Czechoslovakia. Lippmann termed the president, whom he accused of operating a "bastard empire," *pathologically secretive.*

Lowenstein, seen by the journalist David Halberstam as "the ultimate moralist-activist," reached out to both SANE and ADA, where he was a board member and then vice president. ADA's national board chose the Harvard economist and former diplomat John Kenneth Galbraith, a sharp critic of the war, to head it, and adopted a resolution conveying a readiness to back a peace candidate for the presidency from either major political party. SANE's support for an early "Dump Johnson" campaign seemed even stronger. The ADA publication, *World*, which Gans edited, publicly broached the possibility of denying the Democratic Party nomination to the president, presenting "The Issue: Vietnam; The Target: Johnson," in its July 1967 offering. Gans deemed it "of paramount importance that it not be taken for granted that the liberal community will support the President." He also warned, "If there is to be an end to the political polarization that threatens to strain the very foundation of American democracy, it is for the liberal movement to begin to pose another option." Talking to Senator Kennedy on a plane trip to California, Lowenstein offered, "If you want to run we'll let you." Lowenstein explained that the Dump Johnson movement did not involve "Kooks, or the New Left, or just the same old peace people," and would prevent the president from receiving his party's nomination. Kennedy and Lowenstein discussed other possibilities, including retired General James Gavin. "If you get Gavin," Kennedy said, "you've got a new ball game." At the annual convention of the National Student Association, which he had once headed, held at the University of Maryland in mid-August 1967, Lowenstein indicated that the congress could provide "a launching pad for a decision to make 1968 the year when students help change a society almost everyone agrees is headed for destruction." He urged the attendees to constitute "the avant-garde in the effort to deny Johnson renomination."

The Dump Johnson movement was viewed with skepticism or worse by many whose views on the war were little different from those of Lowenstein and Gans. Even friends, reasoning that an incumbent president could not be deposed by his own political party, thought Lowenstein was delusional but he persevered, believing that events could trigger a collapse in Johnson's support. The historian Charles Kaiser offers that radicals viewed it as "a trick to destroy the peace movement," for it would "show how weak" anti-war forces were, thereby playing into the notion that the war was not unloved and could be expanded. Liberals also worried about going against Johnson unless "a major candidate," generally meaning Senator Robert F. Kennedy, were to run against him. Many were pleased by Johnson's domestic agenda, while some considered it "quixotic to break with him," Lowenstein later indicated.

During his travels, Lowenstein saw fit to speak with prominent individuals who were considered opposed to the war, hoping that one would step forward to challenge LBJ. He particularly hoped that Bobby Kennedy, who despised

Johnson and was disliked equally as much in return, would declare his candidacy. He believed Kennedy, in a manner analogous to how Martin Luther King Jr.'s principled moral stance had altered America, "could set things right if he became president," contends Lowenstein biographer Richard Cummings. However, Kennedy continued to resist the entreaty, with his advisers split on whether he should jump into the race or wait until 1972 when his path to the Democratic Party nomination appeared less complicated, at a minimum. In a meeting at the Kennedy home in McLean, Virginia, Bobby acknowledged that Johnson was politically vulnerable, and he agreed with Lowenstein's analysis. "I think Johnson might quit the night before the convention opens. I think he is a coward," Kennedy contended. But he worried about fracturing the Democratic Party and indicated he would run only "under unforeseen circumstances." If he were the first to run against Johnson, charges would fly, Kennedy said, "that I was splitting the party out of ambition and envy. No one would believe that I was doing it because of how I felt about Vietnam and poor people." As Lowenstein departed, he told Kennedy, "You understand, of course, that there are those of us who think the honor and direction of the country is at stake. I don't give a damn whether you think it can be put together or not." Then, Lowenstein stated, "We're going to do it without you, and that's too bad, because you could have become president of the United States."

As Kennedy had suggested, Lowenstein and Gans considered other possible candidates, including Galbraith, General Gavin, Idaho Senator Frank Church, South Dakota Senator George McGovern, who, like many anti-war legislators, faced reelection, California Congressman Don Edwards, and Minnesota Senator Eugene McCarthy. Galbraith was willing, declaring, "This is the year when the people are right, and the politicians are wrong." Two other senators, Oregon's Wayne Morse and Indiana's Vance Hartke, both expressed a readiness to run but Lowenstein and Gans didn't think they were politically viable.

Lowenstein got together with Kennedy yet again for a secret meeting in mid-October, explaining that local organizations were in place in New Hampshire, site of the first presidential primary, and Wisconsin, while the liberal California Democratic Council was committed to backing someone other than Johnson. "I've been across the country thirty times and I can tell you we're going to win," Lowenstein said. "Imagine what we could do *with you*, if we're going to win *without you*! You have to get into it! . . . We are grassroots America. Johnson is finished."

Turned down by Senator Kennedy, Lowenstein and Gans began to consider Eugene McCarthy, who as a second-term congressman from Minnesota had stood up to Senator Joseph McCarthy (who was not related to Eugene McCarthy) in a televised debate in 1952, and then was elected to the Senate in something of a liberal wave six years later. In 1960, McCarthy, a former seminarian and college professor, delivered a stirring nominating speech for Adlai Stevenson, the then darling of American liberals, at the Democratic Party national convention in Los Angeles. McCarthy expected to be picked for the vice presidential slot in 1964, something Bobby Kennedy hoped for himself as well, but President Johnson opted for Humphrey instead.

As US engagement in Vietnam greatly intensified, McCarthy was one of a number of elected officials who called into question the policies of their fellow Democrat Lyndon B. Johnson. Starting in March 1967, McCarthy began to explore the possibility of challenging the president. Anti-war activists encouraged that notion, greeting the senator with signs stating "Peace with McCarthy" and "We Want Gene." He had been appalled to hear Undersecretary of State Nicholas Katzenbach inform the Senate Foreign Relations Committee in mid-August that Congress had to back the president's foreign policy. Following testimony by Katzenbach that the Gulf of Tonkin Resolution amounted to "the functional equivalent" of a congressional declaration of war, McCarthy told a reporter, "This is the wildest testimony I have ever heard." He worried, "There is no limit to what he says the president can do. There is only one thing to do: take it to the country."

On November 30, McCarthy revealed his determination to contest President Johnson's renomination in a series of Democratic primaries. The *New York Times* noted that McCarthy failed to forthrightly declare his own candidacy or indicate he could prevent Johnson from becoming the Democratic Party candidate. But justifying his projected political path, McCarthy pointed to "the evident intention to escalate and to intensify the war in Vietnam," and to avoid compromise or negotiations. "I am concerned that the administration seems to have set no limit to the price which it's willing to pay for a military victory" in Indochina, McCarthy said. He summarized what the war had cost to date. It had ushered in the physical decimation of "a small and weak nation" through a military campaign by the world's most powerful state. It had brought about as many as 150,000 civilian casualties in South Vietnam alone, along with grave devastation to people and property in the North. It had taken the lives of more than 15,000 American soldiers, with close to 95,000 wounded. It cost two to three billion dollars monthly. It had helped to foster "a deepening moral crisis in America," as exemplified by "discontent and frustration and a disposition to take extralegal if not illegal" steps. McCarthy hoped his decision would help assuage "this sense of political helplessness" and alienation particularly rampant on college campuses. At one point, McCarthy, whose relationship with the Kennedy brothers had long been difficult, felt the need to chide Bobby regarding his failure to move early. Ironically as matters turned out, McCarthy held fast to a belief, at least for a time, that Kennedy should undertake a bid for the White House. McCarthy declared that his own challenge shouldn't preclude others from seeking the nomination. Kennedy predicted to his friend and colleague, George McGovern, "He's going to get a lot of support. . . . he'll run very strong in New Hampshire."

Viewed by many as quirky, somewhat disinterested, inclined to dabble in poetry, the deeply moralistic senior senator from Minnesota conveyed his interest in challenging President Johnson. The early response to McCarthy proved heartening, with signs greeting him in Cambridge, "The war is obscene, we want Eugene." He in turn informed gathered throngs, "Vietnam is part of a much larger question, which is, is America going to police the planet?" McCarthy also declared, "There are some things that are just so wrong that you have to take a stand." While remaining doubtful about his own chances, McCarthy thought it essential to demonstrate that the American political system could work. Thomas D. Finney Jr., a top Washington attorney who provided counsel to both JFK and LBJ, believed that McCarthy wanted to offer "a political outlet for a deep dissatisfaction, a deep alienation on the part of a lot of people" often removed from the political scene.

The partnership of McCarthy and Lowenstein, however, soon frayed and collapsed, coming to a head after a rally involving Concerned Democrats, an anti-war group, in Chicago on December 2. McCarthy was furious at the delivery of impassioned oratory by Lowenstein, who spoke for nearly an hour but mentioned the senator only once. That was followed by the "grim-faced" McCarthy's own less-than-impressive speech. McCarthy believed this was hardly "a time for storming the walls, but for beginning a long march," as he later explained. The Vietnam War, he declared in Chicago, was one "in which progress is reported not in terms of the capture of a village or of crossing a river, but rather in terms of the kill ratio." He deemed it "of questionable legality and of questionable constitutionality" and insisted it was "not diplomatically defensible." In characteristic fashion, he presented his vision for the nation:

> In the place of what appears to be doubt, we will establish that the spirit of America is one of trust, and instead of expediency, what this nation seeks is right judgment; instead of ghettos that what we want are neighborhoods and communities in America; instead of disunity or what it sometimes masquerades under consensus, we have dedication of purpose; instead of incredibility, let us have integrity; and instead of murmuring, let us have clear speech and, we hope, America singing again; and in place of that fear of fear, if any have come close to it which is on the edge of despair, let us have hope again.

Life magazine referred to McCarthy's address as "oblique," while the *Wall Street Journal*'s take was equally ambivalent: "Detached. Philosophic. Cynical. Moral. Learned. Lazy." Nevertheless, McCarthy received kudos simply for having challenged the president. *The New Republic*'s analysis was in line with that of several other liberal publications, praising McCarthy for restoring "wit and style to political discourse." *Time* cheered his candidacy for finally affording "legitimate dissenters a civilized voice." Walter Lippmann commended McCarthy for sustaining "the deepest and most cherished values of American political life," and for coming "forward as the defender of the American faith." But the radical journalist I. F. Stone warned that to convince alienated young people, McCarthy needed to stop acting like "a graceful patsy." Consequently, although he feared the senator lacked "guts," Stone wrote, he would "enlist in McCarthy's army," while intending "to keep stirring mutiny until the General stops yawning." Even McCarthy's campaign manager Blair Clark feared "we may have a fraud on our hands."

The senator's performance throughout the month continued to trouble many who might otherwise have supported him, including the previously sympathetic Jack Newfield, who wrote in late December, "Let the unhappy, brutal truth come out. Eugene McCarthy's campaign is a disaster. . . . McCarthy's speeches are dull, vague, and without either balls or poetry. He is lazy and vain. . . . McCarthy earned my vote just by announcing. But he doesn't deserve anything anymore." In addition, McCarthy was still largely unknown to the American public, with polls placing him at tremendous disadvantage when pitted against President Johnson. The anti-war movement itself remained unpopular, with many favoring an escalation of the war.

Bobby Kennedy, Lowenstein's preferred candidate, remained conflicted about whether to enter the presidential race. Evan Thomas, the longtime *Newsweek* reporter and editor, suggests that the anguish over the war experienced by Secretary of Defense Robert McNamara impacted Bobby as well. Kennedy implored McNamara, a close friend, to leave the Johnson administration with "a hell of a bang," but the secretary chose to accept another appointment: presidency of the World Bank. Discussions continued to swirl among Kennedy's friends and advisers as to whether he should run. His brother Edward M. "Ted" Kennedy, now the senior senator from the state of Massachusetts, speechwriter Ted Sorensen, and former White House press secretary Pierre Salinger stood in opposition, worrying Bobby would help elect Nixon while spoiling his own future presidential prospects. Young staff members like Adam Walinsky and Peter Edelman wanted Kennedy to run. The historian Arthur M. Schlesinger Jr., who had served as special assistant to President Kennedy, had recently written to Bobby, confessing that he too had long been against a 1968 campaign, worrying that it would result in a

Nixon presidency. Now, he believed Bobby could take the nomination and he saw Nixon as beatable. In meetings involving Kennedy advisers and friends, Schlesinger reportedly declared, Bobby "owed it to the kids to run, even if he lost."

Protesters and progressive analysts both took Kennedy to task for his indecision. Kennedy found himself heckled on campuses in the United States, which had never before happened. A poster at Brooklyn College read, "HAWK, DOVE, OR CHICKEN?" The syndicated cartoonist Jules Feiffer presented a devastating rendering of "the Bobby Twins." There was, Feiffer's sketch revealed, "a good Bobby" and "a bad Bobby." The first was "a courageous reformer" who employed federal forces to shield civil rights, safeguarded civil liberties, and proved "ill at ease with liberals." The other selected racist federal judges, readily agreed to wiretaps, and was uncomfortable "with grownups." Feiffer warned, "If you want Bobby to be your President, you will have to take both."

In his *Village Voice* column of December 28, 1967, Jack Newfield warned,

> If Kennedy does not run in 1968, the best side of his character will die. He will kill it every time he butchers his conscience and makes a speech for Johnson next autumn. It will die every time a kid asks him, if he is so much against the Vietnam War, how come he is putting party above principle? It will die every time a stranger quotes his own words back to him on the value of courage as a human quality.

Then, Newfield wrote, "Kennedy's best quality is his ability to be himself, to be authentic in the existential sense. This is the quality the young identify with so instinctively in Kennedy. And it is this quality Kennedy will lose if he doesn't make his stand now against Johnson. He will become a robot mouthing dishonest rhetoric like all the other politicians." At their next encounter, Kennedy informed Newfield, "My wife cut out your attack on me. She shows it to everybody." Ethel Kennedy, who would give birth to their eleventh child in late 1968, strongly urged her husband to enter the race.

Many continued to disagree, with Joseph Alsop of the *Washington Post* countering Newfield's assessment. Writing in January, Alsop declared that should Kennedy run, "he will destroy himself. He will destroy his Party. And he will bring into power, perhaps for many years to come, the extreme right wing of the Republican Party." Alsop warned that it would be catastrophic if "the most promising and most richly equipped man of his generation in American politics allows himself to be pressured into self-destruction . . . [by] pretended friends."

During the third week in January, Newfield and Ronnie Eldridge, a businesswoman and activist who worked for Tammany Hall, spent a day with Kennedy attempting to convince him to declare his candidacy. After encountering the Greek actress Melina Mercouri, Kennedy revealed that she asked,

"Did I want to go down in history as the senator who waited for a safer day?" Insisting that the polls and politicians were mistaken, Newfield declared, "This is a crazy moment in history. The anger and alienation are all just below the surface." He bluntly stated, "The problem is Johnson's character, not just his policies, and that is why he is finished. He can't change." Denying that he was concerned about 1972 or helping to elect Nixon, Kennedy admitted, "What bothers me is that I'll be at the mercy of events Johnson can manipulate to his advantage." But as Kennedy dithered, many of his strongest champions went over to McCarthy's camp.

Still, Senator Kennedy continued to criticize the Johnson administration, however obliquely at times, indicating on January 21 that the US was demanding "unconditional surrender" prior to the start of peace talks. Instead, he called for accepting the suggestion by Nguyen Duy Trinh, North Vietnam's Foreign Minister, that discussions would follow the cessation of "bombing and other acts of war." Kennedy himself was said to have been "careful not to shut any doors" regarding a possible presidential bid, finding "it painfully difficult to" respond to young people who wondered why voters would likely have a choice between "hawks" in November: President Johnson, Richard Nixon, and George Wallace, running as a third-party candidate.

Analyzing the political landscape, William V. Shannon of the *New York Times* indicated on January 28 that the McCarthy candidacy was apparently engendering more difficulty for Kennedy than for the president. It was leading RFK's backers to wonder why, if McCarthy could run, Bobby couldn't. At stake too were Kennedy's appeal to the young and his harking to a restoration of JFK-styled idealism. Despite urging from Jesse Unruh, a family friend and speaker of the California State Assembly, Kennedy soon reiterated his disinclination to challenge President Johnson "under any foreseeable circumstances." Unruh was heard to declare "our actions and words must be judged by the human consequences, and the political consequences be damned." A *New York Times* editorial indicated that Kennedy had opted for "prudence . . . over passion," but it considered "less defensible" his tepid backing of Senator McCarthy.

The 1968 presidential race experienced a jolt beginning in late January as the Tet Offensive unfolded in Vietnam. Scenes from the US Embassy, Hue, and other spots struck by North Vietnamese soldiers and Vietcong guerrillas startled the American public, while evidently giving lie to the notion that the war was going well, kindling questions regarding how winnable it actually was. This ironically came amid a new Gallup Poll indicating that the president's political standing had improved, along with his margin over Eugene McCarthy, due to "increased optimism" about "the progress of the war."

But as news of the enemy assault in South Vietnam intensified, McCarthy's campaign in New Hampshire started to gather momentum, with his poll numbers ascending and the president's dropping in like-mannered fashion. In an essay appearing in *Look* on February 6, "Why I'm Battling LBJ," Senator McCarthy focused on one issue: the Vietnam War. The ADA's national board narrowly voted to back his candidacy over that of the president, a move championed by John Kenneth Galbraith, Arthur Schlesinger Jr., and Joseph L. Rauh Jr., a top Washington attorney, who had helped to found the liberal organization. Despite White House attempts to shape the storyline emanating from Vietnam, doubts about US involvement reached unprecedented levels. But in New Hampshire, McCarthy often deliberately downplayed the war, declaring that "national leadership" was at stake, and accusing the president of "eroding and weakening certain structures of government." He also contended that the war drew money away from vital social programs, including those associated with Johnson's War on Poverty and the attempt to usher in the Great Society, neither of which McCarthy unreservedly supported.

On February 8, Senator Kennedy, speaking in Chicago, delivered his strongest condemnation of US policy in Vietnam to date. The Tet Offensive, he declared, had "finally shattered the mask of official illusion with which we have concealed our true circumstances, even from ourselves." The fighting demonstrated that no sector or individual in South Vietnam was immune from Vietcong attacks, as well as how unpredictable the battles presently were. The American people had been taught one thing, which had to be appreciated for the sake of the young American soldiers fighting in Vietnam. "The time has come to take a new look at the war in Vietnam," Kennedy maintained. The US had mistakenly believed there was a military solution to the conflict that actually required the backing and determination of the South Vietnamese people. "It is like sending a lion to halt an epidemic of jungle rot," Kennedy argued. Another illusion involved the perception that American forces would triumph in a manner that the South Vietnamese could not. In truth, the United States lacked a genuine ally in Saigon and was backing a regime lacking support of its own. A third illusion involved the seeking of military conquest, despite the price borne. That had resulted in three years of "horror" and devastation for a "tiny land," which had been pummeled from the air and seen two million of its people rendered homeless. That had led "our best and oldest friends to ask, more in sorrow than in anger," Kennedy declared, "what has happened to America?" The fourth illusion pertained to the notion that the interests of the United States and a "selfish . . . incompetent military regime" were the same. Lessons, Kennedy pointed out, had been learned, including the fact that a complete military victory was not attainable without the "further slaughter of thousands of innocent and helpless people—a slaughter which will forever rest on our national conscience." A political compromise was in order, escalation of the war made no sense, and it was time "to save our most precious stake in Vietnam—the lives of our soldiers."

In an opinion piece appearing in the *New York Times* on February 10, Senator Kennedy referred to the lamentation by the great early-twentieth-century Irish poet W. B. Yeats: "Things fall apart; the center cannot hold; / Mere anarchy is loosed upon the world." Despair was taking hold, Kennedy worried, fed by demonstrations, riots, tanks in American streets, machine guns used against American children, other children starving in the American South, suicides on Native American reservations, 500,000 American soldiers struggling in Vietnam, "millions more of our best youth" failing to understand or accept the war there, alienation, and a feeling of being overwhelmed. Noncandidate Kennedy continued acting as if he were running for something, proclaiming in Neon, Kentucky, the administration's welfare and anti-poverty approaches "unacceptable." A portion of the money being expended in Vietnam, he argued, "should be coming down here to help the people of this area and to help the unemployed in the ghettos."

Backers of President Johnson hardly felt reluctant to go on the offensive, with Senator George A. Smathers of Florida, who had been close to President Kennedy, accusing RFK of performing a disservice to American soldiers in supporting a compromise in Vietnam. Texas Governor John B. Connally Jr. assailed Kennedy for having imperiled US foreign policy. Kennedy's "words and his actions have been a source of discord in this country," Connally charged. "They've had a detrimental effect on the whole attitude of people in this country and an even more disastrous effect insofar as Ho Chi Minh and the communist world are concerned." Businessmen were said to be more opposed to Kennedy's possible candidacy than they had been to any presidential aspirant except of course Franklin Delano Roosevelt.

In the meantime, a dedicated band of young people who supposedly went "Clean for Gene," discarding countercultural apparel for ties or skirts, and seemingly making up a "Children's Crusade," were assisting McCarthy's drive in New Hampshire. The candidate himself continued to evince a disdain for campaigning, and many commentators dismissed his candidacy, notwithstanding "McCarthy's Kids," as hopeless in the face of a likely electoral onslaught. McCarthy also displayed a curiously mixed attitude toward his youthful helpers, clearly favoring student leaders and those from elite schools who hadn't given up on working within the system. Among the most significant of the latter was Sam W. Brown Jr., a graduate student at Harvard's Divinity School and an early participant in the "Dump Johnson" movement.

Fund-raising, McCarthy biographer Dominic Sandbrook offers, constituted no problem, with John Kenneth Galbraith quoted as saying, "Money
was never raised so easily." Wall Street apparently donated more than two
million dollars, while the campaign consumed over five times than much and
nearly triple that of the president. And yet, the campaign managed to fritter
away contributions, always ending up "short of money."

More troublesome were McCarthy's style of campaigning and his delivery
at large rallies, both of which demonstrated disdain for the process, arrogance, and a refusal to cater to the temper of the times. Given the issues
candidates were dealing with, he considered it necessary to display "some
restraint" amid an "atmosphere of shouting and emotion." And in New
Hampshire, whose population was almost entirely white and tilted in a hawk-
ish direction on the war, the cool, professorial demeanor of the former college
professor came across well. The *New York Times*' Steven V. Roberts sensed
this before many other reporters did, noting the appeal of McCarthy's "earnest, low-keyed campaign." A crowd at a high school in New York City
responded enthusiastically to McCarthy's declaration that "the war in Vietnam is an un-American war—it runs contrary to American history and tradition." Those gathered in mid-Manhattan listened as he insisted it was not in
the American vein to employ "our great power and strength against weaker
nations." Talking later at the home of the author Wyatt Emory Cooper and
his wife, the socialite Gloria Vanderbilt, during a get-together attended by
about 200 individuals, many from the artistic, literary, or theatrical worlds,
McCarthy reflected. "It is necessary now to admit to a kind of complete
failure in Vietnam." At the party, the poet Robert Lowell disclosed the establishment of a National Committee of Arts and Letters for McCarthy for President. "These are absolutely desperate times," Lowell explained.

Parrying charges by Generals William Westmoreland and Earle Wheeler
that dissent extended the conflict in Vietnam, McCarthy, a World War II
veteran of military intelligence, deemed such accusations "a vulgar and
improper attempt to degrade the level of the debate." McCarthy continued,
"The brave men who have given their lives in Vietnam did not die because I,
or other senators or the National Council of Churches, or some editors and
columnists, or some intellectuals and students have spoken out—and will
continue to speak out—against this war." Instead, "they died carrying out
military operations under the orders of the President of the United States."
Refusing to back down, McCarthy charged the Johnson administration with
having "deceived" Congress and the American people about the incident in
the Gulf of Tonkin during August 1964 that resulted in initial bombing strikes
against North Vietnam.

After Michigan Governor George Romney, who was somewhat critical of the US war effort, terminated his presidential campaign, McCarthy insisted the choice was clear: to line up with him and his supporters condemning military escalation and backing "an honorable settlement . . . through political means." He insisted, "There is no essential difference between the Vietnam policies of President Johnson and Mr. Nixon." *New York Times* columnist Tom Wicker suggested that McCarthy could be the beneficiary of Romney's withdrawal from the presidential race. Among the prominent figures coming out in support of McCarthy's candidacy was George F. Kennan, the former diplomat who helped to shape the postwar US policy of containment. Speaking to a substantial group of McCarthy backers on February 29, Kennan warned that escalation of American military operations in Vietnam had proven "so destructive to civilian life that no conceivable political outcome could justify the attendant suffering and destructiveness." Kennan saw the South Vietnamese regime as "too weak, too timid, too selfish, too uninspiring to" justify American backing. In an address of his own, Senator McCarthy criticized the new federal budget that called attention to the difficulty of simultaneously waging a war and attempting to mitigate "the hopelessness that leads to riots."

A new poll by Roper Research Associates issued in early March had President Johnson receiving 62 percent of the votes, via write-ins, and McCarthy getting 11 percent. But nearly 70 percent indicated their vote would be determined, at least partially, by a candidate's stance on Vietnam. The press, *New York Times'* columnist Russell Baker wrote, had already written off McCarthy, and anointed President Johnson and Richard Nixon as the virtually surefire candidates of their respective parties.

On Wednesday, March 6, McCarthy accused Johnson supporters of employing "essentially the same tactics" as had Joseph McCarthy's backers. The Minnesotan was referring to recent statements and advertisements slamming him, which suggested that the president's supporters were becoming more worried about the insurgent candidacy. Notwithstanding the Roper poll, a closer reading of New Hampshire politics suggested that more than a third of Democrats were disillusioned with President Johnson. But New Hampshire Governor John W. King blasted McCarthy as "an appeaser" who was "a spokesman for forces of surrender," while King and US Senator Thomas J. McIntyre signed ads warning that Vietnamese communists were following the primary, ascertaining if Americans "at home have the same determination as our soldiers in Vietnam." The ads stated that voting "for weakness and indecision would not be in the best interests of our nation," calling instead for shoring up America's fighting men by writing in LBJ's name, which was not on the Tuesday ballot as the president had yet to officially declare his candidacy. McCarthy noted that many others, including Senate Majority

Leader Mike Mansfield of Montana and George Aiken, Republican senator from Vermont, favored negotiations leading to a coalition government.

Governor King soon went further, declaring that "Ho Chi Minh and his communist friends" were more interested in how well Senator McCarthy was doing. A large vote for McCarthy, King declared, would be happily received in Hanoi "as a sign that the American people are ready to quit." As if in response, McCarthy insisted that he wanted to terminate the conflict "honorably," attend to American slums, and again muster for the United States "the decent respect of mankind."

The CBS evening news broadcast of March 7, presented by anchor Walter Cronkite, reported that Bobby Kennedy was moving "closer than ever" to entering the presidential race. The senator quickly denied that his stance had altered. Helping RFK to reconsider was his brother Teddy's own changed position, although another close adviser, Theodore Sorensen, discounted the report. Cronkite revealed three factors influencing Bobby Kennedy: his disappointment concerning the president's response to release of a report on riots by the President's National Advisory Commission on Civil Disorders, which warned that "Our nation is moving toward two societies, one black, one white—separate and unequal"; his mounting dismay regarding escalation of the war; and encouragement drawn from Senator McCarthy's campaign. On the same day that Cronkite delivered his analysis, Kennedy spoke on the floor of the US Senate, declaring it was "immoral and intolerable to continue . . . what we have been doing" in Vietnam. The next day, Haynes Johnson of the *Washington Evening Star* jotted down, "March 8, 1968—Spent 1½ hrs. with RFK. Certain he will run."

Speaking in Des Moines, Iowa, Kennedy warned that the US "cannot act as if no other nation existed, flaunting our power and our wealth against the judgment and desire of neutrals and allies alike." Democrats were entitled to be proud of their successes but had to acknowledge "our past shortcomings," Kennedy said. Back in Washington, he strongly condemned attacks leveled at McCarthy's loyalty and patriotism. A taped interview conducted with the British Broadcasting Corporation (BBC) revealed Kennedy's call for both terminating US air operations over North Vietnam and meeting with North Vietnamese president Ho Chi Minh. Flying to California, Kennedy broke bread with Cesar Chavez, head of the United Farm Workers Union (UFW), who had been conducting a twenty-five-day fast. Kennedy, who atop a car roof would exhort, *"Viva la huelga!,"* (Long live the strike!) agreed with Chavez's declaration, "Violence is no answer." Flying back East, Kennedy indicated, "Yes. I'm going to do it." Stewart Udall, who served as Secretary of the Interior under both Jack Kennedy and Lyndon Johnson, thought Bobby "was on fire." Udall felt "it was like a Greek tragedy in the sense that events themselves had been determined by fates setting the stage, and that there was really little choice left."

As primary day approached, the *New York Times'* Tom Wicker noted that public opinion appeared to be tilting toward a belief the Vietnam conflict was "a creeping disaster that military means cannot salvage." A new Gallup poll reported that 49 percent of respondents now considered it had been a mistake to introduce US combat troops in Vietnam, while 41 percent thought otherwise; a tenth of those polled remained undecided. More troubling for the administration, 61 percent now believed the war was either being lost or had become a stalemate. Expectations consequently had arisen for McCarthy's showing, while Bobby Kennedy was said to be "reconsidering" his earlier decision to remain out of the race. Talking to a crowd of approximately 400 people in Franklin, New Hampshire, McCarthy urged a change in draft laws to enable Americans who had gone into exile in Canada or Sweden to return to the States without suffering criminal prosecution. Calling for a more expansive interpretation of conscientious objector status, he suggested allowing those exiles to perform alternative service.

Excitement continued to swirl about the McCarthy campaign, much of it fueled by the young people who poured into the state to support the insurgent effort. Reports indicated that college and university students from across the nation were arriving, determined to assist McCarthy's candidacy. Even Republicans, who could cross over for the primary, were impressed, with one calling the youthful volunteers "positively captivating." McCarthy appeared to be riding the crest of a different version of "student power" or "student crusade." As he told enthralled college students, "Nothing like this has ever happened before. You are demonstrating the strength of student power." The *New York Times* applauded the candidate, praising his sensible, calm, rational approach. The paper thought an enthusiastic showing for McCarthy, who was doing well in Minnesota precinct and ward caucuses and in Massachusetts, might compel President Johnson to shift course, thus "making a negotiated settlement in Vietnam a more credible alternative."

The New Hampshire primary produced stunning results, with Senator McCarthy amassing about 42 percent of the vote and President Johnson, relying on write-in votes, failing to top 50 percent. When Republican crossover votes were included, McCarthy came close to besting Johnson, falling a mere 230 votes short, and he snared twenty of twenty-four delegate slots. A subsequent poll indicated that opposition to Johnson, rather than to the war, fueled McCarthy's strong showing but his campaign did appear "to have helped erase the stigma of radicalism and nonconformity from the anti-war movement," however temporarily. While McCarthy affirmed, "I think I can get the nomination," Bobby Kennedy readied to make an announcement declaring his own candidacy. The *New York Times* referred to McCarthy's "remarkable" showing, deeming it a warning to the administration and "a testament" to those who participated in "his campaign for peace." The paper extolled McCarthy for having "rekindled the faith of thousands of intelligent young Americans in democratic machinery and the efficacy of the ballot."

Discussing "the pyrrhic defeat of Lyndon Johnson," the *Times* referred to the explosive impact of the Tet Offensive, as well as the Pentagon's seemingly insatiable demand for greater funding and the move to terminate graduate school draft deferments. McCarthy had occasionally vented emotionally as when he cried out, "In the name of God, let the killing cease." Generally, he calmly indicted the president's "mismanagement of our priorities" and inability to offer "leadership and direction to our nation." Johnson would also hardly be helped in a tax-averse state by the surcharge he had supported to help fund the war. By contrast, the wave of enthusiastic student volunteers greatly aided McCarthy, who also benefited from the slanderous attacks on his patriotism and loyalty. McCarthy came across as a straight-shooter, while LBJ, seen as a "wheeler-dealer," proved disliked. The *New York Times*' Russell Baker termed McCarthy "the Pied Piper of Minnesota or the leader of the Second Children's Crusade."

As Kennedy declared that he was "actively reassessing" a possible run against LBJ, important liberal pundits blasted his purported cynicism and opportunism. Mary McGrory of the *Washington Star* offered, "Kennedy thinks that American youth belongs to him as the bequest of his brother. Seeing the romance flower between them and McCarthy, he moved with the ruthlessness of a Victorian father whose daughter has fallen in love with a dustman." The *New York Post*'s Murray Kempton more angrily presented a column, "Farewell Senator Kennedy," which slammed him as a coward "down from the hills to shoot the wounded. He has, in the naked display of his rage at Eugene McCarthy for having survived on this lonely road he dared not walk himself, done with a single great gesture something very few public men have ever been able to do: In one day, he managed to confirm the worst things his enemies have ever said about him." Unlike McGrory and Kempton, many journalists came to swoon over the second Kennedy brother to run for the presidency.

The results in New Hampshire convinced Kennedy, who lauded the "brilliant job" McCarthy and his devoted young supporters had accomplished, that the Democratic Party was already deeply divided. Announcing his candidacy on March 16 in the Caucus Room of the Old Senate Office Building, where his brother Jack had done so eight years earlier, Kennedy indicated he did not run "merely to oppose any man but to propose new policies," and because he believed America to be "on a perilous course." He was running to initiate new policies that would "end the bloodshed in Vietnam and in our cities" and to bridge the chasm "between black and white, between rich and poor, between young and old" in the United States and across the planet. He sought to ensure that both his political party and his country represented "hope instead of despair . . . reconciliation . . . instead of the growing risk of world war." He intended to draw from his experiences as an adviser to President Kennedy during perilous times involving Cuba, Berlin, Laos, and nuclear arms, when he learned about "the uses and the limitations of military power, about the value of negotiations . . . about the opportunities and the dangers" confronting the United States. Through his service in the Cabinet and the Senate, he had witnessed "the inexcusable and ugly deprivations which cause children to starve in Mississippi, black citizens to riot in Watts, young Indians to commit suicide on their reservations." He had heard young people express rage regarding the war and "the world that they are about to inherit."

In conclusion, Kennedy insisted the issue was "not personal," but rather involved "profound differences over where we are heading and what we want to accomplish." He went on to say, "At stake is not simply the leadership of our party and even our country. It is our right to the moral leadership of this planet." Onlookers foresaw "the bloodiest, bitterest power battles in the Democratic or any other party." Senator McCarthy quickly stated he was "not prepared to deal," intending instead to battle for the Democratic Party nomination. The two men had little love for one another, with Kennedy considering McCarthy "pompous, petty, and venal," and the Minnesota senator seeing RFK as "a spoiled, unintelligent demagogue."

The divisions within Democratic Party ranks were searing, as evidenced by Kennedy's responses to press queries posed during a press conference following declaration of his candidacy. Referring to his recently published book, *To Seek a Newer World*, Kennedy emphasized the need to deescalate the fight in Vietnam. He conveyed support for greater involvement by South Vietnamese forces, an end to the corruption emanating from the regime in Saigon, and negotiations with the National Liberation Front (NLF). He also favored a halt to the bombing of North Vietnam to bring the communist leaders in Hanoi to the bargaining table. At that very same time, President Johnson was fielding requests from General William C. Westmoreland for 206,000 additional troops to be sent to Vietnam. And conflicting news accounts discussed whether Senator Kennedy had earlier promised to remain out of the presidential race if LBJ would create a commission to explore alterations in Vietnam policy. While Kennedy called such reports "an incredible distortion," administration sources had Johnson rejecting the proposal as "wholly and totally unacceptable." Vice President Humphrey proceeded to assail Kennedy for having reversed his earlier stance on the war adopted during Jack Kennedy's administration, finding incomprehensible RFK's charge that US involvement was "immoral."

The first chapter of the "New Politics" of 1968 came to a surprising halt at the end of the same month that Eugene McCarthy nearly defeated an incumbent president from his own party in the year's first primary, soon followed by Bobby Kennedy's entrance into the race and the frenetic response that often greeted him on the campaign trail. Those latter developments were obviously unsettling to Lyndon Johnson, who despised Kennedy and saw him as attempting to win back the throne lost in Dallas four and a half years earlier. Johnson had soldiered on following the near debacle in New Hampshire, informing a crowd in Minneapolis, "Make no mistake about it . . . we are going to win" the war. But Johnson recognized that he and Congress were increasingly at loggerheads and that Kennedy might actually be able to fight more diligently for Great Society programs. On the other hand, a campaign aide recognized, "He will not turn this country over to Bobby—not a chance." However, approval ratings for both the president and the war continued to slide.

Johnson's subsequent decision to withdraw obviously upended the presidential race. Anticipating Vice President Humphrey's entrance into the race, Richard Nixon quickly offered his opinion that the president would not allow RFK to "have the nomination on a platter." Senator McCarthy expressed his belief that President Johnson had "cleared the way for the reconciliation of our people" and the American nation. Referring to the New Politics, McCarthy said "this change in American politics began among the people." Bobby Kennedy initially appeared stunned by the revelation, admitting, "I don't quite know what to say." He soon requested a meeting with President Johnson, while emphasizing the necessity of peace abroad being coupled with "reconciliation at home."

Both McCarthy and Kennedy were among the more eloquent opponents of the war, who possessed the platform of the United States Senate, where criticisms of the administration's foreign policy had already been voiced. The response to RFK's candidacy was much like the reaction many had to the man himself. Support, even of a frenetic variety, poured forth, but so did questions about his character and motivations.

The New Politics associated with both Kennedy and McCarthy suggested that American politics might be transformed, potentially in a radical manner. At the very least, their entrance into the presidential race indicated that the kind of citizen empowerment championed by the New Left might provide a springboard to the highest political office in the land. The undertaking was hardly an easy one, while threatening to tear apart the Democratic Party, the nation's dominant political institution. The quixotic nature of their endeavors was captured by the Kennedy campaign's theme song, "The Impossible Dream," from the musical *Man of La Mancha*, which he loved.

The biggest loser resulting from the advent of the New Politics was Lyndon Baines Johnson, who barely three years earlier had achieved one of the nation's greatest electoral triumphs, engaged in a quest to conduct a War on Poverty, and envisioned ushering in the Great Society. Johnson's skillful handling of the transition to his presidency following the assassination of John F. Kennedy, his key role in bringing about an end to *de jure* segregation in the United States, and his considerable expansion of the welfare state should have warmed the hearts of liberals and of progressives of a more radical stripe. But his insistence on bolstering American operations in Vietnam and continuing the brutal nature of the war waged in the air and on the ground, along with the racial explosions that urban communities endured, shattered his beloved consensus and caused would-be supporters to demand his ousting.

Allard Lowenstein, Curtis Gans, and a small number of other liberal activists did indeed seem to have pulled off the coup they aspired to: the denial of another presidential term for Lyndon Johnson. Although not always comfortable with the ways of the New Left and more militant anti-war and civil rights activists, Lowenstein and Gans helped to spawn the New Politics that rose for a time in the United States. The charisma exuded by Bobby Kennedy added immeasurably to the excitement many felt, notwithstanding the anger and disappointment experienced by Senator McCarthy, who courageously had been the first to challenge LBJ, and participants in the Children's Crusade, whose appearance preceded RFK's entrance into the presidential race. Nevertheless, for a period the twin anti-war candidacies of Eugene McCarthy and Robert F. Kennedy offered the possibility that change, even deep-seated change, might yet be possible in the world's most powerful nation.

5

"We Shall Overcome"

The Dreamer

Dr. Martin Luther King Jr.'s public unveiling as a leading critic of the Vietnam War occurred at the Beverly Hilton Hotel on February 25, 1967, during a symposium hosted by *The Nation* Institute. Speaking to a group of people on "The Casualties of the War in Viet Nam," King referred to "the nightmarish physical casualties," both in Vietnam and in America, with the return of "young men . . . sent home half-men—physically handicapped and mentally deranged." He considered most tragic the plight of children, "mutilated and incinerated by napalm and by bombs." Such casualties, King declared, sufficed "to cause all men to rise up with righteous indignation and oppose the very nature of this war." Equally catastrophic were the "casualties of principles and values," including the United Nations' (UN) provisions about national sovereignty, the idea of self-determination, completion of the Great Society in America, "the humility of our nation," dissent, and a world free of nuclear conflict. His opposition to the war, King explained, was rooted in love for America. He condemned its stance in Vietnam "not in anger but with anxiety and sorrow" and, most of all, due to his "passionate" determination to witness his "beloved" America operate "as the moral example of the world." Disappointment drove him to speak out, particularly regarding his nation's inability to tackle "the triple evils of racism, extreme materialism and militarism."

The present movement toward "a dead-end road" portended "national disaster," King warned. It was necessary to foster "creative dissenters" whose "fearless voices" could override "the blasts of bombs and the clamor of war

Figure 5.1   Dr. Martin Luther King Jr. speaking at an anti-war demonstration in New York City. By early 1967, the great civil rights leader became a fierce, increasingly vocal critic of US policy in Vietnam. Such a stance melded with his commitment to social and economic justice, making King a voice of conscience and critic of the Johnson administration. Library of Congress, Prints and Photographs Division, LC-USZ62-111165.

hysteria." Peace advocates had to organize as well as war hawks did. King agreed with a recent statement historian Henry Steele Commager of Columbia University had delivered to a Senate committee: "We do not have the resources, material, intellectual or moral, to be at once an American power, a European power, and an Asian power." Instead, King contended, America should exude "moral power, a power harnessed to the service of peace and human beings, not an inhumane power unleashed against defenseless people." A choice existed between "non-violent co-existence or violent co-annihilation." King's address, the journalist Thomas Powers indicates, was "a kind of turning point in the country's attitude toward the war." Clearly the readiness of America's foremost civil rights leader to lend his eloquent voice to the anti-war movement was significant, as the Johnson administration unhappily recognized.

By late 1967, Dr. King's reputation appeared on shakier grounds than earlier in the decade. The period began with his position as a major American civil rights leader unquestioned, the initial byproduct of his involvement in the Montgomery bus boycott of 1955 to 1956 that catapulted him to the head of the crusade to end segregation in America and garnered international attention. King's steadfast commitment to nonviolent direct action and the targeted employment of civil disobedience shaped generations of activists, both in the United States and around the globe. His founding of the Southern Christian Leadership Conference (SCLC) in early 1957 provided him with an organizational instrument to broaden the attack on Jim Crow practices. He strongly backed the young activists who participated in sit-ins and freedom rides at the beginning of the 1960s, even when some in organizations like SNCC and CORE chafed at his seemingly dominant stance within the civil rights movement. Setbacks and successes followed, with difficult campaigns in Florida and Georgia offset by great acclaim resulting from a controversial struggle in Birmingham in 1963 and that year's historic March on Washington. Suffering jail, threats on his life, vilification by Southern segregationists and FBI director J. Edgar Hoover alike, King, recipient of the 1964 Nobel Peace Prize, held fast to a determined belief in employing Gandhian tactics throughout the former Confederacy. The civil rights movement, with King remaining at the forefront but with young figures like John Lewis, Diane Nash, and Bob Moses offering leadership as well, provided spurs that culminated in legislative passage of the 1964 Civil Rights Act and the 1965 Voting Rights Act. Those measures, taking place as voter registration occurred in Mississippi and elsewhere and a battle with hardcore segregationists ensued in Selma, helped to bring de jure segregation to an end in the United States.

During the middle of the decade, King initiated a different odyssey, carrying his fight against discrimination and racial prejudice outside the South, with a particular focus on Chicago, which like many cities and towns outside the South remained afflicted with *de facto* segregation. Some of the worst abuse King had received, including of a physical cast, resulted from his new efforts. His standing took other hits when King felt compelled to condemn US involvement in Vietnam, which led to estrangement from the Johnson administration that had previously treated him as an important ally. But belief that the war was both immoral and damaging to his nation's reputation induced King to speak out forcefully by the winter of 1967. From that point, he became one of the most important spokespersons within the anti-war movement, as he condemned the loss of precious lives and resources in the hills, valleys, fields, swamps, villages, and cities of Vietnam. The White House proved infuriated when King, in the midst of large-scale demonstrations against the war, referred to the United States as "the greatest purveyor of violence in the world today." Now insisting that was so, King could "not be silent."

While King rejected efforts to induce him to enter the upcoming presidential race as an anti-war candidate, he strongly supported the peace movement. The Vietnam War, King's biographer Stephen B. Oates writes, "haunted" him by the summer of 1965, as massive escalation of the conflict by the United States continued. The terrible devastation wreaked upon the Vietnamese people and landscape greatly troubled him, along with his own country's failure to appreciate the strength of nationalist fires involving "brown-skinned peoples" around the globe. "The madness of militarism" appalled him. Believing he couldn't simply "sit by and see the war escalate without saying something about it," King reasoned that the war had to be halted. Coretta Scott King strongly supported her husband's anti-war stance, as did Benjamin Spock, who considered the minister "the most important symbol for peace in this country."

Close aides and advisers, including his friend Bayard Rustin, who had been jailed during World War II for his opposition to the Selective Service Act, attempted to dissuade King from voicing displeasure regarding the war. They feared estrangement from the Johnson administration, which was supporting legislation eradicating Jim Crow and ushering in a War on Poverty. However, King saw racial inequities, poverty, and war as "inextricably bound together." Thus, in August 1965, while calling for a halt to the bombing of North Vietnam, he favored negotiating with both Hanoi and the Vietcong. Both moderate civil rights leaders and President Johnson exhibited dismay about King's criticism of the administration's Vietnam policy. The president was also displeased when King contended that peace negotiations should include China.

For a time, King muted his concerns about the war, but occasionally he voiced them. In May 1966, as he spoke of disarmament and the need to suspend nuclear tests, King also worried that the Vietnam conflagration would plunge "civilization . . . into the abyss of annihilation." By the winter of 1966–1967, King wrestled still more with how to respond to the continuation of the Vietnam War, which had only grown bloodier and more brutal. James Bevel, who had served as SCLC's project director, was named the Spring Mobe's executive director. Other Spring Mobe leaders, including David Dellinger and A. J. Muste, hoped that Bevel would help convince King to speak out more forcefully on the war. Bevel asked King, "Are the Vietnamese not your brothers and sisters?" King was troubled by how precious resources were expended in Vietnam rather than employed in a genuine fight against poverty at home. Like many others, he was also dismayed by the fact that blacks were disproportionately fighting and dying in Vietnam.

During a trip to Jamaica, King pored over a copy of *Ramparts*, which contained graphic images of a mother and her infant child, victimized by American weapons, and referred to one million Vietnamese children having "been killed or wounded or burned." He compared himself unfavorably with black militant Stokely Carmichael, who was repeatedly denouncing the war. Returning to the States, King fixated on televised accounts of the fighting and the suffering endured by villagers. He now decided, "I can't be silent. Never again will I be silent." Determining to speak out on the war, he informed President Johnson of his intention. He soon delivered his talk on "The Casualties of the War in Vietnam," which had to have unsettled the administration.

Notwithstanding heated criticism from old allies such as the Urban League's Whitney Young, concerned that the White House would pull back support for the civil rights revolution, King soon became still more pointed in his condemnations of US policy in Vietnam. On March 23, 1967, King declared his readiness to undertake "a much stronger stand" against the war. Talking to reporters in Chicago, King indicated that he planned to become more involved with the anti-war movement. He was doing so, he explained, "because the war is hurting us in all of our programs to end slums and to end segregation in schools and to make quality education a reality, to end the long night of poverty." What was required, he stated, was "a radical reordering of our national priorities." During a rally in Chicago, he called out, "This war is a blasphemy against all that America stands for!" He worried that the United States, which "initiated so much of the revolutionary spirit of the modern world," was now adopting the stance of "an arch antirevolutionary." His own nation, King charged, was meting out atrocities as grave as those committed by guerrilla forces. "We are left standing before the world glutted by our own barbarity," supporting an effort to thwart the tide of history and uphold "white colonialism." Moreover, the Vietnamese adventure was crippling the chances "for a decent America." Like J. William Fulbright, the Senate Foreign Relations Committee chair who had warned about "the arrogance of power," King feared "we often arrogantly feel that we have some divine, messianic mission to police the whole world."

In an interview with the *New York Times* John Herbers, King again underscored how the war was "playing havoc with . . . domestic priorities." Its continuance diminished the likelihood of addressing the issues most affecting African Americans and the impoverished of all races. As King informed Herbers, "The Great Society has been shot down on the battlefields of Vietnam." Consequently, it was essential "to take a stand against it or at least arouse the conscience of the nation against it" to propel movement toward negotiations and the war's end. King also reasoned that his championing of nonviolence within the civil rights movement had to be paired with support for nonviolence globally. He soon urged young people, both blacks and "all white people of goodwill," to file for conscientious objector status.

Along with Commager, Rabbi Heschel, and John C. Bennett, he appeared at a CALCAV gathering at New York City's famed Riverside Church in Morningside Heights on the evening of April 4, delivering the main address, "Beyond Vietnam: A Time to Break the Silence." It was telling, King related, that several important American religious leaders had opted for "firm dissent" rooted in "the mandates of conscience and the reading of history." He had adopted the path CALCAV's executive committee supported, discarding his "own silences," and, speaking "from the burnings of [his] own heart," demanded "radical departures from the destruction of Vietnam." Again referring to the high price African Americans were paying in the war, King noted "the cruel irony" involved in blacks and whites fighting together overseas but being unable to sit "together in the same schools" or to "live on the same block in Chicago."

His attempts to dissuade "desperate, rejected, and angry young men" from resorting to "Molotov cocktails and rifles" led him to express dismay regarding the war. Those young men had asked, "What about Vietnam?" Didn't the United States employ "massive doses of violence to solve its problems, to bring about the changes it wanted?" Reflecting on those questions, "I knew that I could never again raise my voice against the violence of the oppressed in the ghettos without having first spoken clearly to the greatest purveyor of violence in the world today—my own government," King recalled. Additionally, his ministerial path and more recent receipt of the Nobel Peace Prize mandated that he work for "the brotherhood of man." His examination of US involvement in Vietnam also propelled him into the anti-war camp, as he appreciated that Vietnamese nationalists had to view "Americans as strange liberators." The United States was afflicted with "the deadly Western arrogance" pertaining to revolutionary governments in the Third World, denying the Vietnamese the right to an independent state, while backing the repressive, corrupt, and unpopular Southern regime. The war resulted in the plundering of the Vietnamese landscape and its people, especially women, children, and the elderly, through the meting out of massive casualties, the despoiling of water, vegetation, and pasture land, the generating of refugees and the homeless, and the reduction of Vietnamese children to begging and Vietnamese women to prostitution. In the North, American bombing, shelling, and mining further crippled and maimed Vietnam and its people.

King bluntly offered, "Somehow this madness must cease. We must stop now." Furthermore, the United States had to come to terms with the fact that "these are revolutionary times. All over the globe men are revolting against old systems of exploitation and oppression, and out of the wounds of a frail world, new systems of justice and equality are being born. The shirtless and barefoot people of the land are rising up as never before." It was necessary for people residing in the West to back present-day revolutions.

Attacks on King mounted, which admittedly disturbed him. He seemed particularly upset by an editorial in the *New York Times*, "Dr. King's Error," which insisted that the civil rights leader had wrongly melded two "distinct and separate" public issues. His attempt to wed the anti-war and civil rights movements, the paper warned, "could very well be disastrous for both." The *Washington Post* proved equally critical, indicating that King's "usefulness to his cause, to his country, and to his people" had diminished. *Life* magazine derided King's speech as "a demagogic slander that sounded like a script for Radio Hanoi." His longtime adviser Stanley Levinson, controversial due to his ties to the Communist Party, admonished King about his Riverside address: "I do not think it was a good expression of you." Fearful that King would devolve into a "small-time peace leader," Levinson had told him, "I think you will move ten times as many Negroes if you are associated with the Kennedys, the Reuthers and the Fulbrights than you will if you are associated with Norman Thomas and Spock." Harry McPherson, a top presidential counselor, dismissed King as "the crown prince of the Vietniks." Engaged in a continuous campaign to destroy King's reputation, the FBI informed the White House that the minister was "an instrument in the hands of subversive forces seeking to undermine our nation." The Jewish War Veterans of America strongly refuted King's contention that American practices in Southeast Asia could be likened to those of Germany under Adolf Hitler. The board of directors of the National Association for the Advancement of Colored People (NAACP) unanimously opposed King's call to join the civil rights and anti-war movements. Dr. Ralph J. Bunche, another Nobel Peace

Prize recipient, attempted to dissuade him from simultaneously taking a leading role in both the civil rights fight and the anti-war movement. Denying he was striving to unite the two movements, King nevertheless stated, "We can equally believe that no one can pretend that the existence of the war is not profoundly affecting the destiny of civil rights progress."

Important figures, publications, and organizations also praised King. The great theologian Reinhold Niebuhr stated, "I think, as a rather dedicated anti-pacifist, that Dr. King's conception of the nonviolent resistance is a real contribution to our civil, moral and political life." The National Council of Churches' Social Justice Department unanimously applauded King's warnings that the war was diluting the War on Poverty. The *Christian Century* complimented King's "magnificent blend of eloquence and raw fact, of searing denunciation and tender wooing, of political sagacity and Christian insight, of tough realism and infinite compassion." Clearly elated with King's enunciated position on the war, CALCAV named him its cochair and distributed copies of his Riverside speech. James Farmer, CORE's former head, agreed with King's opposition to the war.

On April 15, King joined in a massive anti-war rally conducted at the site of the UN headquarters in midtown Manhattan. Orchestrated by the Spring Mobe, the New York City rally drew as many as 125,000 marchers, while 20,000 congregated in San Francisco. King walked arm-in-arm with Benjamin Spock and Father Frederick Reed, as anti-war protesters headed from Central Park to the UN building. At a press conference in Boston eight days later, King and Spock declared support for Vietnam Summer, which would be led by Lee D. Webb, former SDS national secretary and a conscientious objector who worked for IPS, and CALCAV's Richard Fernandez, and sought to obtain backing within American communities for the anti-war movement. King declared, "It is time now to meet the escalation of the war in Vietnam with an escalation of opposition to that war. I think the time has come for all people of good will to engage in a massive program of organization, of mobilization." In his estimation, the Vietnam War heightened the possibility of a nuclear holocaust. Employing rhetoric adopted by CALCAV, King declared, "There comes a time when silence is betrayal, and today we are involved in one of the most bloody and cruel wars in history. It is poisoning the soul of our nation and has isolated our nation morally and politically." He foresaw 10,000 volunteers, 2,000 of them full-time, organizing and educating the American people in 500 communities across the country. Supporters of King's call included Dr. Spock, the Reverend John C. Bennett, Rabbi Abraham Heschel, the journalist Carey McWilliams, SDS leader Carl Oglesby, and *Ramparts* editor Robert Scheer.

As he acknowledged to the journalist David Halberstam on a flight to the

West Coast, King was adopting a more radical stance, condemning both the war in Vietnam and the "domestic colonialism" that beset America's northern communities. He believed that "reconstructing" the nation might require nationalizing industries, eradicating slums, and providing a guaranteed income for the indigent. It was necessary, King reasoned, to battle "the evils of racism, economic exploitation, and militarism," which he viewed as linked. Encountering disillusioned radical young people only compelled King to dig deeper in order to be able "to speak to and for the alienated," at the same time he attempted to reach "the mass of America." He had been taken aback on encountering a young white radical in Berkeley, who beseeched him: "Dr. King, I understand your reservations about running for president, but you're a world figure, you're the most important man we've got, you're the only one who can head a third-party ticket. And so when you make your decision, remember that there are many of us who are going to have to go to jail for many years, give up our citizenship, perhaps. This is a very serious thing." Through it all, King strove "to remain true to his own," Halberstam believed. King also was compelled to deliver a statement disavowing any intention of seeking political office, as key figures in the anti-war movement, including Scheer and William F. Pepper, the NCNP's executive director, sought to persuade him to run on a third-party ticket, possibly with Dr. Benjamin Spock.

But King felt obliged to criticize General William C. Westmoreland, American military commander in Vietnam, for asserting that anti-war activity aided the enemy. "I think this sinister, evil attempt to confuse the minds of the American people must be stopped," King declared before insisting that "continued escalation" prolonged the war. Later, King charged that President Johnson was employing Westmoreland to help quash dissent. Delivering a sermon at Atlanta's Ebenezer Baptist Church, where he served as pastor, Dr. King lauded heavyweight champion Muhammad Ali for refusing induction into the US Armed Forces and he again urged other young men who considered the war "abominable and unjust" to file as conscientious objectors. Responding to critics of his anti-war stance, King declared, "Ain't nobody gonna turn me 'round."

The summer of 1967 proved troubling with racial conflagrations continuing to bedevil American cities, greatly dismaying King, who had promised "to stir up trouble" in major urban areas, but to do so righteously and nonviolently. The riots in Newark and Detroit were particularly horrific, and President Johnson responded by adopting something of a law-and-order stance. Finding this incomprehensible, King asked how the administration could castigate "the violence of ghetto Negroes" as it provided "an example of violence in Asia that shocks the world?" Conservatives assailed him for having helped pique racial unrest through his own flouting of the law, while the radical journalist Andrew Kopkind, reviewing King's latest book, *Where Do We Go From Here?*, saw him as being "outstripped by his times" and "not ready for the world."

In fact, distressed about the state of the nation and fearing possible race war, King determined that radical change was essential. Having long been sympathetic to the ideals of democratic socialism, he now believed in the need for "a reconstruction of the entire society, a revolution of values." Speaking at the SCLC convention in August, King asked why America possessed forty million indigent individuals. That fact, he continued, led to questions regarding capitalism and wealth distribution. He considered it necessary "to begin to ask questions about the whole society." While perplexed about what to do next, King did suggest SCLC was about to "dislocate" everyday life in urban America. His organization, King declared on August 17, would "very, very definitely" oppose LBJ's renomination unless a shift in war policy occurred.

He also had to fend off seemingly never ending vicious attacks, including one appearing in the September 1967 issue of the widely circulated *Reader's Digest*, Carl T. Rowan's article, "Martin Luther King's Tragic Decision." The African-American columnist assailed King, claiming his ability to help better American race relations was "exaggerated," likening his stints in jail to "publicity stunts," and highlighting how much his anti-war stance had antagonized President Johnson. Responding to Rowan's piece, which also accused him of being influenced by communists, King dismissed the "McCarthy-like" condemnations.

He soon planned yet another campaign, this one intended to "transmute the deep rage of the ghetto into a constructive and creative force." Influenced by the African-American lawyer and activist Marian Wright, King imagined a mass crusade involving civil disobedience occurring near the White House, designed "to cripple the operations of an oppressive society." His longtime ally, Bayard Rustin, conveyed opposition to the plan, and the nation's oldest civil rights groups, the NAACP and the Urban League, declined to express support. Nevertheless, King stated, "Nonviolent protest must now mature to a new level to correspond to heightened black impatience and stiffened white resistance." After delivering testimony to the National Advisory Commission on Civil Disorders (the Kerner Commission—named after its chair, Illinois Governor Otto Kerner Jr.), King spoke to reporters about SCLC's objective of "escalating nonviolence to the level of civil disobedience." That involved encamping in Washington, DC, as the Bonus Marchers had at the height of the Great Depression. Thousands of poor citizens would "camp here and stay," King warned, until Congress passed a massive jobs program or offered guaranteed income for all Americans. Andrew Young, one of King's trusted lieutenants, spoke of the possibility of shutting down Washington, DC, although he didn't appear to favor that tactic. He did believe it was necessary to threaten, in nonviolent fashion, those who held power. Like King, Young saw the nation's problems as systemic, bespeaking "racism, materialism and economic exploitation."

More criticism came his way, with the *Washington Post* charging King's plan amounted to "an appeal to anarchy." This came in the very period when King and several other black ministers readied for a five-day jail sentence in Birmingham, Alabama. The US Supreme Court, in a 5–4 ruling, had upheld criminal contempt convictions involving their protests against Jim Crow practices in that deeply segregated city four years earlier. In their dissent, Justices William Brennan, William O. Douglas, Abe Fortas, and Earl Warren bemoaned the placing of "a state rule of judicial administration above the right of free expression," resulting in "a devastatingly destructive weapon for suppression of cherished freedoms." In a prepared note, King declared, "I am happy to serve this five-day sentence, as I have been happy to enter the jails for the freedom of my people on many other occasions." He affirmed dismay that American resources were being frittered away in Vietnam rather than directed at urban ills. He admitted to near despair on watching Congress refuse the entreaties of the poor and engage in "politics with the war on poverty." The jailing, King wrote on October 30, was "but symptomatic of the ominous clouds which overshadow our national destiny." While behind bars, King outlined a "Bill of Rights for the Disadvantaged."

Meeting in New York City with the Ford Foundation's National Advisory Committee in late November, King bashed American capitalism, and insisted that substantial change was mandated. The Ford Foundation awarded SCLC a $230,000 grant to school 150 African-American ministers in fifteen cities in community organizing techniques. King now stated, "We are not interested in being integrated into *this* value structure. Power must be relocated, a radical redistribution of power must take place. We must do something to these men to change them." As his biographer David G. Garrow records, King offered a similar analysis to his own staff members gathered at a weeklong session for SCLC held near Beaufort, South Carolina. Charging that "the white power structure" remained resistant to change involving race relations and income distribution, King confessed to a lack of confidence. At the same time, he refused to admit defeat, and talked about the need to adopt "new tactics . . . to compel unwilling authorities to yield to the mandates of justice." His beloved nonviolence, King declared, had to "be adapted to urban conditions and mass civil disobedience." Denying that riots were revolutionary, King supported "massive, active, nonviolent resistance to the evils of the modern system" that had to move in a "more person-centered" direction. Referring to his planned "camp-in" in Washington, DC, King revealed, "I'm on fire about the thing." He also disagreed with James Bevel's desire for a more sweeping campaign "to get the war machine to attack us rather than us attacking the war machine." Reasoning differently and notwithstanding his own determined opposition to the war, King argued that the nonviolent struggle had to expand gradually. In a prepared statement, King declared, "America is at a crossroads of history and it is critically important for us, as a nation and a society, to choose a new path and move upon it with resolution and courage." Believing that American civilization, democracy, and honor were at stake, he considered his latest crusade "a last desperate demand" by blacks to stave off "the worst chaos, hatred and violence any nation has ever encountered." King soon named the Reverend Bernard Lafayette Jr., a veteran of sit-in, freedom ride, and voter registration efforts, to coordinate the planned "poor people's campaign for jobs and income." A top NAACP official, Dr. John A. Morsell, predicted King's civil disobedience drive would result in both violence and repression.

As King began planning for the proposed Washington encampment, FBI director J. Edgar Hoover enhanced ongoing surveillance of the civil rights leader. The hatred and disdain Hoover felt for King was longstanding and deeply rooted. But the bugging of King's hotel rooms and the wiretapping of his telephone calls also involved the Kennedy and Johnson administrations. Worried about the Communist Party ties of Stanley Levinson and Jack O'Dell—each a close associate of King—President Kennedy had informed his brother, Attorney General Robert Kennedy, "King is so hot that it's like Marx coming to the White House." During a White House visit in June 1963, President Kennedy told King that Levinson was a "Kremlin agent." Although King promised to relinquish ties to Levinson, he continued dealing with him by way of intermediaries. Due to White House–approved taps on another associate of King, John Kennedy, Bobby Kennedy, and Hoover became aware of the minister's extramarital affairs. On October 10, the attorney general directed the FBI to begin wiretapping King's phones. One FBI document soon referred to him as "an unprincipled opportunistic individual" and a Marxist, while another adjudged King "unfit to serve as a minister of the gospel." President Johnson subsequently heard the tapes, leading him to castigate "that hypocritical preacher."

In public, Hoover, just before King received his Nobel Peace Prize, damned him as "the most notorious liar in the country." Behind the scenes, the FBI implored King—whom it called a "dissolute, abnormal moral imbecile," a "filthy, abnormal animal," and "an evil, abnormal beast"—to commit suicide so that his sexual escapades wouldn't become common knowledge.

Tapes were delivered to the King home in Atlanta, to ensure that Martin's wife Coretta Scott heard them. As King put it, "They are out to break me." The FBI surveillance apparently lightened for a period, reheating as King spoke out against US involvement in Vietnam. In late 1967, Hoover included King and his church-based organization, SCLC, among the targets under the FBI's Counterintelligence Program (COINTELPRO). FBI offices were ordered "to expose, disrupt, misdirect, discredit, or otherwise neutralize the activities of black nationalist hate-type organizations."

In many ways, Hoover was following President Johnson's lead. Having failed to dissuade King from undertaking his Poor People's March, Johnson had promised not "to preside over the liquidation of the American nation or sit fiddling in the White House while Washington burns." Like Johnson, the FBI worried about the possibility of a "massive bloodbath" taking place in Washington, DC. By the end of the year with the Washington protest looming, the FBI sought to renew wiretaps on SCLC supposedly "to obtain racial intelligence information concerning their [sic] plans." Hoover delivered formal requests on January 2, following that up with "a classified blueprint based on informant reports" concerning the nationwide campaign for civil disobedience planned by King, according to the civil rights leader's biographer Taylor Branch. Acting on his own, Hoover instructed his field offices to put together another clandestine effort, POCAM ("poverty campaign"), to be included in COINTELPRO. The FBI also spread rumors about King, ranging from his desire to link up with the Black Muslims to his intention of becoming "a 'Messiah' who could unify and electrify the militant black nationalist movement." A bit later, FBI officials tried to circulate tape recordings purportedly revealing King's "moral turpitude."

Johnson's dismay regarding Dr. King also continued to revolve around the latter's increased expression of support for democratic socialism, albeit behind the scenes, and his fervent opposition to the war. The president had to have been displeased that King, who unknowingly was contending with the presence of FBI informants in his midst, expressed such unrelenting support for the Boston Five, who were indicted on January 5 for supporting draft resistance. At a news conference associated with CALCAV, held in New York City on January 12, King urged backing for an anti-war gathering in Washington, DC, in early February. He indicated, "It is imperative that church and synagogue leaders—clergy and laymen—come to Washington lest persons in the federal government think that men of conscience can be cowed by attack on dissenters or by blunderbuss indictments." Underscoring the religious tenor of the planned rally, King explained, "We want to make this a real witness that takes a stand against a social evil of our times. It is time for clergymen to speak out." He made it clear that there was no intention to repeat the battle against the Pentagon. But he emphasized how important the presidential election was, declaring that the nation would again find "its balance in world politics and its sanity at home or" move in the direction of "more bombs abroad and more arrests at home." To King, the choice was clear: "Either we end the war in Vietnam or many of our most sensitive citizens must be sent to jail."

On January 19, King came to the defense of the African-American entertainer Eartha Kitt, who confronted Lady Bird Johnson while the president's wife hosted a luncheon panel at the White House on urban crime. Kitt exclaimed, "You send the best of this country off to be shot and maimed. They rebel in the street. They will take pot and they will get high. They don't want to go to school because they're going to be snatched off from their mothers to be shot in Vietnam." She then declared, "Vietnam is the main reason we are having trouble with the youth of America. It is a war without explanation or reason." With a trembling voice, the teary-eyed first lady responded that she prayed for "a just and honest peace," but still considered it important to work to improve life in America. The Reverend King considered Kitt's statement a "very proper gesture," and indicative of "the feelings of many persons."

On February 4, he declared that God didn't compel the United States "to engage in a senseless, unjust war as the war in Vietnam." King went on to say, "And we are criminals in that war. We've committed more war crimes almost than any nation in the world." God, King warned, had "a way of even putting nations in their place." Jesus called for employing the drum major instinct differently, by striving "to be first in love . . . in moral excellence . . . in generosity." That hardly endeared Jesus to the general public, which "turned against him . . . called him a rabble-rouser . . . a trouble-maker . . . an agitator." In the final moments of his talk, King turned to the possibility of his own death. He didn't want an elaborate funeral or a celebration of his many accomplishments.

I'd like somebody to mention that day that Martin Luther King Jr. tried to give his life serving others.
I'd like for somebody to say that Martin Luther King Jr. tried to love somebody.
I want you to say that day that I tried to be right on the war question.
I want you to be able to say that day that I did try to feed the hungry.
And I want you to be able to say that I did try in my life to clothe those who were naked.
I want you to say on that day that I did try in my life to visit those who were in prison.
I want you to say that I tried to love and serve humanity.
Yes, if you want to say that I was a drum major, say that I was a drum major for justice. Say that I was a drum major for peace. I was a drum major for righteousness.
. . . But I just want to leave a committed life behind. And that's all I want to say.

Believing that the battle for economic, racial, and social justice in America was tied to the anti-war movement, King remained unrelenting in his criticism of the administration's Vietnam policy. That policy and the "failure to respond to economic problems in the urban areas that are causing riots," he insisted, demanded that the Democratic Party "be demonstrated against" during its national convention in late August. Approximately 2,500 CALCAV members, led by King, Rabbi Abraham Heschel, and Father James B. Shannon of Minneapolis–St. Paul, offered silent prayers on February 6 at Arlington National Cemetery for military casualties in Vietnam. The war, King warned, was wreaking "havoc" on America. "Somewhere along the way we have allowed the means by which we live to outdistance the ends for which we live," King stated.

Criticisms of his approach and leadership continued to fall on King, who met up with local black activists in Washington, DC, including Stokely Carmichael, the former SNCC chair who had helped to spawn the black power doctrine. Accused both "of having sold out the movement at Selma" and of threatening to do so again, King vehemently denied the charge. Whether responding to attacks or not, he quickly issued demands associated with the Poor People's Campaign, including multibillions in appropriations for a genuine assault on poverty. The bare minimum, he declared, involved a commitment to full-employment by Congress, legislation providing for a guaranteed annual income, and construction of a half million low-cost housing units annually.

By mid-February, two months before the planned protests in Washington, King appeared exhausted and possibly doubtful whether his latest efforts could succeed. His nonviolent crusade, which dated back to the Montgomery bus boycott that began in late 1955, had experienced great triumphs, including in that Jim Crow stronghold, the battle to integrate Birmingham, the historic March on Washington, and the breaking down of *de jure* segregation. But King had suffered setbacks along the way, such as the drives that faltered in Georgia and Florida, and the more recent debacle in Chicago, where he attempted to carry his movement outside the South and confronted some of the worst racism he had experienced. He had also encountered challenges to his leadership role within the civil rights movement, particularly as young activists became involved in sit-ins, freedom rides, voter registration drives, and black power factions, all but the latter of which he strongly supported. By early 1968, there were those within the movement and among the media who considered King and his insistence on nonviolence outdated, a man whose best days were behind him and whose influence among other civil rights activists, the Johnson administration, and the general public had waned considerably. Despite those sensibilities, no single figure possessed the aura, the charisma, or the track record of Martin Luther King Jr. He remained the leading proponent of nonviolent resistance, which actually attracted more adherents, including inside the anti-war movement, than ever before.

However, competition for attention, particularly from the media, but also for support from activists, whether white, black, or brown, was fiercer than ever by early 1968. The Resistance and its adult supporters, who included the defendants in the Boston Five, had recently acquired notoriety through draft-card burnings, the March on the Pentagon, actions at draft offices by those associated with what came to be known as the Ultra-Resistance, and the impending trial involving Spock and his codefendants. The UFW's Cesar Chavez was duplicating some of King's tactics, particularly his reliance on nonviolence, in his struggle to improve the lot of some of the nation's most exploited laborers.

Increasingly, more activists in the civil rights, anti-war, and New Left movements were heading in another direction, rhetorically, tactically, and ideologically. Having shifted toward a resistance mode only months before, many of those drawing media attention intensified their demands and aspirations, identifying with revolutionary forces around the globe and favoring the radical transformation of US domestic and foreign policies. Some who had considered reform necessary, and then favored the tactic of resistance, now began talking about the necessity of revolution, both at home and abroad. Other, more recent, members of various political movements dismissed nonviolence as impractical, self-defeating, or impotent. Carmichael and H. Rap Brown had taken SNCC in a very different direction than founders like John Lewis, Diane Nash, and Julian Bond had. The two newer SNCC leaders employed increasingly militant approaches. Although he respected Dr. King, Carmichael felt comfortable challenging the older civil rights leader's insistence on nonviolent tactics. No matter how briefly, Carmichael also joined the Black Panther Party, a self-professed Marxist-Leninist organization extolling community organization and self-defense, which had been founded by two community college students, Bobby Seale and Huey Newton, in the fall of 1966. Portraying the Panthers as the vanguard of the revolution, Seale and Newton soon added Eldridge Cleaver, recently released from a lengthy prison sentence and delivering essays for *Ramparts* magazine, to the party leadership.

By early 1968, Martin Luther King Jr. appeared besieged by antagonists across the political spectrum. His former ally in the White House, President Johnson, continued to be both stung and enraged by King's criticisms of his Vietnam policy and the War on Poverty. The FBI, guided by Director Hoover, maintained its surveillance. Black militants, even some of whom respected King, felt it expedient to assail him in public for his purported moderation, willingness to work with whites, and dogged commitment to nonviolence. Leading newspapers, including those that had offered support for the civil rights movement, blasted his involvement in anti-war demonstrations. Right-wing criticism was expected although it could still prove unsettling such as when 300 picketers gathered in Grosse Pointe, Michigan, where King was speaking to a crowd ten times that size. During his address, protesters called out "commie" and "traitor," resulting in "the worst heckling" he had yet endured.

Indeed, the hatred of King emanating from the right proved especially fierce, even toxically so, as demonstrated by apparent plots on his life considered or actually instigated by hardcore racists. Investigative reporters Stewart Wexler and Larry Hancock refer to "thousands of pages of files" on King gathered by the FBI, which contained "dozens, if not hundreds, of reported threats against" his life. Most were "menacing but harmless," delivered telephonically by "drunks and mentally disturbed individuals." Others were anything but innocuous, including the bombing of the King home during the Montgomery bus boycott, and the unleashing later in the decade by the Alabama chapter of the Ku Klux Klan (KKK) of J. B. Stoner, who had founded the racist, anti-Semitic National States Rights Party. Stoner promised to murder several civil rights leaders, including King and the Reverend Shuttleworth, who headed the Alabama Christian Movement for Human Rights. Law enforcement officials, working with the FBI, prevented Stoner from carrying out his plan. While King was leading a civil rights campaign in Birmingham in the spring of 1963, his headquarters at the A. G. Gaston Hotel was bombed, apparently by an Alabama Klavern, but he had departed from the city. Following the bombing of the Sixteenth Street Baptist Church in September that resulted in the murder of four young girls, another assassination attempt involving right-wing extremists germinated, again featuring Alabama sites. Klansmen fired on a beach cottage King had rented close to St. Augustine, Florida, in May 1964. That summer, the White Knights of the Mississippi Klan, led by Samuel Holloway Bowers, apparently hired a contract killer "to eliminate King" in the state. Bowers was the man who ordered the killing of MFS volunteers James Caney, Andrew Goodman, and Michael Schwerner. President Johnson deemed the threats to King's sufficient to order beefed up federal security for the civil rights leader. The White Knights and Bowers were apparently involved in yet another attempt to kill King, when the march on Selma occurred in early 1965 as part of the campaign to demand black voting rights.

While arrests of individuals tied to plots against King's life seldom occurred, the heavily armed Keith Gilbert, a member of both the militantly antigovernment Minutemen and the racist Church of Jesus Christ–Christian, was captured in Glendale, California, before an impending strike against the minister who was being honored at Los Angeles's Palladium theater for his recent receipt of the Nobel Peace Prize. Another individual arrested that same year was Daniel Wagner, who had been approached by a leading figure in the Ohio KKK, Eloise Witte, and obtained dynamite from James R. Venable, who headed the National Knights of the KKK. The White Knights continued attempting to draw King into a situation that would enable the group to lead him "into a death trap," but also sought to hire outsiders to perform the task. Bounty offers on King's life floating through American jails possibly drew the attention of James Earl Ray, a felon housed at the Missouri State Penitentiary in 1967 before he escaped. Stephen Oates reports that John Kauffmann and John Sutherland, two older supporters of George Wallace, residing in the St. Louis area, promised to pay an assassin who blew away "the big nigger," as Kauffmann referred to King.

Various threads, authors Wexler and Hancock contend, tied together the right-wing plotters who targeted Martin Luther King Jr. Yes, "a deep reactionary form of racism," was part of the mix, but so too, in their estimation, was a supposed religious viewpoint espoused by the Reverend Wesley Swift, a Klan organizer who had created the white supremacist Church of Jesus Christ–Christian. The racist, anti-Semitic Christian Identify movement spawned by Swift eventually transmuted into Aryan Nations. Its members viewed Jews as evolving from a union of Eve and the Serpent, and considered nonwhites "mud peoples" of more ancient vintage.

The plotting against King was ongoing in early 1968, as he geared up for the Poor People's Campaign, the need for which appeared buttressed by release of a report on February 29 by the President's National Advisory Commission on Civil Disorders. In its most telling statement, the Kerner Commission, which pinpointed "white racism" as the trigger for contentious race relations, warned that the nation was racially splintering. Absent marked efforts to rectify the situation, the commission stated, there would exist "a continuing polarization of the American community and, ultimately, the destruction of basic democratic values." Believing the commission's findings confirmed his earlier warnings, Dr. King declared that the nation would suffer "chaos and disintegration" if African Americans were not fully incorporated into American society.

He soon declared April 22 the date when the "nonviolent poor people's march on Washington" would begin. For the initial time, according to *New York Times* reporter Ben A. Franklin, King also "decisively linked" the campaign's "antidiscrimination and antipoverty objectives to" the anti-war movement: "Flame throwers in Vietnam fan the flames in our cities." The demonstrations, scheduled to last several months, would amount to "a lobby-in against Congress," King stated. He subsequently expressed confidence that scores of other "non-Negro minority group organizations," ranging from those representing Native Americans and Chicanos to Puerto Ricans and Appalachian whites, would participate in the Poor People's Campaign. He also refused to declare support for either Eugene McCarthy or Bobby Kennedy for the Democratic Party presidential nomination, calling both "able" and supportive of programs designed to assist America's poor. Believing the war had to be ended, King informed newsmen, "President Johnson is too emotionally involved, and face-saving is more important to him than peace."

By mid-March, King was forced to direct his attention to a labor struggle that was unfolding in Memphis, where sanitation workers, holding signs reading "I AM A MAN," were conducting a strike for union recognition, which was opposed by Mayor Henry Loeb and the white community. On March 18, King appeared at Memphis's Mason Temple, speaking to a large crowd of 15,000 people. He predicted, "I come by here to say that America too is going to Hell, if we don't use her wealth . . . to end poverty, to make it possible for all of God's children to have the basic necessities of life." Referring to the ongoing labor strife, King declared that people

> were tired . . . tired of being at the bottom . . . tired of being trampled over by the iron feet of oppression . . . tired of our children having to attend overcrowded, inferior, quality-less schools . . . tired of having to live in dilapidated, substandard housing conditions . . . with wall to wall rats and roaches . . . tired of smothering in an air-tight cage of poverty in the midst of an affluent society . . . tired of walking up the streets in search for jobs that do not exist . . . of working our hands off and laboring every day and not even making a wage adequate with daily basic necessities of life . . . tired of our men being emasculated. . . . We are tired.

To attain equality, King asserted, it might be necessary "to escalate the struggle a bit," which could lead to "a general work stoppage in . . . Memphis." Believing it essential to maintain pressure, civil rights activists were heading "to Washington to demand what is ours." Rather than wasting precious resources waging war in Vietnam, King said, America must "put God's children on their own two feet." To that end, the Poor People's Campaign would operate "nonviolently but militantly . . . to plague Congress."

In reality, the Memphis movement was far more complicated than King knew. Young activists, enamored with the idea of black power, were susceptible to H. Rap Brown's call to "move from resistance to aggression, from revolt to revolution." Black militants who called themselves the Invaders felt disrespected by the preacher-dominated Community on the Move for Equality that attempted to coordinate backing for striking workers. The historian

Adam Fairclough indicates that the Invaders were determined to embarrass the ministers, who included the Reverend James Lawson, a SNCC founder, as plans continued for a large march in support of the strike. During the next several days, King was in and out of Memphis, while still planning the Poor People's Campaign. Due to plane difficulties, King arrived late for the march, which was slated to begin at 10 a.m. on March 28. The scene was increasingly chaotic by the time King arrived an hour late, and the march quickly degenerated as looting of stores occurred, young people hurled stones, and the police resorted to tear gas. Scores of injuries resulted, four people were wounded by gunshots, and one sixteen-year-old boy was killed. The following day, King met with members of the Invaders, insisting they renounce violence. Speaking to the press, he also emphasized that SCLC had not planned the march and he remained firmly committed to waging a "massive, nonviolent demonstration" in Memphis during his next visit.

But the disastrous march depressed King, who considered calling off the Poor People's Campaign. Negative press coverage hardly helped. The *Memphis Commercial Appeal* cried, "Dr. King's pose as a leader of a non-violent movement has been shattered," and it insisted that "the entire nation" now questioned whether his Washington protest would prove peaceful. *Newsweek* worried that events in Memphis portended what might transpire in the nation's capital. The *St. Louis Globe-Democrat* attacked "the Real Martin Luther King," calling him "one of the most menacing men in America today" and referred to him as "a Judas goat leading lambs to slaughter."

Having returned to Memphis on April 3, King spoke that evening to a small crowd at the Mason Temple. As he approached the close of his speech, he talked about having been stabbed ten years earlier when a crazed black woman drove a blade into his chest, near his aorta, as he sat autographing his first book, *Stride Toward Freedom*, about the Montgomery bus boycott. Countless letters poured into his hospital room, including one from a ninth-grade student, who wrote, "While it shouldn't matter, I would like to mention that I'm a white girl. . . . I read that if you had sneezed, you would have died. And I'm simply writing you to say that I'm so happy that you didn't sneeze." He too was glad that he hadn't sneezed, for he would have missed the sit-in movement, the freedom rides, the struggle in Birmingham, the march to Selma, and the present struggle in Memphis.

Then King referred to threats against his life emanating "from some of our sick white brothers." He admitted not being able to predict what lay ahead, and recognized that a difficult period loomed, but stated that it didn't matter as he had "been to the mountaintop." While he would "like to live a long life," he just desired "to do God's will." Then King declared, "I just want to do God's will. And He's allowed me to go up to the mountain. And I've looked over. And I've seen the Promised Land. I may not get there with you. But I want you to know tonight, that we, as a people, will get to the Promised Land!

Through his life's work—his sermons, lectures, writings, and political engagement—Dr. King provided a living model of commitment to racial, social, and economic justice. He braved vilification, arrests, death threats, and deadly plots, while insisting on the need to aspire to the beloved community that young activists in SNCC and CORE would exalt, at least for a while. He proved willing to relinquish his lofty standing with the Johnson administration, among other civil rights leaders, and in the eyes of the general public, to lend his eloquent, impassioned voice to the campaign opposing US military practices in Vietnam. Long attracted to radical ideals, such as economic democracy or democratic socialism, King also more openly criticized the American economic system during the last months of his too-short life. As urban centers teemed with rage and young people, sometimes side-by-side with their elders, viewed with mounting dismay the horrific reality that was the Vietnam War, King insisted on the need for radical alterations of American domestic and foreign policies. His was a voice of reason in a time when rationality itself increasingly seemed in question, and it was a radical voice at that. Given his own nation's violent nature, both past and present, King's insistence on adhering to nonviolence might have been the most revolutionary act of all. It also may well have been the most farsighted and generous, preventing untold amounts of bloodletting, including that which could easily have befallen African Americans.

6

"We All Want to Change the World"

Springtime of the Young Rebels

During the spring of 1968, on the heels of the Children's Crusade and the arrival of the New Politics, and shortly after the politics of assassination beset the United States once more, American youth again rose to the forefront of public discussion of the era's most contentious issues. The scene was Morningside Heights, skirting the edges of Manhattan's Upper West Side and West Harlem. Many of the young people involved were students at Columbia University, one of the Ivy League schools that long served as a pathway for future American leaders in literature, the arts, the science, and, yes, politics. Graduates of Columbia alone made up a roster of some of the most distinguished Americans, with writers like Isaac Asimov, Allen Ginsberg, and Joseph Heller; artists on the order of Paul Robeson and George Segal; journalists R. W. Apple, Max Frankel, and Norman Podhoretz; physicians Virginia Apgar, Charles Drew, Benjamin Spock, Harold Varmus, and Allen Whipple; scientists Edwin Armstrong and Michael I. Pupin; and political or legal figures Nicholas Murray Butler (who became president of Columbia University), Thomas E. Dewey, William O. Douglas, Charles Evans Hughes, and Harlan F. Stone. Both Theodore Roosevelt and his younger cousin Franklin Delano Roosevelt attended Columbia Law School, but did not graduate, receiving posthumous J.D.s many years later.

By the 1960s, Columbia retained its lofty standing as one of the great American universities, a world-renowned institution that became enmeshed in the era's social tumult. As elsewhere, particularly at elite colleges and universities, activist students began calling attention to the twin traumas of

Figure 6.1   Poster showing Hitler behind the mask of Charles de Gaulle. Across the globe, young radicals demanded change of a transformative nature. From London to Paris, from Rome to Prague, from New York City to Tokyo, they envisioned dramatic alterations of policies in their own countries and abroad. Library of Congress, Prints and Photographs Division, LC-USZ64-6606.

American racism and engagement in Vietnam, but also to the phenomenon that President Dwight D. Eisenhower referred to as the *military-industrial complex*. C. Wright Mills, the late great sociologist who taught at Columbia, had included labor unions and the academy in that development, which dominated American domestic and foreign policies. At Columbia, a pair of radical groups, one black, the other almost entirely made up of white students—the Students' Afro-American Society (SAS) and SDS—now also steered discussion toward the university's continued encroachment on the nearby community, which included many African Americans and Puerto Ricans.

During a span of several years, Columbia had purchased more than one hundred buildings, resulting in evictions of thousands of tenants, most of them black or Puerto Rican. Over a decade earlier, the university, seeking to construct a new gymnasium, began targeting Morningside Heights, which adjoined West Harlem. It promised to offer certain access to community members, but that proved restrictive in a manner viewed by many as insulting to local inhabitants. More recently, Columbia determined to build two gymnasiums, including one for Harlem residents. The community facility was to include a basketball court, a swimming pool, and sections for other indoor sports. Community youth would be able to partake of the facilities without charge, throughout the year. But angered by the seemingly well-intentioned gesture, local activists derided "Gym Crow," while insisting construction be ended. They denounced "separate and unequal facilities."

Ironically drawing on President Eisenhower's admonitions, Columbia SDS had focused on matters related to the military-industrial complex, assailing CIA recruitment during the fall of 1966. Increasingly influenced by the notion of the new working class and the Marxian concept of praxis involving revolutionary activity, SDSers condemned the role played by the university in shaping a new, technologically rooted society. Led by such activists as Mark Rudd, John "JJ" Jacobs, Ted Gold, and David Gilbert, Columbia SDS decried university complicity pertaining to the CIA; the Institute for Defense Analyses (IDA), a leading think tank; and Dow Chemical, the producer of napalm, the jellified gasoline employed to disastrous ends in Vietnam. Members of the "action faction" conducted a sit-in against Dow recruiters beginning on February 23, 1968. Operating in Yippie-like fashion, they engaged in guerrilla theater in March, tossing a pie at a military recruiter.

One of the "actionists," Mark Rudd, a tall, lanky undergraduate, who had grown up in a New Jersey suburb, became chair of the SDS chapter. Rudd was particularly enamored of the late, now martyred Latin American revolutionary Ernesto "Che" Guevara, but also with the Motherfuckers, the anarchist group based on the Lower East Side. Recently returned from Cuba, where he encountered Vietnamese "fighters" and Cubans exalting "their young socialist revolution," Rudd felt inspired by Che, whom he later called "this rifle-toting poet . . . willing to risk his life to free the people of the world." Che's proclamations that "the duty of every revolutionary is to make the revolution" and to "do it, don't just talk about it!" spoke directly to the Columbia undergraduate, who saw himself as "a Guevarista." As Che had, Rudd and like-minded young radicals thought that American imperialism was "crumbling to pieces." Rudd was also aware of Mao's declaration "Political power grows out of the barrel of a gun," and he devoured Frantz Fanon's *The Wretched of the Earth*, which saw revolutionary violence toppling colonial empires.

Almost immediately, a somewhat frenetic Rudd began instituting a series of actions, disrupting campus events, including a memorial service for Martin Luther King Jr. He also fired off an open, much-to-be quoted note to Columbia University president Grayson Kirk, indicating that young people were appalled by the powers that were, in the manner that FSM activists in Berkeley had been. Rudd predicted those same disgruntled youth would "take control of your world, your corporation, your university, and" seek to create a world where "people can live as human beings." He then stated, "Grayson, I doubt if you will understand any of this . . . you call for order and respect for authority; we call for justice, freedom, and socialism. There is only one thing left to say. It may sound nihilistic to you, since it is the opening shot in a war of liberation. I'll use the words of LeRoi Jones, whom I'm sure you don't like a whole lot: 'Up against the wall, motherfucker, this is a stickup.'" Rudd signed off, "Yours for freedom, Mark."

SDS was associated with the nationwide Ten Days of Resistance, which began on April 21 and involved marches, teach-ins, civil disobedience, and a single-day student strike to display opposition to the war. That spring semester would see ten politically motivated bombings or burnings of college or university buildings, according to Kirkpatrick Sale. This was, Sale indicated, the initial "concerted" employment "of such tactics of violence by the student left in this generation," but was then opposed by SDS. Organizational leaders denounced "the Left adventurers" and "the crazies," who were believed to favor sabotage or terrorism. Most members appeared in agreement with a correspondent from *New Left Notes*, the organization's paper, who declared, "We can't succeed with violence. . . . We cannot win an armed revolution—never." At the same time, both "the idea of violence" and its very possibility lengthened, Sale wrote. Notwithstanding or because of that fact, membership soared by the end of the academic year, possibly reaching 100,000 in 350 chapters scattered across the country.

On April 23, 300 students occupied Columbia University's Hamilton Hall, subsequently holding Henry Coleman, acting dean of the undergraduate college, hostage for over twenty-four hours. As Rudd issued a series of demands, Coleman declared, "I have no control over the demands you are making, but I have no intention of meeting any demand under a situation such as this." The demands included ending gymnasium construction, breaking ties to the IDA, halting disciplinary actions pertaining to earlier demonstrations, and terminating a ban on campus disturbances.

A split occurred among the occupiers, with SAS members forcing the white students to leave. The latter proceeded to take over Low Library, where they occupied President Kirk's office. Soon, other buildings were also held by students, not all associated with SAS or SDS. An African-American student, Raymond Wells, explained why black students were barricading themselves in Hamilton: "to protest the white racist university that encroaches on the Harlem Community." The IDA, Wells also contended, "had raped the minds of black people." The administration ordered the campus closed, thereby canceling classes, while the police set up a command post.

Occupied Columbia, as the writer David Caute refers to the 1968 protest at the Ivy League campus, received support from "intellectual tourists." They included the English poet Stephen Spender, Dwight Macdonald, Norman Mailer, and Tom Hayden, who joined the occupiers for a time. But Caute notes that Herbert Marcuse, the philosopher, political theorist, and exile from Nazi Germany later referred to as the "Father of the New Left," hardly appeared supportive of the occupation. In a soon to be published interview, Marcuse explained, "I have never suggested or advocated or supported destroying the established universities and building new anti-institutions instead. I have always said that no matter how radical the demands of the students, and no matter how justified, they should be pressed within the existing universities. I believe . . . that American universities, at least quite a few of them, today are enclaves of relatively critical thought and relatively free thought."

By contrast, Hayden would subsequently write an article, "Two, Three, Many Columbias," playing off Che's exhortation to "create two, three, many Vietnams." Appearing in *Ramparts* in the early summer, the piece supported "raids on the offices of professors doing weapons research," and saluted the Columbia occupiers. To Hayden, Columbia initiated "a new tactical stage in the resistance movement." That involved moving "from the overnight occupation of buildings to permanent occupation; from mill-ins to the creation of revolutionary committees; from symbolic civil disobedience to barricaded resistance." Hayden also suggested that while these tactics were being repeated at other colleges and universities, they were certain "to be surpassed by even more militant tactics."

Having spoken with leaders of both SDS and SAS, Steven V. Roberts of the *New York Times* explained that students in those groups were looking well beyond their college campus. SDS's Nick Freudenberg insisted that Eugene McCarthy and Bobby Kennedy didn't provide "a real choice," contending that even should one of them be able to remove American troops from Vietnam, the United States would still be enmeshed in the affairs of countries like Thailand and Bolivia. Freudenberg said, "What is wrong with this country is the basic social and economic structure," which McCarthy and Kennedy wouldn't change. Many participating in their campaigns, he continued, would eventually sour on liberal politics "and come over to radical politics." SAS's David Anderson believed his organization must "serve as an avant-garde for the black movement across the nation," and he hoped the protest regarding the gym would "spread to other things—such as the war."

John Kifner of the *New York Times* reported that the idea of participatory democracy was guiding the student activists, who continued to insist on amnesty for all demonstrators. However, Fred M. Hechinger, the *Times*'s education editor, viewed matters differently in his op-ed piece, "The Radicals 'Do Their Thing' at Columbia." In contrast to the earlier FSM at UC Berkeley, the Columbia uprising, Hechinger indicated, lacked the support of the general student body. The Columbia activists didn't seem concerned about that, striving for confrontations, while seeking to find "weak spots against which to strike." Radicals also drew on a general feeling, Hechinger wrote, that as recent student challenges against authoritarian rule in Spain, Poland, and Czechoslovakia had been applauded, "the domestic rebellion cannot be too bad either." He noted as well that institutions confronting youth rebellions had to avoid calling in the police. Doing so afforded "radicals a popular rallying point for wider support."

That concern was borne out as 1,000 police began flooding onto the Columbia campus at 1:30 a.m. on April 30, soon driving students out of five occupied buildings. While black leaders in New York City praised the police for the restraint displayed in removing African-American students from Hamilton Hall, a fact-finding commission later charged that "great violence" was meted out to other demonstrators. Over 700 arrests occurred, most following the removal of occupying students. One Columbia University professor, in relaying to *Time* magazine what he witnessed, reported students being "dragged down stairways . . . girls pulled out by the hair; their arms . . . twisted; they were punched in the face"; faculty were "kicked in the groin . . . punched in the eye."

As Charles Kaiser indicates, the demonstrators achieved much of that which they sought. The gymnasium adjoining Harlem was never completed. The university terminated its ties to IDA. Indoor demonstrators were allowed. President Kirk's resignation became effective in August. The university dropped most of the trespassing charges confronting occupiers. Shared governance soon came to the campus. In loco parentis, the parental-like responsibility Columbia had long displayed toward students, ended in the fall. Many student participants looked back fondly at their experiences during the Columbia protests, believing, as the activist Dotson Rader put it, "This was the first event in most of our lives where we felt effective, where what we were doing belonged to us. Never before had I felt as effective as during the Liberation."

Shortly following the Columbia strike, Tom Hayden reflected on what it meant. The students at that elite academic institution, he wrote, had adopted "an internationalist and revolutionary view of themselves in opposition to the imperialism of the very institutions in which they have been groomed and educated." They desired "a new and independent university standing against the mainstream of American society, or they want no university at all. They are, in Fidel Castro's words, guerrillas in the field of culture." Moreover, they "discovered that barricades are only the beginning of what they call bringing the war home."

SDS held its national convention on the campus of Michigan State University in East Lansing from June 10 to June 15. A revolutionary flair colored the massive room where SDS gathered, with images of Vladimir Lenin and Leon Trotsky, along with both hammers-and-sickles and black flags exalting anarchism. In keeping with the temper of the times, Mao Zedong's "Little Red Book," which the Black Panthers sold for profit, abounded. Kirkpatrick Sale notes that delegates attempted to one up each other by expressing revolutionary sentiments. Indeed, the idea of revolution dominated. Put forth as a candidate for inter-organizational secretary, fiery red-headed Bernardine Dohrn, a graduate of the University of Chicago Law School who had worked for the left-wing National Lawyers Guild, demonstrated as much in fielding a question about whether she saw herself as a socialist. "I consider myself a revolutionary communist," she responded, and was unanimously elected.

Young people in particular, whether fair-skinned, bronzed, or darker in hue, both inside and beyond the United States, were increasingly drawn to the possibility of revolution during 1968. They took to the streets in a manner not duplicated except possibly in 1848–1849 and 2011, and arguably with more radical possibilities in mind. While the earlier and later editions of mass revolutionary outpouring generally resulted in challenges to empires or lands formally ruled by empires, the revolutions envisioned in 1968 were more radical, visionary, even utopian in nature. They involved wholesale transformations of social and political orders, and they emerged around the globe. That put them more in line, at least in the imagination of participants, of the revolutionary upheavals that occurred beginning in 1776, 1789, 1917, and

1989. The fact that those visions generally remained stillborn fails to negate the subversive nature of what still baby-faced activists in 1968 contemplated. For whether celebrating socialism, communism, anarchism, or variants of those ideological constructs, the young rebels of 1968 wanted to make over the world in some fashion.

Few looked to the Soviet Union as a model for much of anything, let alone humane socialism. Rather, some considered Mao's China, which was undergoing the Cultural Revolution, as a place where Trotsky's idea of permanent revolution was taking hold. Indeed, China, the Turkish-American historian Arif Dirlik suggests, was viewed as "the center of world radicalism." His British counterpart Roland Fraser sees China, exuding a seeming "religious imperative," as having afforded "an alternative revolutionary model" distinct from industrial capitalist states and ossified Soviet-styled development. Or they looked to smaller "Third World" states, where leaders like Ho Chi Minh and Fidel Castro were challenging the most powerful nation in the world, the first militarily, the other rhetorically. Still turning to Albert Camus, C. Wright Mills, I. F. Stone, and existentialist thought as early New Leftists had, this new crop was increasingly enamored with revolutionary theoreticians, particularly Fanon, Guevara, Debray, Marcuse, the young Marx, and Lenin. Less attractive were the concepts of participatory democracy and the beloved community, which had guided the American SDS and SNCC in the first half of the decade. Instead, they found alluring Castro's prophesy that 1968 would prove "the year of the heroic guerrilla."

The Afro-Caribbean psychiatrist Frantz Fanon (1925–1961), born in Martinique but relocated to France and Algeria, championed decolonization following World War II, particularly supporting the Front de Liberation Nationale that demanded the expulsion of French forces from Algeria. His most famous work, *The Wretched of the Earth*, with a preface by Jean-Paul Sartre, emphasized both the dehumanizing nature of colonialism and the emancipating effect of liberation struggles, including those relying on violence. Seemingly like Mao, Fanon believed in the possibility of "new men," who could be ushered in through revolutionary catharsis.

Ernesto "Che" Guevara, the Argentine physician turned revolutionary, became one of Fidel Castro's most trusted lieutenants in the fight to overthrow Cuban dictator Fulgencio Batista. The handsome, charismatic Guevara became a symbol of the new revolutionary Cuban regime, serving as president of the national bank, minister of industry, and ambassador on a global stage. In 1965, he departed Cuba to export revolution elsewhere, coming up short in both the Congo and Bolivia, where he was captured and murdered by the Bolivian army, which received assistance from the CIA. Just as *The*

Wretched of the Earth proved popular among self-professed radicals and revolutionaries, Guevara's iconic image displaying his dark beret, lengthy hair, and straggly mustache and beard, became a familiar site at institutions of higher learning and in college dormitories around the world.

His writings, including *Guerrilla Warfare* (1960), remained influential, as did his notion of "a new socialist citizen" toiling for society's good and the *foco* theory, which Debray largely derived from Guevara and Castro. A theory that would appeal to many young radicals by the latter stages of the 1960s, focoism indicated that committed revolutionaries, though few in number, could initiate small-scale, mobile guerrilla operations. In Leninist fashion, they would serve as a vanguard for the revolution. Debray (born 1940), a young French intellectual educated at the elite École Normale Supérieure, taught at the University of Havana and produced *Revolution in the Revolution?* (1967), which heralded the guerrilla *foco*. Arrested as a compatriot of Guevara, he received a thirty-year jail sentence from a Bolivian military tribunal. (He would be released after serving three years, thanks to an international campaign that included support from Hannah Arendt, Charles de Gaulle, Nat Hentoff, Dwight Macdonald, Sartre, and I. F. Stone.)

Marcuse, having left Brandeis for the newly established University of California at San Diego, was revered by New Leftists for his best known books, *Eros and Civilization* (1955) and *One Dimensional Man* (1964). A leader of the Frankfurt School, which attempted to link Marxism and Freudianism, Marcuse was drawn to *The Economic and Philosophic Manuscripts of 1844*, the so-called Paris manuscripts, in which Marx highlighted the theme of alienated labor regarding man's estrangement from the workplace. Lenin's contribution to New Left thought, if it can be called that, involved the growing attraction to the notion of a vanguard triggering the revolution. The Black Panthers subscribed to that idea, as did Guevara and Debray.

Revolutionary stirrings that threatened to become fully blown in 1968 arguably first sprouted, ironically perhaps, in a region where socialism had already been embedded: Eastern Europe. There, the young Marx proved influential, but so did liberal inclinations, including those regarding matters that many in the West took for granted: political democracy, the right to engage in dissent, and civil liberties. The Stalinization of the region that had occurred during World War II's final months and its immediate aftermath had in no way ushered in the good society or birthed the new man that socialism seemingly promised. Instead, police states appeared, democracy was quashed even in Czechoslovakia, where it had existed during the interwar period, show trials occurred, and repression was the order of the day. A challenge to Soviet hegemony did take place, as Josip Broz "Tito" began to carve out Yugoslavia's own path to socialism after being denounced for contesting orthodox Marxism-Leninism. While remaining under Tito's firm grip, Yugoslavia flirted with seemingly novel ideas ranging from market socialism to workers' self-management.

There was something of a thaw following Stalin's death in early 1953 and the eventual ascendancy of Nikita Khrushchev in the Soviet Union, but even the hint of a lifting of communism's iron grip threatened party leadership altogether. Riots had broken out in Berlin in 1953, and unrest appeared in Poland and Hungary as Khrushchev suggested that Soviet hegemony would be lightened and especially after he denounced Stalinist terrors in his speech before the 20th Party Congress in February 1956. The failure of the October Revolution in Hungary later that year, however, demonstrated there were stark limits to how far the new Soviet leader would allow client states to curb communist overlordship. Nevertheless, Eastern European leaders operated in different manners over the next dozen years, with some allowing greater or lesser amounts of economic and political liberalization. This occurred even following the removal of Khrushchev from power in 1964 and his replacement by Leonid Brezhnev.

The most promising developments began to crop up in Czechoslovakia by 1967, after a long period of nightmarish communist rule following the coup nineteen years earlier that resulted in party control of government posts, the military, the police, and communications. By the mid-1960s, the Czechoslovakian Communist Party allowed for a weak market system, the exonerating of many purge victims, and the freeing of political prisoners. Intellectuals and young people proved increasingly restless. Critical voices began to be heard, including that of the playwright Vaclav Havel, whose work *The Garden Party* (1963) critically viewed Czechoslovakian society under communist rule. Franz Kafka, the early twentieth century Jewish writer who penned the dystopian classic novel *The Trial*, experienced a rehabilitation of his reputation and republication of his works. Something of a counterculture began to emerge, centered around Prague's Old Town, where young people insisted on freedom and democracy.

Jazz, long banned, made a comeback in Czechoslovakia, while rock 'n' roll, thanks to the Beatles, ushered in the "bigbit" (Big Beat), as the Czechoslovakians referred to it. Arriving during that period, having been invited by students attending Charles University in Prague, Allen Ginsberg appeared in 1965, and university students there named him King of the Czechoslovakian May Day festival, which he celebrated. "And I am the King of May, which is the power of sexual youth, / and I am the King of May, which is long hair of Adam and Beard of my own body / and I am the King of May which is Kral Majales in the Czechoslovakian tongue." He dedicated his coronation to Kafka, who had resided nearby. While the long-deceased Kafka had been considered suspect by the communist regime, so too was Ginsberg, who was denounced by the communist regime, harassed by the Secret Police, and then beaten one night by an individual who derided him as a "'fairy' or 'queer.'" It was Ginsberg, not his attacker, who suffered arrest before being expelled from Czechoslovakia. But following his visit, Prague witnessed more hippies with long hair and blue jeans, an underground club scene developed, rock magazines proved popular, and classrooms discussed Western-styled rock. On May 1, 1966, hundreds marched to Wenceslas Square, in the center of Prague's New Town, crying out, "We want freedom. We want democracy." They also declared, "A good communist is a dead communist."

The dogmatic communist government, led by Antonin Novotny, acted to tighten censorship laws. When Czechoslovakian writers blasted the Soviet treatment of such authors as Yuri Daniel and Aleksandr Solzhenitsyn, government officials banned publications, including the noncommunist literary journal *Tvar*, whose editorial board included Havel. Clashes involving government officials, writers, and young people continued.

On January 5, the Prague Spring began in earnest with the replacement of Novotny as First Secretary of the Czechoslovak Communist Party by forty-six-year-old Alexander Dubček, a Slovak reformer who favored pluralism, democratization, and "socialism with a human face." The intention was to blend socialism and democracy, just as the rebels in Budapest had envisioned. Breaking down Stalinist barriers, Dubček began lifting press censorship, lightening travel restrictions, and rehabilitating many victimized by communist purges. In March, Dubček readily met with concerned students, worried about a possible return to Stalinist rule. When asked for assurances that wouldn't occur, Dubček replied, "You yourselves are the guarantee. You, the young."

Dubček attempted to maintain his nation's good standing with the Soviet-dominated Warsaw Pact, thereby seemingly avoiding the fatal mistake made by Imre Nagy and his reform government during the aborted Hungarian Revolution of 1956. Still, Dubček expressed his intention to accomplish "the widest possible democratization" of his home country, along with the carving out of "a free, modern, and profoundly humane society." On April 5, he initiated the Action Program, which called for a "new model of socialism," one that was both democratic and national, involved a "unique experiment in democratic communism," and included a "new economic model." Under the Action Program, Dubček began a series of reform measures intended to enable Czechoslovakia to chart its own course, internally, including a shift to a consumer-oriented economy and the possibility of a multiparty government. Criticisms of the Soviet Union intensified, while new, noncommunist political clubs appeared.

During May Day celebrations, which featured vast, energized crowds, Czechoslovakian hippies, flowers painted on their faces, were present, while signs praised Israel, democracy, and the idea of making love, rather than war. A banner read, "Of our own free will, for the first time." Slogans condemning socialism and the Soviet Union and celebrating political dissent, even demanding "an opposition party," were heard. *Rude Pravo*, the official organ of the Czechoslovakian Communist Party, applauded "the springlike blossoming of our new public life, the breath of fresh air brought by democratic freedoms." Insisting that Marx had spoken of different paths to socialism, the paper declared, "We are the beginning of a search, which must proceed. There is no other way." That same publication had recently condemned the cult of personality that afflicted communist states, and the "unreasonable transfer of the Soviet experience" to Czechoslovakia. Students were soon reportedly engaged "in large, carnival-like rallies around the country," where they supported "sweeping political reforms" and Dubček, while condemning a Polish Communist Party campaign of anti-Semitism.

In wholeheartedly backing the Prague Spring, young residents of Czechoslovakia differed in certain regards from many of their counterparts in much of the Western world in 1968. Residing in a land that had been sullied by both Nazis and communists, they longed to attain what young rebels in the United States and Western Europe often appeared to take for granted: rule of law, democracy, civil liberties, and the right to dissent, often in provocative ways. Such a political framework remained alien throughout most of the world. So too did the general prosperity that provided an underpinning for radicals in America, Canada, England, France, Holland, Germany, Italy, and Scandinavia, to name a few of the most financially prosperous and democratically stable states.

Student-spawned protest occurred elsewhere in Eastern Europe during the first several months of 1968, but especially in Poland and Yugoslavia. Three hundred students congregated on January 30 at the University of Warsaw to contest the shutting down of the play *Dziady*, whose nationalist tenor pitted native political prisoners confronting tyranny under the Russian tsar. The government, still headed by Wladislaw Gomulka, who was viewed as a reformer but had increasingly adopted a repressive stance toward writers, scientists, and potential dissidents, responded heavy-handedly. This should have surprised no one as the Gomulka regime had clamped down hard after a challenge occurred within the ranks of the party during the middle of the decade. A pair of young intellectuals, Jacek Kuroń and Karol Modzelewski, had inscribed an "Open Letter to the Party," contending the Polish economy was dysfunctional, while blaming the party leaders for bureaucratic malfeasance. Both received prison sentences, resulting in their replacement by

Adam Michnik as leader of disaffected youth. His "commandos" delivered a left-wing criticism of the government, and he was in touch with young radicals in Western Europe. Criticisms of the government again escalated following the release of Kuroń and Modzelewski from prison in 1967. *Dziady*, whose first performance occurred in late November, proved highly popular, troubling the Communist Party ruling strata.

Protests intensified amid what would be called the "March events," leading to a rally in Warsaw's City Center on March 9 by 20,000 students, who suffered violence at the hands of the police. Days of street battles ensued, expanding to cities and towns throughout Poland. At the University of Warsaw, activists produced the Declaration of the Students' Movement, which insisted that censorship be terminated, favored self-government for laborers, called for independent trade unions, demanded a nonpartisan judiciary, and supported the setting up of a constitutional court. However, as the historians Elaine Carey and Jerzy Eisler have recorded, the Polish regime attacked student protesters and abrogated the University of Warsaw's autonomy, shutting down various programs, thereby throwing students out of school, which subjected them to immediate conscription into the Polish army. The government also curbed the festering protest by fueling a vicious, anti-Semitic campaign denouncing Jewish students as international Zionist agents. Michnik, a Jew like several of the intellectuals associated with the movement, saw it as fascism, pure and simple. The student activist Eugeniusz Smolar later indicated, "March 1968 was the last time anyone believed the system could evolve."

Although less well-known than the unrest in either Poland or Czechoslovakia, student protest also occurred in Yugoslavia, which had experienced more amicable relations with the Soviet Union following the death of Joseph Stalin. Yugoslavia remained under the grip of Josip Tito, whose limited tolerance of dissenting thought was demonstrated by his jailing of Milovan Djilas, a top Yugoslav political figure once considered his heir apparent, who warned about a new ruling class emerging in communist states. Nevertheless, Yugoslavia was viewed favorably by many Western observers because of its purported experiments in "workers' self-management" and "socialist democracy." It also adopted a policy of nonalignment, in keeping with India under Jawaharlal Nehru, as articulated at the Bandung Conference held in Indonesia in 1955, and later with Ghana under Kwame Nkrumah. Another important conference of nonaligned states took place in Belgrade in 1961, during which discussion occurred about universal disarmament, peaceful coexistence between nations with disparate political systems, and an end to colonialism.

Despite the treatment afforded Djilas and other dissenters, a band of Marxist academicians delivered criticisms of the Tito regime through both *Praxis*, a magazine that initially appeared in late 1964 and emphasized the early humanist essays of Marx, and a student movement. Gajo Petrović, a young philosopher teaching at Zagreb University, discussed the need for a new journal, while affirming that "socialism is the only human way out from the difficulties in which humanity has entangled itself, and Marx's thought—the most adequate theoretical basis and inspiration for revolutionary activity." Petrovic wrote of the crafting "of an authentic, humanist Marxism" and the fostering of "a really Marxist, nondogmatic and revolutionary approach to" the open issues of our time. He and *Praxis* aspired to the "realization of a humane human community." Influenced by critical thinkers like Petrovic, students in Yugoslavia pushed for reforms in university life, criticized US intervention in Vietnam, and supported their Polish peers who during the spring of 1968 engaged in a "struggle for the democratization" of their nation. Yugoslav students condemned the Polish Communist Party's anti-Semitic campaign.

Young rebels also materialized in Western Europe. As elsewhere, the British New Left began to emerge during the 1950s, with the discrediting of Stalinist communism, the advent of an antinuclear movement, identification with Third World national liberation drives, and a desire for something of a third way, distinct from both Soviet-led Marxism-Leninism and American-dominated capitalism and neocolonialism. Specific triggers included Nikita Khrushchev's denunciation of Joseph Stalin, British and French moves to take control of the Suez Canal in the face of opposition by Egypt's Gamal Abdel Nasser, and the Soviet crushing of Hungary's attempt to chart its own path. English intellectuals, especially historians E. P. Thompson and Perry Anderson, were important pathfinders, as was the journal they were associated with: *New Left Review*. Greater educational opportunities, more affluence, and an end to conscription helped to encourage a youth culture that enabled young people to convey discontent with postwar Britain, indicating the playwright John Osborne's prescience in writing about angry young men in *Look Back in Anger* (1956). Swinging London, the impact of the Beatles and a host of other rock groups, and the readiness with which stirring developments across the globe were recognized, also set the stage for the student activists who appeared in the heart of Great Britain's capital city, as their counterparts did elsewhere in Europe, the United States, Latin America, Africa, the Middle East, and Asia.

On March 17, 1968, the "Battle of Grosvenor Square" unfurled outside the US Embassy in London, as Mick Jagger and Keith Richards would reference in their anthem, "Street Fighting Man." Among those present at a large anti-war demonstration in central London were the actress Vanessa Redgrave and Tariq Ali, one of the leading figures in the British New Left, both of whom spoke at the Trafalgar Square rally. Thousands marched to Grosvenor Square, where they encountered more than a thousand riot police, many on horseback. Fighting ensued, with demonstrators hurling rocks, firecrackers, and smoke bombs, while the police struck with truncheons. Three hundred arrests resulted, and scores were injured. Seventy-five people, a third of them police, landed in the hospital. John Lawlor, who commanded the police, later charged that the organizers failed to rein in the demonstrators and reneged on earlier promises to maintain order. "The demonstration degenerated into a disorderly rabble," he complained. The US ambassador to Great Britain, David Bruce, applauded the forces of law and order: "We are most grateful for the magnificent way the police handled the attack on the embassy."

The appearance of young radicals similarly became quite noticeable in the nations where fascist rule first eventuated: Germany and Italy. Similar and dissimilar factors set the stage for the unrest that percolated among German and Italian students and young workers, including the larger number of university enrollees, anger regarding international events, frustration concerning policies and practices in the academy or at the workplace, and generational considerations. Both German and Italian youth looked back at their parents' generation with concern, even disdain, particularly regarding the enveloping of their countries by the authoritarianism associated with Adolf Hitler or Benito Mussolini.

The German situation was complicated by the division of the state that followed the Allies' occupation at the end of World War II. East Germany became ruled by one of the most authoritarian regimes throughout Eastern Europe, while West Germany largely remained dominated by the Christian Democratic Party, long led by Konrad Adenauer. Chancellor over the course of the West German state's near initial decade and a half of existence, Adenauer became a firm supporter of containment and championed reconciliation with neighbors, particularly France. He also insisted that "all roads of socialism lead to Moscow." During Adenauer's reign, "the German miracle" of economic recovery occurred. But controversies swirled about his government too, especially the reentry of Nazi supporters and even former Nazis into prominent economic or political positions. That enraged the generation coming of age by the latter half of the 1960s, some of whose most impassioned members determined to distinguish themselves from their elders whom they castigated for allowing totalitarianism to engulf their national landscape and wreak terrible havoc across the continent and beyond.

For many young Germans, Axel Springer's press syndicate, including his sensational tabloid, *Das Bild*, served as the embodiment of wrongheaded beliefs and attitudes on the part of the older generation. Despite his anti-Nazi background, Springer was despised for his support of Adenauer and pointed criticisms of German student radicals. The killing of a student by the police during a demonstration attacking the Shah of Iran on June 2, 1967, helped to radicalize the movement, although the general public expressed no sympathy for the twenty-six-year-old victim, Benno Ohnesorg.

The center of the German movement was the Free University in West Berlin, while the most significant student group was the German Socialist Students' League (SDS), which with its tiny band of members had been booted from its parent organization, the Social Democratic Party (SPD), in 1961 for "left deviation." German SDS was part of *die Neue Linke,* which like the New Lefts in Great Britain and the United States, appeared as politically engaged young people desired to create something distinct from the Old Left that seemed so discredited. Student activists were little pleased five years later when the SPD and the Christian Democrats formed a governing "grand coalition." SDS's intellectual forefathers included Rosa Luxemburg, the Polish-German Marxist theoretician and activist who insisted that socialism be paired with democracy, and philosophers associated with the Frankfurt School such as Theodor Adorno, Max Horkheimer, and Marcuse. Luxemburg became a martyr for revolutionary socialists, having been murdered by members of the right-wing paramilitary Freikorps in Berlin after the failed communist-led Spartacus Revolt shortly following World War I. Radical students in West Berlin, in November 1967, established a Critical University that focused on the Third World, direct action, and "the Democratization of School," among other concerns.

They also conducted a "tribunal" in January 1968 that deemed Springer guilty of seeking to reignite German authoritarianism. The next month saw a Vietnam Congress in the same half of the divided city, which paired US atrocities in Southeast Asia with those of the Nazis. Approximately 5,000 students and workers attended that conclave. But the situation became still more explosive in the wake of the attempted assassination of twenty-eight-year-old Rudi Dutschke, the dynamic face of German radicals, by a young right-wing house painter on April 11. Born in the region that became East Germany, Dutschke was denied a university education there after refusing military conscription. Just before construction of the Berlin Wall in 1961, he managed to escape to the Western sector. By 1967, the onetime anarchist Dutschke, who favored an "extra-parliamentary opposition," acquired greater stature within a more robust SDS by coauthoring a paper with Hans-Jurgen Krahl, calling for the group to engage in "sabotage and civil disobedience" to prevent an overbearing state. Supporting the appearance of urban guerrillas, Dutschke believed they could help "destroy the system of repressive institutions." He and like-minded colleagues helped to form a student commune based in part on the ideas of the Austrian-born psychoanalyst Wilhelm. And he was born in a part of Austria-Hungary that is now in Ukraine. Reich, who became another martyr, in his case to the cause of sexual liberation as he was hounded, harassed, and incarcerated by the government of the United States, where he had gone to escape Nazi tyranny. While sympathetic to Marxism, Dutschke believed individuals could help to shape history. He and others in SDS who were similarly inclined favored "provocative action," including that which could cause the police to engage in brutality that would radicalize many. By the fall of 1967, Dutschke supported combining the "propaganda of shooting" championed by Che Guevara and the "propaganda of the deed" lauded by nineteenth-century anarchist Mikhail Bakunin, German activist Volkhard Mosler writes. Dutschke also recognized, "Without provocation we wouldn't be noticed at all."

Early events in 1968, both inside Germany and beyond, made such ideas more palatable for a number of activists, some of whom were quickly drawn to still more radical nostrums. The shooting of Dutschke by a young right-winger who avidly read Springer's newspapers triggered riots in a number of German cities, which coincided with attacks on the press syndicate. The previous year, *Das Bild* had insisted "Germans want no brown and no red SA, no columns of toughs, but peace," then had compared Dutschke and his ilk with street fighters who helped to destroy the Weimar Republic, thereby setting the stage for Hitler's takeover. The tabloid had called Dutschke "Red Rudi," and called for halting "the Terror of the Young Reds!" But as young students and workers protested in the streets of West Germany, the police responded violently and engaged in mass arrests. One of nearly 200 arrested in West Berlin was nineteen-year-old Peter Brandt, the son of Willy Brandt, the former mayor who was the nation's leading Social Democrat and foreign minister in the coalition national government (and later chancellor).

In May 1968, the final large demonstrations took place as student radicals, other left-wing activists, and union members, while conducting a march on the West German capital city of Bonn, condemned the recently promulgated Emergency Laws. Those measures allowed a small group of Bundestag and cabinet members to lead the West German government if exigent circumstances materialized—that is if an attack from outside or grave domestic turmoil occurred. David Caute quotes a professor from Frankfurt University, worried about the public response to student militancy that involved an attempted blockade of the institution and the breaking of windows: "What bothers me is that the rebels tend to bring about the very conditions they oppose. . . . This strengthens the forces of the Right."

Like West Germany, Italy experienced an economic resurgence, another seeming "miracle," during the early postwar period, as per capita income significantly increased. Italy too was politically dominated by center right forces, led by the Christian Democrats, a Catholic party that put together coalition governments. The Italian and the German Christian Democrats offered an anti-communist, pro-capitalist approach, and helped to guide their countries into the North Atlantic Treaty Organization, designed as a military alliance intended to stave off possible Soviet aggression. The Italian political situation was complicated by the presence of strong socialist and communist parties, along with militant labor unions. Adding to the complexity was the continued impoverishment of the southern sector, notwithstanding the post-war boom.

Student activism of a militant cast appeared in Italy during the decade of the 1960s, fueled by attempted educational reforms in the midst of a mush-rooming student population. Unfortunately, too few classrooms existed, text-books were in short supply, teachers weren't adequately trained, and curricula proved outdated. Between 1960 and 1968, the number of students attending universities jumped by 180,000. The much larger pool of students, many from the working class, confronted terrible conditions, including a lack of necessary resources and financial assistance, along with haughty professors, who often failed to hold regular classes or deliver exams, which were gener-ally oral and subjectively evaluated, in a timely fashion. Those professors, moreover, were required to be in the classrooms but one hour a week, and absenteeism proved quite high. Dropout rates passed 50 percent by 1968. The British historian Paul Ginsborg argued, "The decision to allow open access to such a grossly inadequate university system amounted simply to planting a time bomb in it."

The Italian student movement surged in the fall of 1967, as occupations of campus buildings occurred in Catholic universities in Trento and Milan before spreading to large public institutions. The initial occupation at the University of Turin lasted a full month late in the year, then recurred early in 1968. The occupation, which was largely peaceful during its first stage, proved less so after violent forced evacuations. Lectures were increasingly disrupted. The mass-circulation newspaper *La Stampa* adopted an ever more strident tone toward student activists, eventually likening them to Mussolini's supporters while tagging them as dangerous "left-wing fascists." In some-what typical fashion, those students spouted slogans and ideals associated with "Lenin, Mao, Guevara, Fanon, Marcuse, Debray, and Trotsky," writes the British academic Austin Fisher. Important too, as was the case in West Germany, the historical realities of fascism and the fight against it influenced the younger generation.

In mid-February, the Italian student unrest shifted course, with heightened protest in the South, including at the University of Rome, La Sapienza, and in secondary schools. Students were angered by a bill devised by the Minister of Education and introduced in parliament, which called for scaling back university enrollments and establishing little-welcomed restrictions on university programs. The more than 60,000 students attending the University of Rome also suffered from particularly egregious conditions, enrolled as they were in an institution designed to accommodate less than a tenth that number. Ginsborg articulated additional factors leading to the intensified protest, including the greater appeal of anti-capitalist, radical visions at least partially in keeping with the humanitarian papacy of John XXIII. Important too were the examples set by counterparts elsewhere, among those American anti-war activists, Latin American guerrillas, and radical priests in Latin America affiliated with what came to be known as *liberation theology*, which led some to not only identify with the poor and the oppressed but to take up arms against less than sympathetic governments. The appeal of fusing Catholicism and Marxism proved particularly strong. And then there was the failure of Italian institutions, among them the Partito Comunista d'Italia (PCI), to support genuine change. Other analysts contend that the PCI and the Socialist Party had actually grappled with the need for educational reform, and that traditional parties fostered anti-war protests in an attempt to channel youthful militancy.

Takeovers of university buildings proved short-lived, most concluding with the police compelling students to end occupations. The protest at the University of Rome, La Sapienza, was halted at the close of February, but 4,000–5,000 students quickly decided to retake buildings, leading to a violent clash with the police. Large numbers of injuries resulted from the "Battle of Valle Giulia," the last major clash that winter season. Many leaders in the PCI and the party-dominated Italian General Confederation of Labor condemned the student radicals, while the press attacked the movement as "extremist." This stood in sharp contrast to the response by young workers, many of whom identified with student complaints regarding authoritarian control, including within labor unions. During the early part of 1968, hundreds of thousands of workers participated in strikes, particularly concentrated in northern factories. Revolutionary sensibilities intensified following events that suggested the chance for genuine revolution in nearby France.

There, Charles de Gaulle, the World War II hero, offered something of a self-congratulatory account on New Year's Eve. "I greet the year 1968 with serenity. It is impossible to see how France today could be paralyzed by crisis as she has been in the past." De Gaulle could scarcely have been more wrongheaded, as by mid-spring, his regime and the Fifth Republic he had helped to establish a decade earlier tottered with revolution once again threatening as it had in 1789, 1831, 1848, and 1871.

The possibility of revolution beckoned in France during the spring of 1968, however briefly. The center of action eventually, quite naturally, was Paris, including the famed Left Bank, where writers, artists, and rebels long congregated amid students, many from the University of the Sorbonne, one of Europe's most illustrious. The French uprising was a rarity in offering the possibility of a union of students and workers, both of whom participated in massive rallies that threatened to bring down de Gaulle's conservative government. Radical elixirs guided young activists, some of whom were drawn to socialism, anarchism, or Maoism.

The '68ers included charismatic individuals like Danny Cohn-Bendit, Bernard Kouchner, and Bernard Henri-Levi, the latter two acquiring far greater acclaim or notoriety later. The star of the Parisian revolt was "Danny the Red," so labeled both for his left-wing politics that flirted with anarcho-communism and the color of his fiery, disheveled hair. The child of German Jews who had escaped to France as the Nazis gave vent to fanatical anti-Semitism, Cohn-Bendit was studying on a campus considered by students and faculty as unlovely, situated in the suburb of Nanterre, far from the center of Paris. The matter of in loco parentis served as a trigger for student unrest, leading some to contend that hormones as much as ideology caused the young rebels to challenge university officialdom. Also coming to play were the sheer numbers of students attending college and the issues that enraged young people around the globe, particularly the machinations of the two superpowers in their supposed spheres of influence. The French students identified with both Czechoslovakian and American activists, while similarly dreaming large dreams of social and political transformation of their own society.

The young French activists saw themselves as part of the global New Left, which began to emerge in the mid-1950s and early 1960s. In France, the *Nouvelle Gauche* appeared, initially swirling around Claude Bourdet and *The Observer*, which supported a third left-wing path distinct from Stalinism and social democracy. The French New Left attained institutional status with the founding of Parti Socialiste Unifié (PSU), which condemned the brutal attempt to retain control of Algeria, and later incorporated militant groups of gauchistes, who included Trotskyists, Maoists, and anarchists. Ideas associated with all of those sects would be strongly represented during the French student-worker revolt of 1968. The German historian Ingrid Gilcher-Holtey also points to the intellectual influence displayed in such journals as *Socialisme ou Barbarie*, *Arguments*, and *International Situationniste*, which helped to pique reconsiderations of Marxism, offered new visions regarding socialism, emphasized the collective, exalted action, and depicted revolutionary leadership as emanating not from the older version of the industrial proletariat but rather from a purported new working class, young intellectuals, and groups on the fringes of the social order.

Although the initial student strike in Nanterre dissipated, that spring witnessed an outpouring of protest by students and workers that tapped into many of the same concerns that propelled the earlier outburst. The March 22 Movement unfolded in Nanterre, involving a takeover of the dean's office that led to the arrest of several students, including Cohn-Bendit, who were condemning US engagement in Vietnam. Within a month, the March 22 Movement delivered a manifesto that supported "outright rejection of the Capitalist Technocratic University." As conflicts escalated, administrators shut down the university for an indefinite period, while demanding that seven students—one of them Cohn-Bendit—appear before a university board.

On May 3, students at the Sorbonne held a meeting to condemn Nanterre University's closure and to discuss the possibility of a student strike. In the evening, fighting occurred between protesters and police, resulting in hundreds of arrests and scores of injuries. By Monday, May 6, more than 20,000 demonstrators congregated toward the Sorbonne, which had also been closed. Swinging truncheons, the police attacked protesting students. The following day, twice as many demonstrators, who now included students, university lecturers, and workers, marched along the Champs-Élysées, singing "The Internationale" at the Arc de Triomphe. On May 9, students were turned away when they attempted to return to classes at the Sorbonne. Beginning in the evening of May 10, protesters begin constructing barricades. But as the "Night of Barricades" continued into the early morning hours, massive violence resulted from police slamming into students with truncheons, culminating in hundreds of injuries. Prime Minister Georges Pompidou expressed a willingness to meet student demands, and to reopen the Sorbonne. Nevertheless, students undertook an occupation on the campus and by May 13, more than a million people were marching through Paris with more occupations of the Sorbonne ensuing.

Posters displayed images of Marx, Lenin, and Mao, while Trotsky, Castro, and Che were also celebrated. The red and black flag of anarchy was prominent, but so too was the red and blue Vietcong flag, with its yellow star. Influential as well were Abbie Hoffman and Jerry Rubin's Yippies and the Situationists, a small Parisian group founded eleven years earlier, tied to avant-garde artistry. The Situationists were shaped to a considerable extent by a pair of texts: Guy Debord's *The Society of the Spectacle* and Raoul Vaneigem's *The Revolution of Everyday Life*. The Dutch Provos, who had surged in the mid-1960s, were hardly inconsequential, particularly their playful qualities, mixture of political and cultural radicalism, and deliberately provocative nature.

The next day, workers in Nanterre occupied the factory of Sud-Aviation. An Occupation Committee was elected at the Sorbonne, while slogans flourished asserting, "Power to the imagination" and "Be realistic: Demand the impossible." The spread of the movement led to additional strikes and factory closings, with hundreds of thousands refusing to show up for work. By the evening of May 18, two million French men and women were on strike. By the next day, some one hundred factories were occupied, the railroads were not running, and a general strike, long dreamed of by radicals as a step toward the dissolution of capitalism, beckoned. As of May 21, hundreds of factories were occupied, with workers moving to take over many public buildings. Within two days, ten million workers were striking, and the French economy appeared to be grinding to a halt. Even farmers began displaying solidarity with the protesters. On May 24, President de Gaulle, who had seemed to sink into a severe depression, delivered a not-well-received television address during which he sought a "mandate for renewal and adaption," and was followed by another spate of barricades in Paris, where the Bourse, housing the French stock exchange, was burned down.

However, the apex of the French movement had been reached, as divisions on the left and within trade unions became apparent, preventing the solidarity that might have ensured the collapse of de Gaulle's government, which barely survived a parliamentary vote of no confidence. The French Communist Party vacillated, first refusing to back the demonstrators, then seemingly offering support although condemning what it deemed the ultra-left. The latter it dismissed as amounting to "a petty-bourgeois cocktail of Bakunin, Trotskyism, and plain adventurism," in Caute's words. The powerful communist-led Confédération Générale des Travailleurs generally failed to back the striking students and workers. The PSU, headed by François Mitterand, hoped to replace de Gaulle's rule with a Popular Front–style government. By contrast, the Confédération Française Démocratique du Travail, notwithstanding its Roman Catholic origins, was led by Andre Barjoinet, who asserted at the height of the demonstrations, "Today, revolution is possible." The Force Ouvrière, which was closer to the Socialist Party, also proved more supportive.

As organizational forces tied to the parliamentary left pondered what steps to take next, however, de Gaulle became reenergized and spoke again on television, indicating on May 30 that elections would be called shortly. He urged "civic action" to prevent subversion and "totalitarian communism" from prevailing. A newly constituted government outlawed street demonstrations, along with several student groups, and expelled foreign student activists. Cohn-Bendit had already been deported (although he returned in late May). Occupations and strikes ceased, while the general election produced a resounding triumph for de Gaulle and Pompidou. Left in the wake was the spirit of '68, with a number of those influenced later making their mark in French cultural, literary, intellectual, and political circles. Radith Geismar, who was involved with the Paris movement, recalled the emancipatory aspects of 1968, the "tremendous sense of liberation, of freedom," of "a whole system of order and authority and tradition" being "swept aside."

Maoism retained its hold on some for a period, but that soon dissipated. What did not appear in France in the same way it would in Germany and Italy, or even the United States, was the kind of hard left turn that led to the appearance of the Baader-Meinhof gang, the Red Brigades, and Weatherman, all drawn to the old idea of propaganda of the deed with their resort to terrorism and attempts to violently disrupt their societies from within.

Fidel Castro's prediction that guerrilla activity would surge in 1968 proved prescient, but only to a certain degree. The year began with the Vietnamese insurgency dramatically intensifying, but the Chinese Cultural Revolution was actually waning, its violent, disruptive nature compelling Mao to employ the People's Army to push back to ensure matters didn't get out of hand altogether. Elsewhere, guerrilla forces were germinating or continuing campaigns, in Asia, Africa, Latin America, and the Middle East. What was surprising was that the invoking of revolution occurred where it did: in Europe and the United States. Stephen Spender's early encapsulation of 1968 as "The Year of the Young Rebels" proved more accurate, as students, workers, and intellectuals, the same groups Marx had viewed as most drawn to the cause of revolution, demanded change and change of a dramatic sort. Troubled by the quixotic nature of some of those young rebels, Spender most appreciated the activists involved in the Prague Spring, who were striving for fundamental freedoms. In Czechoslovakia, the possibility was again tendered, as it had been in Hungary a dozen years earlier, of fusing socialism and democracy. In France, a dreamy sensibility with anarchist tinges seemed to propel many of the young rebels, but those visionary possibilities quickly became blunted, even among "68ers."

"Burn, Baby, Burn"

Bearing Witness and the Boston Five

Two women and seven men, participants in what soon would be called the Ultra-Resistance, engaged in a new, revolutionary-styled protest on May 17, 1968, targeting the US Selective Service System, considered the bane of existence for so many young Americans. They went inside the Selective Services offices located in Catonsville, Maryland, and proceed to confiscate hundreds of draft records. The nine individuals, all Catholics, and including the activist priests Daniel Berrigan, forty-seven, and his brother Philip, three years younger, carried the files out to the parking lot where they poured homemade napalm over the records before igniting them. As the files began melting down, the demonstrators explained their protest to the media and "prayed for peace." In the fashion of Henry David Thoreau and practitioners of the civil disobedience he extolled, they accepted the fact that arrest awaited them. Following questioning, they were driven to the Baltimore county jail, then refused bail and undertook an eight-day fast before being released. The group came to be known as the Catonsville Nine, and acquired celebrity within the anti-war movement and the New Left.

A clerk, Phyllis Morsberger, explained that she had "thought something was wrong," but was unable to call police, having been restrained by two of the demonstrators. But a maintenance worker heard Morsberger cry out, and he phoned the police, who came upon the protesters praying as the files burned. As a policeman asked, "Who's responsible for this?" one individual expressed his desire "to make it more difficult for men to kill each other," and another explained, "We do this because everything else has failed."

Figure 7.1 Supporters of Muhammad Ali observe a man burning his draft card in Houston, Texas. Draft resisters ranged from Resistance leader David Harris, the former Stanford University student body president, to boxer Muhammad Ali, whose heavyweight title was stripped because of his refusal to be inducted into the US Army. Supporters included members of the Ultra-Resistance, which conducted raids on draft board offices. Library of Congress, Prints and Photographs Division, LC-USZ62-115786.

The group handed out a prepared statement, largely penned by Philip F. Berrigan, which indicated, "We shed our blood willingly and gratefully in what we hope is a sacrificial and constructive act. We pour it upon these files to illustrate that with them and with these offices begins the pitiful waste of American and Vietnamese blood 10,000 miles away." After urging friends in the anti-war and civil rights movements to join in moving "from dissent to resistance," the group sought divine mercy and patience, expressing hope that God will employ "our witness for his blessed designs." The statement also explained that napalm had been employed as it "burned people to death in Vietnam, Guatemala, and Peru, and" might be directed at ghettoes in the United States. As for the destroyed records, Berrigan and his compatriots explained that "some property has no right to exist." Influenced by an encyclical, issued the previous year by Pope Paul VI, which condemned exploitative colonialism, maldistribution of wealth, and warfare, the Catonsville Nine indicated, "We are Catholic Christians who take our faith seriously."

Explaining their action, Daniel Berrigan later wrote, "Our apologies, good friends, for the fracture of good order, the burning of paper instead of children, the angering of the orderlies in the front parlor of the charnel house. We could not, so help us God, do otherwise. For we are sick at heart, our hearts give us no rest for thinking of the Land of Burning Children." Berrigan noted that he and his compatriots acted as they had while the Poor People's March was taking place, with the government planning to engage in increasingly "massive paramilitary means to" stave off urban disorder. The federal government considered the threat so serious that it initially intended to rely on battle-hardened troops, back from Vietnam. Thus the conflagration overseas was increasingly being "brought home," Berrigan warned. But those engaged in the burning of draft cards records determined to "resist and protest this crime," while seeking common cause with their "brothers" across the globe—the indigent, the Vietnamese, and soldiers too, who were ordered to "kill and die, for the wrong reasons, for no reason at all." Philip Berrigan's "Letter from a Baltimore Jail" criticized those unhappy with the practice of civil disobedience and the adoption of radical tactics by priests, who, along with their colleagues, had "experienced intimately the uselessness of legitimate dissent."

Another participant, the anti-war activist George Mische, who had left his job working for the Alliance for Progress due to his anger over US backing of Latin American juntas, also later wrote about the Catonsville Nine. He indicated that the group included, in addition to three priests, two brothers, a nun, and three laypeople. They possessed international experience, having worked in Latin America or Africa, but had also served the poor at home. They took to heart Vatican II and President Kennedy's exalting of public service. Catholics all, they considered it important to take a stand against the Vietnam War, as barely one percent of American bishops had done. Mische was among those particularly disturbed by Cardinal Francis Spellman, the nation's best known bishop, who was a vocal supporter of the war, to the extent of blessing B-52 bombers that pulverized the Vietnamese countryside.

One other member of the Catonsville Nine, "the very fiery" Mary Moylan, a certified nurse and midwife, considered herself "too Irish to be a pacifist." She regarded the American political system as effectively broken, and was influenced by the radical Colombian priest Camilio Torres Restrepo, who had died two years earlier fighting side-by-side with guerrilla forces. Like Philip Berrigan, Moylan believed "you can't play your game by their rules," consequently favoring sharper means of protest.

The protest by the Catonsville Nine would be condemned by supporters of the war, but also by those within the anti-war camp who viewed their approach as too radical. By contrast, many in the Movement viewed them as heroic, as speaking truth to power in previously scarcely imagined fashion. Their consciously illegal operation was intended to call attention to the horrors being committed overseas, and by providing support for the young men who made up the Resistance, many of them unknowingly. The zeitgeist, tied to the era but connected to the anti-war movement more specifically, clearly helped to shape the activists who deliberately broke the law by grabbing draft card records and then setting them afire.

In addition to the general temper of the times, important too were the changes that the Catholic Church had undergone, which many felt were essential in order that it remain viable and meaningful to the committed young. Particularly significant were the reforms associated with the Second Vatican Council, Vatican II, called by John XXIII during his abbreviated papacy (1958–1963). Vatican II urged congregants to be actively engaged, and delivered the message that the church was connected to the modern world. Contesting centuries of anti-Semitism that afflicted the Catholic Church, Vatican II attested to the church's own Jewish roots and covenant with the Lord. Vatican II also emphasized the ideal of religious liberty, condemned civil discrimination rooted in religious strictures, and praised "loyalty to conscience." The historian Garry Wills suggests that Vatican II spurred American Catholics to engage in social and political activism. Yet actual reform within the Church, like that inside American society, continued to be "unfilled," the historian Shawn Francis Peters indicates.

The changes that John XXIII engendered influenced Daniel, a member of the educationally driven Jesuit order, and Philip Berrigan, tied to the Josephites, founded to assist black Catholics, each of whom had already displayed a propensity toward social activism. Both were drawn to the civil rights and anti-war movements, and would be associated with the loose conglomeration known as the Catholic Left. Its participants, Berrigan biographers Murray Polner and Jim O'Grady offer, drew sustenance more from Jesus than from either the American revolutionaries or more modern zealots.

While engaged in seminary work in France in the early 1950s, Daniel encountered "worker-priests," like those who bore witness against Nazism, now charged by traditional church members with possessing communist and revolutionary sympathies. Intellectual influences included the medieval theologian Thomas Aquinas and the French Jesuit priests Henri-Marie de Lubac and Pierre Teilhard de Chardin. A supporter of the Resistance and a fierce critic of anti-Semitism, de Lubac believed in "the struggle for human freedom" and the Church's responsibility to humanity, helping set the stage for the Second Vatican Council. A paleontologist and philosopher who suffered "near-captivity" in Beijing throughout World War II, Teilhard believed man was continually evolving, and attempted to fit together Christian doctrine and modern science. He emphasized humankind's eventual socialization, which would ultimately lead to God. Both Daniel and Philip were also drawn to the Trappist monk Thomas Merton, and his acclaimed autobiography, *The Seven Storey Mountain*. Daniel eventually came to view Merton as both "the conscience of the peace movement of the 1960s" and a firm backer of the nonviolent civil rights campaign.

Attaining a professorship at first Syracuse University and then Cornell, Daniel Berrigan encouraged students to assist CORE in its campaigns in the South, and together with Phil, attempted to participate in a freedom ride, a request turned down by their superiors. During a year of travel abroad in the early sixties, Daniel met up with French Jesuits distressed about US engagement in Indochina. By the time he returned to the States, Daniel was certain the conflict "could only grow worse." Consequently, he started, "as loudly as I could, to say 'no' to the war." Daniel helped to establish both the Catholic Peace Fellowship, which was tied to the Fellowship of Reconciliation, one of the longest-lasting pacifist organizations, and CALCAV, and he knew Roger La Porte, a twenty-two-year-old opponent of the Vietnam War, who engaged in self-immolation in November 1965. After Daniel offered words at a funeral service for La Porte and in the wake of the draft card burning by Berrigan's former student David Miller, Cardinal Francis Spellman evidently convinced the Jesuits to order Berrigan to conduct a "fact-finding" mission in Latin America. That endeavor ended within three months, due to pressure from liberals within the church, outraged at what they deemed a violation of freedom of conscience. *Commonweal* slammed Berrigan's forced exile as "a shame and a scandal, a disgustingly blind totalitarian act, a travesty on

Vatican II." During the March on the Pentagon, Berrigan was among those arrested.

He and the radical historian Howard Zinn traveled to Hanoi in early 1968, where they helped to facilitate release of three American prisoners of war. When American bombs fell, the travelers waited in a bomb shelter in North Vietnam's capital city, as Berrigan explained in *Night Flight to Hanoi* (1968). Arriving back in the United States, Berrigan and Zinn quickly accused the US government of "inept and cold-blooded mishandling" of the release. The American Ambassador to Laos, William H. Sullivan, had demanded the pilots fly from that Southeast Asian country in a military plane, in violation of the apparent agreement with the North Vietnamese. Berrigan and Zinn worried the decision would prevent other captured Americans from being freed. The government contested the charges.

In late March, Daniel Berrigan, David Dellinger, Tom Hayden, Linda Morse of the Student Mobilization Committee to End the War in Vietnam (Student Mobe), and William F. Pepper served as sponsors for a conference called to devise an orchestrated anti-war operation during the election cycle. Discussion occurred about how to respond to the Democratic National Convention, particularly whether to disrupt it. Among those urging such an approach was former SDS leader Rennie Davis, who headed the Center for Radical Research in Chicago.

A veteran of the Battle of the Bulge, Philip Berrigan became influenced by the Catholic Worker Movement and its cofounder, Dorothy Day, who was concerned about both social justice and peace. A member of the Josephite order, Philip, like his Jesuit brother, came to displease his superiors, who transferred him from Washington, DC, then New Orleans, and finally Newburgh, New York, owing to his involvement in civil rights activities. While in Louisiana, Philip was greatly affected by both "the bigotry of white Americans" and the Cuban missile crisis. Serving in Newburgh, his passionate attacks on injustice and the Vietnam War again resulted in a new posting. Before that transpired, both Philip and Daniel were befriended by Thomas Merton, who was considered, along with the Catholic Workers' Dorothy Day, "the most prominent voice for peace in the Catholic Church." In late 1964, Merton asked the Berrigans to participate in a retreat, also attended by A. J. Muste, at the Gethsemani Abbey in Kentucky, highlighting "Spiritual Roots of Protests." A number of participants soon established faith-rooted anti-war groups, including the Catholic Peace Fellowship and CALCAV. Following his latest transfer, Philip quickly established the Baltimore Interfaith Peace Mission, which picketed the residences of Robert McNamara and Dean Rusk in late 1966. Frustration regarding the effectiveness of that kind of protest, however, led members of the organization to opt for more confrontational tactics.

By 1967, a number of American Catholics, like the Berrigan brothers, had joined the ranks of the anti-war movement. Such a stance was in keeping with those of Pope Paul VI and prominent Catholics like Notre Dame professor John McKenzie and Robert Drinan, dean of Boston College Law School. For the Berrigans, notwithstanding their appreciation of the role performed by activists in their nation's history, religious concerns continued to prevail, especially the tenet "Do not repay evil with evil; love your enemies." Later, John Deedy, who had edited the liberal Catholic periodical *Commonweal*, deemed the Berrigans "part of an old Catholic story—people of conscience daring to stand against the state in a witness for life and truth." Focusing on institutions of power, they believed in employing nonviolence creatively.

That same year, Philip Berrigan, increasingly infuriated about the war and determined to make a difference, joined with three others in bearing witness at the Baltimore Customs House. There, the Baltimore Four, as the four activists came to be known, tossed blood, from a duck and their own, onto draft records, declaring they sought to condemn the shedding of human blood in Indochina. The protesters then stated, "We charge that America would rather protect its empire of overseas profits than welcome its black people, rebuild its slums and cleanse its air and water." The four men quoted freely from Henry David Thoreau's manifesto, "Civil Disobedience," deeming its message applicable due to the horrific acts carried out in Southeast Asia. They urged others "to continue moving with us from dissent to resistance," and expressed a readiness to await prosecution. Once again, higher-ups within the Catholic Church conveyed displeasure with a Berrigan brother's politically charged action. The Baltimore Archdiocese termed Father Berrigan's draft card defiling self-defeating, and said it might be viewed "as disorderly, aggressive and extreme," while alienating many desirous "of a just peace." Meanwhile, picketers outside the jail where Berrigan and the artist Thomas Lewis were engaged in a hunger strike referred to them as "political prisoners." On November 7, a federal grand jury indicted the four men involved in the Baltimore Customs House incident, charging them with having damaged government property, destroyed public records, obstructed the Selective Service System, and conspired to violate federal laws.

The Baltimore Four had actually discussed adopting a still more radical approach, indicates Shawn Francis Peters. They thought of blowing up the Baltimore Custom House, where the city's draft records were held. Dissuaded from doing so by Phil Hirschkopf, a progressive attorney they had consulted, they opted instead for his suggestion to throw blood on the draft files. Berrigan initially was quite angry about that proposal, but decided it would enable him and his colleagues "to identify with" those suffering because of the war in Vietnam. Following the Baltimore action, Berrigan reasoned that America required a wake-up call—continuous "social disruption, including nonviolent attacks against the machinery of this war."

In a book that appeared in the late winter, *Protest: Pacifism and Politics: Some Passionate Views on War and Nonviolence*, author James Finn quoted from Philip Berrigan, who indicated, "Peacemaking as a course of both thought and action for the Christian has literally invaded all the areas of human life today. Every human situation, every problem has to be seen in terms of peacemaking or Christian reconciliation." War, racism, and poverty were all threaded together, in Berrigan's estimation. Then on April 3, as Martin Luther King Jr. had returned to support the Memphis sanitation workers' strike, the Resistance spearheaded a third nationally orchestrated draft-card burning. Across the country, 1,000 young men—over 200 in Boston alone, with 15,000 in attendance—submitted their draft cards. The draft resistance movement continued to thrive, but the federal government also remained determined to target those actively engaged in the Resistance, resulting, by year's end, in several hundred being incarcerated. More than 1,000 others had declined to be inducted into the US Armed Forces, subjecting them to possible prosecution.

Also in April, the trial of Father Philip Berrigan, the Reverend James L. Mengel of the United Church of Christ, Thomas Lewis, and David Eberhardt, secretary of the Baltimore Interfaith Peace Mission, took place in United States District Court in Baltimore. The defendants hoped to demonstrate the lesson that should have been learned from the Nuremberg Trials: that individuals could not excuse their role in the commission of atrocities by declaring they had simply been following orders. During his testimony, Berrigan, who had come to believe the Catholic Church should stand "on the side of revolution," acknowledged being "tormented by anger" regarding the Vietnam War's devastation and the need to demonstrate. Arguing that his clients had operated in "the best traditions of American democracy" employing the First Amendment to protest, the defendants' attorney Fred E. Weisgal read from Henry David Thoreau's essay on civil disobedience. The US Attorney for Maryland, Stephen H. Sachs, countered, "American society doesn't permit you to commit a crime if you are sincere or religiously or morally motivated." Having deliberated less than two hours on April 16, the jury reached a guilty verdict. An unrepentant Philip Berrigan urged codefendant Lewis, "Let's do it again," and began planning another action. That one would draw in Daniel, who had previously been reluctant to support, at least fully, his younger brother's revolutionary turn.

The day after the Baltimore Four suffered guilty verdicts, another federal judge, Francis J. W. Ford, ruled against the defendants' contention that the Vietnam War's legality should be taken into consideration in the case of the *United States v. Benjamin Spock* and his codefendants. During pretrial motions, attorney Leonard B. Boudin, representing Dr. Spock, emphasized the war's illegality, and argued therefore that his defendant could not be guilty of conspiring to assist draft registrants in disobeying draft regulations. In the wake of Judge Ford's ruling, the defense attorneys for Spock, William Sloane Coffin Jr., Michael Ferber, Mitchell Goodman, and Marcus Raskin argued that First Amendment protections shielded their clients from prosecution for anti-war activities. At one point, Judge Ford asked Telford Taylor, who had helped to prosecute Nazi war criminals during the Nuremberg Trails following World War II and was serving as a professor at Columbia, "If a defendant believes a law is unconstitutional, that would be an excuse for violating the law?" Individuals should not be prosecuted, Taylor responded, for offering advice about violating laws they deemed unconstitutional. Those who opposed public policies, he went on to say, required publicity and should be granted considerable latitude to employ "symbolic speech" to elicit media coverage.

In an extended analysis in the *New York Times*, legal correspondent Fred Graham bluntly stated that "obvious uneasiness" existed regarding the fact "that so many otherwise law-abiding citizens" were "expressing their views by deliberately breaking the laws." This was apparent in the case of the Boston Five, which included "the world's most famous baby doctor." Graham noted that former Harvard Law School dean Erwin N. Griswold, now solicitor general of the United States, had warned against "indiscriminate civil disobedience." Acknowledging that "a moral right to violate 'unjust laws' " existed, Griswold indicated that nevertheless there existed "no legal right to do so," with those selecting such a method of dissent having to be ready to endure incarceration. Both Griswold and Earl F. Morris, who headed the American Bar Association, insisted that civil disobedience legitimized violence, which had become widespread in the United States. Defendant Raskin, by contrast, recently explained that the Boston Five served as "the focus for dissent when there was nobody else."

As the trial of the Boston Five began, the Ultra-Resistance struck yet again, with the Berrigan brothers and seven accomplices targeting the Selective Service System's offices in Catonsville. Days later, Federal Judge Edward S.

Northrop handed Philip Berrigan and twenty-eight-year-old Thomas P. Lewis six-year sentences, while doling out a sentence half that length to twenty-seven-year-old David Eberhardt, a conscientious objector and ex-teacher who was quickly released on bail. Thirty-eight-year-old James Mengel, a United Church of Christ minister, drew the lengthiest sentence, eighteen years, but received probation and a court order to submit to psychiatric evaluation, which required the "technical maximum sentence." Judge Northrop admonished the defendants: "You have transcended the tolerable limits of civil disobedience. You deliberately set out to use violent means to destroy the very fabric of our society. All of you hide behind words to accomplish your ends—to bring down this society." When the bailiffs escorted off Berrigan and Lewis, cries rang out, "'Justice,' 'Uncle Tom,' and 'Where's the gas chamber?'" An unrepentant Berrigan dismissed those who criticized him and Lewis as "'irresponsible' or 'untrustworthy.'"

Many fretted about the sentences Judge Northrop had delivered, with the *Boston Globe* bemoaning the fact that Berrigan and Lewis had been treated more harshly than "convicted thugs and murderers." A deeply troubled Dorothy Day informed Daniel Berrigan she was astonished "by these harsh sentences," and had become "convinced that sooner or later we are all going to end up in a concentration camp." Still, she was disturbed by the tactics the Berrigans and their colleagues used, and insisted, "We must hang on to our pacifism in the face of all violence." Thomas Merton also worried about the turn to attacking property, fearing it could lead to individuals being hurt or killed. He expressed concerns about participating in "a fake revolution" that attracted individuals ready to engage in "absurd and irrational" acts "simply to mess things up." Merton, who like Day wondered if he too would end up behind bars, believed that the Catonsville action "frightened more than it has edified."

Censured by the Archbishop of Baltimore, Lawrence Cardinal Shehan, Berrigan was also prohibited from delivering Mass in public, preaching, or taking confessions. The Archbishop explained, "I cannot condone and do not condone the damaging of property or the intimidation of government employees." Shehan, who had recently emphasized the "patriotic duties of American Catholics," then indicated that US soldiers should view "themselves as agents of security and freedom." He had, at the same time, supported the right to conscientious objection and demanded the Vietnam War be conducted in a "morally acceptable way," Polner and O'Grady indicate.

More than a year would pass before Francine du Plessix Gray, writing in *The New York Review of Books*, labeled opponents of conscription willing to employ a heightened form of direct action "the Ultra-Resistance." She referred to both the Baltimore Four and the Catonsville Nine, and explained

who made up this new facet of the anti-draft movement and how they determined to act.

> Men and women who believe they have exhausted every other means of protesting
> the Vietnam War raid a draft board, haul out records and burn them, stand around
> singing liberation songs while awaiting arrest. The draft board actions have elements
> of both terrorist strike and liturgical drama. They aim to destruct and to instruct; to
> impede in some small way the war machine; to communicate its evil, at a time
> when verbal and political methods have failed, by a morality play which will startle,
> embarrass the community; to shame the Movement to heightened militancy, perhaps
> to imitation.

Du Plessix Gray indicated that members of the Ultra-Resistance were offering witness in their own fashion, exemplifying "sacrifice and penance . . .
moral primitivism . . . romantic egoism . . . psychological violence."

The response within the Movement to those who were part of the Ultra-
Resistance was mixed. As David Dowd informed Tom Wells, the Berrigans
had "established a model of action which is too heroic to suggest *effective*
steps to ordinary people." But their readiness to risk both their livelihoods,
which in their case involved a calling, and their freedom, appealed to many,
who were, nevertheless, unwilling to replicate their actions. Thus, the
responses to the Resistance and the Ultra-Resistance were similar, with more
admiring them from afar than joining these movements. Had more done so,
the Berrigans might have accomplished what they sought to: obstructing the
war effort.

Meanwhile, the trials of the Boston Five and David Harris, one of the
founders of the Resistance, proceeded apace. On March 26, Harris married
folk singer Joan Baez, who had helped to establish the Institute for the Study
of Nonviolence in Carmel. Baez, along with her sisters Pauline and Mimi,
would appear on a poster in 1968 celebrating the Resistance. Looking demure
with hats on, they sat on a coach with the statement, "GIRLS SAY YES to
boys who say NO," placed above their heads," intended to refute the notion
that draft resisters were unmanly, in some manner. Emphasizing nonviolent
protests rather than her previously thriving musical career, Baez saw Harris
as "Mr. Draft Resistance." Staughton Lynd and Michael Ferber, in their
account of the Resistance, consider Harris its most important figure, helping
to shape its approach and the potency of its message. Harris refused to allow
his attorney to fight his prosecution on technical grounds, believing such an
approach to be hypocritical. After all, he had traveled around the country
urging others to refuse to go along with the Selective Service System and be
willing to suffer the consequences. He had declined to carry his draft card or
to report for duty, both violations of the Selective Service Act. A federal

grand jury delivered an indictment, charging Harris with having declined "to submit to a lawful order of induction." His friend, Dennis Sweeney, a cofounder of the Resistance, had attempted to dissuade Harris from going to jail, warning that he would just become a martyr and ensure that the Resistance collapsed.

The trial began on May 27 in federal court, as Harris appeared with Baez on his arm, and press coverage abundant. Local anti-war and Resistance members, like Sweeney, were present. The judge disallowed testimony regarding the Vietnam War, US foreign policy, the anti-war movement, and the Resistance. Harris did testify for about ninety minutes, during which he admitted to having spoken of tearing the induction center down. "That building is a symbol to me. It is a symbol of death and oppression." Asserting that people had been forced to "live in a politics of fear," Harris called for fighting back against that. "Each of us," he said, "is a seed for the liberation of mankind."

Harris indicated that he accepted the jury's verdict. But he also expressed belief that history "would judge the law . . . guilty," and he contended that his "only crime had been not to commit an even greater crime." The judge allowed that Harris was "motivated by the highest motives, and as such he makes a very outstanding performance, and therefore it's a very difficult thing to find Mr. Harris a criminal under the circumstances. . . . I think he believes in what he is doing, and I think that stems from what he believes to be high motives. I respect him for it. I say so publicly." However, the judge also lectured the defendant: "You have made [this decision], and let it be said that you made it, no one else. . . . You were going to be here or in some other court in this kind of situation, if I may use a term, come hell or high water." Ignoring a joke that Harris attempted, the judge declared that rehabilitation would serve no purpose in this instance "because you don't have to be rehabilitated and you don't want to be rehabilitated and you won't be rehabilitated." Thus, the only purpose for the sentence he was about to impose, the judge admitted, was "punitive" to Harris personally and a warning to others. "It has to be as stark and real and just as hard and tough as you are." Harris was handed a three-year sentence, double that meted out to other draft refusers in the Northern District of California. After pointing out that Harris had spoken repeatedly "about a new world," the judge stated, "Well, I'd like to see it. One thing I'm sure of, it will have to have order, and you can't have order if you break any law you don't like."

As the case of the Boston Five went on, leading pediatricians in that city expressed support for one of the defendants, Dr. Spock, promising in fact to continue backing his peace efforts. They paid for advertisements appearing in leading Boston newspapers that read, "We proudly support our colleague

Dr. Benjamin Spock. We are inspired by his courage as a physician and a citizen." But in the federal courtroom in Boston where the trial took place, thirty-six-year-old Assistant US Attorney John Wall, a Korean War veteran and former paratrooper, dispassionately presented the prosecution's case, quoting from Dr. Spock's conversation with FBI agents during which he stated, "I'll give you evidence that will hang myself." Spock informed the agents he viewed the Vietnam conflict as "immoral and illegal," and intended to "hinder the United States prosecution of the war." He spoke to the agents about having participated in the anti-draft protest at the Whitehall Street induction center the previous December. That action he viewed as merely "symbolic" but reasoned that if it resulted in "young men refusing to be drafted, that would have served my purpose," Spock explained. Conveying a readiness to violate "laws that are contrary to the laws of humanity," he admitted, "If the government were to prosecute me, I'd be delighted." Spock went on to say that if young resisters were being arrested, he should be as well for having "done everything he could to abet" draft resistance.

The first prosecution witness, an FBI agent, referred to the document "A Call to Resist Illegitimate Authority." The jury watched a television film displaying draft cards being burned at Boston's Arlington Street Unitarian Church during the fall. The film contained a scene of the defendant William Sloane Coffin Jr. shaking hands with young men who had set their draft cards on the flame of a tall candle. It also displayed another defendant, Michael Ferber, offering the sermon in which he declared there was "a time to say no" and also referred to "an impulse to purification and martyrdom." Another film presented a news conference two weeks before the March on the Pentagon, in which all defendants were present except for Ferber. Dr. Spock was shown on film footage by ABC News, attacking the Johnson administration's escalation of the war and admitting, "I don't want to be arrested, but I'll do anything I can to oppose the war." Coffin was seen urging churches be used as sanctuaries for draft resisters, and pointing out that if the police grabbed those young men the nation's "moral bankruptcy" would be displayed.

Subsequently, John R. McDonough, assistant deputy to Attorney General Ramsey Clark, testified how Dr. Spock, Reverend Coffin, Mitchell Goodman, and Marcus Raskin all "invited arrest" when they carried a zipper bag—soon introduced into evidence—filled with draft cards to the Justice Department during Stop the Draft Week. As he continued to follow the trial, Homer Bigart, a top reporter with the *New York Times*, indicated this was "the major 'overt act'" purportedly committed by Spock as part of a purported conspiracy to induce draft resistance. The defense, for its part, argued that the defendants were engaged in a type of constitutionally protected "symbolic speech." Leonard Boudin also attempted to prove that New York Mayor John Lindsay and the city's police department had allowed Dr. Spock to "stage a symbolic disruption of the Selective Service machinery" when he sat in front of the Whitehall Street induction center. His arrest, Boudin argued, was designed to convince young people to remain nonviolent during demonstrations against the Vietnam War and conscription. Reverend Coffin emphatically declared that his involvement in the attempt to turn over draft cards to the Justice Department was intended "to precipitate a test case, to challenge the government to a moral confrontation." Encountering a fierce cross-examination, Coffin insisted he had not wanted to convince others to turn over their draft cards, although he recognized an "outside chance" existed that would happen. Dismissing the idea of a conspiracy, Goodman testified instead that the demonstration at the Justice Department involved "rank amateurs." Deeming the war illegal and immoral, and claiming that the United States was employing "violence as a spearhead," Raskin denied any connection with a campaign to spur draft resistance. During his testimony, Dr. Spock explained how he strongly believed his nation had relinquished its standing as leader of the Free World and was presently "despised" around the globe by many who previously looked up to it. He asked, "What's the use of a physician like myself in helping to bring up children to be killed in a cause which is ignoble?" During cross-examination, Spock admitted, "I would be glad if half a million men in the Army and Navy would decide the war is illegal and refuse to obey orders, but I would not advocate it."

The *New York Times'* Fred Graham discussed the defendants' reliance on the theory of symbolic speech. In a recent case involving draft card burning, *United States v. O'Brien*, Chief Justice Earl Warren declared that the judicial brethren could not accept the notion "that an apparently limitless variety of conduct be labeled 'speech' whenever the person engaging in the conduct intends thereby to express an idea." Graham referred to Phillip Berrigan's unsuccessful reliance on the concept of symbolic speech in the case involving the Baltimore Four. Chief Justice Warren wrote that seeming "acts of dissent" could result in prosecution if the government possessed "an important or substantial and constitutional interest in forbidding them, if the incidental restriction on expression is no greater than necessary, and if the government's real interest is not to squelch dissent."

On June 14, in delivering jury instructions, Judge Ford declared, "We are not trying the legality, morality, or constitutionality of the war in Vietnam or the rights of a citizen to protest." Instead, the question to be decided was whether the defendants had "knowingly and willingly conspired." The jury delivered guilty verdicts against Dr. Spock, Reverend Coffin, Michael Ferber, and Mitchell Goodman, on the charge of having conspired to induce draft evasion. Marcus Raskin was declared not guilty. Spock responded: "My main

defense was I believed a citizen must work against a war he considers contrary to international law." Coffin expressed delight with the verdict involving
Raskin, calling it "a real victory for the First Amendment."

A *New York Times* editorial deemed the convicted defendants worthy of
"respect for having had the courage to risk jail in defense of their belief that
they should aid youths unwilling to fight under compulsion in a war they
hated." But the writer and former assistant US attorney Sidney E. Zion indicated that some in the anti-war movement were expressing dismay about the
legal tactics employed by the Boston Five defendants. Many complained that
the defendants had "copped out," favoring a legalistic approach instead of
the long hoped for "moral confrontation with the government over the legitimacy of the Vietnam War." The defendants, one critic complained, "should
have thunderously denounced the war and said it was their legal right and
moral obligation to urge all kids to stay the hell out."

On July 10, Judge Ford announced two-year sentences for the four individuals recently convicted of having conspired to abet draft evasion. Additionally, he imposed $5,000 fines on Dr. Spock, Reverend Coffin, and Mitchell
Goodman, and a $1,000 fine on Michael Ferber. Prior to delivering the sen-
tences, Judge Ford lectured the defendants: "Where law and order stops, obviously anarchy begins." Noting that each week young men were receiving
three-year sentences for draft evasion, he deemed it reasonable to determine
that the defendants had induced "some of these men to flout the law." Ford
went on to declare, "Be they high or low, intellectuals as well as others must
be deterred from violating the law. These defendants should not escape under
the guise of free speech." While Spock and Coffin declined to speak, Ferber
expressed "no regrets" and denied belonging to a conspiracy, stating that
instead he was part of "a movement by my own generation for love of our
country and what it might become." He pledged, "I will not leave that movement. I will remain working in it." Goodman explained he felt it incumbent,
at least in part, to oppose conscription as young men had "grown up in the
strangest and most awful period of our history." Later, Spock stated, "I am
not convinced I broke any law," and pledged to continue with his anti-war
activities. He also warned, "Wake up, America! Wake up before it's too late!
Do something now!" Coffin insisted "those conscientiously refusing induction must find the courage they need and the support they deserve."

On July 11, the *New York Times* contained a celebratory article, "Pediatrician to the World," which indicated that until his unabated anti-war position
alienated some of his countrymen, Dr. Spock was viewed "in a class with
Babe Ruth and Will Rogers as" an American folk hero. The essay noted that
The Common Sense Book of Baby and Child Care, initially published by

Spock in 1946, had sold over twenty-one million copies, with a third revision impending. Presently, "the 'Spock-reared' generation" had come of age, while a favorite comment heard on "the cocktail circuit" indicated, "Well, Spock trained them, and now he's their leader."

Later in the year, the trial of the Catonsville Nine would take place in Baltimore. William F. Kunstler, one of the defense attorneys, acknowledged that the Nine had no faith in the American judicial process. He compared the present trial to the persecutions of both Socrates and Jesus. The trial, the prosecution insisted, did not involve the war or the political views of the defendants, but rather the willful destruction of government documents and interference with the Selective Service System. Arthur G. Murphy, the First Assistant United States Attorney serving as prosecutor, did not contest the argument that a reasonable person could contend the Vietnam War was illegal or immoral, but deemed that irrelevant to the case at hand. After deliberating for only eighty minutes, the jury found all nine defendants guilty. A spectator cried out, "Members of the jury, you have just found Jesus guilty." While acknowledging having been moved by the defendants' views and being desirous of an end to the war, Chief Judge Roszel C. Thomsen stated, "People can't take the law into their own hands." The federal judge issued sentences that varied from two to three and a half years, with both Philip and Daniel Berrigan receiving among the heaviest sentences. Deeming the trial experience "extraordinary for many," Daniel said, "For the nine of us, it was an opportunity without parallel; to 'give evidence' for our lives, to unite with the hundreds in the streets and the millions across the world who are also saying 'no' to death as a social method."

The Resistance, which Dr. Spock and his colleagues supported, and the Ultra-Resistance, featuring the Berrigan brothers and very few others, provided heroic models for those within the Movement. They involved the offering of witness in different ways, but each exposed participants to potential risk in terms of legal liability and sometimes public vilification. It took courage to contest the Cold War culture still prevailing in the United States, the heralding of military service, and the expectation that all men capable of doing so would join their nation's armed forces. An anti-militaristic, anti-war strand also existed in American history, but it had generally been overwhelmed by the widely accepted belief in military service to one's community or nation. Those holding the reins of power by the end of the 1960s were often veterans of the Good War, as Studs Terkel had called World War II, or the Korean conflict. They expected their children would serve when called on, although a fair number themselves became disenchanted with US foreign policy, particularly as American engagement in Vietnam continued.

Various members of the Resistance and the Ultra-Resistance drew on the life and purported thought of Jesus Christ, the effective extolling of conscientious objectors by Henry David Thoreau, the pacifism of peace sects and the great Russian writer Leo Tolstoy, and the anti-militarism of William James, Mark Twain, and Eugene Debs. They also looked to the storied anti-war history of A. J. Muste; Mahatma Gandhi's civil disobedience marches, fasts, and protests; and the practice of nonviolent direct action by World War II draft resisters, anti-nuclear advocates, and civil rights activists like Martin Luther King Jr., John Lewis, and Bob Moses. But notwithstanding such a rich heritage, Resistance and Ultra-Resistance activists still weathered ridicule, ostracism, dismissal as fanatics, and prosecution at the hands of US attorneys. Once again, the federal government turned to the theory of conspiracy to target key participants in these movements within the larger anti-war campaign and the New Left, intending to deliver a scathing warning by way of indictments, prosecution, and incarceration of a select number of leading Resistance and Ultra-Resistance figures. More conspiracy trials would follow.

8

"You Say You Want a Revolution"

Radical Politics and the Counterculture

During the summer of 1968, the American counterculture increasingly grappled with the possibility of revolution. Appropriately enough, discussion of wholesale social and political transformation, as exemplified by the invoking of revolutionary theoreticians or street fighting, cropped up in songs by leading rock musicians. John Lennon, long viewed as the most intellectually inclined member of the Beatles, penned "Revolution," the different versions of which seemed an attempt to dissuade others from going down such a path or at least that of a violent variety. To some at least, the Rolling Stones' Mick Jagger and Keith Richards appeared more in tune with changing political sensibilities on the political left, singing about the need to be "a street fighting man."

In the original version of "Revolution," recorded in early July at Apple Studios, located at 94 Baker Street in Marylebone, London, Lennon spoke to those who favored revolution: a growing number of young people and others associated with various aspects of the Movement and the counterculture. He gently responded that "We all"—clearly referring to political activists and socially conscious hippies—desired to "change the world." Like those who believed this was the natural course of events, Lennon again also conveyed support for social, political, and cultural transformation. But he refused to go along with those who opted for violence, suggesting instead that everything would work out, eventually. He also questioned individuals with a specific goal in mind, and he expressed a desire "to see the plan." Regarding the providing of financial support for the cause, Lennon indicated that he and his

137

Figure 8.1   Allen Ginsberg, Timothy Leary, and Ralph Metzner standing in front of a plaster Buddha preparing for a "psychedelic celebration" at the Village Theater. Facets of the counterculture appeared increasingly politicized, with the Beatles singing about "Revolution" and the Rolling Stones praising the "Street Fighting Man." Library of Congress, Prints and Photographs Division, LC-USZ62-119239.

ilk were already offering what they could but refused to assist those "with minds that hate." Even the notion of constitutional or institutional change he found questionable, declaring it was necessary to alter people's heads and free their minds instead. As for those heading down the path that a number of young people were, whether in Paris or the United States, expressing belief in Maoism, they "ain't gonna make it with anyone, anyhow," Lennon warned.

In contrast to the softly delivered, somewhat drawn out initial recording of "Revolution," the cadence of Jagger and Richards's "Street Fighting Man" was virtually martial in nature, while the lyrics were in keeping with the desire of an increasing number of young people to act now. Influenced by Martha and the Vandellas' spirited "Dancing in the Streets" and recorded in London shortly after the clash between anti-war demonstrations and riot police in the posh Mayfair district near the US ambassador's residence, the song opened with the narrator indicating he could hear "the sound of marching, charging feet, boy." That was followed by the offering that summer had arrived "and the time is right for fighting in the streets, boy." Then, a wry comment was added about what could "a poor boy" do other than perform in "a rock 'n' roll band." That was the case as "sleepy London" afforded no means "for a street fighting man." Nevertheless, Jagger and Richards went on to acknowledge that the timing was auspicious "for a palace revolution," rather than socially acceptable compromise. After repeating the refrain about the quiet English city, they declared the narrator's name to be "disturbance," ready to engage in regicide and to attack those who did the king's bidding.

The Movement and the Vietnam War provided the backdrop to the gestation of the two songs. Remarkably the B side to "Hey Jude," "Revolution" served as Lennon's answer to the call for dramatic social and political upheaval made by self-professed revolutionaries in the West. Written while the Beatles were in India studying mediation under Maharishi Mahesh Yogi, the song was an expression of Lennon's thoughts regarding revolution and the Vietnam War. Earlier, their manager Brian Epstein, who died the previous summer, had precluded their speaking out on political issues. But during one of their last tours in 1966, Lennon decided to express himself.

> I wanted to put out what I felt about revolution. I thought it was time we fucking spoke about it, the same as I thought it was about time we stopped not answering about the Vietnam War. . . . I wanted to say what I thought about revolution. I had been thinking about it up in the hills in India. I still had this "God will save us" feeling about it, that it's going to be all right. That's why I did it. . . . I wanted to tell you, or whoever listens, to communicate, to say "What do you say?" This is what I say.

Lennon went on to assert, "Count me out if it's for violence. Don't expect me on the barricades unless it's with flowers."

Absent the war, Richards acknowledged, "Street Fighting Man" wouldn't have been produced. Jagger later admitted, "The radio stations that banned the song told me that 'Street Fighting Man' was subversive. Of course it's subversive, we said. It's stupid to think you can start a revolution with a record. I wish you could!" He also recalled, "It was a very strange time in France. But not only in France but also in America, because of the Vietnam War and these endless disruptions." Looking back from the vantage point of nearly three decades, Jagger admitted, "I don't really like it that much. I thought it was a very good thing at the time. There was all this violence going on. I mean, they almost toppled the government in France; de Gaulle went into this complete funk, as he had in the past, and he went and sort of locked himself in his house in the country. And so the government was almost inactive. And the French riot police were amazing. Yeah, it was a direct inspiration, because by contrast, London was very quiet."

The responses in many Movement circles to the two songs could hardly have been more different, with the Stones' take on contemporary developments easily preferred and the Beatles' analysis dismissed as counterrevolutionary. While the establishment press was pleased with Lennon's seeming admonitions regarding revolution, underground publications and New Left spokespersons were less than thrilled, comparing his song unfavorably with "Street Fighting Man." They especially would be displeased with "Revolution 1," which included the line, "Count me out," on the *The Beatles* (the double album also known as *The White Album*), released later in the year. *Ramparts* complained, "'Revolution' is a narcissistic little song . . . that, in these troubled times, preaches counter-revolution" and falsely promised "it's gonna be all right." Michael Wood, in an essay on "Revolution 1" appearing in *Commonweal*, declared that the Beatles were insisting that revolution was not necessary. While admitting that might or might not be correct, Wood nevertheless insisted, "It's an absurd statement, if the Beatles intend it flatly." Writing in the *New Left Review*, Richard Merton assailed "Revolution" as a "lamentable petty bourgeois cry of fear." Rock critic Greil Marcus admitted that "Revolution" was "a wild, shouting song that is so immediate and ecstatic that I find myself singing along as my fingers pound out the beat. The music makes me feel happy even though the lyrics depress me."

By 1968, many in the Movement had come to view the Rolling Stones in a different light than the Beatles, as somehow more authentic and radical, for a variety of reasons. That included well-publicized drug busts that were handled differently than when the Beatles got arrested for dope, as Paul McCartney acknowledged. Jagger's presence during the Grosvenor Square demonstration led some to consider him more of a political activist than he actually was. The nearly simultaneous release of "Revolution" and "Street

Fighting Man" led to inevitable comparisons, with the latter received more favorably by those increasingly inclined to a radical viewpoint. *The New Yorker's* popular music critic Ellen Willis, who had likened Lennon's line "Change your head" to Marie Antoinette's "Let them eat cake," admitted that the lyrics in the Stones' song were "innocuous." But she praised its one loud, clear line, which spoke of summer having arrived and revolution appearing imminent. To Willis, "Mick leaves no doubt where his instincts are."

Lennon proved especially troubled, even angered, by the criticism delivered in *Black Dwarf*, a politically charged underground newspaper published in London and edited by Tariq Ali. One full issue was dedicated to *The Bolivian Diaries* by Che Guevara, while another contained both Jagger's handwritten "Street Fighting Man" and "An Open Letter to John Lennon" from John Hoyland. The latter wrote, "Perhaps now you'll see what it is you're (we're) up against. Not nasty people. Not even neurosis, or spiritual under-nourishment. What we're confronted with is a repressive, vicious, authoritarian system." That system, Hoyland cried out, needed to be "ruthlessly destroyed." Patronizingly, he told Lennon, "Now do you see what was wrong with Revolution? That record was no more revolutionary than Mrs. Dale's Diary." Suggesting that Lennon's music, which he compared unfavorably with the Stones', was lacking its edge, Hoyland urged, "Look at the society we live in and ask yourself: why? And then—come and join us."

To the surprise of *The Black Dwarf* staff, the world's most famous rock musician responded with a letter of his own, addressed to "Dear John." "Your letter didn't sound patronising [sic]—it was. Who do you think you are? What do you think you know? . . . I know what I'm up against—narrow minds—rich/poor." Lennon tossed back a question of his own to Hoyland, "What kind of system do you propose and who would run it?" After declaring, "I don't remember saying that 'Revolution' was revolutionary," he urged Hoyland to listen to all three versions of the song. Continuing, Lennon wrote, "You say: 'In order to change the world we've got to understand what's wrong with the world. And then—destroy it. Ruthlessly.' You're obviously on a destruction kick. I'll tell you what's wrong with the world—people—so do you want to destroy them? Ruthlessly?" Until people's minds were altered, there was "no chance" of anything changing, Lennon again insisted. He asked for a single example of a successful revolution, wondering, "Who fucked up communism—christianity—capitalism—buddhism, etc?" Answering his own query, the Beatle said, "Sick Heads, and nothing else." Hoyland felt compelled to get the last word in, lecturing Lennon in effect. "What makes you so sure that a lot of us haven't changed our heads in something like the way you recommend—and then found it wasn't enough, because we simply cannot be turned on and happy when you know that kids are being roasted to death in Vietnam, when all around you, you see people's individuality being stunted by the system."

While the Beatles and the Rolling Stones were recording *The White Album* and *Beggars Banquet*, which contained "Revolution" and "Street Fighting Man," respectively, other leading rock musicians were demonstrating a trend that proved increasingly apparent as 1968 unfolded. The political activism associated with the Movement and the cultural radicalism exemplified by the counterculture intertwined at various points, including in the rock world itself. Jefferson Airplane, already among rock's aristocracy, having produced anthems for the counterculture, "White Rabbit" and "Somebody to Love," began putting together *Crown of Creation* by the winter of 1968. The title song, written by singer-guitarist Paul Kantner, pointed to the ongoing cultural war, in which "the fossils of our time" and hippies proved mutually intolerant.

Recording their album *Waiting for the Sun*, also during the early months of 1968, the Doors, viewed as countercultural icons thanks to songs like "Break on Through (To the Other Side)", "Light My Fire," and "The End," crafted "The Unknown Soldier." Complete with military cadence, the haunting lyrics by Jim Morrison and his bandmates talked about waiting until the war ended. It referred to media coverage of the Vietnam War, its deadly nature exemplified by a bullet flying into a soldier's helmet, and that "unknown soldier" perishing. Released at the beginning of the year, another anti-war song, The Bob Seger System's "2 + 2 = ?," contained a biting delivery and caustic words. The protagonist was a young man yet "old enough to kill," something he didn't want to do but would if he had to. He recalled a high school friend who was now "buried in the mud / over foreign jungle land," which caused grief for his girlfriend, who failed to understand why. Supposedly that friend had "died for freedom," but the protagonist indicated it was "to save your lies." Finding the system at fault, the non-prophet, non-rebel nevertheless asked a simple question: "Why is it I've got to die?"

Few bands exemplified the growing trend toward fusing aspects of the Movement and the counterculture as well as David Peel & the Lower East Side and the Detroit-based band MC5, managed by John Sinclair. Peel's group rawly delivered his songs, including "I Like Marijuana" and "Here Comes a Cop," and an initial album, *Have a Marijuana*, recorded live on New York City streets. Inspired by the Grateful Dead's managers, Sinclair helped to shape MC5, a ramshackle garage band that lived in The Trans-Love commune in Ann Arbor, Michigan, which had featured a banner, "Burn baby burn," as the previous year's riots tore through the city. The MC5 and Sinclair were, he later indicated, "LSD-Driven Total Maniacs in the Universe." "We were fearfully lunatics. We just didn't give a fuck." Although influenced by Malcolm X and William S. Burroughs, the beat-like poet Sinclair and the MC5 didn't feel connected to traditional labor and left-wing groups. Later in the year, Sinclair established the White Panther Party, which sought to follow the Black Panthers' revolutionary lead.

The previous year had been when the American counterculture began to draw more and more attention from the mainstream media. News accounts related stories about strange young people with long tresses and colorful attire congregating in places like San Francisco's Haight-Ashbury district, while celebrating through such events as the Human Be-In in January, the Monterey Pop Festival in June, and the Death of Hippie during the fall. They seemingly had established a community of like-minded sorts in keeping with the Beatles' latest album, *Sgt. Pepper's Lonely Hearts Club Band*, and underground publications on the order of the *San Francisco Oracle* and *The Rag* (Austin, Texas), and the brand-new *Rolling Stone* magazine. Many older people looked askance at this latest version of an American subculture that dated back generations, particularly because of its association with the seemingly unholy trinity of sex, drugs, and rock 'n' roll.

The American counterculture of the 1960s harked back to antebellum bohemians and artistic rebels, including Edgar Allan Poe and Walt Whitman, and late-nineteenth-century celebrants of alternative lifestyles on the order of Bret Harte and William Dean Howells. The Lyrical left of the early twentieth century, featuring John Reed, Louise Bryant, and Max Eastman, among others, lauded socialism, anarchism, syndicalism, anti-militarism, women's rights, and free love. Black bohemians contributed language, sensuality, hip music, and a wry sensibility. The prewar hipsters also employed jive language and a distinct, "underground" look, while the beats, most notably Jack Kerouac, Allen Ginsberg, Neal Cassady, William Burroughs, and Gary Snyder, contested the seeming verities of America's Cold War culture, looking to the East and Buddhism as counters to the sterility they experienced in Judeo-Christian precepts. They viewed little as sacrosanct, including religion, politics, the work ethic, the nuclear family, marriage, monogamy, education, and, on occasion, Western thought.

A freer, even libertine attitude toward sexuality connected different generations of American bohemians. So did a fondness for music, frequently black-rooted, of an unconventional stripe. Both made participants in the American counterculture controversial. But engendering still greater furor was the proclivity toward drug experimentation, which by the 1960s, involved marijuana and hashish, but also psychedelics—psilocybin, mescaline, and LSD—that resulted in perceptual transformations of a wholesale sort. The idea of "tripping" enthralled many involved in the counterculture, while frightening those outside of it, but it was hardly novel. Famed nineteenth-century British writers, for instance, became enamored of opium. Elizabeth Barrett-Browning, Samuel Taylor Coleridge, Charles Dickens, John Keats, Thomas de Quincy, Percy Bysshe Shelley, and Sir Walter Scott all partook of it, as did fictional protagonists like Sherlock Holmes and Lord Henry (in *The Picture of Dorian Gray*). William James, the famed American philosopher and psychologist, experimented with nitrous oxide intoxication, discussing this in his classic work, *The Varieties of Religious Experience* (1902). He wrote about departing from "normal waking consciousness, rational consciousness," and undergoing an alternate form of consciousness, which resulted in "thought deeper than speech!"

The world of psychedelia underwent a revolution of its own thanks to scientific experiments that involved a Swiss chemist, military operatives, and the CIA. In 1938, Dr. Albert Hoffman, a Swiss research chemist, began synthesizing LSD, which he would resynthesize five years later, leading to what would be known as "Bicycle Day" when he grappled with "dizziness, feeling of anxiety, visual distortions, symptoms of paralysis, desire to laugh." During World War II and its immediate aftermath, US intelligence agents conducted a secret research program intended to concoct a drug that would serve as a truth serum, something the American Armed Forces were also attempting to produce. The CIA carried out Project MKULTRA that led to the dosing of unwitting subjects, one involving the Army biochemist Frank Olson who died after suffering "a psychotic state." Aldous Huxley, who had written the dystopian novel *Brave New World*, experienced a series of psychedelic encounters that led to the publication of *The Doors of Perception* (1954) and *Heaven and Hell* (1956). Huxley would become a foremost psychedelic advocate, although he favored its use only by an artistic and intellectual elite, something that appeared to be happening, or so *Time* magazine indicated in discussing the resorting to LSD by the famed English author, Dr. Hoffman, and Hollywood actor Cary Grant.

Harvard University was soon the latest unintended participant in the incipient psychedelic revolution. There, psychologists Timothy Leary and Richard Alpert headed the Psilocybin Project, which acquired considerable notoriety and, eventually, the disdain of the university administration that fired both for doling out drugs to undergraduate students participating in the project. But the two had joined forces with beat poet Allen Ginsberg, having received encouragement from Huxley, seeking to change the world. Along the way, Ginsberg told Cassady, "We are starting a plot to get everyone in power in America high."

Although Leary believed in a controlled environment in which to partake of psychedelic drugs, there were those at the cutting edge of the American counterculture who thought otherwise, particularly a young novelist from Oregon, Ken Kesey, the best-selling author of *One Flew Over the Cuckoo's Nest*, a fictionalized account of his work in a mental institution while participating in drug experiments tied to the CIA's Project MKULTRA, a mind control program. Kesey and his band of followers, the Merry Pranksters, believed in spreading the gospel according to psychedelics in far less discriminating fashion. The Pranksters hosted a series of Acid Tests on the West Coast, and Kesey's compound in La Honda, California, welcoming all comers, including the bad boys of the American subculture of the early postwar period, the Hell's Angels.

As both Leary and Kesey endured troubles with the law, their role as Pied Pipers of the American counterculture began to be superseded by others, including musicians both homegrown and from abroad. Bob Dylan and the Beatles set the pace, through the delivery of musically and lyrically complex recordings, such as *Another Side of Bob Dylan*, *Bringing It Back Home*, *Highway 61 Revisited*, *Rubber Soul*, *Revolver*, and *Sgt. Pepper's Lonely Hearts Club Band*. All demonstrated sophisticated analyses of personal relationships, as well as the influence of drug usage, including of a psychedelic variety.

Other musicians got caught up in the mania of psychedelia, ranging from The 13th Floor Elevators, out of Austin, Texas, and the Los Angeles–based Byrds and the Doors, featuring lead singer Jim Morrison, to the Bay Area groups, many associated with acid rock. The best included Jefferson Airplane, the Grateful Dead, Quicksilver Messenger Service, and Country Joe and the Fish. The Monterey Pop Festival in June 1967 catapulted Seattle-born Jim Hendrix and Port Arthur, Texas, native Janis Joplin into the national limelight. Helping to spread the gospel of the counterculture were the lyrics and music embedded in the the Byrd's "Eight Miles High," Jefferson Airplane's "White Rabbit," the Doors' "The End," Country Joe's "Not So Sweet Martha Lorraine." From overseas, England contributed Donovan's "Sunshine Superman" and Traffic delivered "Dear Mr. Fantasy."

While sex, drugs, and rock 'n' roll provided lures for participants in the counterculture, a nurturing atmosphere also proved significant. That included enclaves appearing in virtually every major city and around college and university campuses, allowing for Kerouac's earlier prediction that "a great rucksack revolution" would occur, involving "Zen Lunatics" given to artistry and "being kind." Leaping past the beat centers in Venice, North Beach, and Greenwich Village, the hippie revolution of the late 1960s was possible because of a demographic explosion known as the baby boom. It could also take place because of the sheer affluence Western society was both blessed with and cursed by, at least in the minds of some. Corresponding and contributory technological advances likewise ensured that the attire, the ideas, even the language associated with the latest version of the counterculture would spread all but globally, and certainly in richer nations, topped off by the wealthiest of them all. That allowed for a profusion of records, books, and newspapers at least loosely associated with the counterculture.

In places like Haight-Ashbury and Greenwich Village, an entire subculture appeared to be germinating by 1968, one that was viewed as at odds with established institutions, practices, and mores. The hippies in the Haight-Ashbury district even contested the idea of money, trying to establish free outlets for food and clothing. Underground newspapers like the *San Francisco Oracle* and the *Berkeley Barb* exalted the counterculture, which included collectives and communes of various sorts. Radical lawyers and physicians adopted a collective approach, while hippies, well known or not, joined communes located both in urban areas and out in the countryside. Networks, such as the Underground Press Syndicate, attempted to thread together both the Movement and the counterculture, which was never as fully apolitical as many commentators believed. By 1968, when talk of revolution was in the air, it proved to be even less so, as some, like those who called themselves Yippies, sought to unite cultural and political radicalism.

As 1968 opened, the influence of hippies on mainstream society was clearly more pronounced. J. Anthony Lukas, one of the nation's most gifted reporters, kicked off a series of articles in the *New York Times* on drug usage in the United States. He opened by discussing Haight Street, situated in the center of the San Francisco hippie scene, in which an easy turn toward marijuana and hallucinogens had taken place. Lukas wrote of the "consciousness altering" aspects of psilocybin, mescaline, LSD, peyote, and DMT (dimethyltryptamine). As for those who had sworn off LSD, many had turned to meditation, especially in vogue in California and sometimes involving gurus such as Maharishi Mahesh Yogi, who had worked with the Beatles and the actress Mia Farrow. Others had become enamored of methedrine or "speed," which had recently coursed through the Haight-Ashbury community, to devastating effect.

Partially to beat a growing dependency on drugs, John Lennon was among those who turned to transcendental meditation, heading to India in mid-February to work with the Maharishi. The Beatles traveled by train to Rishikesh, situated in the Himalayas in the northern sector of India, accompanied by a group of friends, who included Farrow, and the singers Cilla Black, Mick Jagger, and Marianne Faithfull. Already present were the Beach Boys' Mike Love and English folk singer Donovan. Such a journey to the East appealed to many involved with the counterculture, viewing the region as not riddled with many of the problems confronting Western society. While in India, Lennon, Paul McCartney, and George Harrison wrote many of the songs appearing later that year on *The White Album*.

Meanwhile, the increasingly volatile nature of life in the United States resulted in the politicization of hippies on occasion, something that obviously pleased activists like Abbie Hoffman and Jerry Rubin, who were themselves dramatically impacted by the counterculture. The *Village Voice* edition of March 21 presented an article by Sally Kempton, "Yippies Anti-Organize a Groovy Revolution," quoting from Hoffman, who revealed, "We're not leaders, we're cheerleaders." During meetings, Yippies "laugh a lot," while "there is nearly always someone in the back of the room blowing up balloons," Kempton wrote. Hoffman talked of plans for the Democratic National Convention. "We have two alternatives in Chicago, both of them ok. The opposition determines what will happen, they're living actors in our theater." If tolerated, Kempton continued, the Yippies could offer an alternative lifestyle that would be transmitted nationwide. If not, "then they'll face a bloody scene," compelling Yippies to resort to guerrilla tactics as they conveyed the "message of a brutal society." In an interview conducted by John Wilcox for *Other Scenes*, a just-formed underground newspaper in New York City, Hoffman indicated that television images of young people "racing through the streets yelling and screaming" would lead to "blood, violence, boom."

Behind the scenes, unfettered debate occurred among the Yippies about the Democratic National Convention. According to Jonah Raskin, Rubin wanted to pique "a confrontation in which the establishment hits down hard, thereby placing large numbers of people in a state of crisis and tension."[AU: per Life and Times of Abbie Hoffman.—ce] Hoffman countered, "On that theory the only way that Chicago would be a success is if twenty of us got shot to death." Instead, Hoffman preferred guerrilla theater, while arguing with Rubin about the possibility of fascism taking hold in the United States. The Yippies then decided to conduct a demonstration in New York City on March 22.

Days before that event, the *Berkeley Barb* included a letter by Michael Rossman, a longtime Bay Area activist, addressed to his friend Jerry Rubin, warning unhappily "about this Yippie thing." Fearing a bloodbath could ensue in Chicago, Rossman pointed to black radicals residing there who advised white counterparts, "Stay off the street, we won't be able to protect you." The Yippies, Rossman charged, were behaving in a "deeply and dangerously irresponsible" manner. Rubin in particular appeared "surrounded by death," as he turned into "a politico who dropped acid."

On that date, the Youth International Party held a "yip-in" at Grand Central Station in Manhattan, with hundreds of young people who were dressed in costumes, sang, chanted, and released a banner reading "Liberty, Equality, Fraternity." After firecrackers and various objects were tossed in the main waiting area, police charged into the crowd, which countered with cries of "Fascists." The Motherfuckers, a Lower East Side affinity group of anarchists loosely associated with SDS, sought to provoke the police. Countercultural historians Martin Lee and Bruce Shlain refer to them as "acid-fueled fanatics," whose trashing antics "prefigured the paramilitary fad that engulfed the New Left as the decade drew to a close." The Motherfuckers themselves indicated, "We defy law and order with our bricks, bottles, garbage, long hair, filth, obscenity, drugs, games, guns, bikes, fire, fun and fucking."

But despite the presence of the Motherfuckers, one of the yip-in organizers, Paul Krassner, indicated that the participants, many knocked to the ground, "were defenseless." The journalist Michael Stern, writing about "Political Activism New Hippie Thing," offered that the Yippies had hoped for an occasion to enable young people "to share songs, popcorn, jellybeans and love for humanity." Instead, they issued anti-draft pronouncements and drew anti-war statements on the station's walls before being attacked by the city's Tactical Police Force. Scores of individuals were arrested, charged with assault, criminal mischief, resisting arrest, and criminal misconduct. Among those beaten was Don McNeill, the *Village Voice*'s well-regarded young reporter, who warned that the Yip-in was both "a pointless confrontation in a box canyon" and "a prophecy of Chicago." Hoffman happily agreed that it amounted to "a preview of what was gonna happen in Chicago." "The Grand Central Station Massacre," he later wrote, "knocked out the hippie image of Chicago and let the whole world know there would be blood on the streets in Chicago."

In its account of the incident, "Youth: The Politics of YIP," *Time* referred to Yippies as "1968's version of the hippies." The hippie movement, the magazine contended, had suffered a moribund winter but had been revitalized by the Yippies with "their special kind of antic political protest." Abbie Hoffman contended that the Yippies made up "a party," rather than a political movement, while Ed Sanders of the Fugs offered, "It's the politics of ecstasy." That involved a platform of an anarchistic nature, and included "an end to war and pay toilets, legalization of psychedelic drugs, free food, and a heart transplant for L.B.J." Favored as well was "juvenile exhibitionism." By this stage, joining the Yippie bandwagon, kicked off by Hoffman, Rubin, Keith Lampe, Krassner, Sanders, and a few others, were Ginsberg and Timothy Leary. Lampe explained, "Our attitude is basically satirical," involving parodying matters from narcotics raids to US foreign policy.

Ginsberg, who resided in Greenwich Village, refuted the notion that hippies had to withdraw from life. "These people are simply seeking another form of social cooperation. They are trying to start a utopian society, in the midst of a locked-in technological society." Such a mindset, Ginsberg said, "is something beautiful. It really is a return to earlier American values, to the idea of Thoreau and Whitman that the individual is a state higher than the state."

In contrast to the *Village Voice*, which increasingly adopted a negative tone toward the Yippies, the African-American author Julius Lester, writing in the left-wing *Guardian*, expressed appreciation for the new radical group. He welcomed their "techniques of disarming propaganda," and the fact that their roots resided "not in Mao or Che but in the [Dutch] Provos, rock and Lenny Bruce." They wanted to engage others experientially, acting like "Zen monks" who refused to issue "Dos and Don'ts, Right and Wrongs." In *Rat*, a recently formed underground paper in New York City, Jon Moore also viewed the Yippies favorably, suggesting they could "project the convergence of 'cultural' and 'political' consciousness as clear as hippies-flower-love-Haight has last year." Still, he urged those bound for Chicago, "Go with your eyes open."

The Yippies continued targeting the Democratic National Convention to be held in late August in Chicago. They discussed leading a nearly weeklong Festival of Life, to stand in stark contrast to the "National Death Convention." They intended to feature "folk songs, rock bands, 'guerrilla' theater, body painting and mediation." Anticipating "the long hot summer . . . to produce ideal weather for marijuana growing," as they explained in a leaflet titled "People, Get Ready," the Yippies intended to plant "hundreds of thousands of pot seeds" that would sprout by late August. They also looked forward to anointing their own presidential candidate, a now ten-week-old black and white piglet, Lyndon Pigasus Pig, who resided at the commune founded by Hugh "Wavy Gravy" Romney and Jaranara Romney, located in southern California. All sorts of plots were being considered, including a lie-in at O'Hare Field and the use of fake cabdrivers who would transport delegates out of state.

Rubin and Hoffman kept making inflammatory statements of their own, distressing Mike Rossman, Peter Coyote, Allen Ginsberg, and Jim Fourrat. Rossman continued to worry about "irresponsible lies" being imparted by both Movement and countercultural representatives. He was particularly troubled by the Yippies' apparent readiness to allow people to get beaten. Coyote, one of the founders of the San Francisco Diggers, considered the Yippies charlatans, with their false promises of rock bands, park permits, and the like. "This was . . . chicanery," Coyote charged. It was intended to induce "kids from all over the United States to come and get their fucking heads cracked." Ginsberg and Fouratt determined "that Chicago was wrong," also believing "it was just not fair to the young people to manipulate them in this way." Ginsberg told Rubin, "Listen, I don't want to do this unless it's really gonna be pacifist." Rubin convinced the poet that violence "would be the wrong thing for this occasion."

The two top Yippies were, nevertheless, themselves troubled by sentiments expressed by some of their erstwhile allies. During a press conference in the host city of the Democratic National Convention, Timothy Leary announced, "We're gonna burn Chicago down like my great-grandmother, Mrs. Leary. Johnson will not land at that airport 'cause I'll have fifty thousand kids on the landing field." Disturbing too was the attitude displayed by Movement heavyweight Tom Hayden, who purportedly told Rubin and Hoffman, "People are gonna die in Chicago, we're gonna have to be go underground, we'll have to form armed units." Considering Hayden "nuts," Rubin invited him to hang out on the Lower East Side and help to create "a youth culture alliance . . . a whole alternative to America." Hayden countered, "This is serious, fascism is coming."

Yippies based in Chicago were fearful of matters getting out of hand, especially in the wake of the police beating of local activists. Abe Peck's underground paper, the *Seed*, warned, "Don't come to Chicago if you expect a five-day festival of life, music and love." Going further, the *Seed* exclaimed, "The word is out. Chicago may host a festival of blood." Such heated rhetoric angered Hoffman, who insisted, "Those that act peacefully will be treated peacefully." All the while, he, Rubin, and other Yippies were attempting to negotiate with Mayor Richard J. Daley and David Stahl, Chicago's second-in-command, but no permit was forthcoming.

As the Kennedy campaign had gathered momentum, it threatened to derail the Yippies' plans for their Festival of Life. Rubin had conveyed concerns about RFK's impact once he entered the presidential race. "We expected concentration camps and we got Bobby Kennedy," he admitted. "I am more confident of our ability to survive concentration camps than I am of our ability to survive Bobby." Hoffman too considered Kennedy "a challenge to the charisma of Yippie!" Bobby, after all, possessed "the money and the power to build the stage," while the Yippies, Hoffman acknowledged, "Had to steal ours. It was no contest." He wrote, "Every night we would turn on the TV set and there was the young knight with long hair, holding out his hand." And as Hoffman recognized, "When young longhairs told you they'd heard that Bobby turned on, you knew Yippie! was *really* in trouble." Plans were afoot "to disband Yippie! and cancel the Chicago festival."

The politicization of many who considered themselves part of the counter-culture was one of the more striking developments that occurred during the first half of 1968. The media's emphasis on frolicking, long-haired denizens of the Human Be-In, Monterey Pop, and the Haight gave way to more recent stories about Yippies, the Motherfuckers, and hippies supposedly undergoing a shift in perspectives and attitudes in recognizing the need for political engagement. A welter of events threatened to overwhelm Movement activists turned countercultural leaders like Abbie Hoffman and Jerry Rubin, and their plans to stage the era's greatest demonstration as the Democratic Party held its nominating convention in Chicago. The Tet Offensive, the presidential candidacies of Eugene McCarthy and Bobby Kennedy, and the terrible reality of the politics of assassination altered the hopes and expectations of so many, including the leaders of the small collection of Yippies who envisioned holding a Festival of Life in the Windy City. At different points, Kennedy's waging of the New Politics particularly gave pause to Hoffman, Rubin, and Tom Hayden, among others, some of whom considered calling off the protest scheduled for the period when the national convention was being held. Subsequent events, of course, resulted in both the blunting of the New Politics and the decision to proceed with the latest gathering of the tribes, albeit in far different fashion than had eventuated when the hippies first attained widespread attention.

"There's a Man with a Gun over There"

The Politics of Assassination

Figure 9.1   The assassination of Dr. Martin Luther King Jr. touched off riots in over one hundred American cities as grieving African Americans vented rage and frustration, resulting in the most massive civil unrest since the Civil War and leading to forty-five deaths and over 15,000 arrests. Police, National Guard, and US Army troops were mobilized to contain the violence and arson, which reached within two blocks of the White House. Library of Congress, Prints and Photographs Division, LC-U9-18949.

It was perhaps the only assassination of the era that precipitated little mourning. On August 25, 1967, George Lincoln Rockwell, commander of the National Socialist White People's Party (NSWPP), was preparing to drive away from the Econowash laundromat in the Dominion Hills Shopping Center in Arlington, Virginia. Only slightly more than two months before, Rockwell had been the target of a failed assassination attempt when two shots were fired at him in front of his party's nearby barracks. Now, as Rockwell backed out of a parking slot in his 1958 Chevrolet, two bullets crashed through the car's windshield. Wounded in the chest, Rockwell staggered out of the car and pointed at the laundromat roof as he collapsed. The assassin ran the length of the roof, jumped to the ground at the building's rear, and fled. By the time police arrived, Rockwell had died from massive blood loss, as one bullet had severed several major arteries.

Rockwell's notoriety at the time of his death was a product of his extreme right-wing views. These had roots in the McCarthy era of the 1950s, when Rockwell's fear of communism led him to embrace anti-Semitism and Nazism. In December 1959, he founded the American Nazi Party (ANP), which led the US Navy to discharge him after a lengthy term of service. During the early 1960s, Rockwell and his group came to public attention due not only to the Nazi regalia that they regularly sported, but because of his vociferous denunciations of Jews and African Americans. A Holocaust denier and advocate of white power, Rockwell founded Hatenanny Records, which promoted racist music. He and his followers often traveled to rallies in a Volkswagen bus dubbed the "Hate Bus," which was decorated with racist and anti-Semitic slogans. Some ANP rallies turned into riots, as enraged Jewish war veterans and Holocaust survivors attacked the "Führer" and his "storm troopers." As the civil rights movement gained momentum, Rockwell's Nazis worked with the KKK to organize counter-demonstrations and committed his group to a "race war." Given his lengthy record of promoting racial and religious hatred, it came as no surprise that few Americans grieved the death of the man that the BBC labeled "the American Hitler."

Within an hour of the shooting, Rockwell's assassin was arrested at a nearby bus stop and soon identified as former NSWPP member John Patler. He had killed Rockwell with an 1896 model Mauser pistol, the type of German weapon that racist white nationalists tended to favor. As Rockwell was a veteran, his funeral ceremony was to be held at Culpeper National Cemetery, but it quickly became apparent that the controversies surrounding him did not end with his death. When about 150 of his supporters, many sporting Nazi insignia, arrived for the interment, military police and local law officers denied them entry into the cemetery unless the offensive insignia were removed. Foiled by the Secretary of the Army in an attempt to secure burial at a national cemetery, the NSWPP left the cremated remains at a still-unknown site. Patler, whose motive was chiefly resentment and revenge, was convicted of his murder and handed a twenty-year prison sentence.

Though Rockwell stood well outside the political mainstream, his assassination fit into a pattern of political murder in American life. President Andrew Jackson was the target of an assassination attempt in 1832, when a deranged man pointed a pair of pistols at the president's chest as he ascended the steps to the Capitol building. Miraculously, both weapons misfired, and an enraged Jackson thrashed the man with his cane. President Abraham Lincoln succumbed to a head wound inflicted by Confederate sympathizer John Wilkes Booth on April 14, 1865. Less than two decades later, on July 2, 1881, a frustrated applicant for a government job shot President James Garfield in the back at the Washington, DC, train station, leading to Garfield's death some months later.

The twentieth century brought further attempts. In September 1901, an anarchist shot William McKinley at the Pan-American Exposition in Buffalo, New York, resulting in the president's death. His successor, Theodore Roosevelt, was the target of another assassination attempt in Milwaukee, Wisconsin, in October 1912, when he was shot in the chest but survived. Italian-born anarchist Giuseppe Zangara fired five pistol shots at President-elect Franklin D. Roosevelt in Miami's Bayfront Park, on February 15, 1933. Zangara succeeded rather in hitting Chicago mayor Anton Cermak, who died from the gunfire. In September 1935, a political opponent's relative shot and killed Senator Huey Long of Louisiana at the state capitol building in Baton Rouge. Twelve years later, the Zionist paramilitary Stern Gang attempted to send letter bombs to President Harry S. Truman, but bomb experts at the Secret Service defused the threat. In November 1950, pro-independence Puerto Ricans sought to gun down the president at the Blair House, also referred to as the President's Guest House. The police killed one gunman and captured another.

John F. Kennedy remarked more than once on the relative ease with which a determined assassin could succeed and seemed to reconcile himself to that possibility. On November 22, 1963, the threat became reality, as President Kennedy was shot while riding in a motorcade through downtown Dallas, Texas, with his wife Jacqueline, and John and Nellie Connally. Texas Governor Connally also suffered bullet wounds but he would fully recover. The alleged assassin, Lee Harvey Oswald, using a mail-order Mannlicher-Carcano rifle, fired three shots at the president from a window of the Texas School Book Depository overlooking the motorcade's route around Dealey Plaza. Two shots struck the president, the second inflicting a fatal head wound, while splattering blood and brain matter on the first lady and the governor. Across the nation, newspapers resorted to massive-size type to announce some variation of "PRESIDENT ASSASSINATED." Television networks nationwide halted broadcasts and blank screens produced solemn voices warning, "Stand by for a special news bulletin." Americans watched in fascinated horror as the accused assassin, a twenty-three-year-old former Marine who had briefly lived in the Soviet Union and married a Russian woman, was himself gunned down in the basement of the Dallas County jail on live television. The official lying-in-state and funeral ceremonies enabled the nation to collectively grieve the young president's death and slowly come to terms with what had occurred. Controversy and speculation about possible conspiracies continued to swirl regarding the assassination.

The 1960s proved to be a decade riddled with political assassinations in the United States. The momentum of the civil rights movement produced considerable white resistance, especially in the South where violence against activists became commonplace. Organizations like the KKK and White Citizens Councils (WCC) were often behind drive-by shootings, bombings, church arsons, and other acts of terror. On June 12, 1963, only months before the Kennedy assassination, Medgar Evers, an NAACP field secretary, pulled into his driveway at his suburban Bayou Mound, Mississippi, home. As he stepped from the car with an armload of "Jim Crow Must Go" T-shirts, a deadly rifle shot rang out and Evers fell to the ground.

Young civil rights activists Andrew Goodman, Michael Schwerner, and James Cheney, members of both the Council of Federated Organizations and CORE, participated in Mississippi Freedom Summer the following year. On June 21, 1964, police outside Philadelphia, Mississippi, pulled over the car the three were riding in but soon released them. Vigilante forces, which included law enforcement officers, again stopped the car, then abducted and subsequently shot to death Goodman, Schwerner, and Cheney. After President Johnson ordered naval personnel to aid in the search, their bodies were found buried in an earthen dam. Federal charges of civil rights violations led to the convictions of seven men who received jail sentences, while Justice Department investigations continued for decades.

Malcolm X, formerly a spokesman for the Nation of Islam (NOI) and a leading proponent of Black Nationalism, confided to interviewer Gordon Parks in early 1965 that he was being targeted by the NOI because of his break with the organization and criticism of its leader Elijah Muhammad. On February 19, Malcolm's fears were realized. Controversial because of his response to the Kennedy assassination—"the chickens coming home to roost"—and for his insistence that racial justice would be gained "by any means necessary," Malcolm was speaking at Manhattan's Audubon Ballroom when a disturbance broke out in the audience. During this diversion, three gunmen rushed the stage, firing a shotgun and handguns at Malcom, who died shortly afterward. A coroner later identified over thirty entry wounds in Malcolm's body. The gunmen, connected with the NOI, were all arrested and convicted.

A potential assassin struck again the following year as civil rights pioneer James Meredith undertook a personal "March against Fear" from Memphis, Tennessee, to Jackson, Mississippi. On the second day, Aubrey Norvell, a white gunman, sprang from roadside bushes and shot Meredith. A Korean War veteran who helped to integrate the University of Mississippi, Meredith later rejoined the march that was being completed by some 15,000 marchers after the shooting.

In the wake of the Kennedy assassination, the debate as to whether America was a "sick society" took root and grew in subsequent years, driven by violence, politically motivated or not. In 1964, Rod Serling's *Twilight Zone* television series aired an episode titled "I Am the Night—Color Me Black," in which the sun was blotted out and darkness engulfed cities and places where racial hatred abounded. On September 25, 1965, Barry McGuire's "Eve of Destruction" reached the number-one spot on *Billboard*'s record charts. Written in 1964 by P. F. Sloan, the song, banned by some radio stations, referenced the intensity with which war's violence and racial and political hatred had pervaded American society with potentially catastrophic consequences.

As the American political climate grew more volatile and race riots scarred urban centers, the possibility of political violence hovered ominously at the margins of political activity. Anti-war forces and political radicals of varying stripes moved toward increasingly confrontational, even violent tactics by the late 1960s. In 1968, presidential aspirant George Wallace used unrestrained rhetoric, while his supporters often clashed with protesters and hecklers. Still, few could have predicted that the two men who most represented the dreams and hopes for the future would be struck down within a few short weeks of one another, confirming the worst fears about what America had become.

In many ways, James Earl Ray fit the standard profile of a political assassin. Born in 1928 to an indigent family in Illinois, Ray dropped out of school at fifteen, eventually joining the US Army. After being discharged, his life was little more than a continual series of petty crimes: burglary, armed robbery, mail fraud, and theft. In 1967, Ray escaped from the Missouri State Penitentiary and, using a variety of aliases, traveled to Canada and then Mexico, where he unsuccessfully sought to establish himself as a pornographic film director. Ray returned to the United States in November 1967. He was drawn to the presidential campaign of former Alabama governor George Wallace, whose "law and order" theme was a thinly veiled racist "dog whistle." Ray had long nurtured a deep prejudice against African Americans and found much to like in Wallace's segregationist background and railings against federal efforts to advance integration. Motivated, Ray volunteered for the Wallace campaign headquarters in North Hollywood.

It is unclear when Ray decided to act against the nation's foremost civil rights activist, but on March 18, 1968, he left California, heading for Atlanta, Georgia, the site of Dr. Martin Luther King Jr.'s home and church. Once there, Ray bought a map of the city and circled the two locations. He then traveled to Birmingham, Alabama, where, using an alias he purchased a Remington .30-.06 rifle and a telescopic sight. Arriving back in Atlanta, Ray read in the local newspaper of King's plan to return to Memphis, Tennessee, on April 1, to support a local sanitation workers' strike. On April 2, Ray packed up his weapon and departed for Memphis. He rented a room in a rooming house there across the street from the Lorraine Motel, where King was staying.

King and compatriots had resided so often in room 306 of the Lorraine Motel that the room was known to them as the "King-Abernathy Suite." On April 4, King was still recovering from the emotional toll of the previous evening's "Mountaintop Speech." Along with his associates, King focused on immediate issues regarding the sanitation workers' strike. King had also been working on a planned sermon, ominously titled "America May Go to Hell." As evening approached, with plans being finalized for that night's scheduled event, King turned to musician Ben Branch and said, "Ben, make sure you play 'Take My Hand, Precious Lord.'" Then the man who was considered by many Americans to be the last, best hope for racial reconciliation strode out on the motel's second-floor balcony to chat with colleagues.

At 6:01 p.m., Ray, took aim from the bathroom window of his room, fixing King, no more than 200 feet away, in the rifle's telescopic sight. Ray's single shot tore through King's right cheek before breaking his jaw and several vertebrae as it ripped through the jugular vein and other major arteries. King slumped to the balcony floor as those around him, stunned and horrified as they were, began pointing frantically in the direction from which the shot had come. To their dismay, police who had been detailed to provide protection ran toward the balcony, pointing their weapons at the fallen King's cohorts. Witnesses later stated that they had seen a man run from the vicinity of the rooming house. Ralph Abernathy, Andrew Young, and Jesse Jackson were among those who immediately gathered around the now-unconscious King. Young thought King was already dead, but he was rushed to St. Joseph's Hospital where physicians sought in vain to revive him. King was pronounced dead at 7:05 p.m. As news spread, America began to burn.

Although colleagues and friends of King issued calls for calm in subsequent days, their pleas more often than not fell on ears deafened by grief and outrage. For many black Americans, King's violent end was the final testament to the moral rot at the core of a hopelessly racist society. The apostle of peace had fallen victim to the hate and blind rage that he had striven so hard to overcome. Black power advocate Stokely Carmichael took to the radio after the assassination to announce, "White America has declared war on black people. . . . Go home and get your guns." Nearly two weeks of rioting, arson, and death began that April night, with few major cities spared. In the nation's capital, rioting followed immediately upon news of King's death. Buildings burned within two blocks of the White House and a detachment of troops guarded the steps of the Capitol Building. Incoming planes reported that from the air, the city appeared as if it were a war zone, wreathed in the smoke of torched buildings. The death toll in Washington, DC, rose to ten after twelve days of unrest—all but one of the dead was African-American. Journalistic accounts of the magnitude of the rioting varied, but it was reported that as many as 125 inner cities exploded in flames, including sections of Baltimore, Cincinnati, Detroit, and Pittsburgh, with Chicago experiencing some of the worst of the rioting. There on April 5, as looting and arson rapidly accelerated, Mayor Richard J. Daley authorized his police to "shoot to kill" arsonists and "shoot to maim" looters, an order that the state attorney general subsequently claimed was illegal.

There were the exceptional instances in which violence was limited or averted through the actions of individuals. In Boston, the singer James Brown, popularly known as "Soul Brother Number One," helped head off any rioting by offering a free public concert. In Milwaukee, James Groppi, a white Catholic priest, was able to use his influence as an NAACP adviser to help maintain the peace there. In New York City, Mayor John Lindsay, after hearing of King's murder, made a courageous foray into Harlem, which briefly kept violence in check.

Without question, it was Robert Kennedy who most effectively addressed the anguish of black Americans. On the night of April 4, Kennedy was campaigning in Indianapolis's black ghetto when he received word of the tragedy. Realizing that the audience had not yet heard, Kennedy informed his largely black audience that King had been shot and killed. Amid audible gasps and sobs from the crowd of 2,000, Kennedy struggled to articulate the sentiments that might stave off the rage that the murder would likely engender. "For those of you who are black and are tempted to be filled with hatred and mistrust and injustice of such an act, against all white people," he quietly implored in an unsteady voice, "I would only say that I can also feel in my own heart the same kind of feeling." Kennedy reminded his listeners that he had had "a family member killed, but he was killed by a white man." Kennedy assured them that "the vast majority of white people and the vast majority of black people in this country want to live together; want to improve the quality of our life; and want justice for all human beings that abide in our land." In conclusion, the senator asked that those present "dedicate ourselves to what the Greeks wrote so many years ago: to tame the savageness of man and make gentle the life of this world." Almost incredibly, Kennedy's plea worked. The crowd drifted away and Indianapolis was spared the violence that wracked so many other cities. It was a speech, historian Michael Cohen writes, "that no other white politician in America could have given."

King's funeral ceremonies took place on April 8 and 9, even as violent spasms shook the nation's cities. In Memphis, his widow Coretta Scott King led 40,000 marchers in silent tribute to the slain civil rights leader. The following day in Atlanta, services were held at Ebenezer Baptist Church, where King's civil rights colleagues and numerous luminaries, including Robert F. Kennedy and Richard Nixon, were among the mourners. Afterward, a funeral procession drew over 100,000 mourners as it made its way through Atlanta streets to a second service at Morehouse College, King's alma mater, prior to interment. As had been the case with President Kennedy, the nation's three television networks carried the activities live, offering yet another opportunity for collective grieving and soul-searching. Once the violence sputtered out, leaving thirty-nine dead and hundreds of millions of dollars in property damage, the nation attempted to cope with what had transpired.

The vast majority of white Americans were horrified and appalled by the brutal murder of Dr. King and many editorial pages reflected growing concern that America was a "sick society." President Johnson canceled a meeting with military leaders in Hawaii and, following a condolence call to MLK's widow, declared a national day of mourning on April 7. The president also ordered Attorney General Ramsey Clark to begin an investigation into the assassination. It was well known that King had many enemies, not the least of whom was FBI Director J. Edgar Hoover, whose agency fell under Clark's purview. Most public figures expressed shock at King's murder, including presidential candidate George Wallace, who called it a "senseless, regrettable act." Other Southern segregationists failed to rise above their ingrained prejudices. Georgia Governor Lester Maddox, a minor presidential candidate, called King "an enemy of our country" and vowed to restore the lowered state flag to full mast. South Carolina's Senator Strom Thurmond told his constituents, "We are now witnessing the whirlwind sowed years ago when some preachers and teachers began telling people that each man could be his own judge in his own case." The sentiment echoed California Governor Ronald Reagan's assertion that the assassination was the inevitable outgrowth of the new permissiveness that led to people "choosing which laws they'd break." Maryland Governor Spiro Agnew seized the opportunity to summon one hundred black leaders to the state capitol, where in front of television cameras, he lectured them on their responsibility to tamp down black rage.

Unnoticed by many, more assassinations occurred even as the fires first stoked on April 4 continued to burn. On the evening of April 6, Eldridge Cleaver and thirteen other Black Panthers, infuriated by King's assassination, planned to ambush police officers in Oakland, California, in retaliation. After a pair of officers were wounded in an initial shootout with two carloads of armed Panthers, another confrontation occurred when Cleaver and Panther Party treasurer Bobby Hutton holed up in the basement of a nearby building. Realizing their situation was hopeless, Cleaver decided they should surrender, and told Hutton to strip down to his underwear so that the police could see that he was unarmed. What followed has been disputed by both sides. Police insisted that Hutton tried to run and ignored orders to stop. Cleaver claimed that the unarmed Hutton was the victim of a police assassination. Whatever the truth, Hutton ended up dead, his body riddled by twelve police bullets. "Li'l Bobby" became an instant martyr to black militants.

The events of late March and early April transformed the contest for the Democratic presidential nomination. Vice President Hubert Humphrey officially entered the race on April 27 as the instant front-runner, who claimed the support of his party's establishment, which in 1968 still held the upper hand for candidate selection. State party meetings, where powerful urban bosses and party leaders parceled out delegate credentials, were far more important than primaries, which served chiefly to demonstrate a candidate's popular strength. As challengers to a decades-old system, Kennedy and McCarthy had to rely on state primary contests and hope that their performances would be impressive enough to sway party officials.

Kennedy's strength lay in his broad appeal to farm workers, working-class whites, and minorities, including his overwhelming support from black Americans. Shortly after King's death, civil rights activist John Lewis had commented, "We still have Bobby Kennedy. We still have hope." One of the greatest challenges that Kennedy faced during the grueling primary season was appealing to a broader range of white Americans leery of his emphasis on racial and economic justice, which seemed to demand greater federal spending and a heavier tax burden. In an April 26 speech to students from the University of Indiana's Medical School, Kennedy faced heckling from a largely white, privileged audience that took umbrage at his proposals for better health care for the poor. At one point he was challenged by a student who shouted, "Where are you going to get the money?" Without pause, Kennedy responded, "From you. . . . I look around this room and I don't see many black faces who will become doctors," he lectured. "I don't see many people coming here from the slums, or off Indian reservations. You are the privileged people. . . . You sit here as a white medical student, while black people carry the burden of the fighting in Vietnam."

For many white Americans, however, especially in an era of intensified racial conflict, the more pressing matter was law and order. As Kennedy prepared to confront McCarthy in the Indiana primary, it seemed increasingly urgent that his campaign message speak to this concern. McCarthy had won the Pennsylvania primary on April 23 and the Massachusetts contest a week later; Kennedy did not directly compete in either instance. Aware of Kennedy's vulnerability in Indiana, the McCarthy team began to characterize him as the candidate who saw America as merely "a combination of separate interests . . . or groups" whereas the senator from Minnesota believed the nation's ills could be resolved only by calling "upon everyone to be as responsible as they can be."

As the Indiana contest neared its conclusion, a shift in Kennedy's language became evident as he started presenting himself as a law and order candidate. He had been the nation's "chief law enforcement officer," and one who understood "the importance of obeying the law," he boasted. Kennedy also moved away from his earlier focus on the need for sacrifice on the part of privileged white Americans and spoke less about the need for racial integration at the community level. "We've got to get away from the welfare system, the handout system and the idea of the dole," he declared. Privately, Kennedy rationalized his swerve to the right as a product of political necessity. "Now are we trying to win votes," he chastised his querulous staff, "or are we trying to drop dead here?" Though the shift in tone was not without some later cost, Kennedy won the Indiana primary on May 7 with 42 percent of the vote despite the candidacy of the state's governor, Roger Branigan, who ran as a stand-in for Johnson. McCarthy finished a distant third.

Kennedy's changed stances did not go unnoticed. Richard Nixon and Ronald Reagan both joked that the liberal politician seemed to be echoing their positions. McCarthy likewise noted the new direction of Kennedy's speeches, but was heartened on soon topping *Time*'s national presidential poll. He had always disdained Kennedy's campaign style, which he saw as overly dependent on the candidate as celebrity, seeking the adulation of overexcited crowds. On the campaign trail, he now began to articulate a substantive critique of Kennedy's positions, arguing that the latter's proposals for fixing America's inner cities were woefully inadequate. Ignoring the likelihood of white backlash, McCarthy argued that inner city poverty could only be eliminated by integrating minorities into white communities and allocating even more federal funds to urban issues. McCarthy likewise sought to differentiate his foreign policy positions from Kennedy's, lamenting the cost of being "the world's judge and the world's policeman." This repudiation of Cold War policy was a radical stance that McCarthy would expand on in subsequent weeks, ultimately arguing for the withdrawal of US forces from "the land of thatched huts."

Relieved at having easily won the potentially problematic Nebraska primary on May 14, Kennedy continued to aim the bulk of his attacks at Vice President Humphrey, an ardent defender of the administration's war policies. Humphrey had proven a less than adept candidate, as when he ad-libbed about "the politics of happiness, politics of purpose, and the politics of joy." The statement seemed especially incongruous at the moment, given the recent assassination of King, the subsequent devastation in America's inner cities, and ongoing protest regarding the Vietnam War. Yet the vice president seemed determined to maintain the demeanor of a man unfazed by America's tribulations, forsaking the harsh and often profane rhetoric of the era for quaint expressions such as "my goodness!" As much as he was mocked for his seeming obliviousness to the nation's turmoil and for his subservience to Lyndon Johnson, Humphrey possessed the advantage almost from the day of his announcement. By late May, media sources reported that Humphrey was close to or already had the number of delegates to clinch the nomination.

Pushing on, Kennedy confronted McCarthy in the Oregon primary, amid less than favorable circumstances. Forsaking the grassroots approach of the New Politics in Oregon, Kennedy relied on a traditional path of seeking support from the party establishment. Most damaging to Kennedy, however, was his obvious reluctance to debate McCarthy. In a defeat described by political journalist Rowland Evans and Robert Novak as a "disaster," Kennedy lost the Oregon vote, the first electoral setback for the Kennedy brothers.

The two men next approached the all-important California primary with differing expectations. The state's large Hispanic and African-American populations worked to Kennedy's advantage, while McCarthy relied on 150 local headquarters and the enthusiastic backing of many college students. Both candidates toured with Hollywood celebrities, making for an unusually festive campaign.

Kennedy's most memorable campaign moment occurred on Wednesday, May 28, when he rode in a motorcade through an area South and East of Downtown Los Angeles. The frenzied nature of the crowds seemed to confirm that the Kennedy charisma endured, as the convoy of cars was frequently halted by surging throngs seeking to touch the smiling, waving candidate. On several occasions, the cheering, shrieking mob pulled the senator out of his convertible, much to his personal security detachment's dismay. Films and photographs of the event captured Kennedy's undeniable appeal to the coalition that he hoped would propel him to the presidency: working-class whites, blacks, Asian Americans, Latinos, and the young.

On June 1, Kennedy and McCarthy traveled to ABC's studio in Los Angeles for what would be a surprisingly unilluminating affair. Seated at a table with television journalists, the candidates fielded an initial question about how they would bring peace in Vietnam. McCarthy proposed a deescalation of the war, a new government in South Vietnam, and recognition of the National Liberation Front as prerequisites to negotiations. Kennedy suggested letting the South Vietnamese troops "carry the burden of the conflict" and implied that McCarthy was forcing a communist government on South Vietnam. McCarthy then alleged Kennedy remained saddled with the kind of Cold War mindset that had drawn the nation into Vietnam. Little of significance emerged from the subsequent give-and-take and the moderator moved on to social policy, where the candidates retreated to well-established positions on how to alleviate inner-city poverty. When Robert Clark remarked that he perceived a difference in the candidates' proposals for housing, McCarthy, who seemed calm "to the point of inertia," as one historian notes, denied that there was any. Somewhat flustered near the debate's conclusion, ABC's Frank Reynolds demanded, "Where do you disagree?" McCarthy again brought up Kennedy's connection to Dean Rusk and other foreign policy advisors who had pressed intervention in Vietnam, while Kennedy responded that he preferred not to deal in personalities.

Afterward, both camps claimed victory, though post-debate polling placed Kennedy in the lead by a 55–38 percent margin. Although it appeared momentum was swinging away from McCarthy, each man entered the final days of the California contest hoping to triumph.

Kennedy devoted the final day to campaigning by motorcade in San Francisco, San Diego, and Los Angeles, including a quick sweep through Watts. On June 4, Primary Day, Kennedy relaxed at the Malibu Beach home of director John Frankenheimer, before returning to his suite at the Los Angeles Ambassador Hotel around 8 p.m. As Kennedy watched election results on television, it became increasingly evident that he would prevail. Support from previously undecided voters and massive African-American backing eventually enabled Kennedy to win by a few percentage points. Assured by 11:30 p.m. that the vote in Los Angeles County would put him over the top, Kennedy prepared to head to the Embassy Room, where throngs of enthusiastic supporters awaited.

The senator stepped up on the dais in the Embassy Room around midnight, greeted by some 1,500 cheering, screaming supporters. Kennedy advisor Milton Gwirtzman was actually alarmed at the crowd's demeanor, sensing "an almost frightening suppressed violence." The crowd's frenzy, he recounted, "was almost too strong, dangerously strong, the crowd an object for a demagogue." Gwirtzman "had never seen an intensity, in one room, in one election night, before or since." Quieting the clamor, Kennedy proceeded with a speech that, while spontaneous, masterfully summarized the hopes that he evoked among his supporters. "I think we can end the divisions in the United States," he asserted. "What I think is quite clear is we can work together in the last analysis." The violence, the disenchantment, divisions between black and white and rich and poor, Vietnam, all of these contentious issues could be resolved, he promised: "We can start to work together." Wrapping up his remarks, Kennedy declared, "We are a great country, an unselfish country and a compassionate country," he asserted. "And I intend to make that my basis for running." Then came those final words that ever after served as prelude to the calamity lurking only moments away: "We want to deal with our own problems in our country and we want peace in Vietnam. So, my thanks to all of you, and it's on to Chicago and let's win there."

With that, Kennedy lifted two fingers in the victory or peace sign, then made his way through the crowd of reporters huddled near the stage to head for a press conference in the Colonial Room. Kennedy aides and the maître d'hôtel sought to usher the candidate through a mass of journalists, supporters, and campaign workers by passing through the kitchen. There, as Kennedy paused to shake hands with busboy Juan Romero, Sirhan Sirhan, a Palestinian immigrant aggrieved by the senator's support for Israel, pushed past aides and began firing a .22 caliber Iver-Johnson revolver at RFK. The small room erupted in chaos, as former FBI agent William Barry hit Sirhan in the face, and the assassin was pinned against a steam table by a half dozen men, still firing his gun. Barry stooped over the fallen senator and saw that Kennedy had been hit in the back of the head. Romero pushed a rolled-up coat under Kennedy's head and pressed rosary beads into his hand. Kennedy asked, "Is everyone okay?" Journalist Pete Hamill recalled that Bobby "had a kind of sweet, accepting smile on his face, as if he knew it would all end this way." His wife Ethel was soon at his side. As emergency medical personnel arrived and began to transfer Kennedy to a stretcher, he uttered his last words, "Don't lift me." He was taken first to Central Receiving Hospital, where physicians detected a heartbeat and sent him on to Good Samaritan Hospital.

When word of the shooting in the kitchen reached the ballroom, pandemonium replaced the jubilation of only moments before. Shrieks of horror and disbelief filled the air as staff and supporters wept and clutched one another, unable to accept that the unimaginable had in fact happened. In the kitchen area, Sirhan had only been disarmed with difficulty, as former NFL great Rosey Grier, author George Plimpton, and others sought to wrest the revolver from his hand. Sirhan's wild shots had wounded five people in addition to Kennedy, though fortunately no one else suffered life-threatening injuries. As the shooting took place in the early hours of June 5, the majority of Americans did not see the first television reports. CBS had ended its coverage of the Kennedy victory party and ABC was running closing credits when the by now dreaded announcement warned viewers to "stay tuned for a special bulletin." The network's Howard K. Smith came back on the air to announce, "A disturbing report that Senator Kennedy has been shot," and other networks soon echoed the terrible news. Most Americans learned of the latest victim of a violent year on the morning of June 5.

Initial hopes that Kennedy's wounds might not prove fatal faded as surgeons assessed the degree of damage. Though three bullets struck Kennedy, the most serious wound was from the bullet that hit Kennedy in the back of the head and fragmented in his brain. Extensive surgery to remove the fragments and repair the damage proved futile. Senator Robert F. Kennedy, yet another in the too-long line of victims of the politics of assassination, died at 1:44 on the morning of June 6. President Johnson, whose relationship with Kennedy was described as one of "mutual contempt," nevertheless offered a moving public eulogy, privately conceding that the tragedy was "too horrible for words." The Dream had died with King in April. Now only two months later, it seemed that the nation would have to come to grips with the murder of Hope.

By 1968, Americans were all too familiar with the ceremonies of national loss and collective grief. As the country reeled from the shock of Kennedy's death, yet another pageant of mourning played out on millions of television screens. Following an autopsy, Kennedy's body was flown to New York City, where thousands slowly filed through St. Patrick's Cathedral to say goodbye prior to a funeral mass. In a memorable eulogy, with his voice wavering, Senator Edward M. Kennedy, the lone remaining brother, told the mourners, "My brother need not be idealized, or enlarged in death beyond what he was in life; to be remembered simply as a good and decent man, who saw wrong and tried to right it, saw suffering and tried to heal it, saw war and tried to stop it." Kennedy continued, "As he said many times, in many parts of this nation, to those he touched and who sought to touch him: 'Some men see things as they are and ask why. I dream things that never were and say why not.'"

From New York, RFK's remains were transported by train to Washington, DC, for interment at Arlington National Cemetery. Along the route of the funeral train, thousands spontaneously appeared at the trackside waving, weeping, bearing flags, and saluting as the train rolled along. At the nation's capital, the funeral procession passed near Resurrection City, a shantytown remnant of King's Poor People's campaign. Pausing briefly at the Lincoln Memorial, members of the procession were joined by residents of Resurrection City in a rendition of "The Battle Hymn of the Republic," before moving on to Arlington, where forty-two-year-old Robert F. Kennedy was laid to rest next to the grave of his assassinated brother. That same day, June 8, James Earl Ray, alleged assassin of Martin Luther King, Jr., was arrested at London's Heathrow Airport and was soon extradited to Tennessee.

Coming as it did on the heels of King's murder, the assassination of Robert Kennedy disillusioned many Americans who had placed their faith in the possibility that new leadership might guide the nation toward a better future. Journalist Jack Newfield best captured the feeling of irreplaceable loss and hopelessness that engulfed many young Americans in "that murderous spring of 1968." "We are the first generation that learned from experience, in our innocent twenties," he was to write, "that things were not really getting better, that we shall not overcome. We felt, by the time we reached thirty, that we had already glimpsed the most compassionate leaders our nation could produce, and they had all been assassinated." "From this time forward," he feared, "things would get worse."

10

"The Whole World is Watching"

Czechago

Figure 10.1   Only days after Warsaw Pact forces invaded Czechoslovakia in August to suppress the Prague Spring movement, leftist radicals and anti-war demonstrators collided in the streets of Chicago during the Democratic National Convention. The peaceful confrontation shown here between a youthful protester and a National Guardsman was soon superseded by violent televised clashes on city streets between protesters and Mayor Richard J. Daley's Chicago police, whose excesses were later deemed to constitute a "police riot." Library of Congress, Prints and Photographs Division, LC-U9–19759-4/4A.

At 10:30 p.m. on August 21, a Soviet aircraft touched down at Prague's Ruzyne Airport, taxied to a stop, and unloaded a group of men, some in

Russian Army uniforms, who proceeded to waiting cars and departed. Soviet troops soon took control of the airport and parts of the city. Red Army parachutists dropped into Prague suburbs. Red Army formations split into three columns at the city's outskirts with orders to seize the ancient Hradčany Castle, residence of Czechoslovakian president Ludvik Svoboda, as well as to occupy the prime minister's office and the headquarters of the Czechoslovakian Communist Party's Central Committee (KSC). This was the launching of a Soviet-led Warsaw Pact invasion, dispatched to put an end to the newfound freedoms inaugurated during the Prague Spring.

The Russian troops arriving at Ruzyne Airport merely hinted at the invasion's full magnitude. During the night of August 21–22, five Warsaw Pact nations sent a combined 165,000 troops, made up of Soviet, Polish, East German, Hungarian, and Bulgarian forces, along with 4,600 tanks and 250 planes. Knowledgeable observers agreed that the invasion was carried out with frightening efficiency. At 1:10 a.m., Prague Radio responded, informing citizens of what had occurred and asking that civilians "maintain calm and not . . . offer resistance to the troops on the march." Many listeners were dispirited to hear that "our army, security corps and people's militia have not received the command to defend the country." It was March 1939 all over again, as Czechoslovakia laid down its arms in the face of superior force.

Soviet troops quickly moved to seize strategic facilities and key Czechoslovakian leaders. Prime Minister Olditch Czernik was arrested and handcuffed in his office. A tank column led by a black limousine surrounded the Central Committee headquarters, where an angry crowd of defiant Czechoslovakians had gathered. Russian soldiers fired on the crowd, killing one man while the nation's political leadership watched from upper windows. Some hours later, Alexander Dubček and other KSC leaders could again only watch in horror as a squad of Soviet soldiers burst into their meeting room and ripped all the telephone cords out of the wall. Dubcek, Josef Smrkovsky, chair of the National Assembly, and František Kriegel, another powerful political figure, were ordered to raise their hands and face the wall. Escorted out of the building by the troops and KGB (Komitet Gosudarstvennoy Bezopasnosti, or Committee for State Security) officers, the three were herded into an armored car where they were restrained in painful positions. The KSC leaders were driven across the border, stopping in the Hungarian border town in Munkacs, Ukraine, where they were reunited with Czernik, who had been flown in from Prague. No doubt the fate of the Hungarian leader Imre Nagy, who following the failed 1956 uprising in Budapest, had been arrested, flown to the Soviet Union, and executed by a firing squad, was in the minds of all.

Barely four months had passed between the heady days of April, when in the middle of the month, the Dubček government proclaimed the ambitious and wildly popular Action Programme, and the Warsaw Pact invasion. The plan stirred the Kremlin's worst fears about the direction of the Prague Spring, with its promises of basic freedoms, fair elections, a more diversified economy, closer ties with the West, and a gradual transition to democratic socialism or, as Dubček had famously referred to it at a meeting of the KSC Presidium, "socialism with a human face." The traditional May Day celebrations in Prague were further cause for concern for Soviet and Eastern European communist leaders.

In meetings at the Kremlin, Soviet officials harshly chided Dubček and his compatriots. The Soviets likened events in Czechoslovakia to those in Hungary before the revolution there twelve years earlier. Pleading that they too were alarmed by the drift in their nation's politics, the Czechoslovakian Communist leaders promised to stem the tide of reform. The Czechoslovakian Ministry of Interior did ban opposition parties, but the Dubček government continued with plans for a federal union of Czechs and Slovaks and sought to better relations with Western European communist parties. At the end of the month, Warsaw Pact forces began to arrive in Czechoslovakia, ostensibly for previously discussed maneuvers.

June brought additional indications that a confrontation between reformers and hardliners was impending. Late in the month, Slovak Party Secretary Alois Indra sent telegrams to all local party organizations warning about "counterrevolutionary incitements." Particularly worrisome to hard-liners was the publication of a statement afterward known as the "Two Thousand Words," authored by the formerly dissident writer and journalist Ludvík Vaculík and signed by seventy prominent individuals. Although the document only pleaded for the populace to carry on the struggle for greater freedoms and to support the state's legitimate goals and institutions, it provoked a deluge of warnings from angry Soviet officials. Concerned the "Two Thousand Words" might lead to a Warsaw Pact occupation, Dubček and fellow party leaders vigorously denounced the document. At the end of the month, as Warsaw Pact forces withdrew, Soviet forces remained on Czechoslovakian soil, citing "abnormal traffic patterns" for their continued presence.

As of July, tensions persisted, with the Soviet Politburo agreeing that the Czechoslovakian situation would have to be resolved in one of three ways: Dubček would fulfill his promises to crack down on the reformers, a coup d'état by hard-liners would establish a new pro-Soviet government or, least desirable, Czechoslovakia would be brought to heel by force. At a meeting on July 3, Leonid Brezhnev and Hungary's Janos Kadar agreed that the racial and political unrest in the United States precluded interference from that "disintegrating society," regardless of what was done about Czechoslovakia. Within days, the Czechoslovakian leaders received written demands to attend a summit meeting to consider the threat posed by the "Two Thousand Words" manifesto. Viewing this as an unacceptable intervention in Czechoslovakian internal affairs, the leaders declined, despite the continued presence of Soviet troops. Tensions heightened when an article in *Pravda* on June 11 claimed the situation in Czechoslovakia was analogous to that in Hungary in 1956. Following a Warsaw Pact gathering on July 15, a joint memorandum demanded that Prague suppress the reform movement, impose party control over all mass media, and undertake a party purge.

The proposed meeting was scheduled for July 28 at Cierna, a town perilously close to the Soviet border. Many feared betrayal and the arrest of the Czechoslovakian attendees, but following the event, Dubček reassured his countrymen that there had been a general accord and that they were to be permitted to continue "the route opened in January 1968." Their "Soviet comrades" reportedly sought only minor concessions: the Czechoslovakian government would prevent media criticisms of the Soviet Union, foreign policy matter discussions would be limited, and there would be closer cooperation with the Soviet-bloc Council for Mutual Economic Assistance (COMECON). A subsequent meeting on August 3 in Bratislava designed to assuage the concerns of hardliners Walter Ulbricht of East Germany and Poland's Wladislaw Gomulka seemed to conclude favorably for the Czechoslovakians, producing a communique allowing every fraternal communist party the right to solve questions of socialist development according to specific national conditions. However, the Russians, convinced that Dubček would never be willing to tame the anti-socialist counterrevolution that he had helped unleash, and having solidified the support of the other Warsaw Pact countries, decided to opt for an invasion, supposedly sought by Czechoslovakian hard-liners.

On the night of August 20, Karel Hoffmann, in charge of telecommunications, ordered Radio Prague to shut down. At midnight, a second collaborator in the attempted coup demanded the Czechoslovakian News Agency transmit a worldwide statement proclaiming that a "revolutionary government of workers and peasants" had seized power and had requested Warsaw Pact aid in suppressing a counterrevolution. Loyal Czechoslovakians prevented the transmission and instead announced to the world that their nation was being invaded and solicited aid from any quarter. Early on the morning of August 21, remaining hopes the Soviets had to install a compliant puppet regime collapsed when two pro-Soviet Czechoslovakian party leaders confronted President Svoboda at Hradčany Castle and demanded that he accept a list of hardline communists who would form a new government. Svoboda responded, "Get out!" Warsaw Pact forces were already taking control of the city's streets, but they would do so without the support of the pro-Soviet government that the Kremlin anticipated.

The Soviet soldiers participating in the invasion had been informed that they were carrying out their "international duty" against "counterrevolution-aries" who would try to incite them to violence. Yet events in the streets of Prague, Bratislava, and countless other towns and villages told another story. Even as occupying forces secured their hold in Prague and elsewhere, hundreds of delegates to the Fourteenth Party Congress, scheduled to meet in September, arrived in the capital and gathered secretly in a factory. They unanimously voted to condemn the invasion and demand withdrawal of the Warsaw Pact troops and release of the Czechoslovakian political leaders. The delegates then escaped before the Russians could determine their location. Likely through the use of smuggled tape recordings, President Svoboda continued broadcasting to his nation, urging the withdrawal of occupying troops while simultaneously affirming Czechoslovakia's commitment to "the program of the Communist Party." "Do not lose faith," he counseled. "We must remain united in our struggle for a better life in our country."

Popular resistance against the invaders, which took many forms, clearly demonstrated the true feelings of patriotic Czechs and Slovaks alike. Warsaw Pact troops found themselves frustrated by the disappearance of almost all road and highway signs. The Czechoslovakian Secret Police cleared their headquarters of all police files rather than permit them to fall into the hands of the KGB. Czechoslovakian radio and television transmitters managed to continue broadcasting for a surprisingly long period of time, pleading for passive resistance, noncooperation, and foreign support.

The most visible opposition in the days following the invasion occurred in the streets, where events recorded on film soon found their way around the world, revealing the courage and determination of the protesters, who regularly faced injury and death. Protesters hurled bricks and Molotov cocktails at Warsaw Pact armored vehicles, jammed poles into tank gun barrels, and spray-painted swastikas on the offending vehicles. A major confrontation took place outside the Prague Radio Building, where protesters used grade-school Russian to try to convince the tank crews, often comprised of ill-educated young peasants, to withdraw. Eventually overwhelmed by the situation, several of the tankmen opened fire on the crowd, touching off a wild melee during which fire bombs torched several tanks. The arrival of a massive tank ended the confrontation, as the protesters' barricades were pushed aside and the radio station seized, ending its live coverage of the events. For days on end, protesters jammed historic Wenceslas Square, circulating underground pamphlets and holding daily hour-long strikes while staring down tank crews. Though Warsaw Pact troops had orders not to open fire unless fired upon, there were incidents in which discipline broke down and lives were lost. The youthful protesters quickly learned that the Russian tanks would rarely halt for human barriers, making any such confrontations potentially deadly.

Resistance also flared up in rural villages and, perhaps most surprisingly of all from the Russian viewpoint, in the Slovakian regions of the country. Reasoning that the less affluent Slovaks would be more receptive to the Russians than the Western-oriented Czechs, Soviet officials were dumbfounded when major opposition broke out in Bratislava. Slovak resisters left upturned pitchforks in the path of Russian tanks. In the city, young women hiked up their skirts to distract gawking Russian tank crew members while male protesters attacked from the opposite direction, smashing lights and equipment, and setting vehicles ablaze. Boxes of pornography delivered by ostensibly friendly Slovaks distracted a Russian tank group posted to a Bratislava park from its duties. Soviet troops quartered in a city museum found their water supply mysteriously cut off. A confrontation on the Danube bridge between Soviet armored forces and university students quickly turned violent, producing multiple casualties. The tanks soon controlled streets throughout the nation, but graffiti proclaimed that the resistance lived through slogans such as "Ivan Go Home," "Socialism, Yes; Occupation, No," and "This is not Vietnam."

Czechoslovakian television managed to smuggle about forty-five minutes of film about the invasion out of the country before being taken off the air, and its dramatic images, showing the full breadth of popular resistance to the invasion, were soon broadcast abroad. The film easily countered Soviet claims that the Czechoslovakians had welcomed the troops as liberators and made clear that the "youth revolt" of 1968 had crossed the Iron Curtain. In the United States, news of the invasion competed for media coverage with the Democratic National Convention and another deadly week in Vietnam. The gravity of the quashing of the Prague Spring led to longer televised news coverage, as public television temporarily filled the gaps that the commercially funded national networks left, given the half-hour time constraints traditionally imposed on news programs. At CBS, Walter Cronkite expanded his program to an hour on August 22. Though CBS and other networks refused to commit to a permanent hour-long newscast, CBS did agree to a one-hour "news magazine" that would air twice monthly—the popular and widely viewed *60 Minutes*.

As dramatic film images from Czechoslovakia made their way around the world, reaction in the United States and other Western democracies was uniformly critical. In the UN Security Council, a majority voted in favor of a resolution condemning the invasion, but the Soviet delegate vetoed it. More surprising was the reaction from some communist nations and parties. Yugoslavia's Josip Tito, whose nation had been excommunicated from the Soviet bloc in 1948, denounced the invasion, as did Romania's Nicolai Ceauşescu. Even more surprising, both governments encouraged popular demonstrations against the invasion. Communist parties in France, Italy, and Japan also denounced the invasion. Support for the crackdown came from Fidel Castro's Cuba, North Korea, and North Vietnam. Polish and East German officials blamed "Zionists" for the unrest in Czechoslovakia.

Meanwhile, as Warsaw Pact armor and troops controlled Czechoslovakian streets, the remaining question involved the fate of the Dubček government and that of Czechoslovakia. President Svoboda continued to demand release of the detained Czechoslovakian leaders, refusing to meet Soviet emissaries in Prague. In Moscow, an enraged Brezhnev confronted the four Czechoslovakian leaders, berating and charging they had fostered counterrevolution. The resolution he proposed was grim: the Czechoslovakians could accept a "Polish variant," which meant the permanent presence of Soviet troops and the full suppression of basic freedoms, such as those of press, speech, and assembly. A possible alternative was the destruction of Czechoslovakia, which would be split into Czech and Slovak regions, parts of which would be absorbed into the Soviet Union. On August 23, President Svoboda joined his colleagues in Moscow for four days of contentious and emotionally draining negotiations with the Soviet leadership. Both sides desperately needed a resolution that would defuse the situation—the Soviets because they required some justification for the invasion, and the Czechoslovakians because they feared their reform program and even their nation faced extinction. The subsequent "Moscow Protocol" of August 26 was a severe setback for Czechoslovakian hopes for any semblance of political liberalization and national autonomy. While the Czechoslovakian leadership would temporarily remain in office, occupying troops would be withdrawn only in conjunction with *normalization*, a term that signaled to Czechoslovakians that the freedoms enjoyed during the Prague Spring would be markedly circumscribed if not ended altogether. A shaken Dubcek informed his people that the only way to preserve their nation was to comply. Seventy-two Czechs and Slovaks had died during the invasion. Some seventy thousand soon fled the country while the opportunity still presented itself. Another three hundred thousand followed later, as winter swept away the Prague Spring.

By 1968, television, which poignantly relayed many of the developments in Czechoslovakia, played a significant role in American life, especially in the dissemination of news. Though the print media remained influential in conveying information and shaping opinion, the immediacy of television, together with its ability to deliver moving images, greatly enhanced its impact. Televised images of the civil rights demonstrations in Birmingham, Alabama, in the summer of 1963 made clear to many Americans the moral bankruptcy of racial discrimination, fostering a major shift in public opinion. Televised coverage of the assassination of President Kennedy and its aftermath in the fall of 1963 brought the nation together in unprecedented fashion, permitting a type of collective grieving. The Vietnam War became the most divisive foreign conflict in the nation's history in part because it quickly became a "living room war," the brutality of which was brought into individual homes on a nightly basis through television screens. 1968 was replete with events that gained dramatic intensity through television: the Tet Offensive, Lyndon Johnson's withdrawal from the presidential contest, the assassinations of Martin Luther King Jr. and Robert Kennedy, and protests at home and abroad. As much as any of these events, televised coverage of the 1968 Democratic National Convention in Chicago shaped public memory and national politics for years to come.

Canadian professor and media theorist Marshall McLuhan, who gained considerable celebrity with books such as *Understanding Media* (1964) and *The Medium is the Message* (1967), described television as a "cool" medium that required the viewer to "uncover and engage in the media" in order to "fill in the blanks" and determine meaning. This concept was central to a film being shot in Chicago during the fateful August days in 1968. *Medium Cool*, directed by Haskell Wexler, sought to explore the idea of the medium as the message through the story of a reporter covering the Democratic convention. The director could not have known that the scripted film would intersect with actual protests and confrontations between police and protesters, so much of the film presented raw documentary footage, both inside and outside the convention hall. In the final scenes, viewers heard protesters shouting the soon-to-be iconic chant, "The whole world is watching! The whole world is watching!"

Historian Todd Gitlin offers a succinct explanation for events emanating from the 1968 Democratic convention. "What exploded in Chicago that week," he writes, "was the product of pressures that had been building up for almost a decade: the exhaustion of liberalism, the marauding vengefulness of the authorities, the resolve and recklessness of the movement, the disintegration of the Democratic Party." Indeed, Democratic liberalism had seemed triumphant as recently as 1965, but racial conflicts and the Vietnam War helped to taint both the nation's leading political party and the ideology itself.

Robert Kennedy's assassination in early June was a devastating blow to anti-war elements in the party, while Eugene McCarthy proved dispirited as the Democratic Party national convention approached. Little impressed with McCarthy, Norman Mailer, in his account of the presidential campaign, pointed to the candidate's "deadness of manner, blankness of affect and suggestion of weakness in each deep pouch beneath each eye." Mailer notes too that McCarthy was oddly dismissive of the Warsaw Pact invasion of Czechoslovakia.

South Dakota Senator George McGovern, who emerged as the last best hope of anti-war Democrats, confided privately that what distinguished him from McCarthy was that "Gene really doesn't want to be president and I do." The previous year, McGovern had rejected Allard Lowenstein's proposal that the South Dakotan seek his party's nomination. Only days after the Republican convention folded, McGovern agreed to enter the Democratic race to represent the delegates pledged to the martyred Robert Kennedy. Whereas McCarthy had invariably offered only vague notions about ending the Vietnam War, McGovern's proposal was forthright and radical: he would withdraw 300,000 troops within sixty days while the remaining 250,000 were repositioned to safer coastal enclaves. However, despite the intensity of discontent on the part of dissident Democrats, the odds as of August clearly favored the administration's candidate.

Hubert Humphrey had compiled extensive liberal credentials in the course of a lengthy political career, but his tenure as vice president tarnished his reputation. Since his election to the second highest political office in the land, he had endured numerous humiliations inflicted by President Johnson, who had a well-earned reputation for demanding unconditional loyalty from those around him. Rarely shrinking from either vulgarity or bragging, LBJ boasted that he had "Hubert's balls in my pocket." Humphrey proved a loyal soldier when Johnson aspired to the Great Society, and as Democratic discontent with the Vietnam War had grown, he remained a steadfast public defender of Johnson's policies. When Johnson withdrew from the presidential race in late March 1968, Humphrey joined the contest fully aware that most of the elements comprising the "old politics" would ensure his nomination. Having avoided the primary season, Humphrey focused instead on gathering delegates in non-primary states and shoring up backing from labor unions and powerful Democratic political machines such as that directed by Chicago mayor Richard J. Daley. By the eve of the Democratic convention, however, it was increasingly clear that the nomination would not be his without a potentially disastrous intraparty fight.

Humphrey's chief problem was his inability to divorce his candidacy from the Johnson administration's Vietnam policy. Though Humphrey devoted considerable effort to formulating a position that would satisfy both the hawks and doves in his party, Johnson made it clear that any deviation from his policy would incur his wrath. "He just won't bend on Vietnam," confided an administration insider. "He wants personal vindication, even if it wrecks the party, which it may." All too familiar with Johnson's vindictive nature, Humphrey feared any attempt to shed the albatross of the president's Vietnam policy. Owing to his evident political timidity, Humphrey was increasingly viewed by many Democrats as a flawed candidate, whose natural buoyancy appeared incongruous during a year marked by death and violence. A Gallup poll taken at the outset of the convention showed barely a majority of Democrats favoring Humphrey. Mayor Daley initially withheld support while privately calling Humphrey "a lousy candidate." When the vice president arrived at Chicago's airport on August 25, there was no crowd or significant city official awaiting him.

As the likelihood of a contentious Democratic convention grew, so did plans to protest the event. City officials were chiefly fearful of black militants and possible race riots, but influential African Americans like Jesse Jackson and comedian/activist Dick Gregory warned blacks to maintain their distance from whatever fray erupted. Two groups, both appreciative of the reputation of the Chicago police, played chief roles in organizing and directing the protests that August. The Yippies, led by Abbie Hoffman and Jerry Rubin, were masters of the arts of political satire and guerrilla theater, with their published calls to action prior to the convention calculated to alarm city officials. Despite the clearly absurd nature of their threats, Deputy Mayor David Stahl wrote a memo warning that the Yippies had arrived to "start a revolution along the lines of the recent Berkeley and Paris incidents."

The other major protest group planning for the convention was the National Mobilization Committee to End the War in Vietnam. Its leaders, pacifist David Dellinger, Rennie Davis, and Tom Hayden, had laid the groundwork for the Chicago protest in late 1967. The Mobe remained committed to protest based on "a creative synthesis of Gandhi and guerrilla." Hayden called for a more confrontational approach, asserting that it was time for activists to "risk our necks to take democracy back, a time no longer for visionary platforms but for suffering and physical courage." "We are coming to Chicago," he declared, "to vomit on the politics of joy, to expose the secret decisions, upset the nightclub orgies, and face the Democratic Party with its illegitimacy and criminality." In July, Mobe plans for mobilizing demonstrators were augmented by Allard Lowenstein's announced goal of bringing 100,000 McCarthy supporters to the city under the auspices of his Coalition for an Open Convention.

Chicago Mayor Richard J. Daley, however, had no intention of allowing hippies and radicals to disrupt his party's nominating convention in his home town. The protesters' hair, clothes, language, beliefs, and behavior set them apart from a police force with largely working-class backgrounds and high school levels of education. The demonstrators seemed to denounce and defile everything traditional and patriotic. Given that this was a police force not known for its sensitivity, the likelihood of violent confrontation was already present when the Daley administration refused most march permits or to allow protesters to sleep in city parks.

By late August, Chicago appeared as if it were an armed camp. Taking seriously the threat of tens of thousands of protesters, Daley announced that the 12,000 police force would be put on twelve-hour shifts, backed by 6,000 Illinois National Guard troops. Held in reserve would be 6,000 regular Army troops. Rumors floated that 1,000 FBI undercover agents were circulating, along with military intelligence operatives. The convention site, the Chicago Amphitheater, was so heavily fortified with barbed wire and armed guards that reporters and delegates alike referred to it as "Fort Daley" and "Stalag 68." *Chicago Sun-Times* columnist Mike Royko wrote, "Never have so many feared so few," while the *Seed*, Chicago's underground paper, warned readers of the possibility of a "Festival of Blood." On August 22, Chicago police shot to death seventeen-year-old Dean Johnson, who had drawn a gun on officers after being stopped for a curfew violation. Surprisingly, his would be the only fatality of the week to come, but the episode undoubtedly primed police to expect more life-threatening violence and set the tone for their aggressive behavior in subsequent days.

In Lincoln Park, by Saturday, August 24, it was evident that the expected tens of thousands had failed to show up for the revolution. Confronted by police, the few hundred who did come were herded out of the park by the 11 p.m. curfew, led by Allen Ginsberg, one of several notable intellectuals, including the French writer Jean Genet and Robert Lowell, who had come to observe the likely political conflagration. The Festival of Life's actual kickoff began on August 25, featuring music by the MC5. Marchers from a Mobe-sponsored protest that began in front of the Conrad Hilton, where delegates were housed, and then moved to Grant Park for a rally, had joined the Lincoln Park crowd by early afternoon. The "good vibes" created by free food, free drugs, and free music soon gave way to skirmishes between police and the youthful crowd. At 11 p.m., provoked by shouted obscenities and hurled objects, the police charged into the crowd, arbitrarily beating anyone within reach. Some were heard chanting "Kill, kill, kill the motherfuckers." Afterward, Hayden and Rubin were jubilant, believing that the police violence would prove radicalizing. "This is fantastic," Rubin told a friend, "and it's only Sunday night. They might declare martial law in this town." Rubin's hopes for a declaration of martial law went unfulfilled, but for the next three days, a pattern developed in which demonstrators would fill the park during the day, only to be driven out before midnight by club-wielding police who pursued them through neighborhood streets, spreading chaos nightly.

The repression in the streets was in keeping with the atmosphere inside the overcrowded convention hall, where over 6,500 delegates sweated amid a constant din as the event convened on August 26. Daley insisted that dissident Democrats such as the McCarthy and anti-war delegates not be permitted to disrupt the proceedings or embarrass the Johnson administration. Delegates used magnetized floor passes for entry or exit and security guards, not averse to using physical force, aggressively responded to any complaint or deviation from protocol. Virtually the only signs allowed were those that read "We Love Mayor Daley." Band music drowned out shouts and chants generated by dissident delegates. Convention planners seated anti-war delegations at the rear of the hall, handing them microphones that often proved defective. Even standing in place to converse on the convention floor could bring squads of burly security men. Media personnel encountered special security and rough handling. Security guards physically assaulted CBS correspondents Dan Rather and Mike Wallace. Anchor Walter Cronkite observed on the air, "I think we've got a bunch of thugs down there, Dan." Convention chair Carl Albert of Oklahoma, the House majority leader, aggressively relied on his gavel to squelch any potential disruption inside the hall. As of Tuesday evening, the party's internal divisions precluded any significant action on agenda items. The night's activities ended when Mayor Daley made a throat-slashing gesture to notify Albert to gavel the session to a close before peace delegates could seize microphones to denounce Chicago police violence.

All of the emotions that had been simmering for nearly a week reached critical mass on Wednesday, August 28, offering a national television audience an unprecedented spectacle. Two noted public intellectuals, conservative William F. Buckley Jr. and leftist Gore Vidal, served as commentators for both the Republican and Democratic conventions for ABC News, but their exchange that evening revealed both barely concealed mutual disdain and the raw nature of public discourse. In the course of their discussion, Vidal called Buckley a "crypto-Nazi," which sent the usually mild-mannered *National Review* founder into an uncontrolled fit of rage. "Now listen, you queer," Buckley fumed, "I'll sock you in your goddamn face and you'll stay plastered." Unruffled, Vidal could barely conceal his joy at having successfully provoked the often-pretentious Buckley. The exchange would not be the only thing that shocked television audiences that day.

The day began unexceptionally enough with news from the amphitheater that chances for an anti-war candidacy were rapidly slipping away. McCarthy essentially conceded defeat and McGovern appeared a long shot at best. At

4:30 p.m., following three hours of emotional debate, the delegates voted on the "peace plank," a moderate statement that sought to move the party away from the administration's Vietnam policy. The vote failed 1,567 to 1,041, disappointing those who had labored for an end to the war. Anti-war delegates were reduced to singing "We Shall Overcome" and maintaining chants of "Stop the war," while the reality of their defeat took hold. The convention was to reconvene that evening at 8 p.m., when the nomination would be handed to Humphrey.

Protesters gathered that same day at Grant Park, where the only permit to demonstrate had been granted, and took seats at the bandshell where speakers such as Norman Mailer, William Burroughs, and Dick Gregory denounced the Vietnam War. In late afternoon, however, when a young man attempted to climb a flagpole and lower the American flag, helmeted riot police took it as a cue to launch a general assault on the crowd. Rennie Davis was singled out and beaten bloody. The attack became a strategic mistake on the part of the police, leading Hayden to encourage the crowd to leave the park and march to the Hilton. "Let us make sure that if our blood flows," he shouted, "it flows all over the city." The stage was set for what would be called "the Battle of Michigan Avenue."

In a violent confrontation beginning at about 8 p.m., angry, profanity-spouting demonstrators faced off against police lines and formations of national guardsmen in front of the Hilton. Chaos broke out when police suddenly charged into the intersection, indiscriminately beating protesters, bystanders, and journalists. Police pushed one group of bystanders through the plate-glass window of the Haymarket Inn, then poured inside to continue the beatings, which extended to those seated at the bar. Outside, arrestees were dragged by their pants and hair, and beaten again as they were pushed into paddy wagons. Camera crews and journalists reported being targeted for assault. From their suites high above the carnage, the party's anti-war candidates watched in horror as ten minutes of anarchy unfolded. An incredulous McGovern asked, "Do you see what those sons of bitches are doing to those kids down there?" McCarthy compared what was happening below to America's treatment of Native Americans. By contrast, Humphrey, whose eyes watered from tear gas that had seeped into the Hilton, denounced the protesters, proclaiming that they "don't represent the people of Chicago." As what the Walker Report would later describe as "a police riot" continued unabated, the protesters again took up the haunting chant, "The whole world is watching! The whole world is watching!" Observing from the Hilton, veteran political journalist Theodore White wrote in his notes, "The Democrats are finished."

In one of the most compelling coincidences in American history, the Battle of Michigan Avenue occurred even as the Democratic convention was voting on a presidential nominee. Not only were delegates watching broadcasts of the violence on portable televisions, but the three national networks began to intersperse live coverage of the convention events with films of the carnage downtown. The only memorable speech from that evening was delivered by Connecticut Senator Abraham Ribicoff, who had taken the podium for McGovern. Speaking to an increasingly restive audience, Ribicoff declared, "With George McGovern as president, we wouldn't have Gestapo tactics in the streets of Chicago!" As the audience exploded, both in support and outraged, cameras panned to Chicago's mayor, who could distinctly be seen mouthing his response: "Fuck you, you Jew son of a bitch, you lousy motherfucker, go home!" The raw underside of American politics was there for all to see, as Ribicoff, staring at Daley, rejoined, "How hard it is to accept the truth. How hard it is."

Hubert Humphrey displayed jubilation over his nomination, but he was an adept enough politician to understand what had transpired. As Humphrey's speech writer confided, "There was nothing to celebrate that night but wreckage." Humphrey's doctor found the nominee in the hotel suite's restroom weeping. Police violence continued through the night and into the next day, when a squad broke into the rooms of those manning McCarthy's Hilton headquarters, beating the young staff members and volunteers there.

Despite the damage that the Chicago police had done to his presidential chances, Humphrey remained a resolute defender of both Mayor Daley and President Johnson. In his acceptance speech on August 29, Humphrey reduced the Chicago debacle to "the lesson that violence breeds more violence." Before leaving the city, Humphrey told CBS's Roger Mudd, "We ought to quit pretending that Mayor Daley did anything wrong." The presidential candidate claimed that the demonstrations "were planned, premeditated by certain people in this country that feel all they have to do is riot and they'll get their way." Unsurprisingly, Daley remained unrepentant and polls showed public support on his side, notwithstanding his misspoken comment at a press conference that "the policeman isn't there to create disorder; the policeman is there to preserve disorder." In a later interview with Walter Cronkite, who noted that many victims of police brutality were journalists, Daley retorted, "Many of them are hippies themselves. They're part of this movement."

The Democratic Party limped away from Chicago, haunted by the prospect of having nominated a flawed candidate under the most inauspicious circumstances. The prospects for ending the Vietnam War through the political system seemed all but nonexistent. Abbie Hoffman was likely at least partially correct when he proclaimed, "Because of our actions in Chicago, Richard Nixon will be elected president."

In August 1968, two decades into the Cold War, the principals on both sides of the ideological conflict were compelled to confront disaffection within their respective political systems. In the Soviet bloc, the rigid dogmas of Stalinism seemed increasingly bereft of vitality to a younger generation of Czechs and Slovaks, who yearned for even a vestige of humanism in the system imposed on them. The Soviet response to liberalization of Czechoslovakia was military intervention and repression, bringing death and injury. In the United States, the established political order seemed determined to maintain its grip on national policy and leadership, through police violence if necessary. For a brief moment, the discontents in both nations seemed to display a growing weariness with ideological rigidity and the world that it had created.

11

"R-E-S-P-E-C-T"

People Power

It would prove to be one of the most iconic moments during a decade that abounded in them. On the podium alongside the auburn-haired Australian stood two handsome, ebony-shaded young men, with close cropped hair and Fu Manchu mustaches, each holding a single gloved fist in the air and looking to the ground as the Stars and Stripes headed up the flagpole and the American anthem played. Both were attired in dark blue uniforms, which had red and white stripes at the cuffs and the jacket bottoms, and contained the initials USA along with their individual numbers. Each man was barefoot, to protest the widespread poverty still afflicting African Americans, and wore beads to condemn lynchings. On the right flank with his left arm raised was bronze medal winner John Carlos, the twenty-three-year-old sprinter who had won each of his three earlier rounds and ran 20.10 in the final of the 200-meter dash, placing him .04 of a second behind the Australian runner, twenty-six-year-old Peter Norman, who stood on the opposite side. Norman, who temporarily held the Olympic record for the event after his second heat, was the only medal recipient looking straight ahead. All three men boasted the patch of the Olympic Project for Human Rights, Norman to display solidarity with his fellow competitors. Norman had told them, "I'll stand with you," not displaying to Carlos the fear he had expected to see. "I saw love" instead, Carlos remembered. In the middle, with his right arm fully extended, was twenty-four-year-old Tommie Smith, who had broken the Olympic mark during each of the preliminary rounds, then shattered the world record, becoming

Figure 11.1   Black Power protest at the Mexico City Olympics, 1968. Following the slaughter by the Mexican Army and riot police of an untold number of young protesters in Mexico City, US sprinters Tommie Smith and John Carlos raised their fists in the black power salute during the awards ceremony. Library of Congress, Prints and Photographs Division, LC-USZ62-10718.

the first man to officially run under twenty seconds (19.83). Carlos had actually run 19.7 during the Olympic Trials, held at Utah's Echo Summit, but it was not ratified because of his use of unsanctioned footwear. Smith's run was so blistering that it held up as the world record for nearly eleven years.

The black power salute delivered by Smith and Carlos was deliberately displayed, demonstrating the quiet dignity of the two San Jose State students who were following the lead of another young man with considerable gravitas, their African-American mentor and coach, twenty-five-year-old Harry Edwards, who headed the OPHR. Having completed a graduate degree in sociology at Cornell University, Edwards was teaching part-time at San Jose, and was very much influenced by the black power movement that had recently divided civil rights activists and supporters alike. A former student-athlete at San Jose, Edwards recognized the problems confronting young black athletes on college and university campuses, including de facto segregation in approved housing, restaurants that discriminated, social restrictions on interracial relationships, and even stereotypes regarding appropriate academic majors.

Changes in American race relations were and were not taking place, including within the sporting realm. The major professional sports—baseball, football, and basketball—had long been integrated, although even star performers were still bedeviled by racism that affected residential patterns and career opportunities, especially of the management variety, including in the very sports they had starred in. Blatant racial prejudices continued to confront athletes, including arguably the most famous in the world, Muhammad Ali. The undefeated heavyweight boxing champion, whose name change from Cassius Clay and confirmation of his association with the Nation of Islam remained enormously controversial, had his title stripped following his refusal to accept induction into the US Armed Forces. Black athletes, among them UCLA (University of California at Los Angeles) star center Lew Alcindor (later Kareem Abdul-Jabbar), Boston Celtic player-coach Bill Russell, and retired Cleveland Browns running back Jim Brown, came to Ali's defense during a press conference held in Cleveland in early June 1967. Looking back fondly at the event, Alcindor recalled being "very flattered and proud to" have been asked to participate alongside professional athletes. Moreover, "I was one hundred percent behind Muhammad's protesting what I thought was an unjust war. Jim Brown took the lead in the discussion. . . . He told us that our stature as heroes in the black community could help gather support for Ali."

Alcindor adopted a more militant stance that fall, when he attended the OPHR workshop hosted by Harry Edwards. As he later explained, Edwards and those joining his protest sought "to establish an organic link with the struggle of Dr. King, the struggle of Malcolm X, the struggle of SNCC, the struggle of CORE, the struggle of the Panthers." The Olympic Games, Edwards recognized, offered a stage "second only to the UN as an international political forum" and the only one "grassroots blacks had access to." Tendering his support for an Olympic boycott, Alcindor discussed a recent experience in his home city of New York:

> Everybody knows me. I'm the big basketball star, the weekend hero, everybody's All-American. Well, last summer I was almost killed by a racist cop shooting at a black cat in Harlem. He was shooting on the street, where masses of black people were standing around or just talking a walk. But he didn't care. After all we were just a bunch of niggers. I found last summer we don't catch hell because we aren't basketball stars or because we don't have money. We catch hell because we are black. Somewhere each of us has got to take a stand against this kind of thing. This is how I make my stand—using what I have. And I take my stand here.

Edwards reported that "fifty or sixty" athletes "voted unanimously" to join an Olympic boycott, and he contended that black athletes could help to recast the civil rights movement, in a manner no other group could. The idea of such protest dated back several years, when Dick Gregory, the black comedian and activist, and middle-distance runner Mal Whitfield, the African-American three-time gold medal winner, both supported a boycott of the 1964 Tokyo Games. Criticism cascaded upon would-be participants in such a boycott, who received hate letters and were denounced as unpatriotic, even traitorous. Many journalists such as the *Los Angeles Herald Examiner* sportswriter Melvin Durslag condemned the idea of a proposal triggered by "the black nationalist group," and attacked black athletes for supporting Ali. By contrast, the *New York Times'* sportswriter Robert Lipsyte mentioned the "tricks and tokenism" directed at African Americans, including inadequate civil rights legislation, a failing anti-poverty program, and "political oppression and police-state tactics on the street." African Americans were themselves split, with track legend Jesse Owens, the winner of four gold medals during the 1936 Berlin Olympics, asserting, "There's no place in the athletic world for politics." While doubting the effectiveness of a boycott, Jackie Robinson, the great black star who had shattered the twentieth century color barrier in organized baseball, acknowledged possessing admiration for the "youngsters," and declared, "I feel we've got to use whatever means, except violence, we can to get rights in this country."

OPHR's founding statement expressed an unwillingness to accept business as usual, including the token employment of blacks to demonstrate that the United States was addressing its racial conundrum. Signatories asserted, "We must no longer allow the Sports World to pat itself on the back as a citadel of racial justice when the racial injustices of the sports industry are infamously legendary." Any African American allowing himself to be utilized in such a fashion was "a traitor to this country because he allows racist whites the luxury of resting assured that those black people in the ghettoes are there because that is where they want to be." The statement articulated five key demands: restoring Ali's heavyweight title, firing Avery Brundage as US Olympic Committee chair, disinviting athletes from apartheid South Africa and Rhodesia, boycotting the less-than-progressive New York Athletic Club, and hiring more black coaches.

In February 1968, Alcindor, Mike Warren, and Lucius Allen, all stars on UCLA coach John Wooden's national championship basketball squad, declared their intention not to participate in the Mexico City Olympics. Criticism again fell on the athletes, most of it directed at Alcindor, college basketball's greatest star. When questioned that summer about his decision not to play for the US national team, Alcindor responded that America was "not really my country." Once more, hate mail, replete with racial epithets, was directed at Alcindor. Having pored over the vicious letters, *Los Angeles Times* columnist Charles Maher admitted, "One wonders how these people can expect the black man to take great pride in calling himself an American when they still take perverse satisfaction in calling him a nigger."

The International Olympic Committee (IOC) defused the threat of a widespread boycott by banning Rhodesia and South Africa from the Mexico City Games. Thus, when Tommie Smith and John Carlos appeared on the podium during the medals ceremony after the 200-meter dash, their well-thought-out protest was largely isolated. Avery Brundage ensured that the two were summarily dismissed from the US Olympic team, depriving them of a chance to compete in the 400-meter relay, which, barring an unfortunate accident, the American squad was virtually assured of winning. Justifying the reprisal, Brundage claimed, "They violated one of the basic principles of the Olympic Games: that politics play no part whatsoever in them."

The statement was wholly absurd, as the modern Olympic Games had been riddled with political intrigue since its inception seventy-two years earlier. War had resulted in the cancellation of five Olympic Games: the summer contests in 1916, 1940, and 1944, and the winter ones in 1940 and 1944. Germany had staged the 1936 Olympic Games as a celebration of Adolf Hitler's Nazi regime, while the Soviet Union did not participate until 1952, at which point the Games became another Cold War venue. Brundage himself had been involved in controversial moments, including opposing a boycott of the 1936 Summer Games and bringing pressure against the entry of Jewish athletes in Berlin.

But Smith and Carlos were the ones cast as villains by many. The *Los*

Angeles Times charged that the two sprinters had delivered a "Nazi-like salute" and dismissed "the sorry business of a Black Power fist gesture." The *Chicago Tribune* deemed the act "an embarrassment . . . contemptuous of the United States" and "an insult to their countrymen." *Time* magazine delivered a feature article, presenting the Olympic logo with the slogan "Faster, Higher, Stronger" replaced by "Angrier, Nastier, Uglier." The young sportswriter Brent Musburger wrote, "One gets a little tired of having the United States run down by athletes who are enjoying themselves at the expense of their country." He went on to denounce Smith and Carlos, whom he called "juvenile" and "ignoble," as "a pair of black-skinned Stormtroopers." On the other hand, he affectionately referred to Brundage as "Avery." After winning the gold medal over a Russian foe, heavyweight boxer George Foreman went around the ring holding a small American flag, an apparent slap at the protest by Smith and Carlos.

However, a number of American athletes expressed solidarity with the two runners. Wyomia Tyus, who anchored the women's 4x100-meter relay, declared, "I'd like to say that we dedicate our relay win to John Carlos and Tommie Smith." Long jumper Ralph Boston, who won a bronze medal in his signature event (having taken the gold medal and the silver medal, respectively, in the two previous Summer Olympics), also was barefoot during the medals ceremony and offered, "They are going to have to send me home, too, because I protested on the victory stand." Gold-medal recipient Bob Beamon, who shattered the world record by more than a foot and a half with a 29-foot-2.5-inch leap, stood at the podium with his sweatpants rolled up, displaying black socks. That was intended to demonstrate he too was "protesting what's happening in the U.S.A." The three medal winners in the 400-meter run—Lee Evans, Larry James, and Ron Freeman—sported black berets in a silent act of protest on the podium. The US rowing team, all white students from Harvard, offered full support: "We—as individuals—have been concerned about the place of the black man in American society in their struggle for equal rights. As members of the US Olympic team, each of us has come to feel a moral commitment to support our black teammates in their efforts to dramatize the injustices and inequities which permeate our society."

The protest by Tommie Smith and John Carlos during the 1968 Summer Olympics occurred in a city that had been experiencing a great deal of strife over the previous several months, to the dismay of the long-governing Partido Revolucionario Institucional (PRI). Notwithstanding its name, the PRI had long ceased standing for the ideals associated with the Mexican Revolution (1910–1920), particularly following the reform administration of General Lazaro Cardenas (1934–1940). Indeed, to enable the games to go on as scheduled and to quash mounting protest, the Mexican government employed army troops and riot police to attack protesters in Mexico City's Tlatelolco Plaza, resulting in a massacre of an untold number of people, the arrest of thousands of others, and the disappearance of several student leaders.

The surge in opposition to President Diaz Ordaz's PRI government was in keeping with growing unrest characterizing much of Latin America in 1968. Discontent with existing regimes proved widespread, some fueled by national liberation movements elsewhere, but also due to the apparent stranglehold on power by conservative elements tied to large landowners, the Latin American military and police, and reactionary elements within the Catholic Church. Providing a starkly different model were Cuba, which had defied the "Colossus of the North," and its revolutionary leaders, Fidel Castro and the recently deceased Che Guevara. Che's image, in particular, appeared "ubiquitous," the historian Jeffrey L. Gould has indicated. By early summer, students, faculty, and workers joined in a "March for University Autonomy" in Bolivia, condemning the "military boot." In Ecuador, students attacked and torched buses, in a display of anger regarding increased fares, while in Venezuela, they marched to protest budget cuts. In Chile, fighting in the streets of Santiago took place after the arrest of several students. In Brazil, "pitched battles" occurred between students and the police and the military. Protests involving both students and workers followed police efforts to quash demonstrations supporting university autonomy. A state of siege existed in Uruguay, but protests continued. In Uruguay, long stable and prosperous, the urban guerrilla group, the Tupamaros, now moved beyond robberies to the kidnapping of well-placed individuals, in an effort to expose the government's impotence. According to Gould, the 1968 protests in Latin America were matched only by those during the Wars of Independence and an array of strikes that followed the end of World War I.

The Catholic Church, which had long been aligned with conservative, even reactionary elements in Latin America and still contained stridently anti-radical clergy, nevertheless provided support for the liberation movements in the hemisphere. The Conference of Latin American Bishops convening in Medellin, Colombia, in August 1968, asserted that the church, in keeping with Vatican II, needed to demonstrate a "preferential option for the poor." That directive served as a spur for the creation of base Christian communities particularly in indigent neighborhoods, organized by clergy and laypeople alike, and for articulating the theology of liberation, which called for assisting the poor and oppressed in economic, social, and political spheres. Some priests and nuns would go so far as to join the ranks of guerrilla forces determined to topple oligarchies, military juntas, and even the conservative church leadership.

The repression that was meted out in Mexico City as the Summer Olympics approached foreshadowed later waves of atrocities committed in Latin America, including in Chile, Argentina, and Uruguay, where thousands were murdered and right-wing military regimes prevailed for extended periods. The turn toward the iron fist in Mexico gradually developed as protest continued over the span of several months. Protest largely involved high school and university students, their numbers having soared in recent years, as the nation experienced greater affluence and the emergence of a middle class. Students, indeed, comprised the lone group not under the thumb of the PRI, which kept even labor unions in check. Mexican universities retained a large measure of autonomy, in keeping with a tradition that had largely been adhered to in Latin America. But the regime of President Gustavo Diaz Ordaz viewed the budding unrest as imperiling the Mexico City Olympics, designed to showcase Mexico as a modern state. He was even more concerned as protesting French students, workers, and professionals threatened Charles de Gaulle's hold on power. Mexican students, in turn, were enthralled by the events playing out in France. The attraction of radical ideas, including Trotskyism, further worried President Diaz Ordaz, who feared that "an international conspiracy of revolutionaries" existed.

In late July, less than three months before the start of the Olympic Games, violent confrontations ensued in downtown Mexico City, pitting student demonstrations against riot police. In a manner that could only have intensified Diaz Ordaz's paranoia, student manifestoes celebrated movements involving their peers taking place throughout the world. A National Strike Council emerged, and students in Mexico City, angered about the arrival of riot police at universities, conducted a general strike. By early August, hundreds of thousands of students, holding revolutionary banners, were appearing in mass rallies.

Nevertheless, President Diaz Ordaz insisted only weeks before the Olympic Games were to open that Mexico remained "an untouched island," untroubled by the youthful revolt elsewhere. However, the student movement continued, with demands for release of political prisoners, abrogation of a Penal Code criminalizing "acts of subversion, treason and public disorder," termination of the special riot police, and compensation for victims of security forces. In mid-September, government troops began occupying the National Autonomous University, arresting many faculty members and students. The police and the army entered onto the campus of National Polytechnic Institute, shooting at students, who purportedly fired back.

A mass rally took place on October 2 at Tlatelolco, in the center of Mexico City's historic and cultural district. Both soldiers and police suddenly began firing on the crowd, killing an untold number, estimates varying from one hundred to thousands, while thousands more were beaten, tortured, and incarcerated. Others were kidnapped, never to reappear, becoming *los desaparecidos*. The crushing of the student movement set the stage for Mexico to host the Olympic Games.

Ten days following what came to be called the "Night of Sorrow," the opening ceremony for the 1968 Summer Olympics was held in Mexico City, the first Olympic Games to take place in Latin America and in a developing country. Amid great fanfare, which included the lighting of the Olympic Cauldron by the Mexican national champion in the 80-meter hurdles, Enriqueta Basilio, the first woman to perform that feat, President Diaz Ordaz declared the games open. Nearly 5,500 athletes from 112 countries competed in the Mexico City Olympics, with an abundance of world records set in an array of different events. But the 1968 Summer Olympics continues to be best remembered for the carefully orchestrated protest carried out by Tommie Smith and John Carlos.

Like their mentor Harry Edwards, Smith and Carlos were clearly influenced by the growing attraction of black power within the civil rights movement. Particularly following the assassination of Martin Luther King Jr., no group, however loosely tied to that movement, drew more attention than the Black Panther Party. Barely a year old when 1968 began, the party remained a tiny sect at that point, still led by founders Huey Newton and Bobby Seale, as well known for its distinctive attire as anything else. Smartly dressed, the Panthers sported dark leather coats and pants, along with black berets. The Panthers had issued a Ten-Point Program that demanded self-determination for African Americans, a guaranteed income, slavery reparations, decent housing, and empowering education. It also called for exemption from fighting for "a racist government," black self-defense groups in black communities, release of black prisoners, fair trials, and the right to revolt against tyrannical authority.

They initially entered the national limelight during a showdown at the California State Capitol in Sacramento, where a group of thirty Panthers appeared in May 1967, holding rifles and shotguns, as lawmakers prepared to restrict public displays of such weapons. Likening police oppression in America to US military engagement in Vietnam, Seale condemned the "repression, deceit and hypocrisy" that confronted black citizens. The Panthers had already taken to riding in their cars, with their firearms visible, and copies of the US Constitution also at the ready. The legislation passed, signed into law by Governor Ronald Reagan, a darling of American conservatives who increasingly became fixated on "gun rights."

The notoriety acquired by way of the Sacramento incident temporarily escaped FBI director J. Edgar Hoover as he issued a directive to field offices on August 25, 1967. He demanded that operations be conducted against supposed Black Nationalist groups, then explained: "The purpose of this new counterintelligence endeavor is to expose, disrupt, misdirect, discredit, or otherwise neutralize the activities of black nationalist, hate-type organizations and groupings, their leadership, spokesmen, membership, and supporters." The targeted organizations included Martin Luther King Jr.'s Southern Leadership Conference but not the Black Panthers.

More attention came the way of the Panthers in late 1967 and throughout the following year, because of their association with charismatic individuals, a number of whom had trouble with the law. Former SNCC chair Stokely Carmichael, one of the earliest black power proponents, became the Panthers' prime minister, insisting, "We must cut ourselves off from white people." Eldridge Cleaver, a writer for *Ramparts* soon to become a best selling author, served as minister of information, and in August 1968 would become the presidential candidate of the Peace and Freedom Party. Bobby Seale was present in Chicago during the Democratic National Convention, ending up as one of eight individuals charged with having conspired to incite a riot at that point. Huey Newton remained the face of the Black Panther Party, and the individual around whom much of the acclaim and controversy associated with it would swirl. A photographic image of Newton, dressed in leather garb and black beret, holding a rifle and a spear, while sitting on a peacock chair, became one of the era's most enduring.

On October 28, 1967, Newton had been involved in a shootout that resulted in his trial for the murder of John Frey, a white Oakland police officer. Newton's arrest led to Cleaver's effectively taking control of the still-tiny band of Panthers. San Francisco police officers, at 3:30 on the morning of January 16, battered down the front door of the apartment where Cleaver was residing with his wife Kathleen. In February, Cleaver helped to set up a number of "Free Huey Newton" rallies, with many activists, both black and white, contending Newton was being railroaded. Berkeley police officers, at 2:00 a.m. on February 25, broke into the home of Bobby and Artie Seale, charging the couple with a murder conspiracy. In early March, FBI director J. Edgar Hoover informed his staff of the need to "prevent the coalition of militant black nationalist groups," as part of COINTELPRO. That same month, Newton, sitting in jail, issued his Executive Mandate No. 3, directing all Panthers to acquire firearms, and to use them against any uninvited individuals seeking to come into their domiciles without displaying a valid warrant. On April 5, one day following the murder of Dr. King, Cleaver spoke in Berkeley, insisting that the slain civil rights leader, whom he little respected, would be avenged.

The next evening was the occasion when police surrounded Cleaver and another Panther, seventeen-year-old Bobby Hutton, who was purportedly killed when he and Cleaver came out with their hands up, Cleaver, already wounded in the leg, escaped the same fate as it was apparent he had discarded any weapons. *Ramparts* magazine issued a statement questioning whether Cleaver, who had been charged with assault with intent to kill, could receive "fair treatment in jail or in the courts," given "the open hostility of the Oakland police for black militants." At the memorial service for Hutton, Ronald Dellums, a black city councilman from Berkeley, warned that the United States was "going 1,000 miles toward militarism and fascism" while scapegoating black people. Another shootout with police occurred in Los Angeles on August 5, resulting in two dead Panthers. By September, FBI internal memos finally pointed to the Black Panther Party, deeming it "extremist," warning that it was "rapidly expanding," and demanding counterintelligence efforts to disrupt it.

Amid great publicity, the trial of Huey Newton for murder and other charges took place in September, leading to his conviction for voluntary manslaughter, an obvious compromise verdict. Newton had testified on his own behalf, denying that he shot either the murdered policeman, whom the defense sought to portray as a racist, or another cop who had been wounded in the Oakland shootout. As the jury deliberated, Newton told an interviewer, "We feel it necessary to prepare the people for the event of an actual physical rebellion." Labeling Che, Mao, Ho Chi Minh, and Jomo Kenyatta, who headed the Mau Mau guerrillas in Kenya, his teachers, Newton expressed a desire "to become a revolutionary" himself. He praised white revolutionaries who supported the Panthers, calling their dedication inspirational. Hoover, for his part, condemned the Black Panther Party as the "greatest threat to the internal security of the country." After Newton was sentenced to two to fifteen years in prison, one Panther warned, "In a few days there is going to be war." Another declared, "From this day on the war is on until black people are free."

Shortly following the Newton trial, the African-American reporter Thomas A. Johnson examined "Black Panthers: Angry Men 'At War' With Society." He discussed party chapters that desired full employment, the termination of consumer exploitation, fair housing, true education, exemption from military service, and an end to both police brutality and the killing of black citizens. The Panthers drew in young African Americans, Johnson stated, by appealing "to their manhood, status, pride and the need to protect one's own." Interestingly, he compared that appeal with the one offered by elite American military regiments. For those who complained about black people being armed, one young Panther asserted that blacks were no longer going to be submissive.

Controversies continued to follow the Panthers, with both California Governor Ronald Reagan and Speaker Jesse M. Unruh of the State Assembly condemning an invitation by the University of California for Eldridge Cleaver to speak on campus. Reagan denounced Cleaver as "an advocate of racism and violence," while Unruh suggested that faculty who wanted to bring Cleaver to Berkeley harbored a "death wish." UC Regents soon unveiled a new policy applicable to visiting lecturers, generally limiting them to a single appearance. Two thousand students at a meeting responded by voting unanimously to allow Cleaver to present ten lectures on racism, as originally planned.

In a related development, the California State College trustees voted eight to five to suggest to the recently hired president of San Francisco State College, Robert R. Smith, that he remove George Mason Murray, a Black Panther Party member who had just returned from a visit to Castro's Cuba, from a position teaching English to incoming students deemed culturally deprived. While uncertain if he would do so, Dr. Smith indicated, "The odds are against it."

San Francisco State College had experienced turmoil for over a year, starting during the presidency of John Summerskill, a forty-two-year-old clinical psychologist and opponent of the Vietnam War who had worked at Cornell. But Summerskill's liberal credentials hardly served him well during his brief tenure. The college endured a sit-in at his office by students protesting disclosure of academic standing to the Selective Service System; picketing by students and faculty of administrative offices; a physical attack on staff members of the campus newspaper, faculty advisers, and a *San Francisco Examiner* reporter, by black students; occupation of the administration building; the president's closing of the campus to avoid police being called in; and his unanticipated resignation in February 1968, which was to become effective in September.

Genuine tragedy occurred early that same month on the other side of the country when police in deeply conservative, primarily rural Orangeburg fired on students from historically black South Carolina State University, who were conducting a protest against a segregated bowling alley. The incident took place on the university campus where students constructed a bonfire that a police officer tried to extinguish before being injured by a projectile hurled from a crowd. After another officer attempted to subdue the crowd by firing a shot into the air, other police officers, fearing they were being attacked, began shooting at the students, wounding twenty-seven and killing Samuel

Hammond, Delano Middleton, and Henry Smith. Nine officers eventually were tried in federal court but a jury quickly agreed to acquit them during deliberations. Civil rights leaders continued to refer to the terrible incident as "the Orangeburg Massacre."

In March, Bobby Seale told a large crowd in the main auditorium at San Francisco State College "that the only power blacks have is with a gun." That same month, members of Third World Liberation Front, comprised of black, Latino, and Filipino-American groups, occupied the campus YMCA office. Controversy continued regarding the black playwright LeRoi Jones's serving as a visiting professor that spring. Police removed 400 students who were occupying the administration building, demanding Air Force ROTC be removed from campus, 400 indigent students be admitted in the fall, nine minority faculty members be hired to assist minority students, and the sociologist Juan Martinez, who supported the Black Students Union, be retained.

As more protests occurred in late May, the chancellor requested Summerskill's immediate resignation. He was replaced by Robert Smith, a professor of education. On September 18, Smith revealed that the college had established a Black Studies Department. But the request to reassign George Mason Murray caused Smith all sorts of problems. Trustees were enraged to learn that Murray had exclaimed to students at Fresno State College, "We are slaves and the only way to become free is to kill all the slave masters." Murray had also supposedly indicated that black students at San Francisco State College needed to bring weapons to campus to ward off racist administrators. Finally yielding to pressure from the chancellor, President Smith suspended Murray on November 1. Five days later, the longest-running student strike in the history of American higher education began. Following confrontations between students and the police, the campus was shut down for several days, leading Governor Reagan to demand its reopening, something that the trustees ordered President Smith to do. On November 26, Dr. Smith resigned, and the trustees named S. I. Hayakawa, a noted linguist and semanticist, as acting president. After closing the campus, Hayakawa reopened it, while a clash with student and faculty protesters soon resulted. Trying to prevent students from employing a sound truck, Hayakawa attempted to disconnect speakers. He engaged in a verbal battle with the novelist Kay Boyle, a faculty member, telling her, "You're fired," while she responded by dismissing him as "Hayakawa Eichmann." Campus disturbances continued, while Hayakawa, with his dismissive attitude toward critical students and faculty, became a favorite of conservatives across the state and nation.

As the San Francisco State College student strike continued, the Black Panthers remained in the news, with a grand jury in the city purportedly preparing to carry out "a sweeping investigation" of the group. Mayor Joseph L. Alioto wanted the grand jury to decide whether the organization's leaders should face indictments "for conspiracy to commit murder." He declared, "The public has the right to know whether this is an organization along political lines or another Murder, Inc., or a bunch of thugs." The grand jury declined to carry out the investigation. However, the Senate Permanent Investigating Subcommittee, chaired by Arkansas's John L. McClelland, began an examination of the Panthers.

Kathleen Cleaver indicated on November 26 that her husband, Eldridge, the source of much contention at the Berkeley campus, "isn't going back to prison." The Black Panthers, she warned, would prevent that from happening "by any means necessary," including through the use of guns. Thurgood Marshall, the great litigator for the NAACP's Legal Defense and Educational Fund and the first African American to sit on the US Supreme Court, declined Cleaver's bid for a stay of the order placing him back behind bars for having violated his parole agreement. Bobby Seale attacked Marshall as "an Uncle Tom, a bootlicker, a nigger pig, a Tonto and a punk." The following day, thirty-three-year-old Eldridge Cleaver was deemed a fugitive. As it turned out, he fled, resulting in the revoking of a $50,000 bail bond, the start of a seven-year odyssey that carried him to Algeria, North Korea, North Vietnam, the Soviet Union, China, and France.

The publicity induced by the legal tribulations of Huey Newton and Eldridge Cleaver, and the violent confrontations with the police that often involved lesser known Panthers, ironically spurred growth of the Black Panther Party. Eventually, scores of chapters existed across the country, while the membership reached 2,000–5,000. The Panthers soon became known for their free breakfast program for schoolchildren, free medical centers, and *The Black Panther* newspaper. But the fiery leaders—Newton, Cleaver, Bobby Seale, Kathleen Cleaver, and Elaine Brown—earned the greatest attention and attracted loyal followers. That created the potential for disaster, as such strong-willed individuals and others with similar temperaments invariably clashed, setting the stage for internecine squabbles. That propensity was exacerbated by the relentless campaigns waged against the Panthers by government and police agents, determined to prevent the Panther version of black power from amassing greater traction. Criminal trials, police raids, employment of agents provocateurs, the spreading of false but scurrilous rumors, and massive egos crippled the Panthers at the very moment they achieved iconic status inside the New Left and the latest version of the civil rights movement.

Black power probably reached its pinnacle in 1968, with the Panthers, proponents of an armed version of that idea, achieving considerable notoriety. Inside the Movement as a whole, Panthers like Newton, Eldridge Cleaver, and Seale were figures whom many cared to emulate, setting the stage for a hard turn leftward and in the direction of supporting radical, even revolutionary action. A heightened version of the exalting of People Power that characterized the entire decade, black power appeared in other guises, as during the Mexico City Olympics.

The protest conducted with such elegance by Tommie Smith and John Carlos cast a global light on black power, to the dismay of the IOC, the Mexican government, and an array of others upset by the seeming lack of respect and purported ingratitude displayed by the two young men. They suffered dismissal from the US Olympic team, brickbats from sportswriters, and condemnations from other commentators who questioned their patriotism, sanity, and basic decency. In reality, they acted adroitly, bearing witness in their own fashion, avoiding angry rhetoric, charged verbiage, and accusatory language, all of which they would ironically experience because of their silent protest.

The 1968 Summer Games went on, starting in the wake of the Tlatelolco massacre designed to silence the version of People's Power displayed by Mexico's young in the streets of the capital city. The discontent with the ruling party's monopolistic hold on power, its ever greater distance from the ideals of the Mexican Revolution that once helped to sustain it, and the spending of valuable resources on the Games themselves threatened to spill over into Mexican society as a whole, which could have endangered the PRI's unbroken reign. The Mexican government opted to shoot down its own children in the streets of one of the world's great cities, which was hosting the quadrennial Summer Olympics a week and a half later. Protests by students on their high school and university campuses and in the streets were in keeping with the global unrest displayed throughout 1968, when change seemed imminent, and change of a radical, even revolutionary sort beckoned.

American educational institutions similarly continued to experience clashes involving Establishment forces and young people desirous of alterations in their society's makeup. That was seen earlier in the year at Columbia and again at San Francisco State College, where a long-running student strike was carried out, which involved discussion of revolution, the Black Panthers, student power, fear of anarchy, political posturing, and so much more. The strike would endure until the spring when it finally ended, but questions of power in no way abated. Talk of the need for People's Power would continue and heighten at times over the next few years, before subsiding as if a fever had broken.

12

"The Personal Is Political"

Sexual Revolutions

Well known to the staff and patrons of Andy Warhol's Factory, situated just off New York City's Union Square, Valerie Solanas arrived at the building's entrance on June 3, 1968, to confront the pop artist. Paintings of mundane objects such as a can of Campbell's soup and artsy films had assured the openly gay artist of considerably more than his "fifteen minutes of fame" by 1968. The Factory, Warhol's disordered studio, hosted a transient group of eccentrics, including Viva, Ultra Violet, Holly Woodlawn, Joe Dallesandro, Edie Sedgwick, and Candy Darling, proclaimed "superstars" by their white-haired, soft-spoken mentor. It was not always evident what their talents were other than being famous, but in Warhol's universe that was a signal achievement.

Solanas had haunted the Factory long enough to appear in two Warhol films and had approached him the previous year to produce her unorthodox play *Up Your Ass*, which dealt with the sordid activities of a prostitute. Increasingly wary of obscenity charges, Warhol remembered, "I thought the title was so wonderful and I'm so friendly that I invited her to come up with it, but it was so dirty I think she must have been a lady cop." Nevertheless, Warhol accepted the script and upon hearing Ultra Violet read it, enthused that Solanas is "a hot water bottle with tits. . . . She has a lot of ideas." Solanas's faith in Warhol took a downward plunge, however, after he confessed to having "lost" the play in the chaotic stacks of paper in the Factory. In the fall of 1967, Warhol and Viva had spotted Solanas at a nightclub and taunted her, Viva telling her, "You're a dyke! You're disgusting."

By the spring of 1968, the slightly built, brown-haired Solanas, whose

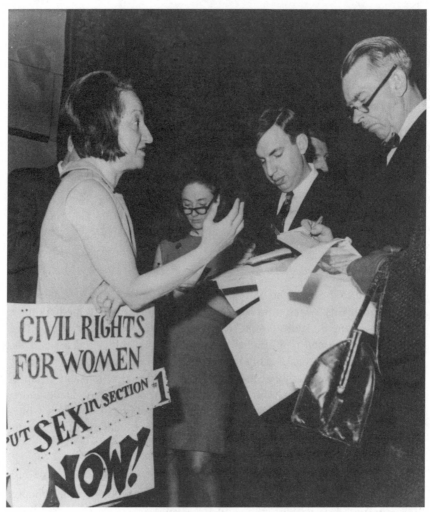

Figure 12.1   A founder of the National Organization of Women (NOW) in 1966, Betty Friedan raised eyebrows when she vowed to "put sex into the New York constitution" in 1967. Within a year, NOW was rapidly outpaced by younger, more radical feminists who demanded far broader and deeper changes in American society than Friedan and her associates advocated. Library of Congress, Prints and Photographs Division, LC-USZ62-122632.

wandering existence had included poverty, living on the street, and prostituting herself in Greenwich Village, became convinced that Warhol was plotting with Olympia Press publisher Maurice Girodias to steal and publish her work, including the radical feminist *SCUM Manifesto*. Wearing a raincoat over a sweater despite the warm weather and uncharacteristically sporting makeup, Solanas, clutching a brown paper bag, told Warhol film director Paul Morrissey that she was there to "get money" from Warhol and ignored Morrissey's claim that the artist would not be in that day. At 2:00 p.m., she succeeded in gaining entry to the building and rode the elevator up to the studio, but was ejected by Morrissey.

Solanas then rode the elevator until Warhol arrived and they strode into the latest edition of the Factory, which boasted white walls, polished wood floors, and retro-chic furniture. Though Warhol complimented Solanas on her appearance, Morrissey continued threatening to eject her. Seated at a desk, Warhol accepted a phone call while Morrissey headed for the restroom. After a brief wait, Solanas drew a .380 semi-automatic pistol from the bag (or perhaps from her coat, accounts differ) and fired three shots at the unsuspecting Warhol. As the first two shots missed, Warhol screamed, "No! No! Valerie, don't do it!" The third bullet struck him, piercing his left lung, spleen, stomach, liver, and esophagus before tearing through his right lung. As Warhol collapsed, Solanas shot visiting art critic Mario Amaya in the hip before pointing the weapon at Warhol's manager Fred Hughes's head, but the gun jammed. Amid the resulting chaos, Solanas walked out of the studio, leaving behind the paper bag. Her fifteen minutes of fame had begun.

Public fascination with Solanas and the attempted assassination of a famous pop artist began as soon as headlines like the *New York Post*'s "Actress Shoots Andy Warhol" hit the newsstands. The event brought together numerous contemporary issues in a compelling narrative: the counterculture, pop art, the cult of fame, lesbianism, feminism, gun violence, and a distinct version of the politics of assassination.

As Warhol slowly recovered from his wounds after a five-hour-long operation, the often blurry details of Solanas's life took shape in newspaper reports. For several years, Solanas roamed the streets panhandling, prostituting herself, and holing up in cheap dives like the Hotel Earle, considered a refuge for lesbians, transvestites, and a variety of down-and-out street people. Solanas sought to establish herself as a writer, publishing an article in *Cavalier*, although the hip men's magazine rejected her proposal to write a regular column, "Lesbian at Large." Increasingly obsessed with the intertwining of sex and power, she wrote *Up Your Ass*. Having lost the script, Warhol paid her $25 to appear in his film *I, a Man*, in which she played a male role.

SCUM Manifesto likely took shape in 1967. The opening sentence suc-
cinctly summarized what the document represented: "Life in this society
being, at best, an utter bore and no aspect of society being at all relevant to
women, there remains to civic-minded, responsible, thrill-seeking females
only to overthrow the government, eliminate the money system, institute
complete automation and destroy the male sex." The introductory paragraphs
made clear Solanas's disdain for the male sex, which she blamed for all
humankind's ills. Because of male egocentrism, man was, she wrote, "an
utter bore, an inoffensive blob. . . . He is trapped in a twilight zone halfway
between humans and apes, and is far worse off than the apes." Women certainly did not require men for sexual fulfillment, she insisted, noting that "the
male is unfit even for stud service."

Though indicted following the shooting, Solanas was declared mentally
incompetent in August and remanded to a state hospital for insane criminals.
Reevaluated in January 1969, Solanas was diagnosed as a chronic paranoid
schizophrenic, though she was deemed fit for trial that June. Representing
herself, she was found guilty and sentenced to three years in prison. Unrepentant, Solanas declared the shooting "a moral act." "And I consider it
immoral," she added, "that I missed. I should have taken target practice."

It would have been easy to dismiss Valerie Solanas as a crank and a lunatic,
but her attempted murder of Andy Warhol produced serious commentary
about her and *SCUM Manifesto*. Ti-Grace Atkinson, president of the New
York Chapter of the National Organization of Women (NOW), hailed Solanas
as "the first outstanding champion of women's rights" and "a heroine of the
feminist movement." According to cultural critic Marcie Frank, "Solanas's
writing and her example prompted . . . Atkinson to describe a form of radical
feminism, to investigate the Amazon legend to do so, and to express the
necessary relations between lesbianism and feminism."

By 1968, the women's movement was dynamic and diverse, encompassing
an expanding body of theory and action that was reflected in a proliferation
of organizations dedicated to realizing women's rights and sexual equality.
Moving far beyond the objectives and accomplishments of those who preceded them, second wave feminists proved willing to view American society
from a radical vantage point. Though the Stonewall Riot was a year in the
future, 1968 also proved to be a foundational year for the homosexual movement, which drew strength and encouragement from the flood of rights movements that blossomed that year.

Already apparent by the mid-1960s, although few recognized this at the
time, the women's movement contained distinct wings, one fundamentally
radical in nature, the other more in keeping with liberal reform efforts. In
late 1964 and the following summer, Sandra Cason Hayden and Mary King,

two white women who were SNCC veterans, proved instrumental in shaping a pair of seminal documents: "Student Nonviolent Coordinating Committee Position Paper: Women in the Movement" and "Sex and Caste: A Kind of Memo." The two papers decried the sexism that afflicted the Movement regarding tasks, leadership roles, "condescension and paternalism." Even the female activist was caricatured, Hayden and King pointed out, as "unthinking, pliable, an ornament to please the man." They found it troubling that "nobody is writing, or organizing or talking publicly about women, in any way that reflects the problems that various women in the movement come across and which we've tried to touch." They concluded, less than prophetically, "Objectively, the chances seem nil that we could start a movement based on anything as distant to general American thought as a sex-caste system."

Founded in 1966 by Betty Friedan, Pauli Murray, and other activists, NOW, by contrast, offered a statement of purpose that was a classic of liberal feminism. It declared, "The time has come for a new movement toward equality for all women in America, and toward a full partnership of the sexes." NOW was dedicated, the document announced, "to the proposition that women are first and foremost human beings, who, like all other people in our society, must have the chance to develop their full human potential." The organization also pledged to "protest and endeavor to change the false image of women now prevalent in the mass media, and in the texts, ceremonies, laws and practices of our major social institutions." NOW focused on legislative solutions to gender-based workplace discrimination, and endorsed the right to an abortion.

For years to come, NOW leaders worried about conflicts involving liberal feminists such as Friedan, the author of the pathfinding book *The Feminine Mystique* (1963), and the growing number of radical feminists who drew from the ideas articulated by Hayden and King. Friedan and NOW's national leadership feared a loss of public support if their organization were associated with radical perspectives. Another divisive issue involved the presence in NOW ranks of lesbians, whom Friedan at one point deemed "the lavender menace."

Although NOW retained a prominent place in the women's liberation movement, the momentum by 1968 was clearly with radical feminists. Many of these women had grown disaffected with both the civil rights movement and the New Left. Some who had participated in the civil rights movement detected an unspoken resentment on the part of black women unhappy with sexual relationships involving black men and white female activists. To others, like Hayden and King, it seemed as if sexism pervaded New Left organizations such as SNCC and SDS. Participation in SDS's campaign to reach out to indigent whites in Chicago led some women activists to denounce the pandering of their male counterparts. The women were appalled by the "swaggering and violent posturing" of the "hillbillies." They were also upset that SDS men pressured them to have sex with those same poor whites. SDS women were additionally displeased by how they were assigned seemingly menial tasks: telephoning, running mimeograph machines, and making coffee. Worse, their viewpoints received little attention during group discussions. SDS women addressed their male counterparts in a resolution conveying their grievances, which appeared in *New Left Notes* in 1967, conceding, "We recognize the difficulty our brothers will have in dealing with male chauvinism," and offering to "help resolve the contradiction." The article was published alongside a clearly derisive cartoon depicting a young woman with a sign reading, "We Want Our Rights and We Want Them Now."

The final straw for many radical women came in August 1967 at a gathering in Chicago of the National Conference for New Politics. A women's caucus composed a resolution, but the conference chairman brushed the women off, declaring "We don't have time for a resolution about women." The women's caucus worked overnight to produce a revised resolution asking for women to have a majority of committee slots and votes. The next day, an unenthusiastic male speaker read the resolution at the convention, and it was approved by voice vote only after initial cries of derision. Enraged and shocked at the condescension they encountered, the Chicago women produced a letter titled "To the Women of the Left." Appearing in New Left publications, the document was essentially a declaration of independence and marked the point when many radical feminists determined to abandon the New Left in favor of their own organizations.

On January 15, 1968, members of the New York Radical Women (NYRW) mounted an "alternative protest event" at a protest organized by the Jeannette Rankin Brigade, an outgrowth of Women Strike for Peace, a coalition of women's groups opposed to the Vietnam War. The NYRW had been founded the previous fall in New York City in one of the first manifestations of radical feminist disillusionment with New Left organizations. Among the leaders were women destined to play major roles in radical feminism, including Robin Morgan, Shulamith Firestone, Pam Allen, Carol Hanisch, and Kathie Sarachild. Hanisch, a former civil rights activist and member of Gainesville Women's Liberation, helped to define the philosophical dimensions of second-wave feminism when she coined the slogan "the personal is political," which introduced the radical concept that there were political dimensions to private life. This outlook demonstrated that power relations determined roles in marriage, the bedroom, the kitchen, the nursery, and the workplace. Kathie Sarachild, another civil rights worker and peace activist, contributed a second major element, popularizing the term *consciousness-raising*, referring to women coming together in small groups to acknowledge and debate the political aspects of personal life. Consciousness-raising encouraged women to question the origins and legitimacy of seemingly mundane acts, such as why it was considered appropriate for women to wash dishes while men cut the grass. Why, they found themselves asking, were women encouraged to be nurses and men encouraged to be physicians? Revelations delivered in consciousness-raising sessions often transformed and radicalized participants. As historian Ruth Rosen writes, "Suddenly one 'got it'. . . . What until that moment had seemed so 'normal' suddenly appeared artificial, not to say coercive." Perhaps more astonishing was the realization that no woman was alone, that millions of others had similar experiences, anxieties, and unfulfilled needs.

Much like their male counterparts in the New Left, NYRW women came to believe that peaceful, nondisruptive protests such as those organized by the Jeannette Rankin Brigade were ineffective in bringing the Vietnam War to an end. As 5,000 radical women gathered in Washington, DC, their criticisms seemed borne out. The Brigade was not allowed to petition Congress when Vice President Hubert Humphrey invoked a precedent prohibiting that legislative body from doing any business prior to the State of the Union Address. The majority of the demonstrators was left standing outside in the snow as a small delegation, which included former Montana congresswoman Jeannette Rankin and Coretta Scott King, was allowed to present a petition to House Speaker John McCormack and to visit the office of Senate Majority Leader Mike Mansfield. Several hundred of the younger women were sufficiently outraged to abandon the Brigade in favor of "militant mass action."

The NYRW's criticisms of the Jeannette Rankin Brigade went beyond concluding that peaceful demonstrations and petitions would not end the war. The radical women objected to the idea of an all-women's protest, which seemed to perpetuate traditional images of women as innately pacifist and as chiefly motivated by traditional, socially prescribed gender roles. Shulamith Firestone proclaimed, "They came as wives, mothers and mourners . . . tearful and passive reactors to the actions of men." She urged radical women to "change the definition of femininity" as a path to political power. Other NYRW leaders insisted that women come together "not as passive supplicants" but rather to embrace united political activism. Ultimately, women's groups from Chicago and Washington, DC, joined with NYRW for the alternative protest, organizing a funeral procession to Arlington Cemetery bearing an effigy of "Traditional Womanhood," which Firestone described as "a larger-than-life dummy . . . complete with feminine get-up, blank face, blonde curls and candle." Firestone recalled that the effigy's "bier" was adorned with "such disposable items as S&H Green Stamps, curlers, garters and hairspray." An accompanying banner urged, "DON'T CRY: RESIST!" Though the protest garnered little media attention, it was a remarkably prophetic demonstration of where second-wave feminism was headed: challenging traditional female roles, attire, accoutrements, and consumerism.

Despite the lack of media coverage, the events of January 1968 had a galvanizing effect on what would increasingly be known as the women's liberation movement. To counter the Rankin Brigade's meeting, some 500 radical women met for a convention in the capital, where as one historian notes, there was no agenda—"no one was prepared for such a massive response and there was chaos." The chaos did not preclude subsequent meetings, organizations, and publications, however, from originating across the country. What quickly became apparent was that there was much disagreement about how the movement should be organized and what its tactics and goals should be.

In March, Jo Freeman examined a fundamental question in her article "What in the Hell Is Women's Liberation Anyway?" appearing in *The Voice of the Women's Liberation Movement*. Freeman sought to distance women's liberation from liberal feminism, declaring that "women's liberation does not mean equality with men." "Equality in an unjust society," she argued, "is meaningless." Radical women, she asserted, should seek "equality in a just society." Seeking common ground between the politicos, who viewed capitalism as inherently exploitative, and the feminists, she argued that women should remain within the Movement while organizing around their own interests. Freeman did not speak directly to the question of which struggle should predominate, but others were willing to address that contentious and divisive issue.

That June, NYRW women produced a publication of their own titled "Notes from the First Year." Rejection of the politico position was explicit in SDS activist Anne Koedt's article, "Women and the Radical Movement." There, she argued that radical women must demand the Movement commit to fighting male supremacy. Radical women, she wrote, had to "begin to expose and eliminate the causes of our oppression as women." This, she asserted, took precedence over "storming the Pentagon as women or protesting the Democratic Convention as women." She saw the oppression of women as an outgrowth of the idea that woman "was at all times secondary to men . . . that her life is defined in terms of him." Ultimately, Koedt came to believe that the psychological dimension of women's oppression was paramount. This perspective was not uncontested. Two months after publication of Koedt's article, Evelyn Goldfield of Chicago's Westside group challenged its premise in an article in the August issue of *The Voice of Women's Liberation*, "Towards the Next Step." Goldfield dismissed consciousness-raising as less important than direct action and questioned the exclusion of men from the women's liberation struggle. Men should not be banned "as a matter of principle," she argued, but only if it were determined that some women hesitated to express themselves in male company.

The quest for women's liberation, Goldfield contended, should unite radicals. Otherwise, she feared, women's issues would become ghettoized, subject for discussion only within women's groups, when these were "questions of life-style, sex, community [and] personal relationships" that required exploration by both genders. While believing that only women were currently capable of discussing these topics in "an organized, coherent manner," she argued that they were ultimately human issues, and it was the responsibility of women to help men change.

Additional voices demonstrated the variety of opinion that was rapidly taking shape within an increasingly diverse and vibrant women's liberation movement. "The Florida Paper" by Judith Brown, a member of both SDS and CORE, blasted the politico "desegregation model" and attacked those who "refuse to acknowledge that for a time at least, men are the enemy." "In the life of each woman," Brown wrote," the most immediate oppressor, however unwilling he may be in theory to play that role, is 'the man.'" "He is still," she insisted, "the foreman on the big plantation of maleville." Arguing that women's liberation groups should work in conjunction with the Movement to formulate positions on war, racism, and "the Savage Society," Brown maintained that the women's movement had to "begin to dismantle this system's deadly social and military toys, and stop the mad dogs who rule us every place we're at." She observed, "The most serious problem for the moment is not war, the draft, the presidency, the racial problem, but our own problem."

Brown offered a thoroughly radical perspective on male-female relations. In order to "revitalize their commitment to their sex and to the liberation movement," she urged, some women should remain single and others should periodically take sabbaticals from their marriages. She also advocated that committed radical women live in all-female communes, learn karate, and practice "self-imposed celibacy" for the purpose of "getting themselves together." Brown warned that radical women's "continued fear of homosexuality may be the one last stand by which the male order can pull us back into tow." She also recognized the possibility that gender differences might be rooted in biology.

By the summer of 1968, the debate over women's liberation's meaning and direction was intense. NYRW, Chicago's Westside group, Gainesville

Women's Liberation, and a Washington, DC, women's liberation group loosely affiliated with the Institute for Policy Studies were all representative of the dynamism of the women's liberation movement during a year when radical politics pushed the boundaries of the possible. Influenced by Valerie Solanas's *SCUM Manifesto*, the Boston-based radical feminist group Cell 16 denounced men as worthless and "subhuman" and demanded women remain apart from them.

Given the different backgrounds and outlooks of radical women, it was inevitable that fractures would develop as they had within the broader Movement. Some advocated the adoption of Yippie-style tactics such as guerrilla street theater, while others insisted on a more "serious" approach that sought to identify and correct the roots of gender discrimination through thoughtful analyses of social, political, and economic institutions. Ironically, tensions within the women's liberation movement reached a breaking point in the course of a protest action that brought the movement its widest audience to date.

The initial idea for a protest of the Miss America Pageant scheduled for Atlantic City, New Jersey, in September came from NYRW's Carol Hanisch. She saw the pageant as a prime opportunity to advance the cause, as "up to this time, we hadn't done a lot of actions yet" and "it was kind of a gutsy thing to do," given that "Miss America was this 'American pie' icon." Robin Morgan undertook many of the organizational tasks and, drawing on her earlier career as a child television actress, skillfully used media contacts. A press release urging women to "reclaim ourselves for ourselves" served as a call to arms and presented a series of ideas that the protest would address. Among the more provocative themes, calculated to ensure media attention, were "The Degrading Mindless-Boob-Girlie Symbol," "Miss America as Military Death Mascot," "The Unbeatable Madonna-Whore Combination," and "The Irrelevant Crown on the Throne of Mediocrity."

By September 7, some 400 feminists from New York City, Florida, Boston, Detroit, and New Jersey had gathered to demonstrate on Atlantic City's famous boardwalk. The radical women walked a picket line and performed guerrilla theater, crowning a sheep as "Miss America." Male reporters attempting to question the participants were ignored, with activist Marion Davidson explaining, "Why should we talk with them? It's impossible for men to understand." The more subtle goal was to compel newspapers to take female reporters off their usual fashion and society beats and assign them to cover something politically relevant. Meanwhile, some of the activists chained themselves to a life-size Miss America effigy to call attention to women's enslavement to artificial beauty standards.

The event that garnered the greatest media coverage, however, and established a myth that persisted for years, grew out of a plan to toss "instruments of torture to women" into a "Freedom Trash Can." Demonstrators threw bras, girdles, curlers, hairspray, false eyelashes, high-heeled shoes, typing books, and copies of *Playboy* and women's magazines into the container. The inspiration for this action may have been a NOW Mother's Day protest months earlier where aprons were tossed onto a trash pile as part of a demand to ratify the Equal Rights Amendment. Though the initial plan had been to set the discarded items on fire, organizers were told that the city would forbid it out of concern that the boardwalk might be at risk. To preclude violence, they decided to abide by the injunction. "We don't want another Chicago," Robin Morgan told a reporter. A secondary consideration was that the NYRW lacked the financial resources to post bail. Thus, despite the fact that nothing was torched during the protest, the myth of "bra-burning, man-hating radical women" soon entered the national consciousness.

While protesters outside the Miss America Pageant venue paraded with posters reading "Up Against the Wall Miss America," "Miss America Sells It," and "Miss America is a Big Falsie," sixteen protesters infiltrated the Pageant auditorium by "wearing 'straight' clothes and lots of makeup." As the outgoing Miss America delivered her farewell speech, some of the radical women unfurled a banner reading "Women's Liberation" and began chanting "Freedom for Women!" and "No More Miss America!" The activists were quickly ushered out by security guards and five were arrested.

In terms of generating media attention, the Miss America Pageant protest was undeniably successful. Certainly some of the reportage was unfavorable and derisive, but the radicals of second-wave feminism had made their presence known in no uncertain manner.

Coverage of these events overshadowed a second protest at the pageant. Civil rights activists held the first Miss Black America Pageant to protest the racism inherent in the all-white pageant. The first Miss Black America, nineteen-year-old Saundra Williams, explained the rationale behind the protest: "Miss America does not represent us because there has never been a black girl in the pageant. With my title, I can show black women that they too are beautiful. . . . for so long none of us believed it. But now we're finally coming around."

Ironically, Saundra Williams's achievement indirectly represented one of the many fault lines in the women's liberation movement and presented numerous questions. Did black and white women suffer from fundamentally different forms of oppression? Was race a greater barrier to the advancement of black women than gender? Could black and white women agree upon and work toward common goals? As significant as these questions were, they took second place to others raised in the course of the Miss America Pageant protest. The politicos, who often described themselves as "pro-woman," argued that too often the protest derided the contestants who were, after all, women suffering from male chauvinism themselves.

Perhaps the most significant immediate negative consequence of the Miss America protest was NYRW's splintering, as feminists stressed the need for consciousness-raising while politicos enthused over their protest activities. Subsequently, "approximately 13 heretical women," including Robin Morgan and other NYRW activists, broke from the NYRW to form the Women's International Terrorist Conspiracy from Hell (W.I.T.C.H.), intended as an action-based group. The new organization held its inaugural action on Halloween, when members dressed as witches gathered in the Wall Street district to cast a "hex" on the financial district. Morgan, facetiously or otherwise, insisted that the curse had the effect of causing a sharp decline of the Dow Jones Industrial Average the following day. More seriously, she defined the protest as a demonstration of solidarity with the working-class struggle against capitalism, an issue that W.I.T.C.H. would regularly address.

One issue of many that remained unresolved within the women's liberation movement was that of sexual orientation. NOW founder Betty Friedan, for example, did not endorse accepting open lesbians into the movement until 1977. Advocates of rights for gay men and women faced immense obstacles. Social, cultural, and religious barriers were only some of the challenges that gay activists faced; in many states, homosexual sexual activity was illegal. Government agencies considered homosexuals uniquely vulnerable to blackmail and regularly refused them employment. Being "outed" as a gay man or women in the initial decades after World War II still meant humiliation, social ostracism, and limited employment opportunities. Derisive language and jokes about "fags" and "queers" and "lesbos" remained culturally acceptable.

As the modern civil rights movement surged in the postwar years, gay Americans began to organize to claim fundamental rights as citizens and to seek social acceptance. The Mattachine Society had been founded in 1950 and sought to unify, educate, and assist the nation's gay minority, as well as to educate heterosexuals about their fellow citizens who were gay. Given the conservative social climate of the 1950s, the Society was organized along the same lines as the CPUSA, with cells and discretion considered crucial. An organization to defend lesbian civil rights, the Daughters of Bilitis (DOB), came into being in 1955. Like the Mattachine Society, the DOB set up chapters across the nation and it embraced the goal of educating the public about gay women and establishing safe places for gay women to socialize, as police often raided lesbian bars. Both organizations grew in number, but confronted considerable public resistance and prejudice into the 1960s, even as ideas about the extension of constitutionally guaranteed rights for minority groups.

The prelude to gay America's great leap forward may well have been the 1966 organizational meeting of the groups that would comprise the North American Conference of Homophile Organizations (NACHO). Meeting in Kansas City, attendees from fourteen groups set up a legal defense fund and began a newsletter. In a subsequent national convention in San Francisco, the first fault lines appeared when lesbian attendees voiced fear that their concerns would not be fully understood by male members and that men would inevitably dominate the organization. In August 1968, NACHO members met again in that city, embraced the slogan "Gay is Good" and adopted a Homosexual Bill of Rights. The five-point document proclaimed that sex between consenting adults should not be a criminal offense; solicitation for sexual acts should not be an offense unless one of the parties filed a complaint (this was to prevent police sting operations); sexual orientation and practices should not be a factor in security clearances, visas, or granting citizenship; sexual orientation should not decide military service, discharge status, or veterans benefits; and sexual orientation should not determine public or private employment. It was a courageous, sweeping statement, but NACHO continued to encounter lesbians' complaints that their concerns were being overlooked.

Other actions in defense of gay rights occurred that year. On March 17, Los Angeles gay men held a public protest of police entrapment and harassment. On April 23, the Student Homophile League at Columbia University picketed and disrupted a psychiatric panel discussion of homosexuality to protest the designation of homosexuality as mental illness. Homophile organizations held a "gay-in" at Griffith Park in Los Angeles on May 30. Two months later in the same city, Lee Glaze, owner of the gay bar The Patch, responded to the arrest of a pair of his patrons by buying out the inventory of a nearby flower shop. He then organized supporters to drive to the relevant police precinct, drape the station in flowers, and bail out their compatriots. These isolated acts revealed a burgeoning gay rights movement that was increasingly less intimidated and more often willing to act. The Stonewall Riots were less than a year away. The gay and lesbian revolution was on the verge of establishing a national presence that, like the civil rights and women's rights movements, would defy seemingly insurmountable odds and demand to be heard.

13

"Goin' Up the Country"

The New Environmentalism

By the 1960s, America possessed a well-established and influential body of nature writing. Henry David Thoreau, John Muir, Aldo Leopold, and Rachel Carson were among the notable writers whose works shaped American thinking about nature, conservation, and wilderness, as well as helping to devise national policy. In 1968, a new addition to this distinguished body of literature appeared under the title *Desert Solitaire: A Season in the Wilderness*, although its author repeatedly asserted that he had no wish to be considered chiefly a "nature writer." *Desert Solitaire* would later become a cherished classic for those who loved the outdoors, and especially America's desert Southwest. The author was Edward Abbey, who at forty years of age had led a wandering existence, roaming the American Southwest, performing military service in Italy, studying philosophy and English at the University of New Mexico, holding a variety of jobs, weathering several failed marriages, and publishing two novels by the late 1950s.

Born in Indiana, Pennsylvania, on January 27, 1927, Abbey quickly developed a disdain for authority and rules. As early as 1947, he became the subject of an FBI file, which ballooned in ensuing decades when Abbey did things like posting letters urging young men to burn their draft cards. Abbey was hired by the National Park Service in 1956 as a seasonal ranger at the then-isolated Arches National Monument, just outside the small town of Moab, Utah. Drawing on his experiences there and elsewhere in what had once been referred to as the "Great American Desert," Abbey produced what would eventually be acknowledged as a compelling defense of wilderness for

Figure 13.1   The Windows formation in Arches National Park, Utah, where environmental activist and writer Edward Abbey served as a park ranger for two seasons. The experience contributed to Abbey's appreciation for the wilderness, which he expressed in *Desert Solitaire* (1968), a book that subsequently deeply influenced those activists who embraced the New Environmentalism. As well as exalting the spiritual and restorative qualities of wilderness America, Abbey warned of the likely degradation that "industrial tourism" would bring. Library of Congress, Prints and Photographs Division, LC-DIG-highsm.

its own sake as well as an eloquent celebration of the beauty of the desert Southwest. His *Desert Solitaire* presciently hinted at new directions for American environmentalism when it was published in 1968.

The heart of *Desert Solitaire* was drawn from diaries that Abbey kept during his two seasons in 1956 and 1957 as a ranger at what is now Arches National Park. The book's opening chapters reflected his attraction to the austere beauty of the place, as well as his thoughts about the wildlife and plants that defied the harsh desert conditions. Much in the tradition of Thoreau's *Walden*, *Desert Solitaire* captured the author's fascination with and admiration for nature's balance, which Abbey saw as threatened even at this early juncture. Also like Thoreau, Abbey found much solace in his generally solitary life. He therefore experienced considerable irritation with motor tourists who interrupted it, and who invariably posed three basic questions: "(1) Where's the john? (2) How long's it take to see this place? (3) Where's the Coke machine?" Though access to the park was relatively limited during the late 1950s, thanks to the paucity of paved roads, Abbey feared that he was witnessing the beginning of what he derided as "Industrial Tourism." The growing demand for greater public access to accommodate the "Wheelchair Tourists," as Abbey deemed those who were at once "the consumers, the raw material and the victims of Industrial Tourism," would, he worried, decimate America's wilderness. The future for wilderness was made equally dire, he insisted, by unrestricted immigration and population growth. Abbey despaired of "a completely urbanized, completely industrialized, ever more crowded environment." "For my own part," he declared, "I would rather take my chances in a thermonuclear war than live in such a world."

Abbey's more immediate remedy for preserving the wild in national parks was quite radical in an era in which American society was enamored of its thriving automotive culture. Cars should be banned from national parks, he insisted, regardless of how that might inconvenience children, the elderly, and the infirm. There should also be a ban on future roadbuilding in national parks, which would encourage hiking to enliven the wilderness experience. Finally, Abbey suggested that park rangers, whom he characterized as "lazy, scheming loafers," should be put to work leading planned hikes and rescuing city-dwellers from natural hazards, rather than manning air-conditioned entrance stations and handing out pamphlets. An authentic wilderness experience also came from accepting that time and distance from "civilization" necessarily defined "wilderness," Abbey contended. "We are preoccupied with time," he wrote, "if we could learn to love space as deeply as we are now obsessed with time, we might discover a new meaning in the phrase *to live like men*."

Desert Solitaire touched on Abbey's experiences involving the land, joined with philosophical expositions on the significance of wilderness and the threats it faced. One of the more notable chapters, "Down the River," chronicled his boat trip down the Colorado River only months before the much-reviled Glen Canyon Dam overwhelmed that stretch of the river, an event that compelled many environmentalists to act.

Abbey's deepest commitment was to the preservation of the wilderness from which he drew spiritual strength. "Wilderness is not a luxury but a necessity of the human spirit, and as vital to our lives as water and good bread," he wrote. "We need wilderness whether or not we ever set foot in it." In an especially heartfelt passage, Abbey indicated that love of the wilderness "is also an expression of loyalty to earth, the earth which bore and sustains us, the only home we shall ever know, the only paradise we ever need—if only we had the eyes to see." The "true original sin," he wrote, "is the blind destruction for the sake of greed of this natural paradise which lies all around us—if only we were worthy of it."

Desert Solitaire spoke to strikingly relevant contemporary developments in 1968. *Desert Solitaire* quickly became, as the writer Russell Martin described it, "a kind of *Catcher in the Rye* for the coming-of-age of the environmental movement." At the same time, Abbey was in many ways unique. He was by no means a stereotypical New Age tree-hugger. In *Desert Solitaire*, he celebrated the rifle as "the weapon of democracy" and declared, "An armed citizenry is the first defense, the best defense and the final defense against tyranny." Later, Abbey proved willing to consider more radical methods to protect the wilderness, promoting "monkeywrenching," the intentional sabotage of developmental projects.

In many ways, 1968 marked a turning point for American environmentalism, which by then had become a mass popular movement, thanks to unprecedented numbers of supporters, activists, and organizations. Increasing numbers elected to take more radical steps in defense of an environment that encountered growing threats. By the late 1960s, the New Environmentalism emerged, addressing the dangers of environmental degradation, the need for greater governmental regulation, and the awareness of a direct relationship between environmental problems and human society.

Since the late nineteenth century, individuals such as John Muir and organizations like the Sierra Club, which he founded in 1892, insisted on the need to conserve natural resources and preserve wilderness. During the Progressive Era, political leaders like Theodore Roosevelt played key roles in addressing these issues. Roosevelt set up the US Forest Service, established 150 national forests, supported federal legislation enabling the irrigation of arid regions, created five national parks, and signed the 1906 Antiquities Act, which authorized the president to designate eighteen national monuments. During his presidency, Roosevelt placed some 230,000 acres of land under federal protection.

Although political enthusiasm for environmental protections waned during the 1920s, when conservatism dominated, the movement gained new proponents during the ensuing decade with the presidency of Franklin D. Roosevelt, who, like his distant cousin Theodore, possessed an affinity for the natural world. Under his watch, the number of national forests, parks, monuments, and wildlife refuges dramatically increased. FDR also put 3.4 million young men to work under the auspices of the Civilian Conservation Corps, which "built 13,000 miles of trails, planted more than two billion trees and paved 125,000 miles of roads," according to the journalist Clay Risen.

Environmental concerns generally took a back seat during both World War II and the early postwar period. By the start of the 1950s, American materialism and belief that science, through artificial chemicals and even nuclear energy, could ensure "better living," prevailed. The federal government's Project Plowshare produced proposals for using atomic blasts to enlarge the Panama Canal, connect aquifers in Arizona, and level mountain ranges to accommodate the construction of an interstate highway. Fortunately, these projects went unrealized and public attitudes about the dangers of what the government called "Peaceful Nuclear Explosions," chemical pollutants, and the despoliation of the natural environment, both casual and resulting from industrial practices, began to shift during the 1950s. Ardent conservationists emphasized the dangers of a "psychology of waste," the necessity of "the land ethic," and the interconnectedness of people and nature.

Marine biologist Rachel Carson did much to awaken the public to the environmental dangers posed by chemicals like DDT (dichlorodiphenyl-trichloroethane) with her book *Silent Spring* (1962), as well as to promote the concept of the "connectedness" of various ecosystems within the global environment. Through the mid-1960s, the Kennedy and Johnson administrations acknowledged the importance of environmental issues, and supported corrective measures, including legislation. At the same time, environmentalism acquired greater popularity, resulting in rapidly expanding organizational memberships, widening awareness of the extent and magnitude of environmental concerns, and activists believing new, more radical tactics and strategies were in order.

1968 began on a hopeful note for those concerned about the environment. On the first day of the New Year, the Redwood National Park was established in California. Later in the year, Congress passed the Wild and Scenic Rivers Act, aimed at restricting the construction of dams, and it enacted the National Trails System Act. At the start on his presidential campaign, Senator Robert F. Kennedy, speaking at the University of Kansas on March 18, worried that the gross national product of the United States "counts air pollution and cigarette advertising, and ambulances to clear our highways of carnage. . . . It counts the destruction of the redwood and the loss of our national wonder in chaotic sprawl."

In 1968, Stanford Research Institute meteorologist Elmer Robinson and R. C. Robbins drew greater attention to atmospheric pollutants, warning that rising carbon dioxide concentrations in the atmosphere "may be the cause of serious world-wide environmental changes." The Sierra Club prepared for the final rounds of a lengthy struggle to halt one of the most dramatic and, in retrospect, bizarre proposals that the Bureau of Land Management had ever put forth: to dam the Grand Canyon.

By 1968, the Sierra Club, under the executive directorship of David Brower as it had been for the past fifteen years, had grown immensely in membership and influence. Brower and environmentalist allies were present at a series of House hearings between 1965 and 1967 and at a Senate session regarding government plans to construct a pair of dams on the Colorado River inside the Grand Canyon. With press and public opinion running heavily against the proposals, the Sierra Club helped to mobilize opposition, publishing one of its by now famous coffee-table "big books" featuring wilderness issues, *Time and the River Flowing: Grand Canyon*. *Life* magazine offered a major article by Brower. The Sierra Club also placed full-page announcements in the *New York Times*. Government officials soon conceded that the public response was unprecedented. A spokesman for the Bureau of Reclamation noted, "Ninety-five percent of them said we'd better keep our hands off the Grand Canyon and a lot of them quoted the Sierra Club." Within twenty-four hours, coincidentally or otherwise, the Internal Revenue Service (IRS) notified the Sierra Club that it could lose its tax-exempt status if it continued lobbying against the dams.

Undeterred, Brower joked that whether or not Americans had strong feelings about the Grand Canyon, they certainly had them about the IRS. A second series of announcements soon appeared in the *New York Times*. In one of the final congressional hearings, Brower emphasized his unwillingness to compromise. Shortly afterward, Utah representative Morris Udall, a strong dam proponent, conceded defeat, and the proposal to dam the Grand Canyon never came to a vote. Pro-dam forces made one final attempt in 1967, favoring expansion of Grand Canyon National Park, along with elimination of the Grand Canyon National Monument and the construction of a single dam on the canyon's Colorado River. The Sierra Club again turned to the *New York Times* as well as other papers with an advertisement reading "Grand Canyon National Monument is Hereby Abolished—from a bill submitted in Congress 15 days ago by Rep. Wayne Aspinall." Colorado's Aspinall was among those deluged with the tear-off coupons and letters urging opposition that the Sierra Club organized. In 1968, Congress approved of the Central Arizona Project, which led to construction of a diversion dam and included a ban on dams in the Grand Canyon. It was one of the environmental movement's greatest achievements.

The Sierra Club's Brower is also credited for having helped to suggest the writing of one of 1968's most controversial books. *The Population Bomb*, by Stanford University professor Paul R. Ehrlich and his wife Anne (who was uncredited), appearing in a year during which Americans already faced an array of crises. Everything about the book was calculated to be alarmist. The publisher, Ballantine Books, believed the original title, *Population,*

Resources, and Environment, sounded too academic and insisted the title be changed to suggest imminent catastrophe. Early editions of the book began with an apocalyptic assertion: "The battle to feed all of humanity is over. In the 1970s hundreds of millions of people will starve to death in spite of any crash programs embarked upon now. At this late date nothing can prevent a substantial increase in the world death rate." Ehrlich's willingness to subordinate statistics to the rhetoric of "an Old Testament Prophet" heightened the book's impact, a reviewer observed. Ehrlich's theory about an impending global catastrophe garnered an unusually large audience as a result of an astute marketing campaign that included an appearance on Johnny Carson's popular late-evening program, *The Tonight Show.*

The Population Bomb focused on the global environment's imperiled state and the resulting food security crisis, which Ehrlich saw as dire. Much of the world's population was either underfed or improperly fed, he argued, and as the global population expanded it would be unreasonable to expect that situation would improve. The press of population further degraded all aspects of the natural world. Posing the obvious question, "What needs to be done?," Ehrlich proposed rapid reduction of the world population through zero or negative population growth. Only then would any effort to increase the food supply be effective. There were several ways to achieve these goals, he suggested, arguing that the United States should assume the lead internationally. This was because Americans consumed a disproportionate amount of the world's food supply. Additionally, any US-initiated program of population control or reduction would have to be implemented at home to avoid allegations of racism.

For his countrymen, Ehrlich considered the use of "temporary sterilants" introduced into water and food supplies as one means of population control. Financial and tax incentives might be employed to convince men to undergo voluntary sterilization, or families to limit the number of children they had. More children, for example, would result in tax penalties. Such ambitious policies required some sort of governmental administration. To that end, Ehrlich envisioned a US "Department of Population and Environment," which, he declared, "should be set up with the power to take whatever steps are necessary to establish a reasonable population in the United States and to put an end to the steady deterioration of our environment." This agency would be empowered to undertake research into population control and to develop more effective contraceptives. In a more Orwellian vein, Ehrlich proposed that such an agency develop "mass sterilizing agents" and prenatal sex determination, as many families continued to have children until a male was born. He also favored legislation guaranteeing the right to abortion and expansion of sex education.

If these suggestions were not controversial enough, Ehrlich's recommendations for the wider world were guaranteed to provoke charges of racism.

Ehrlich drew some of his ideas from William and Paul Paddock's *Famine 1975!* (1967), which called for providing food aid only to countries with adequate pollution controls. Nations like India that "were so far behind in the population-food game that there is no hope" would have such assistance eliminated. Ehrlich lauded the Paddocks for their "courage and foresight."

Having offered a range of often draconian solutions to the crisis he feared, Ehrlich instructed his readers on how to respond. This included pressuring political leaders to take necessary steps. Unsurprisingly, *The Population Bomb* drew significant criticism, chiefly for its apocalyptic tone, neo-Malthusian approach, reckless predictions, and careless employment of statistics. Whatever its shortcomings, Ehrlich's book sold over two million copies and drew the nation's attention to population and environmental issues.

1968 also witnessed the founding of Friends of the Sea Otter (FSO), a group concerned about the precipitous decline of the California sea otter. FSO was dedicated to protecting a thriving colony of some 650 otters on the California coast. The United Nations Educational, Scientific and Cultural Organization (UNESCO) held its Biosphere Conference of 1968, in Paris, from September 9–14, indicating rising global concern about the environment. The 238 delegates from sixty-eight member states met to plan a coordinated international program to combat environmental issues. The attendees agreed on a dozen recommendations for discussion and action.

That same year, science fiction author Philip K. Dick published a novel foretelling a future in which few animals remained alive after a catastrophic war. *Do Androids Dream of Electric Sheep?* (loosely adapted in the 1982 film *Blade Runner*) was set in post-apocalyptic San Francisco during the aftermath of World War Terminus, whose radioactive fallout rendered much of the Earth inhospitable. The novel depicted a future in which advanced robotics perpetuated certain biological life forms, and humankind was apparently creating its own successor race in the powerful and intelligent androids required for the labor-intensive aspects of deep-space colonization. Aided by highly advanced androids, many people fled to distant colonized planets. Those remaining on Earth sought to carry on life amid a poisoned atmosphere and chaotic weather patterns producing continual darkness and dampness.

Most animal species either became extinct or were reduced to near-extinction owing to multiple nuclear exchanges. Live animals were rare, costly, and much-desired status symbols. The chief character, detective Rick Deckard, like most people, could at best afford robotic animals, such as the "sheep" that he and his neighbors had "grazing" on their apartment rooftop. The novel concluded with the protagonist fleeing to the Oregon wilderness, where he was thrilled to find a toad, which had long been thought to be extinct. The amphibian too, however, proved to be a robot, leaving the reader to contemplate the consequences of catastrophic environmental destruction, brought on by humankind's unthinking hubris.

Stewart Brand's *Whole Earth Catalog*, which initially appeared in the fall of 1968, also displayed attention to a variety of environmentally related issues. A compendium in keeping with the back-to-the-land wing of the counterculture, the *Catalog* sparked interest in "organic farming, solar power, recycling, wind power . . . mountain bikes," according to the *Guardian* newspaper. The *Catalog* pointed to the need for "Understanding Whole Systems" and to attend to "Shelter and Land Use." Its cover, a satellite photo shot by NASA (National Aeronautics and Space Administration), displayed a striking image of the "Whole Earth."

The pressing need to address environmental issues on a global basis was made clear through the Apollo 8 mission to the moon in the final month of 1968. This was the first manned orbital voyage to the moon, which guaranteed public interest. Crammed into a small capsule launched from Cape Kennedy on December 21, the three astronauts—Frank Borman, James Lovell Jr., and William Anders—anticipated completing a variety of scientific tasks during a twenty-hour period circling the Moon. Christmas Eve activities included an exceptionally moving telecast, broadcast around the world. Orbiting the moon's barren surface, the crew took turns reading verses from the first chapter of Genesis before signing off with the statement, "Good night, good luck, a Merry Christmas and God bless all of you—and the good planet Earth." More than one astronaut had previously remarked on the unique feelings produced by viewing the Earth from space.

After Apollo 8 completed its flight and splashed down in the Pacific on December 27, a remarkable reminder of the voyage began to circulate. On Christmas Eve, astronaut William Anders had taken a dazzling color photograph of the Earth rising above the moon's horizon. Soon known by the title *Earthrise*, the photograph revealed Earth as a unique, glowing, blue oasis in an infinite darkness, stunningly beautiful and terrifyingly isolated. *Earthrise* was included in *Life* magazine's *One Hundred Photographs that Changed the World*, where wildlife photographer Galen Rowell described it as "the most influential environmental photograph ever taken." Indeed, many who viewed the breathtaking photograph and seriously pondered its significance possessed new conceptions of Earth's uniqueness and humankind's tenuous place in the universe. *Earthrise* confirmed what many environmentalists attempted to convey—that we were all passengers on spaceship Earth and thus all had a stake in its protection and survival. Subsequently, *Earthrise* was the subject of a popular poster that bore the caption, "One Earth, One Chance." And so, while 1968 was a year that brought so much agony and despair, it would end with a small but bright glimmer of hope.

14

"Your Day, of Course, Is Going to Be Over Soon"

The Backlash

The heated 1968 presidential campaign season was in its final days when former Alabama governor George C. Wallace arrived at New York City's Madison Square Garden for a campaign rally on October 24. This amounted to a foray into enemy territory for the American Independent Party candidate, whose slogan "Stand Up for America" had drawn surprising support since early summer, demonstrating that his message of populist outrage resonated far beyond the Deep South. Some 20,000 Wallace partisans swarmed into the arena, the largest crowd there since an appearance by President Franklin D. Roosevelt in 1936. Outside on the street, the fringe elements energized by Wallace's candidacy gathered to declare their support: members of the KKK, the paramilitary Minutemen, and the American Nazi Party. Emblematic of the year's polarization, leftist demonstrators from SDS and the communist Workers World Party assembled to shout derisively at the segregationist, who stressed his role as a "law and order" conservative. Inside, what had come to be a typical Wallace rally took shape. A band played patriotic songs, drawing the loudest cheers for renditions of "Dixie," prior to Wallace's appearance at 8 p.m.

The short, glowering candidate had barely begun his standard speech when a black protester stood up with a sign depicting a Klansman holding a noose, bearing the slogan "Law and Order—Wallace Style." When another demonstrator heckled Wallace with a bullhorn, the crowd erupted in a frenzy of outrage. Surrounding the protesters, fans of Wallace yelled, "Kill 'em! Kill

Figure 14.1   Alabama Governor George C. Wallace speaks to the Democratic National Convention in 1964. Encouraged by his showing in primary elections that year, Wallace embarked on an independent campaign for the presidency in 1968. Capitalizing on the latent rage of white working-class voters, Wallace identified "the angry white man" as a crucial constituency, while railing against hippies, black militants, war protesters, welfare cheaters, and an intrusive federal government at rallies that often degenerated into riots. Though he won only 13 percent of the popular vote in the November election, Wallace identified an electoral strategy that was successfully embraced by the Republican Party in subsequent years. Library of Congress, Prints and Photographs Division, LC-DIG-ppmsca-31590.

'em!'" After police rescued the protesters, Wallace, who welcomed such inter-
ruptions, launched into an assault on "anarchists" and promised, "When
November comes, the first time they lay down in front of my limousine, it'll
be the last one they'll ever lay down in front of!" "Their day is over!" Wallace
thundered. The crowd roared its approval, as it did when he spoke to "a few
anarchists, a few activists, a few militants, a few revolutionaries, and a few
communists" residing in the country. "Your day, of course, is going to be
over soon," Wallace warned with a threatening tone.

That a presidential candidate would deliver such statements was testament
to the raw emotions characterizing national politics in 1968, and no candidate
more effectively employed such charged and at times violent rhetoric than
did George Wallace. In the course of his New York speech, Wallace assailed
the "sick Supreme Court" for its permissive rulings, drawing a supposed
connection to surging crime rates and social disorder. "We don't have riots
in Alabama," Wallace asserted. "They start a riot down there, first one of 'em
that picks up a brick gets a bullet in the brain, that's all." Wallace's supporters
were perfectly clear as to who "they" were—lawless blacks who had turned
American cities into urban battlegrounds. The journalists following the third
party candidate were alarmed at the Wallace phenomenon, stunned at the
magnitude of the conservative backlash that he had identified and mobilized.
"There is menace in the blood shout of the crowd," wrote the *New Republic*'s
Richard Stout, who likened Wallace rallies to what had occurred in "Berlin
in the '30s." Wallace was "the ablest demagogue of our time," Stout admitted.

Wallace was arguably the most extreme personification of the growing
backlash against the political, social, and cultural tumult that peaked in 1968.
The reaction came in several modes, and was most broadly perceptible in the
rising alarm and fear associated with the group presidential candidate Richard
Nixon deemed the "Silent Center"—mostly working- and middle-class white
Americans who saw themselves as responsible citizens and patriots and who
viewed self-proclaimed radicals as endangering sacred values and the American way of life. To this disaffected group, flag-burning anti-war protesters
denouncing America as imperialistic, pot-smoking hippies promoting free
love, gun-toting black militants, and family-endangering feminists were the
shock troops of a new, frightening vision of America that was antithetical to
everything the country had supposedly always represented.

From the local to the national level, conservative politicians were quick to
denounce the radical trends of the late 1960s, in some instances gaining
national prominence even before the cataclysmic events of 1968. By that
year, the American people had endured years of social and political unrest,
taxing institutions and nerves alike. Through the print media, and perhaps
more importantly, television, Americans witnessed the unraveling of the

social fabric that had seemed so sturdy in the immediate postwar years. By the mid-1960s, the turbulence emanating from the civil rights movement and the resistance to it revealed deep social tensions. The rise of black militancy further stoked the fears of white Americans, as did the bloody "ghetto rebellions" that began to sweep through major cities. As the anti-war movement adopted more militant rhetoric and tactics, as clashes with authority figures accelerated, as the excesses of the counterculture became more evident, and as talk of a national crime wave proliferated, many Americans began to feel that they were under siege. A *Time* magazine cover in 1968 conveyed a popular concern by asking, "Has Violence Become an American Way of Life?" Some blamed the seemingly permissive child-centric methods associated with Dr. Benjamin Spock for the young radicals' impudent behavior. Others deemed liberalism responsible for the collapse of authority, while viewing it as synonymous with an intrusive federal government, which threatened local autonomy and individual liberty, pandered to minorities, and ignored hard-working whites.

Often at the forefront of national trends, California produced some of the first significant spokesmen representing the backlash that approached fever pitch by 1968. Max Rafferty initially came to attention as a public school administrator in the early 1960s through his denunciations of public education policies and practices that supposedly produced teenagers who became "booted, sideburned, ducktailed, unwashed leather-jacketed slobs," before turning into "spineless, luxury-loving" student radicals. Elected in 1962 as state superintendent, Rafferty attacked liberal State Board of Education president Thomas Braden, a former operative with the wartime Office of Strategic Services and its successor, the CIA, as a "Comsymp" and homosexual, before focusing verbal assaults on UC Berkeley. He charged that the nation's foremost public university featured professors who taught "a four-year course in sex, drugs and treason."

This mantra, which helped Rafferty win a Republican senate primary before losing to the Democrat Alan Cranston in 1968, was adopted by Ronald Reagan during his 1966 bid for the California governorship. Previously a New Deal liberal, Reagan swung rightward during the early Cold War. His film career waning, Reagan became a host on television programs and a pitchman for General Electric, as well as an advocate for small government, unfettered capitalism, and fervent anti-communism. Blasting socialized medicine, Reagan supported Barry Goldwater's hard-right presidential candidacy in 1964, delivering a late campaign address, known in right-of-center circles as "The Speech," which articulated conservative principles.

Backed by wealthy businessmen, Reagan defeated incumbent Democratic Governor Edmund "Pat" Brown, having relied on standard conservative charges, many drawn from Goldwater. These include accusations that "arson and murder" accompanied inner-city riots such as the one in Watts in 1965, American soldiers were "being denied the right to victory" in Vietnam, the costs of welfare programs were burgeoning, big-government liberalism amounted to tyranny, and hippies and treasonous radicals were running amuck, creating the "mess at Berkeley."

Reagan regularly leavened the harshness of his rhetoric with crowd pleasing humor, often aimed at the counterculture. "A hippie," Reagan joked on multiple occasions, "is someone who dresses like Tarzan, has hair like Jane and smells like Cheetah." On other occasions, referring to protesters carrying signs reading "Make Love, Not War," Reagan quipped that they did not look as if they could do either. According to polls, Californians' top concerns were crime, drugs, and juvenile delinquency, and the Reagan campaign was soon on a victorious trajectory, much to the dismay of the state's liberal elements. His election as governor in 1966 prefigured a conservative groundswell that would gain in strength in subsequent years, demonstrating the latent power of both right-wing populism and celebrity.

As governor, Reagan bolstered his popularity by posing as a defender of civil order and morality against the threats posed by hippies, radicals, and their faculty defenders on California campuses. Addressing a hostile student crowd at Berkeley as "Ladies and gentlemen, if there are any," Reagan made it clear that he intended to represent the people of California, and not accede to the demands of a small group of radical agitators. He helped to orchestrate the dismissal of UC president Clark Kerr, seen as having acquiesced to student demands and tolerated campus disruptions. The governor insisted that campus conduct and faculty hiring be more closely scrutinized and he charged that lazy professors did not teach enough. When they did, much of what they taught was un-American. Every bit as bad, Reagan complained, universities seemed to be "subsidizing intellectual curiosity." Following disturbances at San Francisco State College, Reagan delighted in the appointment of S. I. Hayakawa as the new president, calling him "my Samurai."

Much of the public applauded his crackdown on campus protests and denunciations of hippies, but Reagan found that the realities of governing precluded realization of his promises to reduce taxes and the size of the state government. Budget realities compelled him to sign the largest tax increase in the history of American states and oft-denounced social welfare programs remained in place, while the state bureaucracy grew. Still, Reagan's reputation as a staunch Goldwater Republican, as well as his proven ability as a dynamic spokesman for conservative causes, led him to believe that he might somehow grab the Republican presidential nomination in 1968.

Though refusing to declare his candidacy, Reagan undertook an extensive nationwide speaking tour, aiming humorous barbs at the Democratic opposition. "We can't really blame the president alone for the mess we're in," he told an audience. "A mess like that takes teamwork." By May 1968, however, Reagan's speeches took a more ominous tone. "This nation is totally out of control," he warned a gathering in New Orleans. America was torn apart, he suggested, by urban riots, despoiled by growing demands for wasteful social spending, undermined by draft dodgers, and crippled abroad by the absence of resolve to succeed in Vietnam.

Reagan also warned that civil order at home was threatened by those who believed that "Negroes need not obey the law." Throughout his tenure, Governor Reagan intimated that growing racial unrest was the product of radical agitators or possibly foreign influence. In the aftermath of the 1967 Newark and Detroit riots, he remarked, "It would be pretty naïve to believe that these riots are just spontaneous. I believe there is a plan." His suspicions about the influence of militants were undoubtedly bolstered by the events at the State Capitol in Sacramento in May 1967, when armed Black Panthers marched into the building.

Reagan's belated bid for the 1968 Republican nomination predictably came up short. Traveling to the party's August convention in Miami, the California governor found himself bested by Richard Nixon's sophisticated political apparatus. Reagan won only 182 delegate votes to Nixon's 692, but he refused to be discouraged, telling an acquaintance, "This wasn't our turn."

Across the country, many concerned Americans were drawn to similar voices that promised "law and order" in a nation that seemed to be coming apart. Despite this, George Wallace's rise to national prominence by 1968 surprised many, given that the Alabaman was chiefly known for his aggressive defense of racial segregation as governor from 1962 to 1966. A former state legislator and circuit court judge, Wallace first sought the governorship in 1958. Dismayed by his loss to segregationist John Patterson in 1958, who characterized his opponent as "soft" on segregation, Wallace privately told supporters, "Well, boys, no other son of bitch will ever out-nigger me again." True to his word in subsequent years, Wallace unapologetically defended segregation and encouraged violent white resistance to integration.

Wallace railed against the tyranny of the federal government and a Supreme Court that served, as he saw it, the interests of "convicted criminals, Communists, atheists . . . and left-wing minority groups." This message, initially crafted in defense of segregation, proved to have wider appeal when subtly altered to emphasize the federal government's seeming bureaucratic ineptitude and intrusiveness into the lives of hardworking taxpayers. Running in a small number of Democratic presidential primaries in 1964, Wallace displayed surprising strength in the North and East, where working-class whites embraced this message and his charges that the federal government favored minorities and coddled criminals.

Wallace's ambitions were only momentarily stymied by term limits prohibiting him from seeking the Alabama governorship again, but that problem was resolved by running his wife Lurleen in his place in 1966. Speaking at a rally for his wife, Wallace denounced the elitist national press and attacked the editor of the Montgomery *Alabama Journal* as "one of them Harvard-educated editors that sticks his little finger in the air when he drinks tea and looks down his nose at the common folks of Alabama." As his wife sat quietly on stage, Wallace pledged to stay in public life to fight against the "liberal, left-wing punks," the "judicial dictatorship," and a "government bureaucracy run by folks a thousand miles away with beards and goatees." The enemy, he thundered, was "the liberals and beatniks and socialists." Referring to a nearby Confederate flag, Wallace proclaimed that where you found it, "you won't find college students taking up money for the Vietcong and giving blood to the Vietcong or burning draft cards." Two years later, Wallace brought this same message, only marginally shorn of its neo-Confederate tenor, to a national audience.

Recognizing that he had little chance of winning the Democratic Party presidential nomination, Wallace set about building a third-party movement in early 1968. Thousands of enthusiastic volunteers gained the necessary signatures to ensure his spot on the ballot in all fifty states. Wallace hoped to draw enough electoral votes to throw the election into the House of Representatives.

In June, the Wallace movement rapidly gained momentum as the candidate traveled across the country speaking to the resentments of self-proclaimed patriotic, hardworking Americans who feared their country was under assault. Wallace's shotgun style targeted a wide range of miscreants: welfare cheaters, dope-smoking hippies, flag-burning radicals, liberal judges, "bearded Washington bureaucrats" whose briefcases Wallace vowed to "throw into the Potomac," and, perhaps most famously, "pointy-headed intellectuals who couldn't park a tricycle straight." During a California speaking tour, Wallace denounced "pro-communist, long-haired hippies" and the "pseudo-intellectuals" who defended criminals by "saying that the killer didn't get any watermelon to eat when he was 10 years old." Speaking to journalist James J. Kilpatrick, Wallace snarled, "People were fed up with the sissy attitude of Lyndon Johnson and the intellectual morons and theoreticians that he has around him," as well as with the "sorry, no-account Supreme Court." Absent was Wallace's earlier overt racism. His invective was now aimed more subtly at "rioters," welfare abuse, and federal policies deemed to unfairly favor minorities. The complexities of the Vietnam War did not faze

Wallace. "I think we got to pour it on," he declared. "We've got to win this war." Such sentiments proved surprisingly attractive in 1968 and by September, he drew over twenty percent in presidential polls, along with crowds as large as 25,000 people, at rallies across the country.

Not everyone viewed the Wallace phenomenon favorably. Reporters and journalists from national media that Wallace regularly assailed were increasingly alarmed at what they encountered. Some commented on Wallace's menacing appearance. Theodore White noted that "his close-set eyes were shrunken into deep, dark hollows under the great eyebrows." Others focused on Wallace's uncouth manners, such as spitting into a handkerchief during speeches and drenching all his meals in ketchup. Garry Wills grants that Wallace had "the dingy, attractive air of a B-movie idol, the kind who plays a handsome garage attendant." but otherwise found him repellent.

Wallace's selection of Curtis LeMay as his running mate did little to assuage growing concerns regarding his candidacy. Formerly chief of the Strategic Air Command, LeMay was well known for his advocacy of America's nuclear capability and his embrace of preemptive nuclear war. The cigar-chewing LeMay was likewise remembered for his casual use of such apocalyptic terms as "catastrophe bonus" and "killing a nation." His professed solution to North Vietnamese aggression was to "bomb them back to the Stone Age." During his first press conference, LeMay complained that Americans had "a phobia about nuclear weapons" before stating that he viewed their use as no worse than "a rusty knife." Wallace's efforts at damage control did little to lessen doubts about the trigger-happy former general.

Decidedly more problematic for the Wallace campaign, however, was growing public dismay at the accelerating violence that increasingly characterized his rallies. Wallace had long sought to whip up his supporters by challenging hecklers and protesters at his rallies and deriding them with taunts like "the only four-letter words they don't know are w-o-r-k and s-o-a-p!" On other occasions, he promised protesters a free haircut, or to "autograph your sandals." Inevitably, angry exchanges between his supporters and protesters escalated into physical violence. In Omaha, protesters hurled various objects at Wallace supporters, triggering something of a riot. In Minneapolis, a rally erupted in fistfights that compelled police to use mace and nightsticks. At a September rally in Cicero, Illinois, Wallace supporters surrounded and threatened a group of five young protesters, decrying them as "homos," lesbians, whores, and "the kooks that hate us," before grabbing their anti-Wallace placards. In Detroit, as Wallace fans and hecklers fought with fists and folding chairs, the candidate drawled from the podium, "Well, you asked for trouble and you got it!"

In November, the "Stand Up for America" campaign produced 13.5 million votes for Wallace. Alabama's "Fighting Little Judge," as the state had known him in the 1950s, won the forty-five electoral votes of five Southern states, and he received one vote from North Carolina. The American South, a Democratic political enclave since Reconstruction, was in the midst of a transformation that would radically reshape national politics for decades to come. Though Wallace failed to achieve his most immediate objective, he had identified a constituency that grew in importance in subsequent years. Angry white men, especially those in the South, became a core constituency in Republican electoral strategy, as working-class white men steadily abandoned the Democratic Party. Wallace was, consequently, in the words of biographer Dan T. Carter, "the most influential loser in twentieth-century American politics." Elaborating on this theme, historian Michael A. Cohen notes that "no politician did more to change the narrative and language of American politics than Wallace," adding that the Alabaman's "populist, anti-government, anti-elitist rhetoric has become the template for American conservatism."

Richard Nixon also saw the potency of the "law and order" theme as he contemplated a bid for the Republican nomination in 1968. A complex individual who at times allowed his manifold resentments and suspicions to surface, Nixon was nevertheless an astute political strategist. At the same time, Nixon had suffered two devastating political losses: the first to John F. Kennedy, the second to Pat Brown in the 1962 California gubernatorial contest. Having carefully analyzed Barry Goldwater's failed presidential effort, Nixon recognized the need to appeal to the escalating far-right elements in the Republican Party without alienating the moderates and liberals who still dominated the then ideologically diverse party. "I know the liberal fringe and the conservative fringe have no use for me," Nixon conceded, "but they tolerate me, where they don't tolerate others." For the next four years, he undertook a balancing act as he quietly set about reestablishing his role in Republican party ranks. His rehabilitation was part cosmetic, part behavioral. He shaved three times daily because of his heavy beard, and hired Paul Keyes of *The Jack Parr Show* to write jokes for him. Nixon strove to be more relaxed in public, offering self-deprecating humor. In print and speech, he cultivated the image of a thoughtful and knowledgeable statesman. By 1966, the gradual rehabilitation bore fruit, evident in increasingly positive coverage in the national press. The *New York Times* noted that the New Nixon was "better than ever," appearing "tanned, fit, and relaxed" while effectively "parrying questions about his political future." Nixon appeared on the cover of *Newsweek* with the caption, "Can the GOP Come Back?"

Focused more intently on the balancing act that was critical to his own comeback, Nixon cultivated Southern Republicans, voicing his opposition to segregation while insisting that the national party should not dictate state party platforms. He proclaimed support for federal civil rights acts and simultaneously denounced "mob rule," implying that black demonstrators were out of line. Rejecting ample evidence that South Carolina Senator Strom Thurmond was a racist, Nixon publicly defended the longtime Democratic Party officeholder who had recently switched parties, in a bid for his support. Further courting a Southern base for both his and the Republican Party's future, Nixon proclaimed "a new concept of states' rights," arguing that the traditional battle cry of segregationists could be "instruments of progress." With no evident sense of irony, Nixon chastized the Democrats as the party of "racial demagogues." Nixon threw his weight behind Republicans in the 1966 congressional cycle, when his party made substantial gains. The following year, he traveled abroad extensively, augmenting his foreign policy credentials.

That same year, *Reader's Digest* published Nixon's article "What Has Happened to America?" in which he blamed rising crime, decline of respect for authority, drugs, riots, and campus unrest on "teachers, preachers and politicians [who] have gone too far in advocating the idea that each individual should determine what laws are good and what laws are bad and that he should then obey the law he likes." This was the genesis of a message that would widely resonate two years later.

On the increasingly central issue of the Vietnam War, Nixon criticized the gradual escalation, but claimed that the US effort should be ramped up, while above all insisting on the need for victory. Now a master of vagueness, he promised to "end the war and win the peace" without straying into the minefield of specifics. In a December 1967 interview with the *Los Angeles Times*, the as-yet-to-be-announced candidate dismissed both the "superhawks" and the "wooly-headed doves," insisting that American policy should focus not on "how we lose in Vietnam" but rather "how we win." In another instance, Nixon proclaimed that "under no circumstances should a man say what he will do in January," effectively shielding himself from the need to elaborate on his prescriptions for the war.

Nixon had long pondered the reasons behind his political setbacks, and came into the 1968 campaign with carefully crafted ideas about how to present himself to the electorate. During the autumn of 1967, as he prepared to appear on *The Mike Douglas Show*, Nixon complained to a young producer about how absurd it was that politicians had to subject themselves to indignities like talk shows. The producer, Roger Ailes, who later headed Fox News, warned Nixon that such an attitude would prevent him from becoming president. The brief exchange had consequences far beyond 1968, as Nixon added

Ailes to his campaign team, which quickly embraced the idea of a largely electronic campaign. "We're going to build this whole campaign around television," Nixon proclaimed to his staff. The medium had worked wonders for Nixon during the 1952 presidential campaign when he was accused of having a slush fund, though it had failed him eight years later. This time, Nixon employed a team of professionals to carefully craft a televised image of a steady, practiced, and seasoned leader, someone with the ability to lead the nation out of its current crisis.

The campaign drew additional strategic direction from a memo drawn up by young party activist Kevin Phillips. In "Middle America and the Emerging Republican Majority," Phillips, acknowledging that elections were won by catering to popular resentments, concluded that what most stoked discontent among ordinary Americans was the new cultural elite, made up of condescending liberals whose social theories, realized in policy, were seemingly at the root of the nation's troubles. Republicans should strive to be the party of populism, appealing to "the great, ordinary, Lawrence Welkish mass of Americans from Maine to Hawaii." Nixon was uniquely suited to this task. On more than one occasion, he had made clear that he proudly embraced his image as a "square" who foreswore everything considered "hip." In a May 1968 radio address, Nixon asserted this identity, reaching out to "the millions of people . . . who do not demonstrate, who do not picket or protest loudly." "This silent center," Nixon intoned, had been transformed "from a minority into a majority."

Certain issues were paramount: Vietnam, racial unrest, and apparently escalating "crime and lawlessness." Nixon determined that offering vague promises of strength and resolution pertaining to Vietnam would suffice, while the "law and order" factor demanded greater attention. In a radio address shortly before the New Hampshire Republican primary on March 7, Nixon presented himself as the standard-bearer of law-abiding whites. He warned of "a war in the making in our own society" and the need to "meet force with force if necessary." Black resentments were justified, Nixon continued, but agitation leading to civil disorder was not. "Our first commitment as a nation in this time of crisis and questioning," he intoned, "must be a commitment to order." On March 8, Nixon celebrated his New Hampshire victory, where he garnered 79 percent of the vote, which seemed to validate his new status as the Republican Party frontrunner.

Subsequent events, of course, upended all calculations about the trajectory of the presidential election: LBJ's withdrawal from the race, Martin Luther King Jr.'s assassination, and racial explosions. While Reagan callously responded to King's murder by blaming "those people [who] who started choosing which laws they would break," Nixon traveled to Atlanta to offer condolences to the King family. But Nixon was aware that many white Americans resented the implication that they were somehow to blame for King's murder. The *Chicago Tribune* captured the sentiment perfectly in an editorial, which while demanding King's assassin be brought to justice, insisted, "The rest of us [were] not contributory to this particular crime." The editorial then delivered a broad indictment of a lawless and permissive society. "We are knee-deep in hippies, marijuana, LSD and other hallucinogens," the *Tribune* lamented. "If you are black, so goes the contention, you are right, and you must be indulged in every wish. If you are white, you are wrong. Feel guilty about it."

The student occupations at Columbia University in the spring of 1968 provided Nixon with an opportunity to speak to Middle America's resentments. Nixon reacted quickly, warning that the Columbia unrest was "the first major skirmish in a revolutionary struggle to seize the universities . . . and transform them into sanctuaries for radicals and vehicles for revolutionary political and social goals." Across the nation, Nixon claimed, "every potential revolutionary or anarchist" was watching to see if campus authorities would submit to the forces of disruption. In his campaign speeches, Nixon melded the issue of campus unrest with a more general condemnation of crime and lawlessness, citing alarming statistics and promising that as president, he would "restore order and a respect for law in this country." Otherwise, he warned, the "city jungle" would become "a barbaric reality." Poverty played only a marginal role in criminality, he insisted.

By the summer of 1968, it was evident that Nixon's path to the Republican nomination was clear. His road to the White House also seemed smoother, following the assassination of Senator Robert F. Kennedy in early June. An endorsement from Barry Goldwater secured Nixon's right flank, while Strom Thurmond helped to sell Nixon to Southerners. Thus it was Richard Nixon who accepted his party's nomination in a Miami Beach convention. During the opening ceremonies on August 5, Miami's archbishop established an ominous mood, noting "a heavy cloud of fear hangs over many of our citizens." John Wayne offered the evening's inspirational reading before affirming the importance of "old-fashioned" values. Kevin Phillips later privately explained the cynical rationale for Wayne's inclusion: "He sounds great to the schmucks. . . . The people down there in the Yahoo Belt."

On August 8, the overwhelmingly white delegates listened as their nominee offered a grim vision of contemporary American life: "Cities enveloped in smoke and flame . . . Americans dying on distant battlefields . . . Americans hating each other; fighting each other; killing each other at home." The resolution of this crisis, Nixon proclaimed, lay with "the great majority of Americans, the forgotten Americans . . . the non-shouters, the non-demonstrators."

This great majority "was not racist or sick," he stated. "They are not guilty of the crimes that plague the land." Laying considerable blame for the nation's ills on the incumbent Democrats, Nixon offered no specifics as to how these problems could be addressed, but concluded with an uplifting version of the trials he had faced and overcome. "The time has come for us to leave the valley of despair and climb the mountain so that we may see the glory of the dawn—a new day for America, and a new dawn of peace and freedom in the world."

Looking ahead to the fall campaign, Nixon intended to rely on his running mate, Maryland Governor Spiro Agnew to deliver political sledgehammers. Nixon's selection of Agnew baffled the press—"Spiro who?" was a common reaction. Having undertaken a hard turn rightward following racial disturbances in Cambridge, Maryland, Agnew was chosen as part of Nixon's evolving strategy of appealing to frightened white voters and Southerners. Nixon realized that the Maryland governor could play to the resentments of white voters in a crass manner while he remained above the fray. In other words, Agnew could perform the same tasks that Nixon had for Dwight D. Eisenhower, while adopting a far darker racial quality. Nixon aide Patrick Buchanan had advised the candidate not to worry about black voters: "They're not our voters; and if we go after them, we'll go down to defeat chasing a receding rainbow."

Agnew proved his worth in this role, holding rallies in the South before enthusiastic crowds. Questioned as to why he did not take his campaign into impoverished inner cities, Agnew responded, "When you've seen one slum, you've them all." Seemingly untroubled by casual racism, Agnew referred to a Hawaiian reporter as a "fat Jap" and tossed off the term "Polack" in a Polish neighborhood in Chicago. He was equally willing to unleash harsh verbal assaults on Nixon's Democratic opponent, Hubert Humphrey, denouncing the vice president as "soft on inflation, soft on Communism, and soft on law and order." He adopted a Wallace-like response to hecklers, telling one, "You can renounce your citizenship if you don't like it here," and predicting that after the election, troublemakers would "dry up and disappear." Agnew denounced anti-war protesters as "spoiled brats who never have had a good spanking" and declared that they "take their tactics from Gandhi and their money from daddy." Meanwhile, Nixon employed a relatively high tone in his campaign rhetoric, offering, as one reporter noted, "oratory so evenhanded as to be meaningless."

By October, the campaign's greatest surprise was not the rapid erosion of Wallace's support, but rather Hubert Humphrey's surge. The Democratic candidate had been hamstrung throughout the campaign by the Johnson administration's refusal to allow the vice president to support any Vietnam policy that deviated from the president's. Johnson's stubbornness prevented Humphrey from reaching out to anti-war Democrats, whose support he badly needed. Only in late October, when chances for successful peace negotiations with both South and North Vietnam improved, did Johnson seize the initiative by announcing a bombing halt. The possibility of a negotiated end to the war greatly enhanced Humphrey's electoral chances and he began closing the polling gap with Nixon. This momentary hope, along with Humphrey's chances, collapsed when the South Vietnamese government balked.

Unknown at the time, the South Vietnamese had backed away after being approached by Anna Chennault, who, acting at Nixon's behest, convinced the Saigon government that it would obtain better terms under a Republican president. Clearly a violation of the 1799 Logan Act, which prohibits private citizens from conducting negotiations with a foreign power, this cynical tactic foreshadowed Nixon's behavior in the White House. Meanwhile on the campaign trail, Nixon promised "peace with honor in Vietnam" and a pledge to "bring us together."

On Election Day, Nixon won the electoral vote handily, though the popular margin was razor-thin: 43.4 percent for Nixon, 42.7 percent for Humphrey, and 13.5 percent for Wallace. Having learned the political value of playing to popular resentments and demonizing opponents, President Nixon would embrace a policy of "positive polarization," pitting the Silent Center against the vocal minority, and presiding over a nation in which the divisions of 1968 only seemed to heighten.

The reactionary voices and activities that surfaced in opposition to the revolutionary tide of 1968 did not diminish with the year's passing. Many of the conservative political careers and movements spawned in that tumultuous year proved enduring, fundamentally reshaping American politics and society for decades to come, with often problematic results. The final legacies of 1968 would not be fully understood until years later.

15

"The Revolution Will Not Be Televised"

Legacies and Conclusion

In spite of the rightward turn suggested by the presidential election results, talk of revolution, whether in the United States or beyond its borders, hardly vanished altogether as 1968 wound to a close. The revolutionary surge in Europe did diminish, in one sense, as the possibility of wholesale transformation suggested by the Prague Spring and the surge of '68ers in France dissipated during the summer of 1968. But terrorist groups appeared in Germany and Italy, with small bands of disaffected radicals joining the Red Army Faction (RAF), also called the Baader-Meinhof Group, or the Red Brigades, by 1970. Urban guerrillas, the Red Army Faction and the Italian Red Brigades, drew on the experiences of the Uruguayan Tupamaros and Palestinian militants. The two European groups resorted to bank robberies, bombings, and arson. They also kidnapped and murdered well-known politicians and businessmen. Two RAF members helped Palestinians guerrillas hijack an Air France jetliner. Following the crumbling of the East German regime, revelations emerged about support the Red Army Faction had received from the Stasi secret police. The most notorious action by the Red Brigades involved the kidnapping and killing of former prime minister Aldo Moro.

In early October 1968, the plight of Irish Catholics, heavily outnumbered by Protestants in Northern Ireland, spilled over into the streets of Derry, where a civil rights march drew widespread radio and television coverage. Later viewed as the start of the "Troubles," the march on October 5 was halted by the baton-charging Royal Ulster Constabulary. Two days of rioting by irate Catholic residents followed. Two thousand Queen's University of

Figure 15.1   "You Don't Have to Be Vietnamese to Smell a Rat" proclaims this Yippie
poster inviting protesters to attend the presidential inauguration of Richard Nixon. The
year 1968 came to an end not with the triumph of liberal or radical politics, but with
the narrow election of Republican Richard Nixon, who ran as a "law and order"
candidate who promised to bring "an honorable end to the war in Vietnam." As the
radical Left splintered and outrage against the Vietnam War and racism grew, the
nation was bedeviled by often violent protests even as the Nixon administration
resorted to criminal activities to silence critics. Though he had confided to aides in
early 1969 that the war in Vietnam could not be won, Nixon cynically continued the US
role in the conflict until early 1973, by which time some 58,000 Americans and around
two million Vietnamese had died. Library of Congress, Prints and Photographs Division,
LC-USZ62-127544.

Belfast students conducted their own protest regarding police brutality, but ran into a counter-demonstration headed by the fiery Protestant minister Ian Paisley, a staunch unionist who had established paramilitary groups. Attempted reforms by the Labour-led British government of Harold Wilson proved unavailing, and the Provisional Irish Republican Army (IRA), a republican paramilitary organization, appeared in 1969. The IRA demanded the termination of British control of Northern Ireland and Ireland's reunification. Starting in 1970, the IRA conducted a "Long War" that included bombings, assassinations, and ambushes, seeking to carry out terrorist strikes in Britain and on the European continent. The pushback by British troops was often fierce, leading to the infamous Bloody Sunday on January 30, 1972, when thirteen Catholic demonstrators were killed by British paratroopers.

Similar tactics to those employed by the Red Army Faction, the Red Brigades, and the IRA were adopted by guerrilla forces around the globe by the end of the 1960s and throughout the 1970s; some groups had employed guerrilla warfare for considerably longer. Those in the Middle East ranged from the Palestinian Liberation Organization (PLO), led by Yasser Arafat, to the largely secular Fedayeen-a Khala and the Islamist Mujahideen-e Khalq in Iran. The Japanese Red Army, established in 1969 by Fusako Shigenobu, sought to overthrow the national government, wipe out the monarchy, and help pique revolution worldwide. The Red Army engaged in bloody attacks in Japan, Europe, and the Middle East, while carrying out bombings, hijackings, shootouts with the police, and deadly internecine squabbles. The PLO murder of eleven Israeli team members during the 1972 Olympic Games held in Munich was among the most startling acts of terrorism in the post-1960s era. One of the most enduring campaigns took place in apartheid South Africa, where the African National Congress, led by the jailed attorney Nelson Mandela, employed both civil disobedience and guerrilla warfare. Mass arrests and the banning of political parties came about, along with the formation of cells and armed caches by opponents of the separatist government.

Insurgencies also evolved in Latin America, where a spate of right-wing, military-dominated coups overturned democratically elected governments, often resulting in wholesale repression involving labor activists, leftists, intellectuals, socially engaged priests and nuns, and even reform-minded soldiers. Brutal regimes intensified in Nicaragua, El Salvador, Guatemala, and Brazil, but also appeared in Argentina, Uruguay, and Chile, violating lengthy periods of democratic governance in the latter two nations. Drawing on the inspiration of Fidel Castro, Che Guevara, and Camilo Cienfuegos, guerrillas sprang up in both urban areas and the countryside, sometimes initiating decades-long struggles. According to the historian Donald Hodges, they were connected to a series of "insurrectionary waves," with some of the most serious campaigns initially taking place in Colombia, Guatemala, and Venezuela. Attempts to create "a guerrilla nucleus (foco)" occurred in Brazil, Argentina, Uruguay, Peru, and Nicaragua, among other locales. The "turn to armed struggle" included Chile, where the democratically elected government of Dr. Salvador Allende, a Marxist who favored an evolutionary path toward socialism, was overthrown in 1973, resulting in the terribly repressive regime of General Augusto Pinochet.

The drive toward revolution continued in Southeast Asia, as Vietcong guerrillas and North Vietnamese soldiers maintained their fight against the US-backed South Vietnamese government, which finally concluded in the spring of 1975. That same year also saw communist forces prevail in both Laos and Cambodia, which proved particularly tragic in the latter instance, when the Khmer Rouge, led by Pol Pot, who had studied in Paris, engaged in a fanatical insistence on systematically altering Cambodian society. That led to the capital city of Phnom Penh being emptied, with millions compelled to toil on communal farms, and mass killings resulting from torture, execution, starvation, disease, and exploitation.

Many of the key American figures and forces that demanded change—and change of a revolutionary nature—in 1968 remained prominent during the period ahead, while others surfaced as well. The Movement hardly abated, although it also splintered, with the mass media focusing on different crusades. College and universities experienced more takeovers and violence, while SDS's membership soared, heading toward 100,000. The protest at San Francisco State continued into the spring, while startling scenes occurred in April 1969 on two Ivy League campuses, Harvard and Cornell. In Cambridge, Massachusetts, Harvard students led by SDS sat-in to demonstrate their determination to drive out ROTC, with the *Harvard Crimson* declaring, "ROTC is based on the notion that the country's universities should serve the needs of the warfare state." The student newspaper warned, "Over-expansion of the American military machine has become perhaps the greatest threat of all." After 400 police officers arrested more than one hundred protesters, students initiated a strike. In Ithaca, New York, student members of the Afro-American Society (AAS) occupied Willard Straight Hall, Cornell's student center, following extended confrontations in which the group demanded the setting up of a black studies program and amnesty for AAS students. Worrying that an assault on the building might be impending, the students smuggled firearms into Straight, departing after the university administration acceded to their demands. A photographer for UPI captured the image of weapons-holding AAS students leaving the building.

Students from UC Berkeley and members of the local community associated with the Movement and the counterculture delivered their own statement that same spring, suggesting utopian aspirations. Located off Telegraph Avenue, south of campus, People's Park was birthed on April 20, 1969, following the *Berkeley Barb*'s pronouncement, "The University had no right to create ugliness as a way of life." The underground newspaper was referring to the plot of land, owned by UC Berkeley, intended to house dormitories. But local activists and hippies were determined to occupy the lot and construct a park. A battle took place pitting occupiers against police and highway patrol officers sent by Governor Ronald Reagan to evict them. The police employed birdshot, buckshot, and tear gas, on the lot and in the streets, blinding one young man and killing another. In a televised meeting with faculty and administrators, Reagan lashed out, blaming the protesters for the violence and the university for tolerating, even encouraging it. "All of it began," he lectured his captive audience, "the first time some of you who know better . . . let young people think that they had the right to choose the laws they would choose as long as they were doing it in the name of social protest."

That summer, the leading New Left organization, SDS, which had reached the membership levels previously attained by only a pair of American radical groups during the first several decades of the twentieth century—the early Socialist Party and the CPUSA—tore itself apart. SDS imploded during its national convention, held in Chicago in June 1969, riven by sectarianism and a lefter-than-thou propensity on the part of key members. Groups like Progressive Labor, Revolutionary Youth Movement I, and Revolutionary Youth Movement II battled for preeminence, but ultimately a small group soon calling itself Weatherman ensured the demise of SDS. It included present or past national officers Mike Spiegel, Bernardine Dohrn, Mark Rudd, Bill Ayers, and Jeff Jones. Insisting on the need "to bring the war home," Weatherman identified with the Black Panthers and revolutionaries around the globe. Its members conducted a series of actions in the fall of 1969, culminating in the Days of Rage, during which clashes between hundreds of Weather people and the police occurred in the streets of Chicago in early October. Resulting in hundreds of arrests and costing more than $250,000 in bail money, the Days of Rage nevertheless emboldened some who headed for SDS's last national convention, held in Flint, Michigan, in late December. The "war council" consisted of five days of meetings and rap sessions amid giant posters adorned with images of Che, Mao, Ho, Malcolm X, and the recently slain Black Panther leader from Chicago, Fred Hampton. A large papier-mâché machine gun was suspended above the stage. The 300 or so Weather cadre listened to Dohrn extol Charlie Manson, and celebrate the slaying of the actress Sharon Tate and others by his "family." Weather leaders agreed to head underground and to initiate a terrorist campaign, reliant on bombings that could result in damage to both property and people.

The Weatherman embrace of a terrorist bombing campaign led to bombs being placed close to police stations in Berkeley and San Francisco, resulting in injuries and the killing of one police officer. Weatherman also firebombed the home of a New York State Supreme Court justice, then presiding over a trial in which Black Panthers were the defendants, charged with conducting a bombing campaign of their own in New York City. Bombs were tossed at both a police car in Manhattan and military recruiting centers in Brooklyn. Leading Weather members sought more carnage, discussed kidnapping political figures and police officers in Detroit, and hurled Molotov cocktails onto the front porch of a police detective. Planning to set off bombs at Fort Dix near Trenton, New Jersey, three Weathermen were constructing nail bombs in a fashionable Greenwich Village townhouse, but blew themselves up instead on the early morning of March 6, 1970. Shaken, the Weather leadership nevertheless proved undeterred.

The spate of bombings, committed by Weatherman and other revolutionary groups, scarcely waned in the wake of the Greenwich Village explosion, both on and off college and university campuses. Targets included ROTC buildings but others as well at institutions of higher learning, corporate headquarters, and Army recruiting centers. The ROTC building at Kent State University was torched, soon following by the sending of National Guardsmen onto the campus, which led to the shooting of thirteen students, four fatally, around noontime on May 4. Ten days later, fifteen students were wounded and two killed, as police officers delivered a "barrage of gunfire" at Jackson State College, located in Jackson, Mississippi. There too, an ROTC building had been set on fire, and a riot preceded the calling of police to the largely African-American campus. One Weather leader soon released a tape recorded measure with the greeting, "Hello, this is Bernardine Dohrn. I'm going to read a declaration of war." On August 24, a tiny band also enamored with a vision of bringing the war home, bombed a building—which housed the Army Mathematics Research Center—at the University of Wisconsin, killing a young graduate student, who was himself strongly opposed to the Vietnam War.

The notion that unwanted deaths compelled would-be bombers to resist a turn toward terrorism can be refuted by the sheer volume of bombing incidents that took place over an eighteen-month stretch of time in 1971 and 1972. According to the journalist Bryan Burrough, the FBI traced "2,500 bombings on American soil, almost five a day." In addition to Weatherman and affinity groups, perpetrators included members of Fuerzas Armadas de

Liberación Nacional, the Puerto Rican separatist group; the far-right Jewish Defense League; Omega 7, the Cuban anti-Castro group; and the Black Liberation Army, which splintered from the Panthers and favored armed struggle to bring about the "liberation and self-determination of black people in the United States." Then there was the Symbionese Liberation Army, which murdered an Oakland school superintendent and kidnapped the heiress Patty Hearst.

At various points, particularly beginning in 1967 and 1968, facets of the American counterculture and the New Left had threatened to come together, something feared by political figures and law enforcement officials alike. But that uneasy marriage experienced blows as well, while the counterculture began unraveling, or at least headed away from the flowers, peace, and love moments previously celebrated. In the midst of the Woodstock Music & Art Fair in mid-August 1969, Yippie leader Abbie Hoffman attempted to speak about the travails facing John Sinclair of the White Panther Party. The Who's lead guitarist Pete Townsend forced Hoffman from the stage. Effectively hosted by the Rolling Stones, the Altamont Speedway Free Festival on December 6, 1969, became the anti-Woodstock, with bad trips abounding and the Hell's Angels, hired as security guards, murdering a young concertgoer near the front of the stage. The dark side of the counterculture was there for all to see in the documentary of the Stones' tour, *Gimme Shelter* (1970). Despite the growing propensity of some to "head toward the country," with the establishment of rural communes like Wavy Gravy's Hog Farm outside Llano, New Mexico, the counterculture also suffered the loss of musical super-groups, which rose and departed, including the Beatles, and the death of stars like Jimi Hendrix, Janis Joplin, and Jim Morrison. Harder drugs and guns began appearing in hippie enclaves, including urban communes. A British group, Thunderclap Newman, released "Something in the Air" (1969), which declared "the revolution's here, and you know it's right." Jefferson Airplane's "Volunteers" (1969) sang about what was taking place in the streets, where "volunteers of America" were engaged in a revolution. The band's "We Can Be Together" (1969) assertively declared, "We are all outlaws in the eyes of America," deemed private property a "target for your enemy," and exclaimed, "We are forces of chaos and anarchy."

Other groups engaged in militant actions, including many more in line with the Ultra-Resistance, which had carried civil disobedience to a new level. Women, gays, environmentalists, Latinos, and Native Americans were among those who refused to abandon the revolutionary hopes sparked or intensified by 1968. Redstockings, the radical feminist group that viewed women as "an oppressed class" kept down by men, appeared early the next year, along with the National Abortion Rights League. By 1970, a succession of radical feminist manifestos poured forth: Shulamith Firestone's *The Dia-lectic of Sex*, Germaine Greer's *The Female Eunuch*, Kate Millet's *Sexual Politics*, and Robin Morgan's edited volume, *Sisterhood is Powerful*. Within two years, Congress overwhelmingly passed the Equal Rights Amendment, which seemed destined for quick ratification but soon confronted an anti-feminist backlash. Gloria Steinem's *Ms. Magazine* began publication, provid-ing a forum for modern American feminists. In 1973, the US Supreme Court established in the case of *Roe v. Wade* a constitutional right for safe, legal abortions, especially during the first two trimesters.

One of the most powerful movements to emerge during the 1960s, gay liberation exploded on the scene with the Stonewall riots in 1969. Surfacing in the wake of Stonewall, the Gay Liberation Front (GLF) sponsored "gay-ins," proudly adopted the appellation of "gay," and identified "with all the oppressed," both within and outside the United States. Condemning racism, imperialism, and capitalism, the GLF aggressively called for "coming out of the closet" and deemed itself "a revolutionary homosexual group" that demanded "complete sexual liberation." The Gay Activists Alliance favored the kinds of public "zaps" the Yippies executed, and helped to coordinate the first gay pride parade held in New York City. *Refugees from Amerika: A Gay Manifesto* (1970) by former SDS leader Carl Whitman termed San Francisco "a refugee camp for homosexuals," and insisted "closet queenery must end." Rita Mae Brown, then a little-known writer, called for "a lesbian feminist civil rights movement," and helped to establish the group Radicalesbians. In 1973, the American Psychiatric Association determined that homosexuality was not a mental illness.

Environmentalism received a spur in late January 1969 with a massive oil spill that spewed over 20,000 gallons of crude after a blowout involving Union Oil (later Unocal), despoiling Santa Barbara's pristine coast. The US Geological Survey had granted a waiver enabling the company to avoid meet-ing federal drilling requirements. Congress agreed to the National Environ-mental Policy Act following the ecological disaster, and the next year saw the first Earth Day and Norman Borlaug's receipt of the Nobel Peace Prize for his work extolling the Green Revolution, along with passage of the Clean Air Act. Subsequent legislative achievements included the Clean Water Act (1972) and the Endangered Species Act (1973). But activists demanded more, establishing such advocacy groups as Friends of the Earth (1969), the League of Conservation Voters (1970), Greenpeace (1971), the Earth Force Society (1977, later renamed the Sea Shepherd Conservation Society), and the radical Earth First! (1980). Providing intellectual ammunition for environmentalists were books like Francis A. Schaeffer's *Pollution and the Death of Man* (1970), E. F. Schumacher's *Small Is Beautiful* (1973), Edward Abbey's *The*

Monkey Wrench Gang (1975), David Ehrenfeld's *The Arrogance of Humanism* (1978), and William R. Catton Jr.'s *Overshoot: The Ecological Basis of Revolutionary Change* (1980).

Thanks to a twenty-five-day fast he conducted in early 1968, and breaking bread with Senator Robert F. Kennedy, Cesar Chavez and the Chicano movement acquired far greater acclaim. Six years earlier, Chavez had helped to establish the United Farms Workers Organizing Committee (UFWOC). In late 1965, the UFWOC undertook a nationwide boycott of grapes. The next spring, it carried out a protest march from Delano to Sacramento, California's state capital. Chavez undertook his extended fast beginning in February 1968, to call attention to his movement's need to remain nonviolent. By July 1969, an artist's depiction of Chavez appeared on the cover of *Time* magazine, along with a banner stating "The Grapes of Wrath: Mexican-Americans on the March," and the companion article, "The Little Strike That Grew to *La Causa.*"

"The new Mexican-American militancy," the article noted, had produced other leaders, some considerably "more strident," including Reies Lopez Tijerina, who insisted on the return of land in the American Southwest and West grabbed by American settlers; David Sanchez of the Brown Berets, patterned after the Black Panthers, in Los Angeles; and Rudolfo "Corky" Gonzales, who led "Crusade for Justice" in Denver, which fostered Chicano nationalism. Jose Angel Gutierrez helped to found the Mexican American Youth Organization (MAYO, 1967) in San Antonio, then created La Raza Unida Party in Crystal City, Texas.

Identifying with both Puerto Rican nationalism and the Panthers, the Young Lords Organization (YLO), established strongholds in Chicago and New York City, condemning police brutality and insisting that the needs of Puerto Rican communities be addressed. That led to direct action tactics, including the burning of garbage in the streets and the blocking of traffic in Manhattan. Initially issued in 1969, the YLO's "13-Point Program and Platform" demanded self-determination for Puerto Ricans and all Latinos, "liberation of all third world people," community control of local institutions and land, genuine education, release of all political prisoners, and equality for women. The manifesto condemned racism, capitalism, "The Amerikkkan Military," and anti-communism. It heralded "armed self-defense and armed struggle," as well as the creation of a socialist society.

The product of decades of struggle regarding the mistreatment of Native Americans, the American Indian Movement (AIM) emerged in 1968. Following the lead of civil rights activists, Native American militants resorted to fish-ins, in a defiant display of civil disobedience. In 1968, AIM was established, to compel the federal government to redress long-standing issues of concern to Native Americans. But the American Indian movement failed to garner much attention until the takeover of Alcatraz Island, the site of a former federal penitentiary off the coast of San Francisco, which began in November 1969. The occupation of "the Rock" by "Indians of All Tribes" lasted for over nineteen months, with buildings containing messages reading "Red Power," "Custer Had It Coming," and "Peace and Freedom. Welcome. Home of the Free Indian Land." Indians of All Tribes issued a document addressed to "The Great White Father and All His People," calling for the island to feature a Native American school, museum, and cultural center. Celebrities arrived, including Ethel Kennedy, the actors Marlon Brando and Jane Fonda, the activist Dick Gregory, and the Grateful Dead. Four years after the start of the Alcatraz occupation, another one took place at the dilapidated village of Wounded Knee, South Dakota, the scene of a terrible massacre of Sioux in 1890. The takeover included the holding of eleven hostages, ending with a US Marshall and an FBI agent shot, and two Native Americans killed.

In their hyperkinetic fashion, Yippie activists Abbie Hoffman and Jerry Rubin continued to garner their own headlines, thanks in part to a decision by the Justice Department under Attorney General John N. Mitchell to demonstrate the new Nixon administration's commitment to law and order. His predecessor, Ramsey Clark, had been more inclined to agree with the findings of the Chicago Study Team, led by the attorney Daniel Walker, released on December 1, 1968, which viewed the city's police force as most culpable in instigating the violence that had broken out during convention week. The Chicago police, the Walker Report acknowledged, became "the targets of mounting provocation by both word and act." The police were on the receiving end of "obscene epithets . . . rocks, sticks, bathroom tiles . . . even human feces hurled . . . by demonstrators." But the police, the report indicated, frequently responded with "unrestrained and indiscriminate police violence." More startling still, that violence often came down on those "who had broken no law, disobeyed no order, made no threat," and included nonviolent demonstrators and individuals who simply got caught up in melees. Events on two evenings devolved into what the Chicago Study Team called "a police riot." Predicting that future clashes would occur, the report warned, "And the next time the whole world will still be watching."

Angered by Attorney General Clark's refusal to go after protest leaders, Chicago Mayor Richard Daley exerted pressure, resulting in a grand jury's examination of anti-war leaders involved in convention week demonstrations. A component of the 1968 Civil Rights Act federalized the crossing of "state lines with the intent to incite a riot." On March 20, 1969, a Chicago grand jury issued indictments against a group of radicals, soon referred to as the

Chicago Eight: Yippie leaders Hoffman and Rubin, former SDS leaders Tom Hayden and Rennie Davis, Black Panther Party cofounder Bobby Seale, Goddard College professor John R. Froines, Northwestern University doctoral student Lee Weiner, and David Dellinger, later called "the single most important leader of the national anti-war movement, at its height."

The trial of the Chicago Eight proved sensational, with widespread media coverage and the defendants viewed as Movement representatives. The defendants and their attorneys, William Kunstler and Leonard Weinglass, bantered repeatedly with the septuagenarian Federal District Judge Julius Hoffman, Mayor Daley's former law partner. Enraged by Seale's slurs that he was "a pig, a fascist and a racist," Judge Hoffman ordered the Black Panther physically restrained, with his mouth gagged and his feet chained to a chair. Ultimately, Judge Hoffman severed Seale's case from that of his codefendants. The courtroom clashes never subsided, with particularly sharp exchanges taking place between the judge and his fellow Jews, Abbie Hoffman and Rubin. At one point, Abbie bitingly said to Judge Hoffman, "You are a disgrace to the Jews. You would have served Hitler better." Following extensive jury deliberations in February 1970, the jury found Davis, Dellinger, Hayden, Hoffman, and Rubin guilty of having crossed state lines with the intent to incite a riot. Judge Hoffman added contempt citations against all the defendants and their attorneys, but before the end of the year the US Court of Appeals for the Seventh Circuit tossed out the convictions. The appellate court ruled that Judge Hoffman had blundered on many procedural matters and exhibited marked prejudice against the defendants.

Other trials involving Movement activists had, of course, taken place during 1968. The case of the Boston Five resulted in the conviction of the Reverend William Sloane Coffin Jr., Michael Ferber, Mitchell Goodman, and Dr. Benjamin Spock for conspiracy to abet draft refusal, in violation of the Selective Service Act. The convictions, like those involving the Chicago Eight, would be overturned on appeal. The Boston Five defendants continued to be involved in anti-war activity, with Spock and Coffin particularly remaining at the forefront of opposition to the Vietnam conflict. Nevertheless, the prosecution served the interests of the federal government in tying up resources—material and emotional—required to prevent the defendants from ending up behind bars. Equally important, it provided a warning to others who might have become more involved in supporting draft resistance. After all, if such high profile individuals—and few could surpass Dr. Spock or Reverend Coffin in that regard—were subject to federal prosecution for supporting young men involved with the Resistance, then virtually anyone championing their cause could be as well. Similarly, David Harris, arguably the key figure during the Resistance's short life, adhered to his principles by going to jail for draft resistance, but no mass movement emerged in the manner he and the other founders of the Resistance once envisioned.

Those who came to be known as participants in the Ultra-Resistance recognized this and were willing to suffer a similar fate, if need be, but many others must have had second thoughts about lending public support to draft resisters. The Berrigan brothers, Daniel and Philip, were among the most noteworthy individuals who remained defiant and, in fact, opted for even more radical approaches in the period following their conviction in the case of the Catonsville Nine. They did help to inspire others to carry out similar public acts involving civil disobedience, although again few were willing to follow the Berrigans in openly challenging government authority in that manner. Having received a three-year prison sentence and failing in appellate courts, Daniel jumped bail in early 1970, heading underground, now refusing to adhere to the purported liberal "mythology" indicating there existed a "moral necessity of joining illegal action to legal consequences." After months as a fugitive, he was taken into custody by FBI agents and ended up in Danbury Prison, where Philip was serving time.

Another conspiracy trial soon involved the Berrigan brothers, regarding a charge by the Nixon administration that a plot existed to kidnap National Security Adviser Henry Kissinger, and blow up heating systems in federal buildings in Washington, DC. FBI director J. Edgar Hoover provided testimony to the US Senate indicating that the defendants supposedly sought to curb government operations, compel an ending of the war, and mandate release of all "political prisoners." Philip and his wife, Elizabeth McAlister, a former nun, were among the seven defendants indicted, while Daniel and six others were deemed coconspirators but not charged with the conspiracy. All members of the Harrisburg Seven were religiously motivated anti-war activists and underwent a trial during the spring of 1972 that resulted in a hung jury. Former Attorney General Ramsay Clark headed the defense team.

The Nixon administration also singled out the Vietnam Veterans Against the War (VVAW) for prosecution. Although founded in 1967, the VVAW acquired little attention until it conducted the Winter Soldier Investigation in a Detroit hotel in early 1971, exploring purported war crimes committed by American troops in Vietnam. Veterans delivered charged remembrances of acts they had carried out or witnessed, recounting incidents involving arson, rape, torture, murder, and the destruction of villages. That spring, VVAW participated in mass anti-war rallies in Washington, DC, topped off by the hurling of combat ribbons and medals onto the steps of the Capitol Building, and the testimony before the US Senate by VVAW representative John Kerry. The young veteran poignantly wondered, "How do you ask a man to be the last man to die for a mistake?" He assailed civilian commanders for having "deserted their troops," declaring, "There is no more serious crime in the laws of war." The VVAW, Kerry hoped, would help to enable America to alter course, to engage in a "turning" from Cold War policies.

While attempting to besmirch the reputation of the much-decorated Kerry, the Nixon White House also obtained indictments against eight VVAW members, who participated in anti-war demonstrations during the 1972 Republican Party National Convention in Miami Beach. A grand jury indicted the so-called Gainesville Eight, charging them with conspiring "to organize numerous 'fire teams' to attack with automatic fire and incendiary devices police stations, police cars and stores" with "lead weights, 'fried' marbles, ball bearings, 'cherry' bombs, and smoke bombs." Despite the government's reliance on infiltrators and agents provocateurs, the jury returned a not guilty verdict after only four hours of deliberation on August 31, 1973.

The federal government opted for various approaches, including prosecution, to cripple the Black Panther Party. As demonstrators cried out, "Free Huey!" with party cofounder Huey Newton in jail, convicted of killing a white police officer in Oakland, twenty-one Panthers members were charged with conspiring to blow up the New York City Botanical Gardens and several department stores, and to murder police officers. The case drew the attention of many white liberals and radicals, with famed conductor Leonard Bernstein and his wife Felicia Montealegre, a Chilean actress, holding a fund-raising party at their duplex on Manhattan's Park Avenue in early 1970. That led writer Tom Wolfe to charge that "radical chic" drove well-known, affluent individuals like Bernstein and Montealegre to support the revolutionary black militants. The trial concluded on May 13, 1971, with an acquittal following jury deliberation of less than an hour.

While the US government elected not to retry Bobby Seale for his purported involvement in inciting a riot during the 1968 Democratic Party National Convention, he remained in jail temporarily, having been sentenced to forty-eight months for acts of contempt during the trial of the Chicago Eight. Although that sentence would later be overturned, Seale again was prosecuted, along with several others, including Ericka Huggins, who headed the Black Panther Party's New Haven chapter, for the killing of nineteen-year-old Alex Rackley, suspected of being an FBI informant. The trial of Seale and Huggins became another cause célèbre in New Haven, leading Yale University president Kingman Brewster to admit, "I am skeptical of the ability of black revolutionaries to achieve a fair trial anywhere in the United States." After a lengthy trial and extended deliberation, the jury failed to agree on a verdict, resulting in a mistrial.

Twenty-five-year-old Elmer G. "Geronimo" Pratt, a Vietnam War vet and a Black Panther Party leader in Los Angeles, was convicted of the murder of Caroline Olsen, a young white woman who taught elementary school, and her husband Kenneth, which occurred on December 18, 1968. With Panthers in the northern part of the state ordered by Huey Newton to refute Pratt's alibi, he received a life sentence in 1972. Pratt served twenty-seven years behind bars, before his conviction was overturned because the witness who testified against him had lied about being a government informant. His defense team came across evidence indicating that COINTELPRO had been directed at Pratt.

White Panther Party leader John Sinclair suffered legal harassment and prosecution as well. The MC5 manager and cofounder of the avowedly revolutionary White Panther Party, Sinclair delivered his own manifesto in late 1968, patterned after the ten-point plan of the Black Panthers, which he fully endorsed. It called for "total assault on the culture by any means necessary, including rock 'n' roll, dope and fucking in the streets." It also insisted on the removal of schools and other institutions from corporate dominance and an end to money, "free food, clothes, housing, dope, music, bodies, medical care . . . access to information media." The manifesto demanded the freeing of all prisoners and all soldiers. But Sinclair acknowledged, as he later revealed, "We can't win with guns." Rather, he hoped to foster "cultural revolution" to weaken the existing power structure. The FBI subsequently deemed the White Panthers "potentially the largest and most dangerous of revolutionary organizations in the United States."

White Panther members Sinclair, his wife Leni, and Pun Plamondon were viewed as prime suspects in the bombing of a CIA office in Ann Arbor, Michigan. As Sinclair served a ten-year sentence following his conviction for holding a pair of marijuana joints, public luminaries participated in a "John Sinclair Freedom Rally" held in Ann Arbor in late 1971. Among those present were John Lennon, Yoko Ono, Allen Ginsberg, Ed Sanders, the musicians Phil Ochs, David Peel, Bob Seger, and Stevie Wonder, and the Chicago Eight's Rennie Davis, David Dellinger, Abbie Hoffman, Jerry Rubin, and Bobby Seale. The following year, Sinclair and two other White Panthers were charged with conspiring to carry out the bombing of the CIA office. A defense motion to suppress any evidence obtained through illegal electronic surveillance resulted in a unanimous ruling by the US Supreme Court, which led to the freeing of the defendants.

But others lacking the notoriety of the Boston Five, certain Black Panther leaders, and John Sinclair, continued paying a heavy price for Movement activities that led to assaults on their freedom, sometimes resulting in debilitating incarcerations or worse. In 1968, twenty-eight-year-old Lee Otis Johnson, a SNCC and anti-war activist, received a thirty-year sentence in Houston for purportedly delivering a single marijuana joint to an undercover agent. Campus radicals in Texas yelled, "Free Lee Otis!" but he served four years before a federal judge ruled that a change of venue should have taken place to preclude a prejudiced setting. Unfortunately, as Johnson's sister admitted, "His life deteriorated in prison," as her handsome, brilliant brother left prison a broken man.

Another charismatic young African-American man, twenty-one-year-old Fred Hampton, a leader in the Illinois chapter of the Black Panther Party, which he had joined in 1968, became another victim of the politics of assassination. Hampton set up a community service program, which provided free school breakfasts and medical care. Pointing to the large number of attacks conducted against Panthers, he called for the party "to be an armed propaganda unit" but insisted, "The basic thing is to educate." Determined to bridge racial divides on the political left, Hampton established a Rainbow Coalition, which brought together members of the Panthers, SDS, the Blackstone Rangers, a Chicago street gang, and the Young Lords. Encouraged by FBI director Hoover, law enforcement agents targeted the Black Panthers in Chicago, repeatedly raiding their headquarters, arresting members, and engaging in shootouts with party members. Then, on the early morning of December 4, 1969, police fired as many as ninety-nine bullets into the Black Panther headquarters on Monroe Street, killing both Hampton and twenty-two-year-old Mark Clark, who supposedly had gotten off a single shot of his own. The Panthers soon charged that Hampton had been executed in cold blood.

Martin Luther King Jr. and Bobby Kennedy, two of the great dreamers in the American political pantheon, had also been murdered, victims of the politics of assassination that carved out a deadly path throughout the decade of the 1960s, but at no point more emphatically than in 1968. Their names were added to a roster that contained President John F. Kennedy, civil rights activist Medgar Evers, Black Nationalist Malcolm X, and American Nazi Party chieftain George Lincoln Rockwell. Later, right-wing presidential candidate George Wallace, Allard Lowenstein, who spearheaded the Dump Johnson movement, and John Lennon—all of whose stars shone brightly in 1968—similarly became tragic casualties of a paranoid, hate-filled atmosphere that possibly included conspiratorial aspects. Despite five gunshot wounds, Wallace survived, but was left a paraplegic. The shooters included a young man desperate for fame, a former acolyte and activist, and a crazed fan. While serving as a dean at Stanford, Lowenstein had befriended his killer, Dennis Sweeney, one of the Resistance founders. Lennon's slaying took place after the end to a five-year hiatus of largely remaining out of the limelight, which followed extended political involvement that had led the

Nixon administration to seek his deportation. As if responding to charges in 1968 that his "Revolution" was counterrevolutionary, Lennon had produced a spate of brilliant, politically charged songs, including "Give Peace a Chance," "Working Class Hero," "Power to the People," "Happy Xmas (War Is Over)," "Imagine," "Gimme Some Truth," "Woman Is the Nigger of the World," "John Sinclair," "Attica State," "Luck of the Irish," and "Sunday Bloody Sunday."

As attested by later investigations of the FBI and the CIA, many of these leading activists were among those tracked by intelligence operatives and local police forces. In his later analysis of American political prisoners, J. Soffiyah Elijah, while a clinical instructor at Harvard Law School, discusses the Bureau's continued employment of COINTELPRO in targeting the Berrigan brothers, Dr. King, Malcolm X, Stokely Carmichael, Huey Newton, Fred Hampton, and Native American activist Leonard Peltier, among others.

On March 8, 1971, as Muhammad Ali returned to the ring for the first time in four years, a group of anti-war activists carried out the burglary of an FBI office in Media, Pennsylvania. Proclaiming themselves the Citizens' Commission to Investigate the FBI, the burglars, relying on the massive attention garnered by Ali's fight against the man generally considered the new title holder, Joe Frazier, grabbed over a thousand documents. One such document, the writer Betty Medsger indicates, unveiled the agency's covert COINTELPRO campaign. COINTELPRO operations included an array "of dirty tricks," such as "planting disinformation about anti-war activists . . . planning the murder of a member of the Black Panthers . . . sending innocent people to prison on the basis of false information by agents and informers." The burglars offered various documents to journalists, and a series of articles appeared, including one by Medsger underscoring J. Edgar Hoover's mania about dissenters. Calling for additional interviews of anti-war and student activists, one document suggested that would "enhance the paranoia in these circles," while another spoke of extensive surveillance of African-American college groups.

Later revelations in the Senate demonstrated the systematic nature of FBI abuses, and resulted in increased congressional oversight of intelligence operatives. In its analysis of domestic surveillance, issued in 1975, the Church Committee warned, "Too many people have been spied upon by too many government agencies, and too much information has been collected."

The Church Committee Report and that by the United State House Select Committee on Assassinations, which met between 1976 and 1978, explored the assassinations of President Kennedy and Dr. King. Although inconclusive, the findings suggested that conspiracies led to the murders of those

American leaders, but absolved government agencies from direct involvement.

Those congressional investigations clearly resulted from the anguish caused by events that unfolded in the United States during the 1960s and early 1970s, including assassinations of important political figures, racial conflagrations that beset the nation, the prolonged war in Vietnam that unwound so disastrously, and cultural clashes that divided Americans from one another. 1968 added more to a sense of unease, disillusionment, and distrust of government institutions than any other year during the turbulent decade and a half that followed the start of the 1960s. Later developments also contributed to the troubled sensibilities, topped off by the Watergate revelations of presidential abuse of power involving futile attempts by the Nixon administration to respond to social and political unrest.

The revolutionary possibilities associated with 1968 had, ironically, helped to bring about the Nixon presidency, rather than the New Politics that briefly emerged that year. In addition to returning the presidency to American conservatives, Nixon offered a blueprint for other Republican political figures: veering from apparently well-thought-out rational deliveries to venomous attacks, both personally presented and offered by surrogates. Whereas the American Old Left had previously been the target, along with members of the Eastern Establishment, increasingly liberalism itself was. The same methodology was called on: slurs, innuendoes, questioning of the patriotism of one's political foes, attacks on "the liberal media," and jabs at other institutions ranging from the Democratic-controlled Congress to the US Supreme Court. Nixon's own circumscribed presidency would be replete with attempts to divide the American people, as in his appeal in November 1969 to "the great silent majority" to provide support to their beleaguered president.

The American nation proved the poorer for all this, as the range of political options shrank, rather than expanding in the manner foreseen by those who participated in the New Politics of 1968. In the end and notwithstanding his own inglorious fall from power, Richard M. Nixon became the most immediate beneficiary of the tumult that reached its peak in the United States during 1968. Others followed his lead, culminating with the astonishing turn of events characterizing the 2016 presidential race, won by a clearly ill-informed candidate with a checkered past who drew support from some of the most reactionary elements in American society and, quite possibly, the Russian government of Vladimir Putin. By contrast, only eight years earlier, the country seemed to have surmounted many of the prejudices and fulfilled the promises suggested throughout 1968 that real change of a progressive cast could occur.

Appendix

List of Abbreviations

AAS	Afro-American Society
ABC	American Broadcasting Company
ADA	Americans for Democratic Action
APA	American Psychiatric Association
AP	Associated Press
ARVN	Army of the Republic of Vietnam
BBC	British Broadcasting Corporation
CALCAV	Clergy and Laymen Concerned About Vietnam
CBS	Columbia Broadcasting System
CCD	Conference of Concerned Democrats
CIA	Central Intelligence Agency
COINTELPRO	FBI's Counterintelligence Program
COMECON	Council for Mutual Economic Assistance
CORE	Congress of Racial Equality
COSVN	Central Office for South Vietnam
CPUSA	Communist Party of the United States
DDT	dichlorodiphenyltrichloroethane
DMZ	Demilitarized Zone
DOB	Daughters of Bilitis
ERAP	Economic Research and Action Project
ESSO	East Side Service Organization
FBI	Federal Bureau of Investigation
FDR	Franklin Delano Roosevelt
FSM	Free Speech Movement
FSO	Friends of the Sea Otter
GSVN	South Vietnamese government
HUAC	House Un-American Activities Committee
IDA	Institute for Defense Analyses
IRS	Internal Revenue Service

IOC	International Olympic Committee
IPS	Institute for Policy Studies
JFK	John Fitzgerald Kennedy
KGB	Komitet Gosudarstvennoy Bezopasnosti (Committee for State Security)
KKK	Ku Klux Klan
KSC	Czechoslovakian Communist Party's Central Committee
LBJ	Lyndon Baines Johnson
LSD	lysergic acid diethylamide
LNS	Liberation News Service
Mobe	National Mobilization Committee to End the War in Vietnam
MFS	Mississippi Freedom Summer
MPs	military police
NAACP	National Organization for the Advancement of Colored People
NACHO	North American Conference of Homophile Organizations
NASA	National Aeronautics and Space Administration
NATO	North Atlantic Treaty Organization
NBC	National Broadcasting Company
NCNP	National Conference for New Politics
NLF	National Liberation Front
NOI	Nation of Islam
NOW	National Organization for Women
NSWPP	National Socialist White People's Party
NVA	North Vietnamese Army
NYRW	New York Radical Women
OPHR	Olympic Project for Human Rights
PAVN	People's Army of Vietnam
PCI	Partito Comunista Italiano
PLO	Palestine Liberation Organization
POCAM	Poverty Campaign
PRI	Partido Revolucionario Institucional
RAF	Red Army Faction
RFK	Robert Fitzgerald Kennedy
SANE	National Committee for a Sane Nuclear Policy
SAS	Students' Afro-American Society
SDS	Students for a Democratic Society
SDS—German	Sozialistischer Deutscher Studentenbund
SNCC	Students for a Nonviolent Coordinating Committee
SPDS	Social Democratic Party of Germany

Spring Mobe	Spring Mobilization Committee to End the War in Vietnam
Student Mobe	Student Mobilization Committee to End the War in Vietnam
UC	University of California
UCLA	University of California, Los Angeles
UFW	United Farm Workers
UN	United Nations
UNESCO	United Nations Educational, Scientific, and Cultural Organization
VC	Vietcong
VDC	Vietnam Day Committee
VVAW	Vietnam Veterans Against the War
W.I.T.C.H.	Women's International Terrorist Conspiracy from Hell
WSP	Women Strike for Peace

Bibliography

PREFACE

Albert, Judith Clavir, and Stewart Edward Albert, eds. *The Sixties Papers: Documents of a Rebellious Decade*. New York: Praeger, 1984.

Anderson, Terry H. *The Sixties*. 2nd ed. New York: Pearson/Longman, 2004.

———. *The Movement and the Sixties*. New York: Oxford University Press, 1995.

Berman, Paul. *A Tale of Two Utopias: The Political Journey of the Generation of 1968*. New York: Norton, 1996.

Bloom, Alexander ed. *Long Time Gone: Sixties America Then and Now*. New York: Oxford University Press, 2001.

Browne, Blaine T., and Robert C. Cottrell. *Lives and Times: Individuals and Issues in American History: Since 1865*. Lanham, MD: Rowman & Littlefield Publishers, 2009.

Carey, Elaine. *Protests in the Streets: 1968 Across the Globe*. Indianapolis: Hackett Publishing Company, 2016.

Cottrell, Robert C. *Sex, Drugs, and Rock 'n' Roll: The Rise of America's 1960s Counterculture*. Lanham, MD: Rowman & Littlefield, 2015.

Caute, David. *The Year of the Barricades: A Journey through 1968*. New York: Harper & Row, 1988.

Fraser, Ronald et al. *1968: A Student Generation in Revolt*. London: Chatto & Windus, 1988.

Daniels, Robert V. *Year of the Heroic Guerrilla: World Revolution and Counterrevolution in 1968*. New York: Basic Books, 1968.

Gitlin, Todd. *The Sixties: Years of Hope, Days of Rage*. New York: Bantam Books, 1987.

Kaiser, Charles. *1968 in America: Music, Politics, Chaos, Counterculture, and the Shaping of a Generation*. New York: Grove Press, 1988.

Katsiaficas, George. *The Imagination of the New Left: A Global Analysis of 1968*. Boston: South End Press, 1987.

255

Kurlansky, Mark. *1968: The Year That Rocked the World*. New York: Ballantine Books, 2003.

Marwick, Arthur. *The Sixties: Cultural Revolution in Britain, France, Italy, and the United States, c. 1958–c. 1974*. New York: Oxford University Press, 1998.

Powers, Thomas. *The War at Home: Vietnam and the American People, 1964–1968*. New York: Grossman Publishers, 1973.

Spender, Stephen. *The Year of the Young Rebels*. New York: Vintage Books, 1969.

Wyatt, David. *When America Turned: Reckoning with 1968*. Boston: University of Massachusetts Press, 2014.

CHAPTER 1

Braunstein, Peter, and Michael William Doyle, eds. *Imagine Nation: The American Counterculture of the 1960s and '70s*. New York: Routledge, 2002.

Farber, David R. *Chicago '68*. Chicago: University of Chicago Press, 1988.

Hoffman, Abbie. *The Autobiography of Abbie Hoffman*. New York: Four Walls Eight Windows, 2000.

———. *Revolution for the Hell of It*. New York: Dial Press, 1968.

———. *Soon to Be a Major Motion Picture*. New York: Putnam, 1980.

———. *Square Dancing in the Ice Age*. Boston: South End Press, 1982.

———. *Woodstock Nation: A Talk-Rock Album*. New York: Random House, 1969.

Hoffman, Jack, and Daniel Simon. *Run Run Run: The Lives of Abbie Hoffman*. New York: Jeremy P. Tarcher/Putnam, 1996.

Krassner, Paul. *Confessions of a Raving, Unconfined Nut: Misadventures in the Counter-Culture*. New York: Simon & Schuster, 1993.

———. *How a Satirical Editor Became a Yippie Conspirator in Ten Easy Years*. New York: Putnam, 1971.

Jezer, Marty. *Abbie Hoffman: American Rebel*. New Brunswick, NJ: Rutgers University Press, 1992.

Raskin, Jonah. *For the Hell of It: The Life and Times of Abbie Hoffman*. Berkeley: University of California Press, 1996.

Rosenfeld, Seth. *Subversives: The FBI's War on Student Radicals and Reagan's Rise to Power*. New York: Farrar, Straus and Giroux, 2013.

Rubin, Jerry. *Do it! Scenarios of the Revolution*. New York: Simon & Schuster, 1970.

———. *We Are Everywhere*. New York: Harper & Row, 1971.

Sale, Kirkpatrick. *SDS*. New York: Random House, 1973.

Sloman, Larry. *Steal This Dream: Abbie Hoffman and the Countercultural Revolution in America*. New York: Doubleday, 1998.

Stein, David Lewis. *Living the Revolution: The Yippies in Chicago*. Indianapolis: Bobbs-Merrill, 1969.

Viorst, Milton. *Fire in the Streets: America in the 1960s*. New York: Simon & Schuster, 1979.

Wells, Tom. *The War Within: America's Battle over Vietnam*. Berkeley: University of California Press, 1994.

Zaroulis, Nancy, and Gerald Sullivan. *Who Spoke Up? American Protest against the War in Vietnam, 1963–1975*. Garden City, NY: Doubleday, 1984.

CHAPTER 2

Baskir, Lawrence M., and William A. Strauss. *Chance and Circumstance: The Draft, the War, and the Vietnam Generation*. New York: Random House, 1978.

Coffin, William Sloane Jr. *Once to Every Man: A Memoir*. New York: Atheneum, 1977.

Dancis, Bruce. *Resister: A Story of Protest and Prison during the Vietnam War*. Ithaca, NY: Cornell University Press, 2014.

DeBennedetti, Charles, and Charles Chatfield. *An American Ordeal: The Antiwar Movement of the Vietnam Era*. Syracuse, NY: Syracuse University Press, 1990.

Ferber, Michael, and Staughton Lynd. *The Resistance*. Boston: Beacon Press, 1971.

Flynn, George Q. *The Draft, 1940–1973*. Lawrence: University Press of Kansas, 1993.

Foley, Michael S. *Confronting the War Machine: Draft Resistance during the Vietnam War*. Chapel Hill: The University of North Carolina Press, 2003.

Goldstein, Warren. *William Sloane Coffin Jr.: A Holy Impatience*. New Haven, CT: Yale University Press, 2004.

Gottlieb, Sherry Gershon. *Hell No, We Won't Be Resisting the Draft During the Vietnam War*. New York: Viking, 1991.

Harris, David. *Dreams Die Hard*. New York: St. Martin's, 1982.

Maier, Thomas. *Dr. Spock: An American Life*. New York: Harcourt Brace, 1998.

McNeill, Don. "The Grand Central Riot: Yippies Meet the Man." *The Village Voice*. March 28, 1968.

Mitford, Jessica. *The Trial of Dr. Spock*. New York: Vintage, 1970.

Powers, Thomas. *The War at Home: Vietnam and the American People, 1964–1968*. New York: Grossman Publishers, 1973.

Raskin, Marcus. *Essays of a Citizen: From National Security to Democracy*. New York: Routledge, 1991.

Robbins, Mary Susannah, ed. *Against the Vietnam War: Writings by Activists*. Lanham, MD: Rowman & Littlefield Publishers, 2007.

Useem, Michael. *Conscription, Protest, and Social Conflict: The Life and Death of a Draft Resistance Movement*. New York: John Wiley & Sons, 1973.

Wells, Tom. *The War Within: America's Battle over Vietnam*. Berkeley: University of California Press, 1994.

Zaroulis, Nancy, and Gerald Sullivan. *Who Spoke Up? American Protest against the War in Vietnam, 1963–1975*. Garden City, NY: Doubleday, 1984.

CHAPTER 3

Allison, William Thomas. *My Lai: An American Atrocity in the Vietnam War*. Baltimore: The Johns Hopkins University Press, 2012.

Angers, Trent. *The Forgotten Hero of My Lai: The Hugh Thompson Story*. Lafayette, LA: Acadian House Publishing, 2014.

Bilton, Michael, and Kevin Sim. *Four Hours in My Lai*. New York: Penguin Books, 1993.

Bowden, Mark. *Hue 1968: A Turning Point of the American War in Vietnam*. New York: Atlantic Monthly Press, 2017.

Braestrup, Peter. *Big Story: How the American Press and Television Reported and Interpreted the Crisis of Tet 1968 in Vietnam and Washington*. New Haven, CT: Yale University Press, 1983.

Hammel, Eric. *Fire in the Streets: The Battle for Hue*. New York: Dell, 1992.

———. *Khe Sanh: Siege in the Clouds—An Oral History*. New York: Crown Publishers, 1989.

Herring, George. *America's Longest War*. New York: McGraw-Hill, 2013.

Hersh, Seymour M. *My Lai 4: A Report on the Massacre and Its Aftermath*. New York: Random House, 1970.

Hunt, Michael H. *Lyndon Johnson's War: America's Cold War Crusade in Vietnam, 1945–1968*. New York: Hill and Wang, 1997.

Jones, Howard. *My Lai: Vietnam, 1968, and the Descent into Darkness*. New York: Oxford University Press, 2017.

Karnow, Stanley. *Vietnam: A History*. New York: Viking, 1983.

LaFeber, Walter. *The Deadly Bet: LBJ, Vietnam, and the 1968 Election*. Lanham, MD: Rowman & Littlefield Publishers, 2005.

Mann, Robert. *A Grand Illusion: America's Descent into Vietnam*. New York: Basic Books, 2001.

Maras, Robert, and Charles W. Sasser. *Blood in the Hills: The Story of Khe Sanh, the Most Savage Fight of the Vietnam War*. Guilford, CT: Lyons Press, 2017.

Moise, Edwin. *The Myths of Tet: The Most Misunderstood Event of the Vietnam War*. Lawrence: University Press of Kansas, 2017.

Murphy, Edward F. *The Hill Fights: The First Battle of Khe Sanh*. New York: Presidio Press, 2004.

Nolan, Keith William. *The Battle for Saigon: Tet 1968*. Lanham, MD: Pocket Books, 1996.

Obendorfer, Dan. *Tet: The Turning Point in the Vietnam War*. Baltimore: The Johns Hopkins: University Press, 2001.

Olson, James S., and Randy Roberts. *My Lai: A Brief History with Documents*. Lanham MD: Bedford/St. Martin's, 1998.

Schmitz, David F. *The Tet Offensive: Politics, War and Public Opinion*. New York: Rowman & Littlefield Publishers, 2005.

Sheehan, Neil. *A Bright Shining Lie*. New York: Vintage, 1989.

Smith, George W. *The Siege at Hue*. Boulder, CO: Lynne Rienner, 1999.

Sorley, Lewis. *William Westmoreland: The General Who Lost Vietnam*. Mariner Books, 2012.

Spector, Ronald H. *After Tet: The Bloodiest Year in Vietnam*. New York: Free Press, 1992.

Stubbe, Ray. *Valley of Decision: The Siege of Khe Sanh*. New York: Houghton Mifflin, 1991.

Wilbanks, Jason H. *The Tet Offensive: A Concise History*. New York: Columbia University Press, 2008.

Wirtz, James J. *The Tet Offensive: Intelligence Failure in War*. Ithaca, NY: Cornell University Press, 1994.

Woods, Randall B. *LBJ: Architect of American Ambition*. New York: Free Press, 2006.

CHAPTER 4

Bohrer, John R. *The Revolution of Robert Kennedy: From Power to Protest.* New York: Bloomsbury Press, 2017.

Browne, Blaine T., and Robert C. Cottrell. *Lives and Times: Individuals and Issues in American History: Since 1865.* Lanham, MD: Rowman & Littlefield Publishers, 2009.

———. *Modern American Lives: Individuals and Issues in American History Since 1945.* New York: M. E. Sharpe, 2008.

Burner, David. *Making Peace with the '60s.* Princeton, NJ: Princeton University Press, 1996.

——— and Thomas R. West. *The Torch Is Passed: The Kennedy Brothers and American Liberalism.* New York: Atheneum, 1989.

Califano, Joseph A., Jr. *The Triumph and Tragedy of Lyndon Johnson: The White House Years.* New York: Simon & Schuster, 1991.

Chafe, William H. *Never Stop Running: Allard Lowenstein and the Struggle to Save American Liberalism.* New York: Basic Books, 1993.

Chester, Lewis, Godfrey Hodgson, and Bruce Page. *An American Melodrama: The Presidential Campaign of 1968.* New York: Viking, 1969.

Clarke, Thurston. *The Last Campaign: Robert F. Kennedy and 82 Days That Inspired America.* New York: Henry Holt, 2008.

Cohen, Michael. *American Maelstrom: The 1968 Election and the Politics of Division.* New York: Oxford University Press, 2016.

Cottrell, Robert C. *Izzy: A Biography.* New Brunswick, NJ: Rutgers University Press, 1992.

Cummings, Richard. *The Pied Piper: Allard K. Lowenstein and the Liberal Dream.* New York: Grove Press, 1985.

Dallek, Robert. *Flawed Giant: Lyndon Johnson and his Times, 1961–1973.* New York: Oxford University Press, 1998.

Eppridge, Bill. *A Time It Was: Bobby Kennedy in the Sixties.* New York: Harry M. Abrams, 2008.

Gardner, Lloyd C. *Pay Any Price: Lyndon Johnson and the Wars for Vietnam.* Chicago: Ivan R. Dee, 1995.

Gillon, Steven. *Politics and Vision: The ADA and American Liberalism, 1947–1985.* New York: Oxford University Press, 1987.

Guthman, Edwin O., and Jeffrey Shulman, eds. *Robert Kennedy in His Own Words: The Unpublished Recollections of the Kennedy Years.* New York: Bantam, 1988.

Halberstam, David. *The Unfinished Odyssey of Robert Kennedy.* New York: Random House, 1969.

Harris, Fred, and Tom Wicker, eds. *The Kerner Report: The 1968 Report of the National Advisory Commission on Civil Disorders.* New York: Pantheon, 1988.

Heath, Jim F. *Decade of Disillusionment: The Kennedy-Johnson Years.* Bloomington: Indiana University Press, 1975.

Isaacson, Walter, and Evan Thomas. *The Wise Men: Six Friends and the World They Made.* New York: Simon & Schuster, 1986.

Johnson, Lyndon Baines. *The Vantage Point: Perspectives of the Presidency, 1963–1969.* New York: Holt, Rinehart and Winston, 1971.

Kaiser, Charles. *1968 in America: Music, Politics, Chaos, Counterculture, and the Shaping of a Generation.* New York: Grove Press, 1988.

Kennedy, Robert F. *To Seek a Newer World.* Garden City, NY: Doubleday, 1967.

Kimball, Peter. *Bobby Kennedy and the New Politics.* Englewood Cliffs, NJ: Prentice-Hall, 1968.

Larner, Jeremy. *Nobody Knows: Reflections on the McCarthy Campaign of 1968.* New York: Macmillan, 1970.

Matusow, Allen J. *The Unraveling of America: A History of Liberalism in the 1960s.* New York: Harper & Row, 1984.

Newfield, Jack. *Robert Kennedy: A Memoir.* New York: Dutton, 1969.

Palermo, Joseph A. *In His Own Right: The Political Odyssey of Senator Robert F. Kennedy.* New York: Columbia University Press, 2001.

Reedy, George. *Lyndon B. Johnson, a Memoir.* New York: Andrews and Michael, 1982.

Sandbrook, Dominic. *Eugene McCarthy and the Rise and Fall of Postwar American Liberalism.* New York: Anchor Books, 2005.

Schlesinger, Arthur M., Jr. *Robert Kennedy and His Times.* New York: Ballantine Books, 1978.

Schulman, Bruce J. *Lyndon B. Johnson and American Liberalism: A Brief Biography with Documents.* Boston: Bedford Books, 1995.

Shapley, Deborah. *Promise and Power: The Life and Times of Robert McNamara.* Boston: Little, Brown, 1993.

Talbot, David. *Brothers: The Hidden History of the Kennedy Years.* New York: Free Press, 2007.

Thomas, Evan. *Robert Kennedy: His Life.* New York: Simon & Schuster, 2000.

Tye, Larry. *Bobby Kennedy: The Making of a Liberal Icon.* New York: Random House, 2016.

United States Kerner Commission. *Report of the National Advisory Commission on Civil Disorders.* New York: Bantam Books, 1968.

White, Theodore H. *The Making of the President, 1968.* New York: Atheneum Publishers, 1969.

Witcover, Jules. *85 Days: The Last Campaign of Robert Kennedy.* New York: William Morrow, 2016.

Wofford, Harris. *Of Kennedys and Kings: Making Sense of the Sixties.* New York: Farrar, Straus and Giroux, 1980.

Woods, Randall B. *Prisoners of Hope: Lyndon B. Johnson, the Great Society, and the Limits of Liberalism.* New York: Basic Books, 2016.

CHAPTER 5

Branch, Taylor. *At Canaan's Edge: America in the King Years, 1965–68.* New York: Simon & Schuster, 2007.

———. *Parting the Waters: America in the King Years, 1954–63.* New York: Simon & Schuster, 1988.

———. *Pillar of Fire: America in the King Years, 1963–65.* New York: Simon & Schuster, 1998.

Burns, Stewart. *To the Mountaintop: Martin Luther King Jr.'s Sacred Mission to Save America, 1955–1968.* San Francisco: HarperCollins, 2004.

Carson, Clayborne, ed. *The Papers of Martin Luther King, Jr., and the Modern Black Freedom Struggle*. Stanford, CA: Stanford University Libraries, 1989.

Colaiaco, James A. *Martin Luther King, Jr.: Apostle of Militant Nonviolence*. New York: St. Martin's, 1993.

DeBenedetti, Charles, ed. *Peace Heroes in Twentieth-Century America*. Bloomington: Indiana University Press, 1988.

Fairclough, Adam. *To Redeem the Soul of America: The Southern Christian Leadership Conference and Martin Luther King, Jr.* Athens: University of Georgia Press, 1987.

Garrow, David J. *Bearing the Cross: Martin Luther King, Jr., and the Southern Christian Leadership Conference*. New York: William Morrow, 1986.

———. *The FBI and Martin Luther King, Jr.* New York: Penguin Books, 1981.

———. *Protest at Selma: Martin Luther King, Jr., and the Voting Rights Act of 1965*. New Haven, CT: Yale University Press, 1978.

Jackson, Thomas. *From Civil Rights to Human Rights: Martin Luther King, Jr. and the Struggle for Economic Justice*. Philadelphia: University of Pennsylvania Press, 2009.

King, Coretta Scott. *My Life with Martin Luther King Jr.* New York: Holt, Rinehart and Winston, 1969.

King, Martin Luther, Jr. *The Autobiography of Martin Luther King Jr.*, ed. Clayborne Carson. New York: IPM, 1998.

———. *Stride toward Freedom: The Montgomery Story*. New York: Harper & Row, 1968.

———. *Where Do We Go from Here: Chaos or Community?* New York: Harper & Row, 1967.

Levingston, Steven. *Kennedy and King: The President, the Pastor, and the Battle over Civil Rights*. New York: Hachette Books, 2017.

Lewis, David L. *King: A Biography*. Urbana: Illinois University Press, 1978.

Lischer, Richard. *The Preacher King: Martin Luther King Jr. and the Word That Moved America*. New York: Oxford University Press, 1995.

Oates, Stephen B. *Let the Trumpet Sound: The Life of Martin Luther King, Jr.* New York: HarperPerennial, 1992.

Peacke, Thomas R. *Keeping the Dream Alive: A History of the Southern Christian Leadership Conference from King to the 1980s*. New York: P. Lang, 1967.

Powledge, Fred. *Free at Last? The Civil Rights Movement and the People Who Made It*. Boston: Little Brown, 1991.

Ralph, James. *Northern Protest, Martin Luther King, Jr., Chicago and the Civil Rights Movement*. Cambridge, MA: Harvard University Press, 1993.

Sides, Hampton. *Hell Hound on His Trail: The Electrifying Account of the Largest Manhunt in American History*. New York: Anchor, 2011.

Washington, James Melvin, ed. *A Testament of Hope: The Essential Writings of Martin Luther King, Jr.* San Francisco: Harper & Row, 1986.

West, Thomas R., and James W. Mooney, eds. *To Redeem a Nation: A History and Anthology of the Civil Rights Movement*. St. James, NY: Brandywine Press, 1993.

Wexler, Stuart, and Larry Hancock. *The Awful Grace of God: Religious Terrorism, White Supremacy, and the Unsolved Murder of Martin Luther King Jr.* Berkeley, CA: Counterpoint Press, 2012.

Williams, Juan. *Eyes on the Prize*. New York: Viking Penguin, 1987.

Wofford, Harris. *Of Kennedys and Kings: Making Sense of the Sixties*. New York: Farrar, Straus and Giroux, 1980.

CHAPTER 6

Anderson, Terry H. *The Sixties*. 2nd ed. New York: Pearson/Longman, 2004.

———. *The Movement and the Sixties*. New York: Oxford University Press, 1995.

Avorn, Jerry L. *Up Against the Ivy Wall: A History of the Columbia Crisis*. New York: Atheneum Press, 1968.

Barlow, William, and Peter Shapiro. *The Year of the Monkey: Revolt on Campus, 1968–1969*. New York: McGraw-Hill, 1982.

Bell, Daniel, and Irving Kristol, eds. *Confrontation: The Student Rebellion and the Universities*. New York: Basic Books, 1968.

Berman, Paul. *A Tale of Two Utopias: The Political Journey of the Generation of 1968*. New York: Norton, 1996.

Bloom, Alexander, and Wini Breines, eds. *Long Time Gone: Sixties America Then and Now*. Oxford; New York : Oxford University Press, 2001.

Carey, Elaine. *Protests in the Streets: 1968 Across the Globe*. Indianapolis, IN: Hackett Publishing Company, 2016.

Caute, David. *The Year of the Barricades: A Journey through 1968*. New York: Harper & Row, 1988.

Cohn-Bendit, Daniel, Jean-Pierre Duteuil, Alan Geismar, and Jacques Sauvageot. *The French Student Revolt: The Leaders Speak*. New York: Hill & Wang, 1968.

Daniels, Robert V. *Year of the Heroic Guerrilla: World Revolution and Counterrevolution in 1968*. New York: Basic Books, 1968.

Elbaum, Max. *Revolution in the Air: Sixties Radicals Turn to Lenin, Mao, and Che*. London: Verso, 2002.

Fink, Carole, Philip Gassert, and Detlef Junker, eds. *1968: The World Transformed*. Washington, DC: Cambridge University Press, 1999.

Fraser, Ronald et al. *1968: A Student Generation in Revolt*. London: Chatto & Windus, 1988.

Gilbert, David. *Love and Struggle: My Life in SDS, the Weather Underground, and Beyond*. Oakland, CA: PM Press, 2012.

Gildea, Robert. "A Recipe for Revolution: Could 1968 Happen Today?" *Open Democracy*. July 12, 2013. https://www.opendemocracy.net/ourkingdom/robert-gildea/recipe-for-revolution-could-1968-happen-today.

Gitlin, Todd. *The Sixties: Years of Hope, Days of Rage*. New York: Bantam Books, 1987.

Glaberman, Martin. "Regis Debray: Revolution Without a Revolution." *Speak Out* (April 1968).

Grant, Joanne, ed. *Confrontation on Campus: The Columbia Pattern for the New Protest*. New York: New American Library, 1969.

Hayden, Tom. *The Long Sixties: From 1960 to Barack Obama*. Boulder, CO: Paradigm, 2009.

Hitchens, Christopher, Kay S. Hymowitz, Stefan Kanfer, Guy Sorman, Harry Stein, Sol Stern. "May 1968: 40 Years Later." *City Journal* (Spring 2008).

Horn, Gerd-Rainer. *The Spirit of '68: Rebellion in Western Europe and North America, 1956–1976*. New York: Oxford University Press, 2007.

Isserman, Maurice, and Michael Kazin. *America Divided: The Civil War of the 1960s*. New York: Oxford University Press, 2000.

Kahn, Roger. *The Battle for Morningside Heights*. New York: Morrow, 1970.

Kaiser, Charles. *1968 in America: Music, Politics, Chaos, Counterculture, and the Shaping of a Generation.* New York: Grove Press, 1988.

Katsiaficas, George. *The Imagination of the New Left: A Global Analysis of 1968.* Boston: South End Press, 1987.

Klimke, Martin. *The Other Alliance: Student Protest in West Germany and the United States in the Global Sixties.* Princeton, NJ: Princeton University Press, 2010.

———, Jacco Pekelder, and Joachim Scharloth, eds. *Between Prague Spring and French May: Opposition and Revolt in Europe, 1960–1980.* New York: Berghahn Books, 2011.

Koning, Hans. *Nineteen Sixty-Eight: A Personal Report.* New York: Norton, 1987.

Kunen, James S. *The Strawberry Statement: Notes of a College Revolutionary.* New York: Random House, 1969.

Kurlansky, Mark. *1968: The Year That Rocked the World.* New York: Ballantine Books, 2003.

Levitt, Cyril. *Children of Privilege: Student Revolt in the Sixties: A Study of Student Movements in Canada, the United States, and West Germany.* Toronto: University of Toronto Press, 1984.

Marwick, Arthur. *The Sixties: Cultural Revolution in Britain, France, Italy, and the United States, c. 1958–c. 1974.* New York: Oxford University Press, 1998.

Raimo, John. "Prague '68 and the End of Time." JHIBLOG. https://jhiblog.org/2015/05/18/prague-68-and-the-end-of-time/.

Rudd, Mark. "Che and Me." http://www.markrudd.com/?violence-and-non-violence/che-and-me.htm l.

Rupnik, Jacques. "1968: The Year of Two Springs." *Transit* (May 16, 2008).

Sale, Kirkpatrick. *SDS.* New York: Random House, 1973.

Spender, Stephen. *The Year of the Young Rebels.* New York: Vintage Books, 1969.

Suri, Jeremi. *Power and Protest: Global Revolution and the Rise of Détente.* Cambridge, MA: Harvard University Press, 2003.

Teodori, Massimo, comp. *The New Left: A Documentary History.* Indianapolis, IN: Bobbs-Merrill, 1969.

Wallerstein, Immanuel M. *University in Turmoil: The Politics of Change.* New York: Atheneum, 1969.

Wallerstein, Immanuel M., and Paul Starr. *The Liberal University under Attack.* New York: Random House, 1971.

———. *The University Crisis Reader.* New York: Random House, 1971.

CHAPTER 7

Baez, Joan. *And a Voice to Sing With: A Memoir.* New York: New American Library, 1987.

Carroll, James. "Daniel Berrigan, My Dangerous Friend." *The New Yorker.* May 2, 2016.

Trials of the Resistance. Chomsky, Noam. New York: New York Review Books, 1970.

Chomsky, Noam, Paul Lauter, and Florence Howe. "Reflections on a Political Trial," *The New York Review of Books,* August 22, 1968.

Dancis, Bruce. *Resister: A Story of Protest and Prison during the Vietnam War.* Ithaca, NY: Cornell University Press, 2014.

DeBennedetti, Charles, and Charles Chatfield. *An American Ordeal: The Antiwar Movement of the Vietnam Era.* Syracuse, NY: Syracuse University Press, 1990.

du Plessix Gray, Francine. "The Ultra-Resistance." *The New York Review of Books*, September 25, 1969.

Farber, David R. *Chicago '68.* Chicago: University of Chicago Press, 1988.

Ferber, Michael, and Staughton Lynd. *The Resistance.* Boston: Beacon Press, 1971.

Foley, Michael S. *Confronting the War Machine: Draft Resistance during the Vietnam War.* Chapel Hill: The University of North Carolina Press, 2003.

Goodman, Mitchell, ed. *The Movement Toward a New America: The Beginnings of a Long Revolution.* New York: Alfred A. Knopf, 1970.

Gottlieb, Sherry Gershon. *Hell No, We Won't Go: Resisting the Draft during the Vietnam War.* New York: Viking, 1991.

Hall, Mitchell K. *Because of Their Faith: CALCAV and Religious Opposition to the Vietnam War.* New York: Columbia University Press, 1991.

Hauser, Thomas. *Muhammad Ali: His Life and Times.* New York: Touchstone, 1992.

Krassner, Paul. *Confessions of a Raving, Unconfined Nut: Misadventures in the Counter-Culture.* New York: Simon & Schuster, 1993.

———. *How a Satirical Editor Became a Yippie Conspirator in Ten Easy Years.* New York: Putnam, 1971.

Maier, Thomas. *Dr. Spock: An American Life.* New York: Harcourt Brace, 1998.

Meconis, Charles A. *With Clumsy Grace: The American Catholic Left 1961–1975.* New York: The Seabury Press, 1979.

Mitford, Jessica. *The Trial of Dr. Spock.* New York: Vintage, 1970.

Nelson, Jack, and Ronald J. Ostrow. *The FBI and the Berrigans.* New York: Coward, McCann, 1972.

Peters, Shawn Francis. *The Catonsville Nine: A Story of Faith and Resistance in the Vietnam Era.* New York: Oxford University Press, 2012.

Polner, Murray, and Jim O'Grady. *Disarmed and Dangerous: The Radical Lives and Times of Daniel and Philip Berrigan.* New York: Basic Books, 1997.

Tollefson, James W. *The Strength Not to Fight: An Oral History of Conscientious Objectors of the Vietnam War.* Boston: Little, Brown, 1993.

Tracy, James. *Direct Action: Radical Pacifism from the Union Eight to the Chicago Seven.* Chicago: University of Chicago Press, 1996.

Torgoff, Martin. *Can't Find My Way Home: America in the Great Stoned Age, 1945–2000.* New York: Simon & Schuster, 2004.

Tracy, James. *Direct Action: Radical Pacifism from the Union Eight to the Chicago Seven.* Chicago: University of Chicago Press, 1996.

Williams, Roger Neville. *The New Exiles: American War Resisters in Canada.* New York: Liveright Publishers, 1971.

CHAPTER 8

Braunstein, Peter, and Michael William Doyle, eds. *Imagine Nation: The American Counterculture of the 1960s and '70s.* New York: Routledge, 2002.

Cottrell, Robert C. *Sex, Drugs, and Rock 'n' Roll: The Rise of America's 1960s Counter-culture*. Lanham, MD: Rowman & Littlefield Publishers, 2015.

Coyote, Peter. *Sleeping Where I Fall: A Chronicle*. Washington, DC: Counterpoint, 1998.

Fairfield, Richard. *Communes U.S.A.: A Personal Tour*. Baltimore: Penguin, 1972.

Finder, Henry, ed. *The 60s: The Story of a Decade*. New York: Random House, 2016.

Gleason, Ralph J. *The Jefferson Airplane and the San Francisco Sound*. Arcana, 1969.

Glessing, Robert J. *The Underground Press in America*. Bloomington: Indiana University Press, 1970.

Goldberg, Danny. *In Search of the Lost Chord: 1967 and the Hippie Idea*. Brooklyn, NY: Akashic Books, 2017.

McMillan, John. *Smoking Typewriters: The Sixties Underground Press and the Rise of Alternative Media in America*. New York: Oxford University Press, 2011.

McNeill, Don. *Moving through Here*. New York: Knopf, 1970.

McWilliams, John C. *The 1960s Cultural Revolution*. Westport, CT: Greenwood Press, 2000.

Miller, Timothy S. *The Hippies and American Values*. Knoxville: University of Tennessee Press, 2011.

Moretta, John. *The Hippies: A 1960s History*. Jefferson, NC: McFarland & Company, 2017.

Mungo, Raymond. *Famous Long Ago: My Life and Hard Times with Liberation News Service*. Boston: Beacon Press, 1970.

New Yorker, The. The 60s: The Story of a Decade. New York: Random House, 2016.

Norman, Philip. *John Lennon: The Life*. New York: Ecco, 2008.

O'Neill, William L. *Coming Apart: An Informal History of America in the 1960's*. Chicago: Quadrangle Books, 1971.

Peck, Abe. *Uncovering the Sixties: The Life and Times of the Underground Press*. New York: Pantheon Books, 1985.

Raskin, Jonah. *For the Hell of It: The Life and Times of Abbie Hoffman*. Berkeley: University of California Press, 1996.

Rorabaugh, W. J. *American Hippies*. Cambridge: Cambridge University Press, 2015.

Roszak, Theodore. *The Making of a Counter Culture: Reflections on the Technocratic Society and Its Youthful Opposition*. New York: Doubleday, 1969.

Sinclair, John. *Guitar Army: Rock and Revolution with The MC5 and the White Panther Party*. Port Townsend, WA: Process, 2007.

Stein, David. *Living the Revolution: The Yippies in Chicago*. New York: Bobbs-Merrill, 1969.

Streitmatter, Roger. *Voices of Revolution: The Dissident Press in America*. New York: Columbia University Press, 2001.

Vesey, Laurence. *Communal Experience: Anarchist and Mystical Counter-Culture in America*. New York: Harper & Row, 1973.

Wiener, Jon. *Come Together: John Lennon in His Time*. New York: Random House, 1984.

Wolfe, Burton H. *The Hippies*. New York: Berkley, 1968.

Yablonsky, Lewis. *The Hippie Trip: A Firsthand Account of the Beliefs, Drug Use and Sexual Patterns of Young Drop-Outs in America*. New York: Pegasus, 1968.

CHAPTER 9

Branch, Taylor. *At Caanan's Edge: America in the King Years, 1965–68.* New York: Simon & Schuster, 2006.

Browne, Blaine T., and Robert C. Cottrell, *Modern American Lives.* Armonk, NY: M. E. Sharpe, 2008.

Chester, Lewis, and Godfrey Hodgson, *An American Melodrama: The Presidential Campaign of 1968.* New York: Viking, 1969.

Cohen, Michael. *American Maelstrom: The 1968 Election and the Politics of Division.* New York: Oxford University Press, 2016.

Dyson, Michael. *April 4, 1968: Martin Luther King's Death and How It Changed America.* New York: Basic Civitas, 2008.

Garrow, David. *Bearing the Cross: Martin Luther King, Jr. and the Southern Christian Leadership Conference.* New York: HarperCollins, 1986.

Goduti, Philip A. Jr. *RFK and MLK: Visions of Hope, 1963–1968.* Jefferson, NC: McFarland & Company, 2017.

Heyman, C. David. *RFK: A Candid Biography of Robert Kennedy.* New York: Dutton 1998.

Kurlansky, Mark. *1968: The Year That Rocked the World.* New York: Ballantine, 2003.

Newfield, Jack. *Robert Kennedy: A Memoir.* New York: Penguin, 1988.

Palermo, Joseph A. *In His Own Right: The Political Odyssey of Senator Robert F. Kennedy.* New York: Columbia University Press, 2001.

Perlstein, Rick. *Nixonland: The Rise of a President and the Fracturing of America.* New York: Scribner, 2008.

Smiley, Tavis. *Death of a King: The Real Story of Dr. Martin Luther King's Final Year.* New York: Little Brown, 2014.

Steel, Ronald. *In Love with the Night: The American Romance with Robert Kennedy.* New York: Simon & Schuster, 2000.

Thomas, Evan. *Robert Kennedy: His Life.* New York: Simon & Schuster, 2000.

CHAPTER 10

Appelbaum, Anne. *Iron Curtain: the Crushing of Eastern Europe, 1944–1956.* New York: Doubleday, 2012.

Bischof, Gunter, Stefan Kramer, and Peter Ruggenthaler, eds. *The Prague Spring and the Warsaw Pact Invasion of Czechoslovakia in 1968.* Lanham, MD: Lexington Books, 2010.

Chapman, Colin. *August 21st: The Rape of Czechoslovakia.* Philadelphia and New York: J. B. Lippincott, 1968.

Chester, Lewis, Godfrey Hodgson. *An American Melodrama: The Presidential Campaign of 1968.* New York: Viking, 1969.

Cohen, Michael A. *American Maelstrom: The 1968 Election and the Politics of Division.* New York: Oxford University Press, 2016.

Farber, David. *Chicago '68.* Chicago: University of Chicago Press, 1994.

Gitlin, Todd. *The Sixties: Years of Hope, Days of Rage.* New York: Bantam Books, 1987.

Klimke, Martin, and Jacoco Pekelder. *Between Prague Spring and French May: Opposition and Revolt in Europe, 1960–1980.* New York: Berghahn Books, 2011.

Kovály, Heda Margolius. *Under a Cruel Star: A Life in Prague 1941–1968.* New York: Holmes & Meier, 1986.

Kurlansky, Mark. *1968: The Year That Rocked the World.* New York: Ballantine Books, 2004.

Kusch, Frank. *Battleground Chicago: The Police and the 1968 Democratic National Convention.* Chicago: University of Chicago Press, 2008.

Kusin, Vladimir V. *The Intellectual Origins of the Prague Spring: The Development of Reformist Ideas in Czechoslovakia 1955–1967.* Cambridge: Cambridge University Press, 2002.

Mailer, Norman. *Miami and the Siege of Chicago.* New York: Random House, 1968.

Perlstein, Rick. *Nixonland: The Rise of a President and the Fracturing of America.* New York: Scribner, 2008.

Schneir, William, ed. *Telling It Like It Was: The Chicago Riots.* New York: Signet, 1969.

Schultz, John. *No One Was Killed: the Democratic National Convention, August 1968.* Chicago: University of Chicago Press, 1969.

Schwartz, Harry. *Prague's 200 Days: the Struggle for Democracy in Czechoslovakia.* New York: Frederick A. Praeger, 1969.

Stien, David Lewis. *Living the Revolution: Yippie in Chicago.* Indianapolis, IN: Bobbs-Merrill, 1969.

Stolarik, M. Mark. *The Prague Spring and the Warsaw Pact Invasion of 1968: Forty Years Later.* Mundelein, IL: Bolchazy-Carducci Publishers, 2010.

Vondorova, Jitka. *The Prague Spring 1968: A National Security Archive Documents Reader.* Budapest: Central European University Press, 1998.

Walker, Daniel. *Rights in Conflict.* New York: E. P. Dutton, 1968.

Williams, Kieran. *The Prague Spring and Its Aftermath: Czechoslovak Politics, 1968–1970.* Cambridge: Cambridge University Press, 1997.

Zeman, Z. A. B. *Prague Spring: An Eyewitness Report on Czechoslovakia before the August Invasion.* New York: Hill & Wang, 1969.

CHAPTER 11

Anthony, Earl. *Picking Up the Gun: A Report on the Black Panthers.* New York: Dial Press, 1970.

Barlow, William, and Peter Shapiro. *The Year of the Monkey: Revolt on Campus, 1968–1969.* New York: McGraw-Hill, 1982.

Biondi, Martha. *The Black Revolution on Campus.* Berkeley: University of California Press, 2014.

Blackstock, Nelson. *Cointelpro: The FBI's Secret War on Political Freedom.* New York: Pathfinder, 1988.

Bloom, Joshua, and Waldo E. Martin Jr. *Black against Empire: The History and Politics of the Black Panther Party.* Berkeley: University of California Press, 2014.

Boyle, Kay. *The Long Walk at San Francisco State, and Other Essays.* New York: Grove Press, 1970.

Brown, Elaine. *A Taste of Power: A Black Woman's Story.* New York: Pantheon, 1992.

Carey, Elaine. *Plaza of Sacrifices: Gender, Power, and Terror in 1968 Mexico.* Albuquerque: University of New Mexico Press, 2005.

Caute, David. *The Year of the Barricades: A Journey through 1968.* New York: Harper & Row, 1988.

Churchill, Ward, and Jim Vander Wall. *The COINTELPRO Papers: Documents from the FBI's Secret Wars against Domestic Dissent.* Boston: South End Press, 1990.

Cleaver, Eldridge. *Soul on Ice.* New York: McGraw-Hill, 1967.

Cosgrove, Ben. "The Black Power Salute that Rocked the 1968 Olympics." *Time.* September 27, 2014.

Daniels, Robert V. *Year of the Heroic Guerrilla: World Revolution and Counterrevolution in 1968.* New York: Basic Books, 1968.

Davis, James Kirkpatrick. *Assault on the Left: The FBI and the Sixties Antiwar Movement.* Westport, CT: Praeger, 1997.

Dean, Sam. "John Carlos: My Black Power Salute at Mexico City Is as Pertinent Now as It Was in 1968." *The Telegraph.* August 16, 2016.

Fink, Carole, Philip Gassert, and Detlef Junker, eds. *1968: The World Transformed.* Washington, DC: Cambridge University Press, 1999.

Foster, Julian, and Durward Long, eds. *Protest! Student Activism in America.* New York: William Morrow, 1970.

Fraser, Ronald et al. *1968: A Student Generation in Revolt.* London: Chatto & Windus, 1988.

Goldblatt, David. *The Games: A Global History of the Olympics.* New York: W. W. Norton & Company, 2016.

Grant, Joanne, comp. *Black Protest: History, Documents, and Analyses, 1619 to the Present.* New York: Fawcett World Library, 1969.

Harris, Glen Anthony. *The Ocean Hill-Brownsville Conflict: Intellectual Struggles Between Blacks and Jews at Mid-Century.* Lanham, MD: Lexington Books, 2012.

Hilliard, David, and Lewis Cole. *This Side of Glory: The Autobiography of David Hilliard and the Story of the Black Panther Party.* Boston: Little, Brown, 1993.

Johnson, Nicholas. *Negroes and the Gun: The Black Tradition of Arms.* Amherst, NY: Prometheus Books, 2014.

Joseph, Peniel E. *Waiting 'til the Midnight Hour: A Narrative History of Black Power in America.* New York: Holt, 2007.

Katsiaficas, George. *The Imagination of the New Left: A Global Analysis of 1968.* Boston: South End Press, 1987.

Kurlansky, Mark. *1968: The Year That Rocked the World.* New York, 2003.

Leonard, David. "What Happened to the Revolt of the Black Athlete?" *Colorlines.* June 10, 1998. http://www.colorlines.com/articles/what-happened-revolt-black-athlete.

Lester, Julius. *Look Out, Whitey! Black Power's Gon' Get Your Mama.* New York: Dial Press, 1968.

Marine, Gene. *The Black Panthers.* New York: New American Library, 1969.

O'Reilly, Kenneth. *"Racial Matters": The FBI's Secret File on Black America, 1960–1972.* New York: Free Press, 1989.

Orrick, William H., Jr. *Shut It Down! A College in Crisis: San Francisco State College, October 1968–April, 1969; a Report to the National Commission on the Causes and Prevention of Violence.* Washington, DC: US Government Printing Office, 1969.

Pearlman, Lise. *American Justice on Trial: People v. Newton.* Berkeley, CA: Regent Press, 2016.

Pearson, Hugh. *The Shadow of the Panther: Huey Newton and the Price of Black Power in America.* Reading, MA: Addison-Wesley Publishing Company, 1994.

Richardson, Peter. *A Bomb in Every Issue: How the Short, Unruly Life of Ramparts Magazine Changed America.* New York: The New Press, 2009.

Seale, Bobby. *A Lonely Rage: The Autobiography of Bobby Seale.* New York: Times Books, 1978.

———. *Seize the Time: The Story of the Black Panther Party and Huey P. Newton.* New York: Random House, 1970.

Smith, John Matthew. "'It's Not Really My Country': Lew Alcindor and the Revolt of the Black Athlete." *Journal of Sport History* (Summer 2009).

Spies-Gans, Juliet. "47 Years Ago, Olympian John Carlos Raised His Fist for Equality." *Huffington Post.* October 16, 2015. https://www.huffingtonpost.com/entry/john-carlos-47-years-olympic s-salute_us_562157efe4b02f6a900c4fa2.

Van Deburg, William L. *New Day in Babylon: The Black Power Movement and American Culture, 1965–1975.* Chicago: University of Chicago Press, 1992.

Wendt, Simon. *The Spirit & the Shotgun: Armed Resistance and the Struggle for Civil Rights.* Gainesville: University Press of Florida, 2007.

Zirin, Dave. "1968: The Year of the Fist." *Edge of Sports.* September 18–21, 2003. http://www.edgeofsports.com/2003–09–18–21/.

CHAPTER 12

Adler, Margot. *Drawing Down the Moon: Witches, Druids, Goddess-Worshippers and other Pagans in America.* London: Penguin, 2006.

Baxandall, Rosalyn, and Linda Gordon, eds. *Dear Sisters: Dispatches from the Women's Liberation Movement.* New York: Basic Books, 2000.

Campbell, W. Joseph. *Getting It Wrong: Ten of the Greatest Misreported Stories in American Journalism.* Berkeley: University of California Press, 2016.

Carden, Maren Lockwood. *The New Feminist Movement.* New York: Russell Sage Foundation, 1974.

Cleninden, Dudley, and Adam Nagourney. *Out for Good: The Struggle to Build a Gay Rights Movement in America.* New York: Simon & Schuster, 1999.

Collins, Gail. *When Everything Changed: The Amazing Journey of American Women from 1960 to the Present.* New York: Little, Brown, 2009.

Davis, Flora. *Moving the Mountain: The Women's Movement in America since 1960.* Chicago: University of Chicago Press, 1999.

Duplessis, Rachel Blau, and Ann Snitow. *The Feminist Memoir Project: Voices from Women's Liberation.* New York: Three Rivers Press, 1998.

Eaklor, Vicki L. *Queer America: A People's GLBT History of the 20th Century.* New York: The New Press, 2008.

Echols, Alice. *Daring to Be Bad: Radical Feminism in America.* Minneapolis: University of Minnesota Press, 1989.

Eller, Cynthia. *Living in the Lap of the Goddess: The Feminist Spirituality Movement in America*. Boston: Beacon Press, 1993.

Evans, Sara. *Personal Politics: The Roots of Women's Liberation in the Movement and the New Left*. New York: Random House, 1979.

————. *Tidal Wave: How Women Changed America at Century's End*. New York: Free Press, 2003.

Faderman, Lillian. *The Gay Revolution: The Story of the Struggle*. New York: Simon & Schuster, 2015.

Fahs, Breanne. *Valerie Solanas: The Defiant Life of the Woman Who Wrote SCUM (and Shot Andy Warhol)*. New York: Feminist Press at CUNY, 2004.

Freeman, Jo. *The Politics of Women's Liberation: A Case Study of an Emerging Social Movement and Its Relation to the Policy Process*. New York: McKay, 1975.

Gallo, Marcia M. *Different Daughters: A History of the Daughters of Bilitis and the Rise of the Lesbian Rights Movement*. New York: Carroll & Graf Publishers, 2006.

Giardina, Carol. *Freedom for Women: Forging the Women's Liberation Movement, 1953–1970*. Gainesville: University Press of Florida, 2010.

Harrison, Cynthia. *On Account of Sex: The Politics of Women's Issues, 1945–1968*. Berkeley: University of California Press, 1988.

Harron, Mary, dir. *I Shot Andy Warhol*. MGM, DVD 2001.

Harron, Mary, and Daniel Minahan. *I Shot Andy Warhol*. New York: Grove Press, 1996.

Linden-Ward, Blanche, and Carol Hurd Green, *Changing the Future: American Women in the 1960s*. New York: Twayne Publishers, 1992.

Maclean, Nancy. *The American Women's Movement, 1945–2000: A Brief History with Documents*. New York: Bedford/St. Martin's, 2008.

Marcus, Eric. *Making Gay History: The Half-Century Fight for Lesbian and Gay Equal Rights*. New York: Perennial, 2002.

Morgan, Robin, ed. *Sisterhood Is Powerful: An Anthology of Writings from the Women's Liberation Movement*. New York: Random House, 1970.

Rosen, Ruth. *The World Split Open: How the Modern Women's Movement Changed America*. New York: Penguin, 2000.

Tanner, Leslie, ed. *Voices from Women's Liberation*. New York: New American Library, 1970.

Watson, Steven. *Factory Made: Warhol and the Sixties*. New York: Pantheon Books, 2003.

CHAPTER 13

Abbey, Edward. *Abbey's Road*. New York: E. P. Dutton, 1979.

————. *Beyond the Wall*. NewYork: Henry Holt, 1971

————. *Desert Solitaire*. Tucson: University of Arizona Press, 1968.

————. *The Journey Home*. New York: E. P. Dutton, 1977.

————. *A Voice Crying in the Wilderness*. New York: St. Martin's Press, 1989.

Andrews, Richard N. L. *Managing the Environment, Managing Ourselves: A History of American Environmental Policy*. New Haven, CT: Yale University Press, 2006.

Brooks, Flippen J. *Conservative Conservationists: Russell E. Train and the Emergence of American Environmentalism*. Baton Rouge: Louisiana State University Press, 2006.

Calahan, James M. *Edward Abbey: A Life.* Tucson: University of Arizona Press, 2001.

Carson, Rachel. *Silent Spring.* New York: Houghton Mifflin, 1962.

Cohen, Michael P. *The History of the Sierra Club 1892–1970.* New York: Random House, 1988.

Gottlieb, Robert. *Forcing the Spring: the Transformation of the American Environmental Movement.* Washington, DC: Island Press, 2005.

Harvey, Mark. *Wilderness Forever: Howard Zahniser and the Path to the Wilderness Act.* Seattle: University of Washington Press, 2007.

Kluger, Jeffrey. *Apollo 8: The Thrilling Story of the First Mission to the Moon.* New York: Henry Holt, 2017.

McClosky, Michael J. *In the Thick of It: My Life in the Sierra Club.* Washington, DC: Island Press, 2005.

Merchant, Carolyn. *American Environmental History.* New York: Columbia University Press, 2007.

Petersen, David, ed. *Confessions of a Barbarian: Selections from the Journals of Edward Abbey, 1951–1989.* New York; Little, Brown, 1994.

Rome, Adam. *The Bulldozer in the Countryside: Suburban Sprawl and the Rise of American Environmentalism.* New York: Cambridge University Press, 2001.

Rothman, Hal K. *The Greening of a Nation?: Environmentalism in the United States Since 1945.* Fort Worth, TX: Harcourt Brace, 1998.

Sale, Kirkpatrick. *The Green Revolution: The American Environmental Movement, 1962–1992.* New York: Hill & Wang, 1993.

Taylor, Dorceta. *The Rise of the American Conservation Movement.* Durham, NC: Duke University Press, 2016.

Turner, Tom. *David Brower: The Making of the Environmental Movement.* Oakland: University of California Press, 2015.

Wyss, Robert. *The Man Who Built the Sierra Club: A Life of David Brower.* New York: Columbia University Press, 2016.

CHAPTER 14

Ambrose, Stephen. *Nixon: the Triumph of a Politician, 1962–1972.* New York: Simon & Schuster, 1989.

Applebome, Peter. *Dixie Rising: How the South Is Shaping American Values.* New York: Harvest, 1996.

Blackstock, Nelson. *COINTELPRO: The FBI's Secret War on Political Freedom.* New York: Pathfinder Press, 1988.

Cannon, Lou. *Governor Reagan: His Rise to Power.* New York: Public Affairs, 2005.

Carter, Dan. *The Politics of Rage: George Wallace, the Origins of the New Conservatism and the Transformation of American Politics.* New York: Simon & Schuster, 1995.

Chester, Lewis, Godfrey Hodgson, and Bruce Page. *An American Melodrama: The Presidential Campaign of 1968.* New York: Viking, 1969.

Churchill, Ward. *Agents of Repression.* Boston: South End Press, 2002.

Cohen, Michael. *American Maelstrom: The 1968 Election and the Politics of Division.* New York; Oxford University Press, 2016.

Flamm, Michael. *Law and Order.* New York: Columbia University Press, 2007.
Frady, Marshall. *Wallace.* New York: Dutton, 1969.
Hodgson, Godfrey. *The World Turned Right Side Up: A History of the Conservative Ascendancy in America.* Boston: Houghton Mifflin, 1996.
Kurlansky, Mark. *1968: The Year That Rocked the World.* New York: Ballantine, *2003.*
Lesher, Stephan. *George Wallace: American Populist.* Boston: Addison-Wesley, 1994.
McGinniss, Joe. *The Selling of the President.* New York: Penguin, 1968.
Mitchell, Mark, dir. *Berkeley in the Sixties.* First Run Features, 1990. DVD
Parmet, Herbert. *Richard Nixon and His America.* New York: Little, Brown, 1990.
Perlstein, Rick. *Nixonland: The Rise of a President and the Fracturing of America.* New York: Scribner, 2008.
Rosenfeld, Seth. *Subversives: The FBI's War on Student Radicals and Reagan's Rise to Power.* New York: Farrar, Straus and Giroux, 2012.
Sherrill, Robert. *Gothic Politics in the Deep South.* New York: Ballantine, 1968.
Weiner, Tim. *Enemies: A History of the FBI.* New York: Random House, 2012
White, Theodore. *The Making of the President: 1968.* New York: Atheneum, 1969.
Wills, Garry. *Nixon Agonistes: The Crisis of the Self-Made Man.* Boston: Houghton Mifflin, 1970.
Witcover, Jules. *The Resurrection of Richard Nixon.* New York: G. P. Putnam's Sons, 1970.
———. *White Knight: The Rise of Spiro Agnew.* New York: Random House, 1972.

CHAPTER 15

Albert, Judith Clavir, and Stewart Edward Albert, eds. *The Sixties Papers: Documents of a Rebellious Decade.* New York: Praeger, 1984.
Anderson, Terry H. *The Sixties.* 2nd ed. New York: Pearson/Longman, 2004.
———. *The Movement and the Sixties.* New York: Oxford University Press, 1995.
Berger, Dan. *The Struggle Within: Prisons, Political Prisoners, and Mass Movements in the United States.* Oakland, CA: PM Press, 2014.
Bingham, Clara. *Witness to the Revolution: Radicals, Resisters, Vets, Hippies, and the Year America Lost Its Mind and Found Its Soul.* New York: Random House, 2016.
Bloom, Alexander, and Wini Breines, eds. *Long Time Gone: Sixties America Then and Now.* Oxford; New York: Oxford University Press, 2001.
Blumgart, Jake "Whatever Happened to Left-Wing Domestic Terrorism?" *Alternet,* April 12, 2013. http://www.alternet.org/tea-party-and-right/whatever-happened-left-wing-domestic-terrorism.
Browne, Blaine T., and Robert C. Cottrell. *Lives and Times: Individuals and Issues in American History: Since 1865.* Lanham, MD: Rowman & Littlefield Publishers, 2009.
Burrough, Bryan. *Days of Rage: America's Radical Underground, the FBI, and the Forgotten Age of Revolutionary Violence.* New York: Penguin, 2015.
Cottrell, Robert C. *Sex, Drugs, and Rock 'n' Roll: The Rise of America's 1960s Counterculture.* Lanham, MD: Rowman & Littlefield, 2015.
Eckstein, Arthur M., *Bad Moon Rising: How the Weather Underground Beat the FBI and Lost the Revolution,.* New Haven, CT: Yale University Press, 2016.

Enstad, Robert. "A Study in Unanswered Questions." *Chicago Tribune*. April 19, 1972.

Gitlin, Todd. *The Sixties: Years of Hope, Days of Rage*. New York: Bantam Books, 1987.

Marwick, Arthur. *The Sixties: Cultural Revolution in Britain, France, Italy, and the United States, c. 1958–c. 1974*. New York: Oxford University Press, 1998.

Means, Howard. *67 Shots: Kent State and the End of American Innocence*. Boston: DaCapo Press, 2016.

Nadeau, Barbie Latza. "How Europe Won the '70s War on Terror." *Daily Beast*. January 25, 2015. http://www.thedailybeast.com/how-europe-won-the-70s-war-on-terror.

Powers, Thomas. *The War at Home: Vietnam and the American People, 1964–1968*. New York: Grossman, 1973.

"Red Brigades." http://web.stanford.edu/group/mappingmilitants/cgi-bin/groups/view/77.

Sale, Kirkpatrick. *SDS*. New York: Random House, 1973.

Thompson, Heather Ann. *Blood in the Water: The Attica Prison Uprising of 1971 and Its Legacy*. New York: Vintage, 2016.

Toebin, Jeffrey. *American Heiress: The Wild Saga of the Kidnapping, Crimes, and Trial of Patty Hearst*. New York: Anchor Books, 2017.

Unger, Irwin, and Debi Unger. *The Movement: A History of the American New Left, 1959–1972*. New York: Dodd, Mead, 1974.

Zaroulis, Nancy, and Gerald Sullivan. *Who Spoke Up? American Protest against the War in Vietnam, 1963–1975*. Garden City, NY: Doubleday, 1984.

Index

About the Authors

Robert C. Cottrell is professor of History and American Studies at Cal State Chico and has written over twenty books, including *Sex, Drugs, and Rock 'n' Roll* (Rowman & Littlefield Publishers, 2015).

Blaine T. Browne is Emeritus Professor at Broward College and is the author of numerous articles and books, including *Modern American Lives: Individuals and Issues in American History, Lives and Times: Individuals and Issues in American History,* and *Uncertain Order: The World in the Twentieth Century.* He currently teaches at Oklahoma City University.